Celebrating Ethnicity and Nation

EUROPEAN STUDIES IN AMERICAN HISTORY
General Editor: Michael Wala

Celebrating Ethnicity and Nation
American Festive Culture from the Revolution to the Early 20th Century
Edited by Jürgen Heideking, Geneviève Fabre, and Kai Dreisbach

Constructing Identity in America
Self, Group, and Nation
Edited by Michael Wala

CELEBRATING ETHNICITY AND NATION

*American Festive Culture from the Revolution
to the Early Twentieth Century*

Edited by

Jürgen Heideking, Geneviève Fabre
and Kai Dreisbach

Berghahn Books
New York • Oxford

First published in 2001 by
Berghahn Books

© 2001 Jürgen Heideking, Geneviève Fabre and Kai Dreisbach

All rights reserved.
No part of this publication may be reproduced in any form or by any means without the written permission of Berghahn Books.

Library of Congress Cataloging-in-Publication Data

Celebrating ethnicity and nation: American festive culture from the Revolution to the early twentieth century / edited by Jürgen Heideking, Geneviève Fabre and Kai Dreisbach.
  p. cm.
Papers from the biennial conference of the European Association for American Studies, held in Lisbon, Portugal, April 1998.
  ISBN 978-1-57181-237-7 (hardback) -- ISBN 978-1-57181-243-8 (paperback)
  1. Festivals--United States--Congresses. 2. Nationalism--United States--Congresses. 3. Ethnicity--United States--Congresses. I. Heideking, Jürgen, 1947- II. Fabre, Geneviève. III. Dreisbach, Kai. IV. European Association for American Studies. Conference (1998 : Lisbon, Portugal)

GT4803 .C45 2000
394.269--dc21

British Library Cataloguing in Publication Data

A catalogue record for this book is available from the British Library.

ISBN: 978-1-57181-237-7 hardback
ISBN: 978-1-57181-243-8 paperback

Contents

Editors' Preface   vii

Introduction
    Geneviève Fabre and Jürgen Heideking   1

CHAPTER 1
Celebrating the Constitution: The Federal Processions of
    1788 and the Emergence of a Republican Festive Culture
    in the United States
    Jürgen Heideking (†)   25

CHAPTER 2
The Nation as Spectacle: The Grand Federal Procession in
    Philadelphia, 1788
    Dietmar Schloss   44

CHAPTER 3
Revolutionary Festivals and Political Violence: The Impact
    of the French Revolution in America
    Marie-Jeanne Rossignol   63

CHAPTER 4
From Celebrating Victory to Celebrating the Nation:
    The War of 1812 and American National Identity
    Michael Wala   74

CHAPTER 5
Performing Freedom: Negro Election Celebrations
    as Political and Intellectual Resistance in
    New England, 1740-1850
    Geneviève Fabre   91

CHAPTER 6
Italian Americans and Columbus Day: A Quest for
    Consensus between National and Group Identities,
    1840-1910
        Bénédicte Deschamps   124

CHAPTER 7
"... to divide their love": Celebrating Frenchness and
    Americanization in San Francisco, 1850-1909
        Annick Foucrier   140

CHAPTER 8
Charity on Parade: Chicago's Jews and the Construction
    of Ethnic and Civic "Gemeinschaft" in the 1860s
        Tobias Brinkmann   157

CHAPTER 9
Demonstrating the Values of 'Gemüthlichkeit' and 'Cultur':
    The Festivals of German Americans in Milwaukee,
    1870-1910
        Heike Bungert   175

CHAPTER 10
Halloween—a "Reinvented" Holiday: Celebrating White
    Anglo-Saxon Protestant Middle-Class America
        Adrien Lherm   194

CHAPTER 11
Climate, Identity, and Winter Carnivals in North America
        Bernard Mergen   215

CHAPTER 12
Creating and Instrumentalizing Nationalism: The Celebration
    of National Reunion in the Peace Jubilees of 1898
        Fabian Hilfrich   228

CHAPTER 13
Historical Bonding with an Expiring Heritage: Revisiting the
    Plymouth Tercentenary Festivities of 1920-21
        Udo Hebel   257

List of Contributors   298

Index   302

Editors' Preface

THIS VOLUME REPRESENTS the collective effort of a group of scholars from several nations who met in April 1998 at the biennial conference of the *European Association for American Studies* in Lisbon. Under the general topic of "Ceremonies and Spectacles: America and the Staging of Collective Identities", our workshop was devoted to the problems of "Festive Culture and National Identities in the United States from 1787 to 1900."

This project is based on an interdisciplinary approach, combining the perspective of historians and literary European scholars on a topic of increasing academic interest in the United States. The individual essays in this volume demonstrate the enormous range and complexity of this field of research, and they present some of the methodological approaches that can be applied. The time frame extends from the late colonial period to the early twentieth century. The range of topics includes distinctively "American" celebrations, as well as festive traditions of European immigrants and Afro-Americans. These different aspects of festive culture in the United States illustrate the pluralistic nature of an evolving American national identity.

The editors wish to thank all the authors for obeying the dictates of a rigorous timetable. We also want to thank Berghahn Books, our publisher, for professional cooperation and support for this project. We greatly benefited from the scholarly comments and wise guidance of the series editor, Michael Wala, whose initiative made possible the publication of this project as the first volume of the series "European Studies in American History."

We are hopeful that this volume will stimulate further discussion and research on both sides of the Atlantic.

Geneviève Fabre, Jürgen Heideking, Kai Dreisbach
August 1999

We dedicate this book to Jürgen Heideking, whose sudden death in March came as a shock to all of us. We will always remember his kindness; we admire his dedication, the passion and the energy he brought to his work, and we feel great respect for the scholarship he so generously shared with us.

Geneviève Fabre and Kai Dreisbach
August 2000

INTRODUCTION

Geneviève Fabre and Jürgen Heideking

Festive Culture as a Creative Force

DURING THE PAST decade, public festivals and civic celebrations have become a favorite topic of scholarly investigation. This growing academic interest has been stimulated by great commemorative events such as the Bicentennials of the United States Constitution and the French Revolution as well as by the revival of radical nationalism and ethnic violence in Europe after the end of the Cold War. Political and social scientists are rediscovering ceremonies, rituals, myths, and symbols as keys for the understanding of deeply held popular attitudes and values as well as for the mechanisms of social integration or exclusion; philosophers try to define the "public sphere" (as an intermediary space between the political sphere of governments and the private sphere of individuals) where citizens communicate, reflect on or "negotiate" the meaning of their common experiences, and carry out social activities; anthropologists and cultural historians ask new questions about the ways in which political systems are legitimized, and about the nature, formation and transformation of collective identities, memories, and emotions.[1]

In contrast to the United States, France has a long tradition of scholarly research on the importance of festivals and celebrations for revolutionary politics, national identity, and nationalism. Beginning in the late nineteenth century, historians such as F.A. Aulard, Albert Mathiez, and Albert Soboul devoted monographs or chapters of books to the rituals, ceremonies, symbols, and myths of the French Revolution. Often, however, these phenomena were mainly understood as reflections or ideological expressions of under-

---

Notes for this section begin on page 22.

lying social forces and economic interests. The publication in 1976 of Mona Ozouf's book *La fête révolutionnaire*—which twelve years later appeared in an English translation—marked a fresh beginning.[2] Ozouf's approach was strongly influenced by sociological and psychological theories. She distinguished two types of public rituals: celebrations of transgression, collective excitement, and release (terms borrowed from Freudian psychoanalysis), and celebrations of unity and collective self-expression, which according to the sociologist Emile Durkheim are part of the religious life of any social group or community. Ozouf's principle aim was to explain the ambiguous relationship between revolutionary violence and the conjuration of national unity. In this context, she put great emphasis on a process which she calls "le transfer de sacralité", the transfer of sacrality from the religious feastdays of the Old Régime to the new national festivals and civic life of the Republic, from traditional religion to the quasi-religious legitimation of revolutionary institutions and post-revolutionary politics. By exploring the religious dimension of festive culture, Ozouf contributed indirectly to a deeper understanding of American "civil religion", first described and analyzed by Robert N. Bellah. In later writings, in which he strongly condemned the United States' involvement in the Vietnam War, Bellah reaffirmed his conviction that "civil religion" does not mean "the worship of the American nation but an understanding of the American experience in the light of ultimate and universal reality."[3] In his famous *Daedalus* article of 1967,[4] Bellah took his clue from Rousseau's *Contrat Social*, and defined "civil religion" as an ensemble of common beliefs, symbols, and rituals which give expression to the collective identity of a nation. He quoted from American sermons and political speeches to illustrate the deeply rooted idea that the United States plays a special role in God's order of salvation, and that the history of the American people reveals a universal, transcendent truth.

The works of Bellah and Ozouf have inspired a lively debate which is being nourished by new approaches in neighboring disciplines such as cultural history, literary studies, linguistics, and anthropology. Meanwhile, there exists a broad scholarly consensus that spontaneous as well as ritualized periodic public celebrations constitute a fundamental aspect of social life, revealing deeply held attitudes and values. In addition, they fulfill essential albeit ambivalent functions for every community: they guarantee and legitimize the existing social order, but by mobilizing popular participation they can also threaten the cohesion of societies and the rule of established elites; they fuse the sacred and the profane and thereby contribute to the building of "imagined communities" ranging from small homogeneous groups to diverse nations; and they act as seismographs of consensus and conflicts within a society.[5] In this sense, public celebrations do not just "reflect" social practices and reality, but they possess the power to "construct" political concepts and create cultural meaning. Festive culture must therefore be seen as an integral part of the historical process which shapes and transforms power relations, social structures and popular mentalities.

By focussing on the complex interaction of collective identities on the local, regional and national level, this volume tries to evaluate the impact of festive culture on the process of nation-building in the United States. In particular, a close look at a variety of public celebrations from the Revolution to the early twentieth century will help to answer the question of how Americans responded to four historical challenges: 1) the dissolution of the colonial order and the creation of a new constitutional and political system based on popular sovereignty; 2) the transformation from a predominantly agrarian to an expanding commercial, market-oriented society, accompanied by the growth and differentiation of an immigrant population; 3) the conflicting pressures of centralization and national integration on the one hand and sectionalism, regionalism, and ethnic or religious particularism on the other; 4) the reunion of North and South after the devastating Civil War and the assimilation of millions of new immigrants into a society characterized by industrialization and urbanization.

American Festive Culture from the Revolution to the Civil War

It has been argued that during the Revolution the American settlers "celebrated themselves into an American future," and that these celebrations, publicized by the patriot press, for the first time created a sense of common destiny and American identity.[6] After independence from Britain was achieved, the egalitarian tendencies of radical republicanism were balanced by a different version of civic republicanism, which put more emphasis on order, self-discipline, regularity, and social harmony. This new republican festive culture found expression in the Grand Federal Processions of 1788, huge parades in cities from Boston to Charleston on the occasion of the ratification of the United States Constitution, which projected the concept of a sovereign, self-governing people onto the streets.[7] The Declaration of Independence and the new Federal Constitution served as symbols of an emerging American nation. This cult of the founding documents and the reverence of George Washington marked the beginnings of a secular "civil religion", which did not clash with traditional beliefs and practices but supplemented the religious life experienced by Americans in their various denominations. This process climaxed in George Washington's famous landing at Murray's Wharf on April 23, 1789, and in his inauguration at Federal Hall in Manhattan on April 30.

However, the relative consensus and harmony of the late 1780s did not last. This was mainly due to the French Revolution, which radicalized the political discourse in the United States during the 1790s and fueled a debate between Federalists and Republicans over the meaning of the Constitution and the "true republican way" of celebrating. In most cities, the artisans, mechanics, and tradesmen shifted their allegiance to the Jeffersonian Republicans, and they tried to preserve the form, if not the spirit, of the grand processions in the annual Fourth of July celebrations. Their preference for "sound republican simplicity", their Jacobinial toasts and radical songs pointed to a more democratic style of politics and festive culture. The Federalists, on their part, began to put even more emphasis than before on the themes of order and stability. They did this in particular by moving the image of George Washington, the war hero and first president, into the center of public ceremonial life.[8] These divergent styles of festive culture reflected the broader pattern of conflict within consensus which characterized the early national period. Federalists and Republicans interpreted the Constitution differently, and they claimed to defend the political and social order against open attacks and subversion by the other party. The tension between the two different republican ideologies was further complicated by undercurrents of resentment and protest on the margins of the republican society, and there was no consensus as to which celebration should prevail. In New York, Evacuation Day, celebrating the Treaty of Paris and the departure of British troops in 1783, rivaled the Fourth of July at the turn of the century, even though both feasts had been sponsored by the Columbian Order of Tammany Society in 1786. In the big cities and in some rural areas there existed—especially among laborers, new immigrants and blacks—alternative rituals and ceremonies; some remained connected with the "plebeian" culture of the colonial period, others like Pinkster or Election Day were distinct African American civic events;[9] still others became major parades like St. Patrick's Day. St. Patrick's Day, at first a Protestant event (1762), was taken over by Irish Catholics in the 1820s; it not only survived anti-Irish feelings but flourished and became a model for other ethnic groups.

Although Thomas Jefferson's election as President in 1800 did not cause a civil war, as some contemporaries had feared, the national cohesion remained fragile. It was again tested by the dispute over Jefferson's embargo policy, and it almost collapsed during the War of 1812 when bitter partisan and regional clashes paralyzed American military operations. The relatively successful outcome of the war, however, revived American nationalism and added some new symbols and commemorative dates to the repertoire of American festive culture: Francis Scott Key's—still unofficial—national anthem; Andrew Jackson's victory over the British at New Orleans; and

Uncle Sam as the personification of an American "national character". The gradual return of conciliation and national consensus after 1815 was certainly furthered by the "Washington myth" which had meanwhile taken roots in the American consciousness. The fiftieth anniversary of the Declaration of Independence in 1826 was observed in "a climate of general good will", and most Americans interpreted the death of John Adams and Thomas Jefferson on July 4, 1826, as a sign from heaven confirming the providential role and mission of the American people.[10]

Since the Revolution, a distinctive calendar of public ceremonial events had taken shape without any central direction or planning. It contained annual national holidays (the Fourth of July and Washington's birthday), important political events such as the inauguration of a president; local holidays with national relevance (especially the anniversaries of battles of the War for Independence and the War of 1812), and days of fasting and prayer proclaimed by state governments and churches. To this calendar were added one-time events that became prominent like grand funeral processions or receptions organized to honor state visitors—a tradition that endured throughout the nineteenth century. New York, for example, staged ceremonies for Lafayette in 1824, Andrew Jackson in 1833, Daniel Webster in 1837 and Louis Kossuth, hero of the Hungarian Independence, in 1831. A new element appeared in 1825, when the citizens of the state of New York celebrated the opening of the Erie Canal with a huge parade. The organizers had tried to reaffirm the spirit of civic republicanism and the ideal of a homogeneous society, but the event signaled instead the beginning of a new era characterized by rapid social and economic change. The United States had become the most egalitarian, individualistic, and acquisitive society in the world; American festive culture began to reflect as well as shape this transformation toward a dynamic market economy.[11]

During the antebellum period, the republican festive culture of the early nineteenth century came under additional pressure from various directions. On the one hand, the growing complexity of the American society, caused by the "market revolution", made it increasingly difficult to stage harmonious civic celebrations. On the other hand, in a political climate shaped by democratization and party competition, public celebrations no longer acted as moderating forces but contributed to the escalation of ideological and sectional conflicts. And finally, the mass immigration of the 1840s and 1850s produced ethnic tensions which could not be absorbed by the traditional American festive culture.

At the same time, the annual observance of the national holidays appears to have lost much of its authenticity and popular appeal. The official ceremonies acquired the character of uniform, mechanically observed rituals.

Fourth of July parades degenerated into military spectacles, dominated by militias and marching bands. One writer even tells us that in the 1830s, the Fourth of July became "the butt of national ridicule" and was famous for "the dullness of its soporific oratory."[12] Abraham Lincoln's wish, expressed in his Lyceum Address of 1838, that Americans might revive the spirit of the Declaration of Independence and create a "political religion", illustrates this loss of meaning and direction.[13] As the generation of the Founding Fathers was passing away, the Revolution acquired the quality of a myth which could be used for different political purposes. The polarization of the Jacksonian era changed the cultural climate of the United States. Fueled by the widening franchise and the formation of popular parties, politics took on the dramatic functions which the old ceremonies and rituals no longer fulfilled. By participating in the election campaigns with their national conventions, mass rallies, processions and jubilees, American voters celebrated "a great democratic festival" and turned it into "a satisfying form of cultural expression."[14] However, there no longer existed a unified celebration of republicanism and national pride. The emotional nature of party politics aggravated the sectional crisis of the 1850s that led to the Civil War.

Already by the 1840s, the participation of immigrants in parades and other public ceremonies had become a source of conflict. In Philadelphia, anti-immigration protesters staged a Grand Native American Procession on the Fourth of July, 1844, that provoked serious rioting.[15] Occasionally, immigrants were excluded from communal activities because of their low social status or their Catholicism. In the 1850s, the growing involvement of Catholics in public festivities accelerated the retreat of the upper classes into a "private sphere", sheltered from intrusions by ordinary folks.[16] This, combined with nativist resistance, induced immigrant communities to organize their own "ethnic" parades and festivals.[17] Parallel to this growing awareness of ethnic identities, were a number of reform movements, especially the Temperance Movement and Abolitionism, which mobilized tens of thousands of Americans by adapting traditional festive forms such as parades and banquets and by creating new rituals and symbols. In the frontier regions, religious revivals and camp meetings pushed secular forms of celebrations into the background. African Americans initiated a long tradition of freedom celebrations reminding Americans that emancipation had become a major issue and a national and international affair after the abolition of slavery in the British West Indies in 1833.

The Mexican War caused an upsurge of nationalist feelings, but only for a short period of time. Even before the victory celebrations ended, it had become clear that the territorial gains, instead of binding the nation together, aggravated the North-South confrontation over the slavery issue. Republican festive culture had given way to a diversity of ceremonial styles and practices employed by different social groups, competing political parties, new ethnic and religious communities, and crusading reform movements. Lacking a common spirit and purpose, festive culture could not act as an integrating, cohesive force; on the contrary, its symbolic power was used to intensify the conflicts over states' rights and slavery that tore the Union apart.

Overlooking the century from the Revolution to the Civil War, we can see that, throughout this time, festive culture formed an integral part of the political process. Since the 1790s, a radical, egalitarian festive culture coexisted with a more conservative style, which emphasized order, social stability, and national cohesion. The first focused on the Declaration of Independence, the second on the Constitution and the role of George Washington as the "father of the country". After the War of 1812, both types again seemed to merge into one common, homogeneous republican festive culture. Soon, however, this harmony dissolved when competing political and social forces created new ways of celebrating or filled old forms with new meaning. To a large degree, the Civil War was fought over two basically irreconcilable constitutional interpretations and world views. With the victory of the North the *national* construction of meaning—as outlined in Lincoln's two inaugural addresses and in his Gettysburg address—triumphed, and slavery disappeared as a legal, constitutionally protected institution. The war with its enormous destruction of lives and property as well as Lincoln's violent death, which immediately elevated the President to national martyrdom, deeply affected American festive culture. The spirit and style of public celebrations changed considerably during the final decades of the nineteenth century, when the themes of sacrifice and regeneration became part of American civil religion.[18] The "new birth of freedom" which Lincoln had proclaimed at Gettysburg bound the Declaration and the Constitution closely together again as central elements of a revived national festive culture of the United States.

Festive Culture from the Gilded Age to the Great Depression

To a certain degree, however, the symbolic tension between the Declaration and the Constitution continued even after the Civil War and the centennial celebration of 1876 when big cities like Philadelphia and New York vied for precedence in organizing public festivities. Alarmed by the difficulties and problems of the Reconstruction period, Northern politicians shied away from strictly enforcing the constitutional amendments against a recalcitrant South, and they closed their eyes to the suppression of black civil rights. The rationale behind this "soft" approach to the race question, however, was the intention of "healing the wounds" of the Civil War and fostering (white) national unity. Historical societies—national organizations such as the Daughters or the Sons of the American Revolution—sponsored many events to uphold patriotism and morality. The dedication of the Statue of Liberty in 1886, presented by the French "Sister Republic" as a gift for the Centennial of the Declaration of Independence, added another powerful national symbol to American festive culture. Offering hospitality, political freedom, and economic opportunity to the world's underprivileged classes, "Liberty" soon became the most powerful expression of the "American Creed." Ironically, the celebration of the statue took place soon after the end of Reconstruction when black codes and disfranchisement denied citizenship to the new freedmen; it also coincided with legislative efforts to restrict the flow of immigration, particularly from Asia and from Southern and Eastern Europe. At the same time, the American middle classes appropriated older festive traditions such as Halloween and Carnival and transformed them into bourgeois community celebrations.[19]

In the new culture, civil servants—the police and street cleaners first, then the firemen—appropriated the parades. Workers, craftsmen and traders, who had marched since the Federal Processions of 1788, became more militant and potentially disruptive with the growth of the Union movement (as can be seen in the Eight-hour March of September 1871, a prelude to the first Labor Day Parade of 1888). Germans were more visible and women, after their exclusion from the dedication of the Statue of Liberty in 1886, became more assertive and claimed their right to appear in the public space. Women's suffrage and labor parades intensified in the 1910s. The more traditional patriotic feelings found their expression in larger civic and "industrial" pageants, celebrating the nation's past or present technological power and achievements. Two events frame that period: The dedication of the Brooklyn Bridge (1883) with its "Nineteenth Century Wonder March" praising modernity and the emergence of a new metropolis and the Hudson Fulton Celebration of 1909, commemorating past discoveries.

The Centennial Celebration of the Constitution, which extended from 1887 through 1889, marked the first conscious effort to "popularize" the Constitution and to establish "constitutionalism" as the main feature of American political culture. The most memorable event was a repeat performance of the Philadelphia Federal Procession of 1788, a magnificent civic and industrial parade organized by the Constitutional Centennial Commission of Pennsylvania, financially supported by the federal government, and attended by President Grover Cleveland and his wife. Similar parades in New York and other cities as far away as San Francisco reflected the desire to revive the spirit of republican harmony in a vastly different, industrializing and urbanizing society. The founding fathers received much praise for their sense of proportion and compromise—virtues now considered as essential for the reintegration of the South as well as for the reconciliation of the working classes with the capitalist system. The Constitution appeared as "the Arc of the Covenant", as a "sacred document", and as "an inspiration from God", formulations that signaled the beginning of a veritable "worship of the Constitution".[20] At the end of the nineteenth century, constitutionalism began to take roots in the public consciousness, and it became an important factor in the concept of American "exceptionalism" so eloquently expressed in Frederick Jackson Turner's 1893 lecture on "The Significance of the Frontier in American History."[21] More and more people acknowledged that it was this constitutionalism—understood as an absolute commitment to the rule of law, devotion to a "higher law" embodied in the Constitution, and obedience to the Supreme Court as final arbiter of legal disputes—which truly set the American people apart from Europe and from the rest of the world. The war against Spain in 1898 gave another boost to the American sense of destiny and national pride. The victory prepared the way for overseas territorial expansion, while the patriotic sentiments at home were instrumentalized to finally "close the wounds" of the Civil War and complete the "reconciliation" of North and South.

During this period, the two founding documents co-existed in a somewhat tense, but generally constructive relationship. The Declaration served as a rallying point for reformers and critics of the established order, from the women's movement of the late nineteenth century and the anti-imperialists of 1898-99 to the intellectuals of the Progressive Era. The Constitution, on the other hand, appealed more strongly to the defenders of property rights, the supporters of a liberal economic order, and to American patriots or expansionists.[22] While intellectuals such as the historian Charles A. Beard regarded the Constitution as an obstacle to the democratization of the American society, other progressives contributed to the flourishing cult of the founding documents. The Playground Association of America inaugurated a campaign for a "Safe and Sane Fourth": the national holiday, which seemingly had turned into a rowdy and (because of the reckless use of fireworks) accident-prone affair of the lower classes, was to be observed in the future with civic pageants, alcohol-free picnics, and edifying oratory. The Association staged a "model celebration" in Springfield, Massachusetts, where in 1908 American citizens of various ethnic and racial backgrounds marched in a parade of nations led by Buffalo Bill Cody's Wild West troupe. Philadelphia celebrated Founder's Week in 1908 in the same spirit. This reform initiative was obviously influenced by the European tradition of historic pageants and reached its climax around the turn of the century.²³ In order to awaken a sense of history and tradition in the American people, the organizers constructed a version of America's past and present that was free of class struggle, racial hatred, and regional hostilities. Another important aim was the assimilation of millions of new immigrants who arrived during these years in the United States: in 1915, for example, the Commissioner of Immigration at the port of New York proposed that the Fourth of July should be celebrated as "Americanization Day", and one year later Congress, in a symbolic act, introduced a special "Constitution Day."²⁴

An image of the aboriginal past was included in pageants to contrast with the technological age—as in the Boston Pageant of 1915. The pageants portrayed its inevitable decline—an end brought not by conquest but by progress—as did the Wood Stevens' Pageant of All Northwest Milwaukee 1911. The Historical Pageant of Illinois presented Indian removal as a legitimate business transaction. Different groups were invited to participate mainly to demonstrate their civic sentiment and their loyalty instead of their distinct ethnic identity. Blacks and Asians were still notably absent except in a Pageant of Nations—in Newbury Port—where public floats depicted life under slavery. When race relations were an issue they were idealized in scenes reminiscent of Old South plantation imagery or blackface minstrelsy. The only pageant that openly criticized the enduring stereotypes of African American history was *Star of Ethiopia* by W.E.B. Du Bois. This "black folk drama" was sponsored by the NAACP and presented from 1913 to 1916 in commemoration of emancipation.

The new pageantry combining recreation and fine arts in support of reform movements expressed many tensions: as parades emphasized diversity and the mobility of the nation, they also reaffirmed Anglo-Saxon supremacy. In a Progressive Era and an age of modernity, their organizers resisted innovations and resorted to old traditions borrowed from colonial or European pre-industrial ages. However, opposition to the framers of this new festive culture became more manifest especially among women and workers: in 1913 for example the Industrial Workers of the World staged a pageant in Madison Square Gardens for the benefit of New Jersey strikers.

It is important to note that, in spite of the increased control of public action by officials, there were significant changes: the new festive culture incorporated plebeian forms and tried to combine politics and business with fun and popular entertainments. Carnivalesque or more burlesque forms that had developed in early nineteenth century clubs and societies were included more officially during the latter part of the century. There were also more exchanges between the theatre and the street—as in Imre Kiralfy's *America*, a show created for the World Columbian Exhibition, or in a Fourth of July at Des Moines that featured New Orleans Mardi Gras. There were also mutual borrowings between the commercial stage and the new pageantry. New terms appeared to describe these festivities: extravaganza, show (Barnum and Bailey's Greatest Show on Earth in 1891), masque (the Masque of Rockport, Mass. where the spirit of nature submits to the spirit of civilization), or holiday play festival as in Pittsburgh in 1909 or Chicago in 1908.

Although the new culture celebrated progress and civilization, it was still mainly commemorative and very much oriented towards the past; in reaction to modern industrial society it sought to revitalize a lost spirit of communal loyalties and artistic participation. It revived old folk dances, crafts, games, and great American myths. Celebrations were conceived as "history lessons", and their function was to contrast with progressive educational theories, thus embedding civic feeling in the past.

The War in Europe and the American participation in the military struggle against the Central Powers (beginning in April 1917) greatly stimulated the trend toward national unity and social homogeneity. The Star-Spangled Banner, the (still unofficial) national anthem, the Declaration and the Constitution all served as rallying points for the newly established patriotic associations; protecting the constitutional order against external and internal subversion became an obsession of politicians, government propagandists, the police and the Judiciary; and the Statue of Liberty figured prominently on millions of posters inviting Americans to buy war bonds. In the realm of international relations, President Woodrow Wilson's League of Nations promised the right to national self-determination and democratic self-government, a system of collective security, and the precedence of the rule of law—in other words, an international constitutional order on the American model. This crusading spirit and idealism were submerged, however, in the public disappointment over the results of the war, in the quest for material gains during the 1920s, and finally in the economic hardship of the Great Depression. The rise of fascism in Europe and the outbreak of World War II presented new challenges which gave strong impetus to the ongoing process of nation-building and again transformed American festive culture.

Case Studies of Festive Culture, Collective Identities, and Nationalism in the United States

To fill this very broad and general interpretative framework with empirical research in order to verify, modify, or negate the underlying assumptions remains a task for the coming decades. Some important contributions have been made by American historians during the 1990s, especially concerning the early national period, and the Lisbon conference provided an additional stimulus.[25] The authors tried to heed the admonitions by some critics of the new literature that one should not exclusively study events on the national level but also take into account the variety and complexity of local and regional political cultures. From the beginning, American collective identities were pluralistic, and American nationalism always developed as a result of tensions between these various levels as well as between a dominant "mainstream" culture and ethnic and religious minority cultures. Festive culture, therefore, cannot be analyzed without a thorough understanding of the social structures, economic interests, party struggles, and ideologies of the time.[26]

It is important to consider in this volume the role that African Americans and immigrants performed in the formation of the political culture and how they did this precisely through festivity. These communities showed that they were eager to participate in the celebrations but wished to do so on their own terms; not only combining elements of the festive culture they met in the new country with elements of their own culture, but also seizing the opportunity thus offered to make their presence more visible and more legitimate. For most of the groups this entry into the public sphere was not to be taken for granted. Excluded at first from the official celebrations, not allowed to take part in pageants or parades except as exotic, decorative or allegorical objects they became aware of the obstacles they would have to overcome as well as of the important stakes involved should permission finally be granted. In a country that had, from its early days, created a calendar of celebrations and a tradition of pageantry, thus vying with old Europe in order to create truly American rituals, admission into that culture surely meant recognition and a form of integration that could open other doors. No wonder then that appearance in the public arena became such a vibrant claim, a battle to fight for in the name of democracy or of the principles set by the nation.

Because of their long exclusion from official celebrations, ethnic communities have been inspired by the grand processions and festivals of American democracy to organize their own ceremonial life and commemorations. They staged their own ritualized events as alternative celebrations with their own distinctive sites. History became a major issue, as something to be set right, remembered, reconstructed, or dramatically reenacted through collective memory; to celebrants, public festivals offered the occasion to reflect upon their own history, long neglected, overlooked, or ignored by others, to claim a past and a future, where they could be real actors and admitted in the new republic as full citizens who would participate in all aspects of the democratic process. Festive life should therefore be instructive and educational, giving them a chance to rehearse and experiment with their new roles. Feasts were conceived as political and civic events, not as mere amusements and entertainments. The question of power was to be taken seriously—in a critical assessment of the way they were ruled, or could win back their freedom, identity and independence.

Celebrations thus became forums where claims were made, grievances voiced, social injustice and inequalities or mistreatment exposed, new ideas and strategies tested. On the one hand, one could see ethnic celebrations as a mirror offered to the mainstream cycle of feasts, in an effort to emulate them and contribute to the forging of a common civic American identity; on the other hand, they were implicitly questioning and challenging this festive culture and the society whose interests it served, pointing at the failure to create true democratic participation that would take into consideration the needs and strivings of all citizens. In that sense the Fourth of July, Independence Day, conveys so many images of freedom and new beginnings, and could create a consensus, yet it was also for some groups a controversial holiday, one that reminded them of the failures of the new era. One is reminded of Frederick Douglass' famous Fourth of July address "What is to us your Fourth of July?" and of the long search on the part of African Americans for other more relevant commemorations (the abolition of the slave trade, state emancipations or abolition of slavery in the West Indies, or insurrections and their heroes).

Immigrant groups have also tried to establish an alternative calendar and create their own national self-celebrative events. In doing so, they have expressed at the same time their enduring loyalty to their country of origin, its beliefs and customs, and their faith in the new nation, always emphasizing that the plurality of voices should be heard. In that sense immigrants have shown the same concerns as the framers of the first republican celebrations, insisting on the innovative New World character of their festivals and inscribing them in the emerging American pageantry, while giving them a definite ethnic imprint borrowing from Old World traditions.

Thus, American festive culture, whether ethnic or mainstream, has displayed rather paradoxical features—affirming the need to break away from the old countries (as the first Americans did after independence) yet reasserting the ties and the roots of identity there; proclaiming Americanness, yet voicing disagreement with the exclusion or mistreatment of newcomers.

Celebrations are a much contested terrain, the object of many negotiations on the choice of sites, on the time and space frame, on who should be the organizers, supporters, main actors, and participants. Interestingly, through these efforts at organization they have been instrumental in creating or developing institutional structures. New forms of leadership have been created that may not have been otherwise so vocal and visible, and these organizations, societies, associations, lodges, and lobbies came to play a major role in shaping the communities or the larger society. Celebrations have also revealed tensions and conflicts between elites that competed for control and prominence, or between the elites and "the people" who disagreed with the constraints imposed upon them—especially under the influence of educators or reformers of the Progressive Era—and who have sought to restore a freer festive mood.

Festivals are a rich field of investigation for historians—as arenas of discussion and the testing of new ideas and of the interplay or confrontation between groups and forces, as matrices for the invention of cultures and the forging of new identities, and as templates of the process of Americanization. They not only reflect the state of a society at a precise historical moment but indicate the feelings the various actors had about the society they live in, their grievances and aspirations, and their ideas of how to bring about some change. The term "celebration" then assumes a new meaning when will and desire come into play, when commemoration is less important than anticipation and an agenda for the future. This dimension of celebrations has often been ignored because festivals have centered on anniversaries, centennials, evocation of glorious deeds, of heroes and victories. Marginal or dissenting voices in the chorus of pride and praise—that took place for example in the grand processions between the opening of the Erie Canal and the Fulton Hudson parade—have pointed to the limits of these achievements. These limits and flaws become manifest if one looks more carefully at the unfolding of the official ceremony, if one is attentive to signs, to the presence or absence of certain groups, to persuasive pronouncements and eloquent silences.

Perhaps one of the obstacles to a deeper understanding of what public celebrations are about and to their use as fundamental source for the study of societies has been the stereotypical form through which they have been reported in journals, newspapers, observers' or more official accounts. One needs to reach beyond these formalistic descriptions to deeper layers in order to grasp the meaning of all these festivals.

The first two articles look from different angles at the "Grand Federal Processions" of 1788 which were the first impressive manifestations of American national festive culture. Jürgen Heideking places these parades into the political context of the intense debate over adoption or rejection of the new Constitution formulated by the Philadelphia Convention between May and September 1787. He analyzes their meaning on different levels: they were used by the supporters of the Constitution for propaganda purposes; they allowed the urban middle classes to voice their demands for an active national trade policy conducive to their economic interests; they gave meaning to the monumental events since the Revolution and served to construct a national identity by projecting the image of a virtuous, self-governing, and self-reliant people onto the streets of the major American cities; and finally they helped to provide legitimacy and "sacrality" to the new political order. It should also be noted that despite a lack of central organization all these parades and celebrations used the same symbols, dealt with the same topics, and showed a similar character. In this way, they gave expression to the American motto of "unity in diversity."

Dietmar Schloss concentrates his attention on Philadelphia's magnificent "Federal Procession" on the Fourth of July, 1788, which came closest to an "official" national parade. His detailed interpretation reveals the coexistence and fusion of two different aesthetic conceptions in this public celebration: while the first part of the parade borrowed heavily from the iconographic and allegorical traditions of English Lord Mayor shows, the second part contrasted this "artificial world of mythology and allegory" with the radical authenticity of artisans and craftsmen performing their work on floats, an innovative conception which Schloss calls "the aesthetics of everyday reality." He relates the tension between these two conceptions to the divergent political orientation of the urban elite and the middle classes as well as to the transformation from classical republicanism to liberalism taking place in post-revolutionary America. The "two different ways of conceiving the nation" reflected in the two aesthetic conceptions were held together, however, by the ideal of economic independence which reserved active participation to "respectable" members of the community.

Marie Jeanne Rossignol's paper deals with American political festivals at the time of the French Revolution and examines the connection between revolutionary festivals, political culture and the birth of new nations. The author focuses first on a specific event, a festival organized in Charleston and Philadelphia in 1793 on behalf of the French ambassador. Incidentally, this inaugurated a tradition of celebrations honoring presidents, state officials or visitors. More importantly, it revealed the impact of the French Revolution on the formation of parties and partisanship in the early republic. Rossignol considers and questions the framework within which revolutionary festivals have recently been studied. Drawing primarily from Mona Ozouf's and Jules Michelet's works as well as from Simon P. Newman's and David Waldstreicher's studies of festive cultures in early America, she sees the 1793 festival as a political middle ground where republican democratic values were being contested at a time of political and social unrest, when the spirit of the American revolution had to be more actively defended. She also describes another revolution in the beginning of that same decade that gave birth to the first black republic in the New World and became the prototype of dangerous and cruel festivals that could encourage slave insurrection. Rossignol argues that the Haitian revolution had enduring effects throughout the antebellum and Civil War era on race relations in the American South and fostered the emergence of new forms of political cruelty and of a new racial order.

By analyzing public celebrations with national connotations such as Independence Day and Washington's Birthday, Michael Wala evaluates the impact of the War of 1812 against Great Britain on the development of American national identity. Since these celebrations had become "public battlegrounds in the contest of ideas and ideologies" there existed in 1812 "no unifying national identity that transcended regional and party differences." The declaration of war aroused patriotic sentiments in some parts of the country, but the long war effort seems to have rather strengthened regional identities, especially in New England. Andrew Jackson's victory in New Orleans and the treaty of peace were celebrated on the local level without becoming immediately common symbols. President Monroe's visit to New England in the summer of 1817, however, instilled a feeling of reconciliation, and the decline of the Federalist Party made it easier to appeal to the common destiny of the American people and to rebuild a still precarious national consensus.

The Negro Election Day examined by Geneviève Fabre is one of the examples of assertive and daring appearances of African Americans—slaves and free blacks—in the public space in colonial and antebellum times. It also demonstrates that they were keen observers of white political practices, were capable of creating their own forms of self-government, and of celebrating their own carefully chosen figures of authority and power. Basing her study on testimonies to be found in diaries, memoirs, and accounts in early histories, Fabre traces the origins, development and decline of this Negro festival and tries to derive from its styles of performance the function and meaning the event may have held for its celebrants as well as its place in the political culture of New England or in the ceremonial life within the diaspora. She relates it to other coronations that occurred in the North, such as Pinkster—or in the South and the Caribbean—the famous JonKonnu festival. The essay further explores the interests, material or symbolic, that were at stake for both blacks and whites in such rituals; it also points at the blending of serious intent and play, of gravity and irreverence or parody, and at the indirect and disguised ways celebrants conveyed their message to their audiences and to the larger society. Taking issue with some interpretations, Fabre shows the role that those who were excluded from official feasts could play by staging their own civic events, and sees this festival as an exemplary ceremonial performance that carried potent political meaning.

Columbus Day is one of the most symbolic festivals in American commemorative culture, celebrating a hero who assumed historical and mythical dimensions; and an event that heralded the birth of a nation and was an inspiration for those who set out to explore a whole new continent. Bénédicte Deschamps traces the history of the celebration from its first observance in 1792 to the early twentieth century. She stresses the part played by successive organizations and committees in promoting the festival: from the Columbus Order to the Knights of Columbus, by newspapers, editors, mutual aid societies, churches, and lobbies. The most striking event was the growing role of the Italian community who began celebrating Columbus in the 1840s. Feeling that they could legitimately claim Columbus as their hero, they also wished to raise him to the rank of national and universal figure, "father of them all", founder of a dynasty of explorers and discoverers, who should be honored with gratitude. This claim gave Italian immigrants more voice and power to fight against the prejudices and discrimination they met in the United States, and to counter their negative image in the American mind. In their rituals they emphasized nobility and virtue, knowledge and civilization first introduced in the Americas by Columbus, a claim in precedence no other group could make; they stressed bonds and common heritage between Italians and Americans, modernity and "Americanness". Deschamps considers the different steps in the process of appropriation and of reinterpretation at the time of Italian reunification and later, when Italian American communities grew in number and spread through the country. She also traces the stages in the elaboration of a new concept of festivity—one that was more sober and dignified. Like most ethnic festivals, Columbus Day became the subject of much controversy, pitting Catholics against Protestants or—within the Italian community—the elite against the crowd of participants. In spite of the factions and dissension, Columbus Day remained a major celebration that sought to achieve consensus and compromise between political and religious groups, and between Italian and non-Italian forces.

Annick Foucrier studies the French celebrations in San Francisco in the context of the development of the city itself and of French immigration to the United States and to the West Coast. Events after the 1789 or the 1848 revolutions—creating then a shift of loyalties between Bonapartists and Republicans whose ideas were later to triumph—or in 1870 with the fall of the empire, were crucial in shaping celebrations staged by French residents or "French Californians". If these celebrations stressed communality between two liberty-loving peoples who honored their heroes, Lafayette and Washington, and sung the two national anthems, there was nevertheless much competition between the Fourth and the Fourteenth of July and much debate as to which revolution offered the most compelling inspiration. Foucrier

examines the problem of language and identity—more acute in the 1880s—
and the responses of other groups: supportive in the case of Irish American
nationalists, or negative on the part of others who joined in the opposition
to foreigners at a time of growing nativist thinking. Celebrations thus
offered either the opportunity to denounce social injustice and inequalities in
the name of freedom or to criticize France and its New World descendants,
deride their alien customs and reanimate old stereotypes. The author is also
attentive to the origin, urban or rural, of the various waves of French immigrants in order to explain internal splits and conflicts in local politics and to
assess the meaning the celebration had for its diverse participants.

Tobias Brinkmann uses the charity parade organized by Jewish immigrants in September 1867 in Chicago as a key to understanding the interrelated processes of assimilation, ethnicization, and community-building in
nineteenth-century America. He describes the celebration, which took place
on the occasion of the founding of a Jewish hospital, as "a powerful statement of civic unity and duty transcending all religious, social, and ethnic and
racial boundaries." For Chicago's Jews, who had immigrated from various
German regions, charitable and philanthropic activities served on the one
hand as a means to overcome their own growing internal theological and
political divisions and to foster "Gemeinschaft." On the other hand, public
gestures such as the opening of the new, modern hospital to citizens of all
denominations and classes constituted efforts to win the acceptance of the
society at large and to counter anti-Jewish prejudices. While Jews in Chicago
after the Civil War formed a separate ethnic group, they maintained a strong
sense of commitment to their new home country, and they continued to
strive for inclusion in a broader civic and national community. In Brinkmann's opinion, therefore, the Jewish parade of 1867 is representative of an
intermediary stage between the "inclusive" civic celebrations of the early
republic and the "exclusive" ethnic festivities which became more common
as the century progressed.

As part of a larger research project on German-American festive culture,
Heike Bungert explores the changing mentality of German immigrants in
Milwaukee, Wisconsin, the so-called "German Athens." Her examples of
large-scale public celebrations include the patriotic "peace jubilees" after the
Franco-Prussian War of 1870-71; the festivities marking the Bicentennial of
German settlements in North America in 1883; the annual meeting of the
North American Gymnasts Union in 1893, and the visit of Prince Henry of
Prussia, the brother of Kaiser Wilhelm II, in 1902. The striving for public
displays of ethnic unity often only barely concealed divisions of interests and
opinions in Milwaukee's very diverse German-American community of sev-
eral hundred thousand people. With considerable ingenuity and creativity,

the organizers adapted the parades and other forms of festive culture to the different occasions and circumstances. At the same time, they constantly stressed certain general themes such as the important German contributions to American prosperity and "national character," the strength and self-confidence of the German-American community, and the specific German values of discipline, industry, and *Gemütlichkeit*. Bungert's sources reflect a growing nationalistic and militaristic spirit but also the development of a German-American "dual identity" based on the belief that Germans in the United States "combined the best of both worlds." Despite their open sympathy for the German Empire, German ethnic leaders in Milwaukee used the festivals as vehicles to better integrate their followers into "mainstream" America. Their eagerness to utilize the parades for commercial and advertising purposes seems to have surpassed even the often derided "Yankee materialism." According to Bungert, Milwaukee's German-American community achieved through public celebrations "a new form of cultural cohesion" which helped to check the sense of insecurity in an increasingly industrialized and individualistic society.

Halloween, an old British custom, transplanted into North America, was singled out as a celebration that could bridge the Old World and the New World. Reinterpreted to fit the new environment, it was also meant to reinforce values and images that were threatened by the arrival of newcomers who had to be reminded of the precedence and dominance of Anglo- Saxon culture. Adrien Lherm's essay traces the linguistic and historical origins of Halloween, compares the old British tradition to the American one and examines all the manipulations and strategies to redirect and control the feast in the 1840s after the long neglect following the War of Independence. Using E. P. Thompson's distinction between plebeian and patrician culture, Lherm analyzes the differences between performers and their audiences, the claims made by the poor on the wealthier, the role of gift-giving in an era of consumerism, and the competition between street and home. After "the battle for Christmas," Halloween was brought home to respectability by the elites in the 1870s in an attempt by educators and social workers to tame and sanctify the festival, and thus save it from rowdiness and lawlessness. It became a site for staging middle class values, in order to foster both a domestic and civil religion and a new national identity. These reorientations met resistance on the part of "revelers" who insisted on keeping the free mood that initially characterized the celebration. In a way, efforts to control it failed. By the early twentieth century, Halloween was no longer an unanimous rite but remained a battlefield paving the way for more reappropriations and interpretations.

When citizens of St. Paul, Minnesota, organized the first winter carnival in the United States in early 1886, they tried to turn the challenge of nature, namely long and cold winters in (what was the) the American Northwest, to their advantage. As Bernard Mergen vividly explains, all festivals, not just carnivals, are a form of play which uses social class, ethnicity, gender, and generation as "shapers of identity." In the case of St. Paul, a festival organized by local businessmen to promote investment and tourism inspired the citizens' fantasy and imagination. This, in turn, helped to transform the identity of the (then) Northwest, a region which shortly before had been better connected with the nation by the Northern Pacific Railroad. By joyfully celebrating winter recreation and amusement, the St. Paul carnival became part of the emerging leisure ethic of the American upper and middle classes. Like all carnivals, the St. Paul festival featured symbolic figures, costumes, and rituals that allowed a temporary reversal of power relations and the projection of a different social order. Some of the sporting activities popularized by immigrants from Northern Europe, especially "tobogganing" with its strong female participation, challenged the patriarchal codes of behavior. Most importantly, however, the citizens of St. Paul succeeded in creating a distinct metropolitan identity which included and protected all the various ethnic, gender, and generational identities. In a fascinating way, therefore, the St. Paul Winter Carnival (which still exists today) reveals the complex interplay of local, regional, and national identities typical of most public celebrations in the United States.

Fabian Hilfrich places the "peace jubilees" following the victory in the Spanish-American War of 1898 in the context of trends of centralization and nationalization during the Progressive Era, including the emergence of a true national public opinion. The main festivities, which took place successively in Chicago, Philadelphia, Atlanta, and Washington, D.C., were manifestations of a more nationalistic and aggressive spirit influenced by intellectual and ideological currents in Europe. With their military and naval parades, reenactments of battles, floral shows, historical pageants, and open commercialism and "boosterism," these events set new standards of quality and complexity for American public celebrations. Surprisingly, however, the main theme dominating the "jubilees" was not the military victory of 1898 but national reunion and reconciliation designed to transcend the bitter memories of the Civil War. By joining in the celebrations, Southerners symbolically accepted the verdict of the Civil War and thus gained "real" readmittance to the Union. As concessions, Northerners accepted the continuing discrimination and segregation of Afro-Americans in the South as well as a reaffirmation of white Southern sectional identity (especially the cult of the "Lost Cause"). President William McKinley, who attended the "peace jubilees" in all four cities, skillfully exploited these occasions to elicit support for his expansionist policies in the Caribbean, the Pacific, and in the

Philippines. The message of national reconciliation, therefore, was combined with an appeal to the American "destiny" of spreading democracy and civilization around the globe. However, the criticism voiced by anti-imperialist and African American leaders disturbed the harmony of the "jubilees" and foreshadowed the political battles of the twentieth century.

The concluding essay by Udo Hebel views the Plymouth Tercentenary festivities of 1920-21 as a rather defiant reaffirmation of New England's cultural hegemony and its dominant version of American civil religion at the crossroads of the "long" nineteenth and the "short" twentieth centuries. Inaugurated as a civic rite during the early phase of the Revolution in 1769, Forefathers' Day commemorated the landing of the Pilgrims at Cape Cod and the signing of the "first American constitution", the Mayflower Compact, in the year 1620. During the nineteenth century, this filiopietistic remembrance became part of the "national calendar" of United States festive culture, and until World War I the "Pilgrim myth" served as a crystallizing focus of nationalist sentiments. The Tercentenary of Forefathers' Day, which was celebrated in and around Plymouth, Massachusetts, for several months in 1920-21 was the climax of this development, evolving into a multidimensional cultural performance planned and organized by local, regional and national committees. Exploring the choreography of these festivities in great detail, Hebel shows (and implicitly criticizes) the underlying homogenized version of American history and the exclusive nature of the concept of white, Anglo-Protestant "Americanism". A careful interpretation of the orations, poems, parades, theater plays, and newspaper reports reveals that the organizers tried to counter the prevailing postwar sense of crisis and disillusionment with a spirit of "national bonding" through time and space, as well as with an affirmation of solidarity with the war-time partner Great Britain. The voices of cultural pluralism and ethnic diversity were barely heard on this occasion, and some Irish-Americans, who demonstrated against British oppression in Ireland, were kept at a distance by the police. Despite this ideological "backward orientation", however, which marks the Tercentenary as an endpoint rather than a beginning, the celebrations contained some original and "modern" elements, first among them the so-called "Pilgrim Spirit" which used historical pageantry as a public ritual of communal self-discovery and meditation. The "Indian Village" in Morton Park, featuring war dances of members of the Passamaquoddy tribe, foreshadowed in a different, more problematic way the entertainment culture and historical tourism of the second half of the twentieth century. While Forefathers' Day lost its grip on the historical imagination of the American people, the Pilgrims still figure prominently in the collective memory of the nation, and Plymouth has emerged as "one of the sacred places of American tourism."

As editors and authors, we are fully aware of the fact that our volume cannot cover all aspects of this particularly rich and fascinating topic. We hope, therefore, that the following essays will further stimulate scholarly efforts to understand festive culture as an integral part of American history and human experience in general. Innovative approaches and perspectives such as these are needed to cross disciplinary boundaries, to find new ways of reflecting on the importance of public celebrations, and to understand the role of the ever-contested "public sphere" in the long-term processes of state-building and the formation and transformation of collective identities.

Notes

1. Important recent contributions include Sean Wilentz, ed., *Rites of Power: Symbolism, Ritual and Politics Since the Middle Ages* (Philadelphia: University of Philadelphia Press, 1985); Aleida Assmann and Dietrich Harth, eds., *Mnemosyne: Formen und Funktionen der kulturellen Erinnerung* (Frankfurt/Main: Fischer, 1991); Assmann and Harth, eds., *Revolution und Mythos* (Frankfurt/Main: Fischer, 1992); Jürgen Habermas, *The Structural Transformation of the Public Sphere: An Inquiry into a Category of Bourgeois Society*, trans. Thomas Burger, with the assistance of Frederick Lawrence (Cambridge, MA: Cambridge University Press, 1989); Stephen Carr et al., *Public Space* (Cambridge: Cambridge University Press, 1992); Craig Calhoun, ed., *Habermas and the Public Sphere* (Cambridge, MA: MIT Press, 1992); Geneviève Fabre, "Lieux de fête et de commémoration," *Revue Française d'Études Américaines* 51 (1992): 7-17; Manfred Hettling and Paul Nolte, eds., *Bürgerliche Feste. Symbolische Formen politischen Handelns im 19. Jahrhundert* (Göttingen: Vandenhoeck & Ruprecht, 1993); Étienne François, ed., *Nation und Emotion* (Göttingen: Vandenhoeck & Ruprecht, 1995); Étienne François, ed., *Lieux de Mémoire: Erinnerungsorte* (Berlin: Centre Marc Bloch, 1996).
2. Mona Ozouf, *La fête révolutionnaire* (Paris: Gallimard Press, 1976); *Festivals and the French Revolution* (Cambridge, MA: Harvard University Press, 1988). Cf. the review essay by Joseph F. Byrnes in *History and Theory* 28 (1989): 112-25.
3. Cf. Bellah's statements in Robert N. Bellah, "Civil Religion in America," *Daedalus* 96 (1967): 18; "American Civil Religion in the 1970s," *Anglican Theological Review* 1 (1973): 8-20; *The Broken Covenant: American Civil Religion in Time of Trial* (New York: Seabury Press, 1975). The debate continued through the 1980s: see James A. Mathisen, "Twenty Years After Bellah: Whatever Happened to American Civil Religion?" *Sociological Analysis* 50 (1989): 129-46; D.G. Jones and R.E. Richey, eds., *American Civil Religion* (San Francisco, CA: Mellen Research University Press, 1990).
4. Bellah, "Civil Religion," 1-21.
5. Benedict Anderson, *Imagined Communities: Reflections on the Origin and Spread of Nationalism* (London: Verso, 1983).
6. David Waldstreicher, "Rites of Rebellion, Rites of Assent: Celebrations, Print Culture, and the Origins of American Nationalism," *Journal of American History* 81 (1995): 37-61; cf.

Peter Shaw, *American Patriots and the Rituals of Revolution* (Cambridge, MA: Harvard University Press, 1981).
7. See the articles by Jürgen Heideking and Dietmar Schloss in this volume. For a detailed interpretation see Jürgen Heideking, *Die Verfassung vor dem Richterstuhl. Vorgeschichte und Ratifizierung der amerikanischen Verfassung, 1787-1791* (Berlin and New York: W. de Gruyter, 1988), 709-87; cf. Heideking, "The Federal Processions of 1788 and the Origins of American Civil Religion," *Soundings* 77 (1994): 367-87.
8. Cf. Barry Schwartz, *George Washington: The Making of an American Symbol* (New York and London: The Free Press, 1987); Simon P. Newman, "Principles or Men? George Washington and the Political Culture of National Leadership, 1776-1801," *Journal of the Early Republic* 12 (1992): 477-507; Joyce Appleby, "Radicalizing the War for Independence: American Responses to the French Revolution," *Amerikastudien/American Studies* 41 (1996): 7-16. In the present volume, this period is dealt with by Marie-Jeanne Rossignol.
9. See Geneviève Fabre's article in this volume. Cf. Shane White, "'It Was a Proud Day': African Americans, Festivals, and Parades in the North, 1741-1834," *Journal of American History* 81 (1994): 13-50; John Saillant, "Lemuel Haynes's Black Republicanism and the American Republican Tradition, 1775-1820," *Journal of the Early Republic* 14 (1994): 293-324; Susan G. Davis, *Parades and Power: Street Theater in Nineteenth-century Philadelphia* (Philadelphia: Temple University Press, 1986), 73-112.
10. On the effects of the War of 1812 on festive culture, see Michael Wala in this volume. For celebrations in the so-called "Era of Good Feeling" see William H. Cohn, "Une fête nationale: le 4 juillet dans l'histoire américaine," *Cultures* 3 (1976): 147-63.
11. Gordon Wood, *The Radicalism of the American Revolution* (New York: Knopf, 1992); Mary Ryan, "The American Parade: Representations of Nineteenth-century Social Order," in Lynn Hunt, ed., *The New Cultural History* (Berkeley, CA: University of California Press, 1989), 131-53; Sean Wilentz, *Chants Democratic: New York City and the Rise of the American Working Class, 1788-1850* (New York: Oxford University Press, 1984); Wilentz, "Artisan Republican Festivals and the Rise of Class Conflict in New York City, 1788-1837," in Michael H. Frisch and Daniel J. Walkowitz, eds., *Working-Class America: Essays on Labor, Community, and American Society* (Urbana, Ill., Chicago: University of Illinois Press, 1983), 37-77.
12. Robert A. Orsi, "Parades, Holidays, and Public Rituals," *The Encyclopedia of American Social History*, 1913-22.
13. Mario Cuomo and Harold Holzer, eds., *Lincoln on Democracy—His Own Words, With Essays by America's Foremost Historians* (New York: Harper Collins, 1990), 20.
14. The year 1840 saw "the most spectacular campaign in which the whole nation had ever engaged ... highly competitive party structures exerted every effort to arouse popular excitement ... the voters were moved to identify strongly with the symbols, personalities, organizations, and myths that taken together constituted their party." Richard P. McCormick, *The Second American Party System: Party Formation in the Jacksonian Era* (Chapel Hill: University of North Carolina Press, 1966), 341-42, 350.
15. Davis, *Parades and Power*, 149-50.
16. Ryan, "The American Parade," 145-47.
17. See the articles by Bénédicte Deschamps, Annick Foucrier, and Tobias Brinkmann in this volume. Cf. Kathleen N. Conzen, "Ethnicity as Festive Culture: Nineteenth-century German America on Parade," in Werner Sollors, ed., *The Invention of Ethnicity* (New York and London: Oxford University Press, 1989), 44-76; Ramón A. Gutiérrez and Geneviève Fabre, eds., *Feasts and Celebrations in North American Ethnic Communities* (Albuquerque, NM: University of New Mexico Press, 1995).

18. Cf. Merrill Peterson, *Lincoln in American Memory* (New York: Oxford University Press, 1994); Garry Wills, *Lincoln at Gettysburg: The Words That Remade America* (New York and London: Simon & Schuster, 1992).
19. See the contributions by Adrien Lherm and Bernard Mergen to this volume.
20. Michael Kammen, *A Machine That Would Go Of Itself: The Constitution in American Culture* (New York: St. Martin's Press, 1986), 142, 148.
21. Frederick Jackson Turner, "The Significance of the Frontier in American History," in Turner, ed., *The Frontier in American History* (New York: H. Holt and Company, 1920), 1-38.
22. See Fabian Hilfrich's article in this volume.
23. Wolfgang Hartmann, *Der historische Festzug. Seine Entstehung und Entwicklung im 19. und 20. Jahrhundert* (München: Prestel, 1976).
24. See the articles by Heike Bungert and Udo Hebel in this volume. Cf. Robert A. Orsi, "Parades, Holidays, and Public Rituals," in *Encyclopedia of American Social History*, 1913-22.
25. See especially David Waldstreicher, *In the Midst of Perpetual Fetes: The Making of American Nationalism, 1776-1820* (Chapel Hill: University of North Carolina Press, 1997); Len Travers, *Celebrating the Fourth: Independence Day and the Rites of Nationalism in the Early Republic* (Amherst, MA: University of Massachusetts Press, 1997); Simon P. Newman, *Parades and the Politics of the Street: Festive Culture in the Early American Republic* (Philadelphia: University of Pennsylvania Press, 1997); Brooks McNamara, *Day of Jubilee: The Great Age of Public Celebration in New York. 1788-1909* (New Brunswick, NJ: Rutgers University Press, 1997); John Seeley, *Memory's Nation: The Place of Plymouth Rock* (Chapel Hill: University of North Carolina Press, 1998); David Glassberg, *American Historical Pageantry: The Uses of Tradition in the Early Twentieth Century* (Chapel Hill: University of North Carolina Press, 1990). The workshop reports of the Lisbon conference are published in *American Studies in Europe Newsletter* 41 (1998): 1-15. For an assessment of the importance of festive culture for American national identity in the twentieth century see John Bodnar, *Remaking America: Public Memory, Commemoration, and Patriotism in the Twentieth Century* (Princeton, NJ: Princeton University Press, 1992).
26. Andrew R.L. Cayton, "We Are All Nationalists, We Are All Localists": Review Essay of David Waldstreicher, *In the Midst of Perpetual Fetes, Journal of the Early Republic* 18 (1998), 521-28. See also Joanne B. Freeman's review of Simon P. Newman, *Parades and the Politics of the Street*, ibid., 315-17.

Chapter 1

CELEBRATING THE CONSTITUTION

*The Federal Processions of 1788 and
the Emergence of a Republican Festive Culture
in the United States*

Jürgen Heideking

Public Celebrations as an Integral Part of the Debate Over the Constitution, 1787-88

WHEN THE CONTINENTAL Congress in Philadelphia resolved that the American colonies should be "free and independent states," Massachusetts delegate John Adams envisaged a national holiday for the new country. He predicted that Independence Day

> will be celebrated by succeeding generations as the great anniversary Festival. It ought to be commemorated, as the day of deliverance, by solemn acts of devotion to God Almighty. It ought to be solemnized with pomp and parade, with shows, games, sports, guns, bells, bonfires, and illuminations, from one end of this continent to the other, from this time forward, forever.[1]

During the following years of war and economic crisis, however, Americans did not find many opportunities for joyful celebrations. It took more than a decade, before John Adams' vision was—at least partially—turned into a reality. This happened in a rather unexpected way, as part of a major politi-

---

Notes for this section begin on page 40.

cal debate over whether the United States' original constitution, the Articles of Confederation of 1777, should be replaced by a new "national" or "federal" constitution. Drafted at the Philadelphia Convention from May to September 1787, this document was to be ratified by the states at specially elected conventions. It could not go into force until approved by at least nine of the thirteen states. Though a few states immediately adopted the new Constitution, among them Pennsylvania and Connecticut, the process of ratification soon stalled. Opposition began forming in the fall of 1787 to protest against the centralist, "consolidating" effects of the Philadelphia plan, and opponents demanded better protection for the rights of the states and their individual citizens. This campaign was so successful that the Constitution was almost rejected in Massachusetts, while several other important states such as Virginia and New York deferred a decision until the summer of 1788. For months, the fate of the "American experiment" of republican self-government hung in the balance. It was in this anxious and emotionally charged atmosphere that a new form of festive culture emerged, characterized by a wave of public celebrations culminating in the great "Federal Processions" of Philadelphia and New York City in July 1788.[2]

The idea of celebrating the ratification with a parade or "Grand Procession" originated in John Adams' hometown of Boston. A caucus of the Boston tradesmen had spontaneously decided to mark the narrow victory won by the Constitution's supporters, the self-styled "Federalists," in the final vote taken at the Massachusetts ratifying convention on February 6, 1788.[3] After two days of preparation, the parade moved down the snow-covered streets of Boston on February 8 "in solemn silence," according to newspaper accounts, punctuated only by the ringing of church bells and by "huzzahs" when the marchers passed the houses of prominent Federalists.[4] The number of participants soon swelled from 1,500 to 4,000, since many spectators decided to join the marching column. The parade was led by a group of ax-swinging lumberjacks symbolically clearing a path to the American West. Then came the horse-drawn and ox-drawn carts of local farmers that had been invited to join in the festivities. At the heart of the parade, however, were the artisans, tradesmen, mechanics, and sailors, organized according to occupation and marching behind the banners of their respective guilds. Groups of artisans riding on colorfully decorated floats demonstrated such skills as rope making, shoemaking, and candlemaking. The greatest attraction was apparently the "Federal Ship," a boat taken from the Boston harbor and loaded onto a wagon drawn by thirteen horses, one for each state in the Union. It symbolized the new "ship of state" that had been launched by the Federal Convention in Philadelphia. Rounding out the procession was a unit of Massachusetts militiamen and a sled containing the members of the organizing committee. After five hours the march ended on the square in front of Faneuil Hall where hot punch and cheese were served and a number of toasts made to the members of the Philadelphia and Boston conventions. The concluding act was performed by the ship carpenters who transported a rotten barge, called "Old Confederation," to the Boston Green and put it to the flames.

This event differed markedly from Fourth of July celebrations held during the 1780s, which generally centered around patriotic speeches and military drills performed by the militia. Accordingly, the "innovative" character of the ratification celebration was stressed in private letters as well as in newspaper articles that were reprinted all over the Union.[5]

As the ratification debate continued in the following weeks and months, other cities, unwilling to be outdone by Boston, entered into competition with each other to see who could put on the most magnificent Federal Procession. Since organizers now had more time to prepare and merchants had begun to provide financial backing, the parades were becoming ever larger and more spectacular. Carpenters in Baltimore built the "Federal Edifice," a tower with thirteen floors, each sporting thirteen columns and thirteen arches. It rested heavily on the shoulders of seven men, representing the number of states that had so far adopted the Constitution. Baltimore merchants donated funds for a great banquet and for the construction of a real ship christened the *Federalist*. On the day after the parade, it sailed up the Potomac to Mount Vernon to be presented to George Washington in honor of his role as commander-in-chief of the Continental Army and president of the Federal Convention.[6]

In Charleston, South Carolina, teachers marched together with their students carrying a globe and holding signs praising the benefits of a uniform, republican education for young Americans. Even slaves were allowed to participate, albeit only as liverymen leading their masters' horses. At the banquet held afterwards, wealthy plantation owners mingled with the common citizens "in the greatest harmony."[7] In Portsmouth, New Hampshire, the published order of procession listed seventy positions, from "Columbus, on horseback" to the "Ship Union, Commander George Washington," and included displays of the exquisite crafts of goldsmiths and silversmiths. Printers worked on a mobile press, distributing specially composed "Federal Songs" and "Federal Poems" among the spectators.[8] The atmosphere in Portsmouth was particularly joyful, since New Hampshire, after a failed attempt in the winter, had become the ninth state to ratify on June 21, 1788, thus fulfilling the conditions for the Constitution to take effect.

The citizens of Philadelphia, who had hosted the Federal Convention as well as the Pennsylvania ratifying convention in 1787, resolved to honor the

States—like the gen'rous vine supported live,
The strength they gain is from th'embrace they giv
THE FEDERAL PILLARS.

UNITED THEY STAND—DIVIDED FALL.

NINTH and the SUFFICIENT PILLAR.

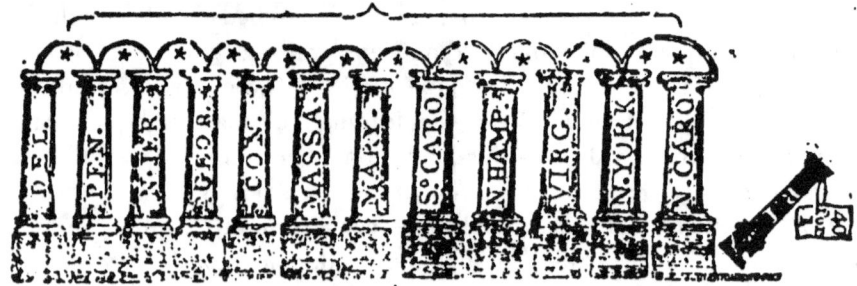

The GREAT PALLADIUM of our happy land
Connects "*the Union*" by a "*golden chain*;"
Which kept entire, these Federal States shall stand
As long as Time's old annals shall remain:
And nations see with joy, the beauteous Dome,
" COLUMBIA's boast, and FREEDOM's hallow'd home."

The Ratification Process in Newspaper Cartoons, Mass. Centinel,
January 16 and June 26, 1788, December 16, 1789.

adoption of the Constitution by nine states by celebrating it on the twelfth anniversary of Independence Day. The centerpiece of this event, Philadelphia's "Grand Federal Procession," set new standards with over 5,000 participants and dozens of floats.[9] Among these were the "Ship Union" with thirteen sailors under the command of an actor posing as George Washington, and the "Grand Federal Edifice," a dome supported by thirteen corinthian columns, thirty-six feet in height, and drawn by ten white horses on which several architects and 450 carpenters had labored furiously for days. The main attraction, however, was the "triumphal car", a float formed in the shape of the American eagle in whose talons were clutched Pennsylvania's Chief Justice Thomas McKean and a copy of the Constitution. Enhancing the splendor of the parade was the work of a number of artists, led by painters Charles Willson Peale and Jacques Louis David, who would later plan and orchestrate French revolutionary festivals. They designed costumes and banners, decorated floats with allegorical figures, and devised so-called "transparencies," translucent paintings illuminated from within depicting scenes from the War of Independence or displaying portraits of George Washington and other revolutionary heroes. Federalist songs and poems were printed in English and German (one third of Philadelphia's 40,000 inhabitants were of German descent) and distributed along the route of the procession.[10] One of the last divisions was formed by clergymen of various Christian denominations and a Jewish Rabbi, all walking "arm in arm with each other, to exemplify the Union."[11] Organizers estimated 17,000 people attended the concluding banquet at Union Green and listened to a speech given by prominent Federalist James Wilson, who expounded on the importance of the new Constitution for America's "public happiness" and the future prosperity of the United States.[12] In the evening, festive illuminations graced the ships in the harbor and the public buildings.[13]

The most conspicuous holdout in the ratification battle at this point was New York, a crucially important state without which no one could seriously imagine a viable American Union. The Federal Procession in New York City was staged on July 23 with an eye to making an impression on the ratifying convention just up the Hudson River in the little town of Poughkeepsie, where delegates, among them Alexander Hamilton and anti-Federalist Governor George Clinton, had been futilely debating the pros and cons of the Constitution for weeks. A committee of merchants and artisans meticulously oversaw every detail of the preparations right down to notices requiring residents to sweep the streets along the parade route. The 5,000 marchers gathered at 8 a.m. and began to form a line that was a mile and one-half long. Six of the ten marching divisions were reserved for artisans, tradesmen, and mechanics. A ship was once again at the center of the procession, this time

New York's "Grand Federal Procession".

a specifically built miniature frigate named *Hamilton* in honor of New York's leading Federalist politician. Next came the "Federal Chair of State," a throne on which allegorical female figures representing "Freedom" and "Justice" held up a copy of the Constitution. In the final section of the parade were professors and students from Columbia University (formerly known as King's University), members of the New York Philological Society propagating American English as a distinct national language, and, finally, the clergy. The official newspaper report, written by Noah Webster, described the parade as "slow and majestic," while "numberless crowds were pressing on every side ... As this splendid, novel, and interesting exhibition moved along, an unprecedented silence reigned throughout the city, which gave a solemnity to the whole transaction suited to the singular importance of its cause. No noise was heard but the deep rumbling of carriage wheels, with the necessary salutes and signals."[14] The march ended at Bayard's farm where French architect Pierre L'Enfant, who a few years later would plan the city of Washington, had arranged ten long rows of dining tables like spokes of a half-wheel (it was hoped that New York would soon become the tenth state to ratify), joined by a 150-foot colonnade with three raised pavilions in the center. The whole construction offered seating for 6,000 guests, a remarkable number for a city with a population of less than 33,000. After dinner, thirteen toasts were drunk, each followed by the firing of ten cannons. At 4 p.m. a salute fired from the *Hamilton* signaled that the return march was to begin, and the participants made their way back to the "The Fields", now City Hall Park.[15]

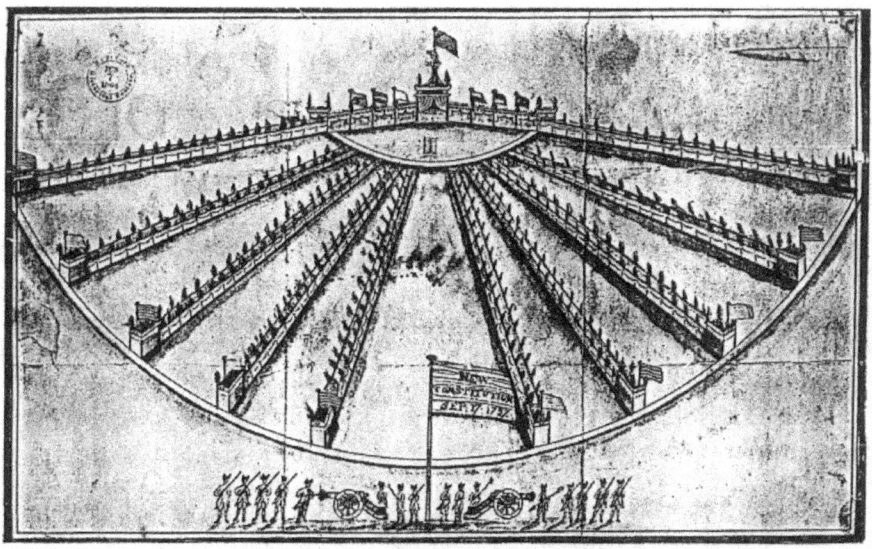

The "Federal Banquet Pavillon" by Pierre L'Enfant.

The Ratification Celebrations as Political Propaganda

The examples selected above may suffice to convey an image of the Federal Processions and the atmosphere in the coastal cities. One has to keep in mind, however, that the parades were just the highlights of a whole wave of urban and rural festivities accompanying the debate over the Constitution. A closer, systematic look at these events reveals a complex pattern of functions, purposes, and meanings. On the first level, that of mundane politics, the Federal Processions and the ratification celebrations in general were effective propaganda ploys. The advocates of the Constitution had laid claim to the term "federal" since the fall of 1787 in order to distinguish themselves as "Federalists" from their adversaries, the "anti-Federalists." The dispute over names was an integral part of the larger debate: the anti-Federalists strongly—yet in the end vainly—resisted this negative party label. They viewed themselves as the "true" Federalists; it was they who were defending the Articles of Confederation against attempts to establish a "national" or "consolidated" government. Across the country the organization of the festivities lay exclusively in the hands of Federalists who took care to ensure that the voice of discord did not disturb their harmonious chorus of praise. Beyond the Federalists' sincere expression of joy and relief at the adoption of the Constitution, their main objective was to break the remaining resistance against a smooth transition to the new system of government. Knowing that the opposition drew most of its support from the agricultural backcountry, the Federalists went out of their way to include farmers in the processions. They were even more delighted when prominent representatives of the "agrarian interests" agreed to participate in the celebrations. One delegate from the western parts of Massachusetts, who had voted against the Constitution at the ratifying convention, wrote to a friend a short time later that he did not regret accepting an invitation to the parade as the citizens of Boston had lavished exquisite food and drinks upon him for days.[16] At about the same time, a female observer predicted that the festivities in Boston would impress the rural population more than even the most eloquent arguments for ratification.[17]

The celebrations were also devised to put psychological pressure on the opposition. The states that had not yet ratified the constitution were often symbolically portrayed as broken pillars, empty tables, unused goblets, or unlit candles. This was understood as a clear warning against continued resistance. At the celebration in New York, threats by the Federalist-dominated city to secede from its anti-Federalist hinterland and join the new Union hung in the air. It was this danger that compelled the delegates at the Poughkeepsie convention to reluctantly adopt the Constitution a few days after the parade.[18] Radical anti-Federalists angrily resented the "pompous" celebrations, recognizing their strong influence on public opinion. A writer using the pseudonym "Maria" compared the processions to a "Royal Homage" in Europe: "Was I a gentleman, I would bear testimony against such proceedings, on such occasions, as I think it tends to the subversion of true republican principles, in as much as it controuls the bias of a citizen's mind, which ought to be free and uncontroulable by party measures."[19] The printer of the *New York Journal*, Thomas Greenleaf, paid a bitter price for having the audacity to publish ironic comments on the city's Federal Procession. The article had barely appeared when an enraged mob stormed his shop and destroyed the printing press. At other places, anti-Federalists organized demonstrations and burned or symbolically buried the constitution—rituals that were reminiscent of the Revolution and the War of Independence. They could not prevent, however, the strengthening of the deep-seated desire for social harmony and national unity. Urban residents from Boston to Charleston had almost unanimously voted for the adoption of the Constitution, and now the backcountry was slowly becoming infected with the spirit of Federalism embodied in the processions. Public support for the Constitution gained momentum as a result, aided by the

Federalists' promise to add a Bill of Rights to the document. The celebrations expedited this swing in public mood, which in turn not only enabled the Constitution to be put into effect, but also secured a clear victory for the Federalists in the first congressional elections in the winter of 1788-89.

The Federal Processions as Expression of Economic Interests

On a second level, the Federal Processions reflected hope for an improvement of the economic situation under the new Constitution. The main impetus came from the urban middle class, the small businessmen and members of artisans' guilds, who comprised a majority of the marchers. These groups had suffered the most during the depression of the 1780s and now expected a more active national trade policy favoring American producers. The parades gave them an opportunity to display their talent, creativity, discipline, and self-confidence, but also to present their demands to the responsible politicians. In this sense, the parades can be regarded as symbolic acts performed both to overcome the perception of crisis looming since the middle of the 1780s, and to summon prosperity associated with the new system of government. A newspaper article on the Baltimore parade expressed this feeling: "In this elegant place ... the American character, emerging from depression, was exhibited in all its glories."[20] Not surprisingly, metaphors of the rising sun, which incorporated the image of a westwardly expanding "American Empire," were exceedingly popular. The "Federal Ships" included in most of the parades symbolized hope for a revival of commerce, crucial to so many of the trades dependent on shipping and shipbuilding.[21]

The participants in the Federal Processions also presented concrete economic demands. The state legislatures should encourage stability and investment, and the future national government should reduce imports from Europe and boost manufacturing and industry at home to create more employment opportunities for Americans. Hence, for example, the protectionist slogan of Baltimore nail-makers: "While industry prevails, we need no foreign nails!"[22] In New York City, several delegations of artisans marched behind a Hamilton-inspired banner: "Americans, encourage your own manufactures!" On one of the floats, blacksmiths were forging an anchor under the motto: "Forge me strong, finish me neat, I soon shall moor a Federal fleet."[23] The push for national self-reliance went so far as to lead to a ban on imported liquors at the banquets, with such "American beverages" as cider and beer being offered in their place. For the merchants involved in overseas trading, this overt protectionism surely went too far. Since they shared the desire for an energetic national government, however, they joined in the festivities and reinforced the people's faith in an economic upturn. In Boston they proved that action was louder than words, placing orders for several new ships just in time for the ratification debate.[24]

Seen from this angle, the course of events exhibited clear parallels to the struggle for independence from Britain. The rebellion against Parliament and King also began in the coastal cities and was initiated mainly by tradesmen's organizations like the Sons of Liberty. For the most part, the same social groups that made up the Federal Processions in 1788 had also organized demonstrations and economic boycotts such as the Boston Tea Party. In newspapers and speeches, the framing of the Constitution was thus often described as a "second American Revolution," this time in favor of an efficient national system of government. The underlying idea was that farming, commerce, and industry should complement each other to fuel economic growth and avoid the volatile social tensions of the kind that had surfaced in the 1780s in Shay's rebellion. The parades were thus indicative of the urban population's increasingly "modern" understanding of republicanism, as opposed to the traditional emphasis on the cultivation of agrarian values such as thrift and simplicity.[25] Benjamin Rush was inspired by the Philadelphia procession to propose that the different trades of the city

> may avail themselves of their late sudden and accidental associations, and form themselves into distinct incorporated societies. Many advantages would arise to them from such institutions, especially if part of the objects of their union should be to establish a fund for the relief of the infirm or decayed members of their companies, and of their widows and orphans.[26]

When the new government under the Constitution was installed in 1789, trade and merchants' associations from several American cities petitioned Congress for legislation promoting commerce and industry.[27]

The Ratification Celebrations and the Construction of National Identity

On a third level, the celebrations not only revealed a desire for national unity but also provided Federalists with the opportunity to forge a stronger sense of common American identity. Five years after the signing of the Peace Treaty with Great Britain, the image of an "English enemy" and the threat of foreign intervention no longer sufficed to draw the citizens together.[28] Now it became more important to depict or construct a common history as a progressive liberation movement, an ascending line from Columbus to the Pilgrims and to Independence under the leadership of George Washington.[29] The symbolic burning of the ship *Old Confederation*, for example, which took place in several cities, branded the Articles of Confederation as a historical aberration, a temporary departure from the path of progress and unity to which the American people were destined by Divine Providence. The Federal Constitution, by contrast, was portrayed as the crowning achievement of the American Revolution, the logical consequence and consummation of American history since the discovery of the "New World." At the parades, the new ship of state was entrusted to George Washington, foreshadowing his election to the presidency. No one symbolized national unity more than Washington, the embodiment of republican virtue and the common good.

The structure of the processions also anticipated the "march of civilization," the famous metaphor coined a century later by historian Frederick Jackson Turner in his essay "The Significance of the Frontier in American History": "Stand at Cumberland Gap and watch the procession of civilization, marching single file—the buffalo following the trail to the salt spring, the Indians, the fur-trader and hunter, the cattleraiser, the pioneer farmer—and the frontier has passed by."[30] What Turner only implied, namely that cities represented the highest form of civilization, was openly proclaimed by the parades of 1788. The city dwellers, who accounted for less than ten percent of the population, saw themselves as a dynamic, progressive force leading the way to prosperity and national greatness. The dominance of the middle classes, who were more thoroughly "Americanized" than the people in rural areas, obviously contributed to the similarity of the parades regardless of state and regional distinctions.[31]

Attempts to construct a "usable past" for a common American future were tied to ideological and cultural ambitions comparing the United States favorably with the "Old World." The artists celebrating the rising glory of the American Empire in pictures, poems, and songs wanted to convince their compatriots of the superiority of the republican political system and culture. Being heavily influenced as they were by European styles and tastes, they were not entirely certain as to how this new culture was to distinguish itself from its European counterpart. The creation of an "American national language" envisioned by Noah Webster and his friends, for example, was more easily said than done. Nevertheless, the celebrations of 1788 can be regarded as a milestone in the development of a uniquely American public culture. The processions themselves were theatrical works of art, productions in which the people emerged from their roles as spectators to become supporting actors in a republican choreography. The organizers of the parades aimed at a visual confirmation of the principles and values on which a common future was to be based: popular sovereignty, participation and consent of the governed, and a government of laws based on a written Constitution.

The ratification celebrations introduced a number of new rituals, symbols, and techniques. Part of the iconography was borrowed from Europe, especially from the Lord Mayor shows in London,[32] but Federalists imbued the traditional forms with a new ideology by setting the processions up as the reflection of a self-governing, harmonious republican society. In the words of Pennsylvania Federalist James Wilson, the parades represented a living image of "a people, free and enlightened, establishing and ratifying a system of government which they have previously considered, examined, and approved."[33] After participating in the Philadelphia Federal Procession, Benjamin Rush proudly compared public life in America with the situation in Europe. Foreigners who had seen "the splendid processions of coronations in Europe, declare, that they all yield, in the effect of pleasure, to our hasty exhibition instituted in honor of our Foederal Government." In marching side by side without any hierarchical order, the various classes, professions, and trades

> seemed to acknowledge by their harmony and respect for each other that they were all necessary to each other and all useful in cultivated society. These circumstances distinguished this procession from the processions in Europe, which are commonly instituted in honor of single persons ... Farmers and Tradesmen are either deemed unworthy of such connections, or are introduced like horses or buildings, only to add to the strength or length of the procession. Such is the difference between the effects of a republican and a monarchical government on the minds of men.

According to Rush, who was strongly interested in educational matters, the procession had "made such an impression upon the minds of our young people, that 'foederal' and 'union' have now become part of the 'house-hold words' of every family in the city."[34] Whereas public festivals in Europe often turned raucous, the participants in the Federal Processions were allegedly the paragons of republican virtue. Almost pleadingly, the newspapers pointed out that Americans avoided the excessive use of alcohol during the events, that there were no fights, much less riots, and that everyone returned peacefully home at the conclusion of the banquets. While that may have been a slight exaggeration, the calls for moderation and discipline definitely contributed to the solemn aura surrounding the public ceremonies. In this way, the processions illustrated the legitimation of the new political order by the principle of popular sovereignty. French artist Jacques Louis David, who after returning to France organized spectacular revolutionary festivities, observed in view of Philadelphia's Fourth of July procession: "National festivals are instituted for the people; it is fitting that they participate in them with a common accord and that they play the principal role there."[35] The citizens themselves had taken center stage, and in becoming actors on the public scene, they were "observing themselves in the process of defining themselves."[36] To a certain degree, this image of a self-governing people and a harmonious community was illusionary, as the "newspaper war" over ratification as well as the confrontation between Federalists and anti-Federalists clearly demonstrated. In addition, substantial parts of the population—women, free blacks, day laborers, the poor—were still reduced to the status of passive spectators, not to speak of the slaves who were not even considered part of the community. Nevertheless, the republican vision projected onto the streets of America's cities in 1788 held the promise of an egalitarian, more inclusive "civil society."[37]

The Federal Processions as Rituals of an American "Civil Religion"

On a fourth and final level, the processions must be seen as semi-religious rituals designed to sanctify the new constitutional order. Many contemporaries believed the settlement of the colonies, the Revolution, the War of Independence, and the crafting of the Constitution were all part of a divine plan. In newspaper articles and speeches, these events were explicitly compared with the Exodus of the Children of Israel from Egypt, Moses' delivery of the Law, and the liberation of the Jews from Babylonian persecution. Again, Benjamin Rush eloquently expressed this feeling—a mixture of religiosity and nationalism—in public:

> I do not believe that the Constitution was the offspring of [divine] inspiration, but I am perfectly satisfied, that the union of the states, in its *form* and *adoption*, is as much the work of a divine providence, as any of the miracles recorded in the Old and New Testament were the effects of a divine power. 'Tis done! We have become a nation. America has ceased to be the only power in the world, that has derived no benefit from her declaration of independence.[38]

There were also many references to other historical precedents: a writer in Rhode Island recalled that the Greeks and Romans had regularly held large "public celebrations" and that such festivities formed part of the "outward or ceremonial religion in every Country."[39] The birth of a nation had always occasioned "public worship of the Deity," explained "An American" in the *Fayetteville Gazette*, and the American nation could not be an exception if it was to be stable and permanent: "Lycurgus and Solon, Romulus and Jereboam, those founders of nations, saw the necessity of calling in the aid of religion to give stability and duration to their newly-established empires ... Human nature is still the same; and the aides of religion are as necessary, as in ancient times." The same writer continued his reflections in the next edition of that newspaper with the controversial demand that public religion [should] be maintained, and the support of it proportioned among all members of the community ... There never has been a nation great or happy, where the subject's obedience to human law did not receive a sanction from the obligation of religion. Hence all legislatures have interwoven religion with their system of law and government ... Religion may be established on principles consistent with perfect freedom.[40]

At the Federal Processions, the Constitution assumed an elevated position as an actual document. Always carried near the center of the parades in the manner of a "holy scripture" on floats or "triumphal cars," it epitomized the concept of justice and the rule of law. This is where the proximity to religious rituals is most striking, inasmuch as *la translation des objects sacrés* is the central element of Christian processions.[41] The effort to sanctify the Constitution, or, in other words, the particular American form of "constitutionalism," was often observed by Europeans visitors to the United States with a certain bewilderment, and actually began even before the ratification of the document.[42] American republicanism, combining the principle of popular sovereignty with respect for the rule of law and the superiority of higher law over legislative and executive actions, did not clash with traditional piety. The great majority of American clergy had supported the struggle for independence, and their active participation in the Federal Processions of 1788 was surely a precondition of the smooth "transfer of sanctity" from the revolutionary order to the new federal system of government. Contrary to the situation in France in the following decade, this sanctity was not wrested from the church and usurped by the republican state; it had merely been extended from the religious to the political sphere in the form of a supra-denominational "civil religion." This took the edge off the enlightenment principle of the separation of church and state, which at this time was beginning to spread from Virginia to the rest of the Union. By their steady and finally successful insistence on a Bill of Rights, the anti-Federalists, too, made a very important contribution to the ratification process. Insofar as these fundamental rights were understood as reflections of the natural and divine law, the inclusion of a Bill of Rights even reinforced the aura of "holiness" surrounding the constitution. Though the First Amendment explicitly forbids Congress to establish a religion, Federalists and anti-Federalists alike did not intend the new government to be indifferent to religious concerns or even irreligious. As the embodiment of a "natural order," American society was bound by the "inalienable rights" ordained by divine law and subject to the will of a Higher Being.

This integration of civil religion in American political culture was furthered by another event that occurred in the spring of 1789, signifying the beginning of the national era: the inauguration of the first president of the

United States in New York City. This occasion was preceded by an unparalleled triumphal procession from Washington's home at Mount Vernon to the seat of the old and the new Congress. Washington was hailed by delegations of citizens at all important stops along the way. The most elaborate of these ceremonies took place in Philadelphia, where Charles Willson Peale had arranged for the bridge over the Schuylkill River to be spanned by six-meter-high arches, creating a *via triumphalis* lined by women dressed in white robes and resembling ancient priestesses. Washington was compelled to ride through this guard of honor on a white horse before being escorted by a solemn procession to City Hall, where he thanked the citizens, including a few words addressed to a delegation from the German Lutheran Church. The final segment of the journey was by water down the Hudson River, where he was accompanied by a flotilla of festooned boats.[43]

The inauguration was held on April 30, 1789, in the presence of Congress and members of the clergy. Washington solemnly swore the oath of office on the Bible, concluding with the phrase "so help me God." In his inaugural address he held forth that the "invisible hand" of an "almighty being" had obviously guided the fortunes of the United States. Virtue and happiness went hand in hand with duties and benefits, honest politics and public prosperity,

> since we ought to be no less persuaded that the propitious smiles of Heaven can never be expected on a nation that disregards the eternal rules of order and right which Heaven itself has ordained; and since the preservation of the sacred fire of liberty and the destiny of the republican model of government are justly considered, perhaps, as *deeply*, as *finally*, staked on the experiment entrusted to the hands of the American people.[44]

The speech was followed by a short church service for the president and members of Congress in the Anglican St. Paul's Chapel. The gravity of the ceremony was enhanced by the fact that one of the first measures of the new government was the proclamation of a national day of fasting and prayer, thus also underlining the cultural and religious continuity from colonial times to the federal republic. Congress had already appointed official chaplains, who were to open each session with a prayer and hold regular church services for the Representatives and Senators. The ceremony concluded with a spectacular display of fireworks, the illumination of New York harbor, and "public rejoicing."

Despite Washington's appeal for national unity and harmony, the political culture of the 1790s was characterized by a clash between two opposing interpretations of republicanism and the Constitution. Though the seeds for both views had been sown during the ratification debate, the conflict was aggravated by the French Revolution. While the Federalists under the leadership of Washington and Alexander Hamilton were first of all concerned with stabilizing the new government and holding the nation together, the Republicans led by Thomas Jefferson and James Madison organized opposition to what they perceived to be monarchical tendencies. The political and ideological differences were also visible in the public celebrations: for the Federalists, both Washington and the Constitution symbolized the nation, and the President's birthday soon became one of the most celebrated events in their annual calendar. It is no surprise, therefore, that the "memorial processions" staged throughout the country following Washington's death in 1799 became the greatest public spectacles since the Federal Processions of 1788.[45]

The Republicans, by contrast, advocated a return to the egalitarian, anti-authoritarian values of the American Revolution. The Fourth of July remained by far their most important holiday, and they tried to "balance" the Constitution with the more radical Declaration of Independence. It was not uncommon during this period for supporters of the respective parties to celebrate national holidays separately, depending on their particular ideological orientation.[46] Public life assumed a dynamic, vibrant quality, and conflict and consensus became two sides of the same coin, as they have remained ever since.

Notes

1. John Adams to Abigail Adams, July 3, 1776, quoted from L.H. Butterfield et al., eds., *The Book of Abigail and John: Selected Letters of the Adams Family 1762-1784* (Cambridge, MA, and London: Harvard University Press, 1975), 140-42. John Adams was thinking of July 2, the day of the congressional resolution; on July 4, Congress formally adopted the Declaration of Independence.
2. The author has analyzed this emergence of a new republican festive culture in greater detail in his habilitation: *Die Verfassung vor dem Richterstuhl: Vorgeschichte und Ratifizierung der amerikanischen Verfassung, 1787-1791* (Berlin and New York: W. de Gruyter, 1988), 709-87. See also Jürgen Heideking, "The Federal Processions of 1788 and the Origins of American Civil Religion," *Soundings* 77 (1994): 367-87; Whitfield J. Bell, "The Federal Processions of 1788," *New York Historical Society Quarterly* 46 (1962): 5-40.
3. Federalists had been able to achieve the result of 187 to 168 in favor of ratification only by promising to introduce amendments, especially a Bill of Rights, after the adoption of the Constitution.
4. The most detailed newspaper report appeared in Benjamin Russell's *Massachusetts Centinel* on February 9, 1788.

5. Benjamin Lincoln felt that the newspaper reports on the procession "would no more compare with the original than the light of the faintest star would with that of the sun." Jeremy Belknap called the parade "a kind of Lord Mayor's show." According to Samuel Salisbury, the procession "was something new and one of the most pleasing sights that ever I saw." For Isaac Winslow, "the like was never seen before," and Thomas Fitch Oliver maintained that the celebrations had been conducted "in an entire new style at least for this Country." Benjamin Lincoln to George Washington, February 9, 1788, Washington Papers, Library of Congress; Belknap to Ebenezer Hazard, February 10, 1788, Mass. Hist. Soc. Collections, 5th Series III (1877), 17-19; Samuel Salisbury to Stephen Salisbury, February 10, 1788, Salisbury Papers, American Antiquarian Society; Isaac Winslow, Jr., to Henry Knox, February 10, 1788, Knox Papers, Mass. Historical Society; Thomas Fitch Oliver to Dr. Benjamin Lynde Oliver, February 11, 1788, Oliver Family Papers, Mass. Historical Society.
6. When the *Federalist* sank during a storm a few weeks later, Washington interpreted this as a bad omen for the future of the Union. Diary, June 9 and July 24, 1788, Washington Papers, LC.
7. *Charleston State Gazette*, May 29, 1788.
8. *New Haven Gazette*, 26 June 1788.
9. For more detail and interpretation, see Dietmar Schloss's article in this volume. Cf. Sarah H.J. Simpson, "The Federal Procession of the City of New York," *New-York Historical Society Quarterly Bulletin* 9 (1925): 39-58; Laura Rigal, "'Raising the Roof': Authors, Spectators and Artisans in the Grand Federal Procession of 1788," *Theatre Journal* 48 (1996): 253-77.
10. Francis Hopkinson, the chairman of the arrangements committee, composed "An Ode" honoring American independence. The last four lines read: "Hail to this festival! all hail the day! *Columbia's* standard on HER ROOF display: And let the PEOPLE'S Motto ever be, 'UNITED thus, and thus UNITED—FREE.'" *Documentary History of the Ratification of the Constitution*, ed. John P. Kaminski, Richard Leffler, and Gaspare J. Saladino (Madison, WI: State Historical Society of Wisconsin, 1976-) 18: 246-47.
11. Benjamin Rush, "Observations on the Fourth of July Procession in Philadelphia," *Pennsylvania Mercury*, July 15, 1788, reprinted in *American Museum*, July 1788; *Documentary History of the Ratification of the Constitution*, 18: 265.
12. James Wilson's oration was printed on 9 July in the *Pennsylvania Gazette* and reprinted in fourteen newspapers by September 6: *Documentary History of the Ratification of the Constitution*, 18: 242-46.
13. Francis Hopkinson, a determined Federalist, wrote a detailed description of the parade and the banquet, printed on July 9, 1788, in the *Pennsylvania Gazette* and in the *Pennsylvania Packet*, and later distributed as a pamphlet. A German version entitled "Die grosse Bundesschaftliche Procezion" appeared on July 15, 1788 in the *Gemeinnützige Philadephische Correspondenz.*
14. Noah Webster's report was published in early August by several New York newspapers.
15. Richard Leffler, "The Grandest Procession," *Seaport* (Winter 1987-88): 28-31.
16. William Widgery to George Thatcher, February 8, 1788, G. Thatcher Papers, Boston Public Library, Boston, MA.
17. Hannah T. Emery to Mary Carter, February 10, 1788, Cutts Family Papers, Essex Institute Library.
18. At the state-wide elections in late April to early May 1788, anti-Federalists had won a two-thirds majority; the final vote in the convention on July 26, however, went 30 to 27 in favor of ratification.
19. *Worcester Magazine*, Massachusetts, February 1788.

20. Baltimore *Maryland Journal*, May 2, 1788.
21. Leffler, "The Grandest Procession," 29.
22. Baltimore *Maryland Journal*, May 6, 1788.
23. New York *Daily Advertiser*, August 2, 1788.
24. *Massachusetts Centinel*, March 26, 1788.
25. For the changing economic interpretation and understanding of republicanism in the late eighteenth century, see Drew R. McCoy, *The Elusive Republic: Political Economy in Jeffersonian America* (Chapel Hill: University of North Carolina Press, 1980).
26. Benjamin Rush, "Observations," *Documentary History of the Ratification of the Constitution*, 18: 264.
27. Heideking, *Die Verfassung vor dem Richterstuhl*, 742, fn.86.
28. Jürgen Heideking, "The Image of an English Enemy During the American Revolution," in Ragnhild Fiebig-von Hase and Ursula Lehmkuhl, eds., *Enemy Images in American History* (Providence, RI and Oxford: Berghahn, 1997), 91-107.
29. "The connection of the great events of Independence—the French Alliance—the Peace—and the name of General Washington, with the adoption of the Constitution, was happily calculated to unite the most remarkable transports of the mind which were felt during the war, with the great event of the day, and to produce such a tide of joy as has seldom been felt in any age or country." Benjamin Rush, "Observation," *Documentary History of the Ratification of the Constitution* 18: 262.
30. The article, originally published in 1893, is reprinted in F.J. Turner, ed., *The Frontier in American History* (New York: Holt, 1920), 1-38 (quote on p.12).
31. Reporting on the celebrations in Philadelphia and New York, the *Massachusetts Centinel* praised these "noble and federal festivals" on August 8, 1788, as "originating in the metropolis of Massachusetts, and extending universally through the Union."
32. Cf. David Cressy, *Bonfires and Bells: National Memory and the Protestant Calendar in Elizabethan and Stuart England* (Berkeley: University of California Press, 1989); David M. Bergeron, *English Civic Pageantry 1558-1642* (Columbia, SC: Arnold, 1971).
33. James Wilson, "An Oration", July 4, 1788, *Documentary History of the Ratification of the Constitution* 18: 244.
34. Benjamin Rush, "Observation," ibid., 263-64, 268.
35. David Lloyd Dowd, *Pageant-Master of the Republic: Jacques Louis David and the French Revolution* (Lincoln: University of Nebraska Press, 1948), 66; Mona Ozouf, *La fête révolutionnaire* (Paris: Gallimard Press, 1976), 51-53, 91-93, 119-20; English translation: *Festivals and the French Revolution* (Cambridge and London: Harvard University Press, 1988).
36. Kenneth Silverman, *A Cultural History of the American Revolution* (New York: Columbia University Press, 1987), 580.
37. Cf. David Waldstreicher, *In the Midst of Perpetual Fetes: The Making of American Nationalism* (Chapel Hill: University of North Carolina Press, 1997).
38. Benjamin Rush, "Observation," *Documentary History of the Ratification of the Constitution* 18: 266.
39. *United States Chronicle*, Providence, July 3, 1788.
40. "An American," *Fayetteville Gazette*, September 14 and 21, 1789.
41. Ozouf, *Festivals and the French Revolution*, 95.
42. Recently, Milton M. Klein explained the reactions to the Watergate affair by referring to "the mystical importance Americans attach to their fundamental charter." "Mythologizing the U.S. Constitution," *Soundings* 78 (1995): 170. The impeachment of President William Jefferson Clinton may be another example of "how persistent the appeal of the Constitution remains."
43. Heideking, *Die Verfassung vor dem Richterstuhl*, 783-87.

44. *Inaugural Addresses of the Presidents of the United States*, ed. U.S. Government Printing Office (Washington, DC: GPO, 1973), 3.
45. Simon P. Newman, "Principles or Men? George Washington and the Political Culture of National Leadership, 1776-1801," *Journal of the Early Republic* 12 (1992): 477-507.
46. Len Travers, *Celebrating the Fourth: Independence Day and the Rites of Nationalism in the Early Republic* (Amherst, MA: University of Massachusetts Press, 1997).

Chapter 2

THE NATION AS SPECTACLE

The Grand Federal Procession in Philadelphia, 1788

Dietmar Schloss

IN 1787, BETWEEN May 25 and September 17, the Constitutional Convention in Philadelphia drew up a plan of government to take the place of the Articles of Confederation, a plan that would then be sent to the individual states for ratification. In some states the new constitutional plan met with strong opposition, and the entire ratification process took more than two and a half years. During this period several state capitals marked their state's adoption of the Constitution with a public parade.[1] The first of these parades took place in Boston on February 8, 1788, two days after the Massachusetts Convention had cast the decisive vote. The idea for the parade had sprung up among local tradesmen and artisans, who formed a committee and managed to organize it within twenty-four hours. The central attraction was a float carrying a "ship" named "*Federal Constitution*," which was fully rigged, and manned by a captain, several officers, and a crew of thirteen. It had been placed on a carriage and was drawn by thirteen horses—thirteen being the number of states in the union. Delegations of various local tradesmen and craftsmen made up the bulk of the parade. Marchers and spectators assembled afterward to partake of punch, wine, crackers, and cheese.[2] The Boston parade provided the model for celebrations in several other cities, most of which, however, were organized not by tradesmen's committees, but by

---

Notes for this section begin on page 60.

members of the Federalist elite. The most extensive and elaborate of these Federal Processions was held in Philadelphia on the Fourth of July in 1788. New Hampshire, the ninth of the thirteen states, had ratified on June 21, and with this ratification the Constitution was now legally in effect. The "Grand Federal Procession" in Philadelphia can thus be regarded as the "official" parade of the United States.

The organization of the Philadelphia parade was placed in the hands of Francis Hopkinson (1737-1791), a prominent, though controversial, Philadelphia citizen.[3] He had been a member of the Continental Congress and a signer of the Declaration of Independence, and had held several public offices, the last of which was judge of the Admiralty Court of Pennsylvania. (He was also the first judge in the United States who was subjected to an impeachment procedure, though he was to be cleared of the charges.) It was not his political position, however, that secured Hopkinson his appointment as organizer of the Federal Parade, but his artistic and literary talents. A well-known poet, essayist, and political satirist, he had participated in several propaganda campaigns in the local press. During the Revolution he had supported the cause of the American patriots; after 1783 he had joined the Federalists and used his pen to support a reform of the Articles of Confederation. Hopkinson was also a distinguished harpsichord player, and composed what are generally considered to be the first "American" songs. In addition, he was an excellent draftsman and painter and designed coins and paper money as well as official seals for various departments of the new government; he was also the designer of the American flag known as the Stars and Stripes. In creating and executing the floats and exhibits of the Philadelphia parade, Hopkinson received the help of the painter Charles Willson Peale (1741-1827), who had already arranged previous patriotic displays such as the celebration of the 1783 Treaty of Paris in Philadelphia and the Federal Parade in Annapolis, Maryland.[4]

The Federal Parades received extensive coverage in the newspapers and magazines. A detailed "Account of the Grand Federal Procession in Philadelphia," written by Francis Hopkinson, appeared in the local press. The "Account" was republished as a separate pamphlet and it was again reprinted in the July 1788 issue of the *American Museum*, which also included the speech delivered on the occasion by James Wilson and an eyewitness account by Benjamin Rush. There was obviously a great desire to have the nation participate in these events.

For a long time the Federal Parades—like public festivals in general—were ignored by academic historians.[5] They were viewed as part of the nation's leisure activities and thus not considered worthy of serious analysis. Also, the elaborate ceremony and lavish decorations employed in some of these parades probably did not square with many historians' idea of what constituted proper public ritual in a democratic nation. The first to draw attention to the whole array of public celebrations in the revolutionary and post-revolutionary era was Kenneth Silverman,[6] and the first serious analyses of the Federal Parades came from labor historians. Observing that there were large contingents of tradesmen and artisans marching in the processions, these historians regarded the parades as instances of an emerging culture of labor in the United States. According to Sean Wilentz and Alfred F. Young, the Federal Processions gave tradesmen and artisans the opportunity to articulate, if not a new class consciousness, then at least a new sense of their own worth.[7]

It was the rise of the cultural studies movement in the later eighties and early nineties that made festivals a popular field of historical research. The newer investigations regard parades and public festivities not merely as "expressions" of political sentiment, but also as "instruments" of political practice. Of the more recent work on American festivals of the period, the studies of Jürgen Heideking and David Waldstreicher deserve particular mention. Heideking gives us the most comprehensive and detailed account of the Federal Parades. He argues that they fulfilled different functions for different political and social groups: first, they were used by the Federalist elite for propaganda purposes; through them the Federalists hoped to exert pressure on the anti-Federalists and win over those who were undecided. Second, they gave the middle classes in the cities the opportunity to assert publicly their importance in republican society. Third, they served to instill in the population a "love" for the newly established nation and were thus exercises in civil religion. Heideking argues that the Federal Parades were powerful instruments for establishing the idea of a national identity in the minds of Americans.[8] Waldstreicher, too, sees festivals and parades as instruments of nationalism; his main focus, however, is on the tensions and the struggles that went into this kind of nation-building. For him, the festivals were arenas of conflict in which different social and political groups were competing to establish their own view of the nation and their own brand of nationalism. As regards the Federal Parades, however, Waldstreicher encounters difficulties with this line of argument. On the surface, there is little conflict visible between the participating groups, which is probably why Waldstreicher prefers to dedicate much more space to the struggles between Federalists and anti-Federalists preceding the parades than to the parades themselves.[9]

So far, then, historians have considered the Federal Parades mainly from a social and political perspective. Little attention has been given to iconographic traditions, and even less to the aesthetic assumptions that stand behind them. It is my aim here to go some way towards redressing the balance. Using Hopkinson's "Account of the Grand Federal Procession in Philadelphia" as my principal source, I will try to analyze the Philadelphia parade from the viewpoint of cultural aesthetics. The parade aspired to be a republican *Gesamtkunstwerk* making visible and real to both marchers and spectators the unity of the new nation. If one looks closely at the pageants and floats, however, one realizes that there are two different aesthetic conceptions employed—a traditional one drawing on allegory and a more modern one which espouses the principles of "realism." Each type of aesthetics implies a different vision of the nation. In the first and official part of the parade, which draws on the allegorical approach, the nation is envisioned along the lines of classical and neoclassical Republicanism, while in the second part, which contains the exhibits of the trades and professions and adopts a "realist" style, the nation is depicted from the viewpoint of Liberalism. Gordon S. Wood and other historians have argued that, after the Revolutionary War, American society began to transform itself from a republican society dominated by an elite of patricians and wealthy landowners to a capitalist market society that was increasingly opening itself to the middle classes.[10] The spectacle of the nation which the Grand Federal Procession presents to us is the spectacle of exactly this transformation.

Francis Hopkinson begins his detailed description of the Federal Parade in Philadelphia by establishing a symbolic frame, both of time and of place.[11] We are told that the procession took place on the Fourth of July. The celebration of the Constitution is thus fused with the celebration of the Declaration of Independence. The Constitution is declared to be the fulfillment of what had been promised by the Declaration. Both the Declaration and the Constitution were debated and voted upon in Philadelphia, which confers to this city a particular status in American history. Hopkinson writes that the rising sun on the morning of the Fourth of July was greeted with the ringing of church bells and the discharge of a cannon from a ship which carried the name *Rising Sun* (57). Thus a correspondence is established between the sun and the ship, nature and art, and this provides an allegorical backdrop to the parade. We are given to understand that the nation to be inaugurated by the parade has its origins in the light of science and knowledge and not in the darkness of despotism. The allegorical backdrop is further enhanced by ten ships anchored in the harbor which were fully decked out and carried white flags with the names of those states that had already ratified the Constitution.[12]

The parade itself consisted of eighty-eight different exhibits and floats and can be divided into three major sections. The first section, composed of twenty-five groups, portrayed the stages of American history. Interspersed among the exhibits were several groups of city and county cavalries. The second section contained the floats and pageants of the farmers, merchants, tradesmen, and artisans; with more than fifty groups, it was by far the largest section of the three. Officials of the city of Philadelphia, members of the professions—doctors, lawyers, clergymen—and students and professors of the University of Pennsylvania marched in the third and final section, which was the smallest. There were no pageants in this third section. However, contemporaries were particularly struck by the sight of the clergymen: the group was made up of representatives of different denominations, including a Jewish rabbi—all walking arm in arm.

Statehouse and Congress Hall

The marchers had assembled at eight o'clock at the intersection of South and Third Streets, and the parade started to move at half past nine. It was one and a half miles long; 5,000 people participated in it. It covered a distance of three miles and reached its destination, Union Green, at half past twelve. The concluding celebrations took place on a spacious lawn made available by a private citizen. The most important pageants of the parade, the "Federal Edifice" (see below) and the ship *Union*, together with the various standards and flags, were placed in the middle of the lawn. From underneath the "Federal Edifice," James Wilson addressed marchers and spectators who were seated at tables arranged in a large circle. He concluded his oration with ten toasts, the first being addressed to the "people of the United States" and the last to "the whole family of mankind" (74). Afterwards food and drink was provided for a crowd of 15,000. By six o'clock in the evening, the lawn was tidied up and all participants and spectators were back in their own houses. All commentators remarked on the orderly conduct of the people taking part in the event. The parade thus seemed to provide a fitting emblem for the new nation united under a republican constitution.

In the first section of the parade, we find representations of the history of American government. At the head of the parade was a group of twelve men swinging axes, symbolizing the first pioneers clearing the land. It may seem surprising that the parade did not begin with the Puritan forefathers, but the organizers had opted for a nonpartisan stance. If they had commemorated Puritanism, that might have been construed as favoring New England. Thus, a "generic" symbol was chosen to portray the beginning of the American state. According to the prevalent political philosophies of the day (Republicanism, Lockean Liberalism, Scottish Enlightenment thought), civil society begins with the clearing of the land and the establishment of agriculture; agriculture signals the emergence of private property, which requires the protection of the law. The other displays in this section referred to more specific events in recent American history: prominent Philadelphia citizens on horseback held up flags and signs commemorating the Declaration of Independence, the French Alliance, and the Peace Treaty of Paris. One citizen carried a sign with the name George Washington written on it; another was dressed as a herald proclaiming the "New Era." One rider commemorated the 17th of September, 1787, the day on which the Constitution was adopted by the Constitutional Convention. He was followed by a band playing the "Grand Federal March," composed for the occasion by Alexander Reinagle.

The first float of the parade was a wooden structure in the form of a large eagle—thirteen feet high—which had been placed on a carriage and was drawn by six horses. The breast of the eagle was decorated with 1thirteensilver stars and thirteen red and white stripes. The right foot clutched an olive branch; the left grasped thirteen arrows. Pennsylvania Chief Justice Thomas McKean and two other judges stood on a ladder inside this structure and held a copy of the Constitution in their hands. The float was followed by one representative from each of the ten states which had already ratified the Constitution; they walked arm in arm—"emblematical of the union," as Hopkinson wrote (58). The next group consisted of a delegation of consuls and representatives of foreign states. It was followed by a carriage containing two men; one was wearing regular clothes, and the other was dressed as a Native American, both smoking from a calumet. It may be surprising that the American Indians did not figure in the pioneer stage of the parade. But as the parade dramatized the genesis of the new American government, and as Native Americans were considered to belong to the pre-civilized stage, they were, thus, not a part of the parade's principal domain. That the Native American figure was placed near the foreign legations shows that American Indians were regarded by contemporaries primarily as members of independent nations and partners to treaties, rather than as potential citizens.

The way in which the American nation is presented as a spectacle in this first, quasi-official part of the Grand Federal Procession is reminiscent of the triumphal marches of Imperial Rome and of the coronation celebrations and royal pageants of monarchical Europe. Although the organizers avoided displays glorifying the power of military or civic leaders and opted for images representing the state as a collective entity, they were obviously striving for the grand gesture.[13] This desire for pomp and ceremony can be explained in two ways: first, although Americans firmly believed in the novelty of their political system and were convinced of its superiority to the governments of Europe, they nevertheless wished to compete with European public celebrations. From colonial times on, Americans had felt a sense of inferiority about the great European achievements in the arts and sciences, suffering as they did from the stigma of cultural provincialism. However, even before the Revolution, poets had heralded the "rising glory of America," announcing the coming of a new "golden age" and a flowering of the sciences and the arts on the American continent.[14] The new nation as created by the Constitution seemed to bring the United States closer to this goal. In fact, the Federal Parades were considered by contemporaries as works of art and were regarded as fulfilling this promise of a cultural renaissance in the West.

Second, the desire for the grand spectacle was also motivated by traditional Republicanism, the dominant ideology during the Revolutionary and post-Revolutionary periods. As historians have pointed out, in Republicanism the state was conceived of as a community of virtue rather than as a system of laws and institutional arrangements.[15] In order to function, a republic needed loyal and virtuous citizens who could only be produced through a process of education. The federal processions were considered as lessons in republican virtue and patriotism. The fact that they appealed not only to the intellect but also to the senses increased their pedagogic effect in the eyes of many contemporaries, which explains why artists such as Francis Hopkinson and Charles Willson Peale were appointed to supervise the events. As Kenneth Silverman writes, "the participation of so many cultural figures in the political rejoicing marks the fullest expression in eighteenth-century America of the Whig view of the reciprocal relation between liberty and the arts."[16]

Drawing on the resources of art to teach citizens virtue, public parades were considered powerful instruments of political education, as is made apparent in the following passage taken from James Wilson's speech which is included in Hopkinson's "Account":

> Public processions may be so planned and executed as to join *both* the properties of nature's rule. They may *instruct* and *improve*, while they *entertain* and *please*. They may point out the *elegance* or *usefulness* of the *sciences* and the *arts*. They may preserve the *memory*, and engrave the *importance* of great *political events*. They may represent, with peculiar felicity and force, *the operation* and *effects* of great *political truths*. The *picturesque and splendid decorations around me*, furnish the most *beautiful* and most *brilliant* proofs, that these remarks are FAR FROM BEING IMAGINARY. (73)

In what was one of the major political sourcebooks of the American republicans, *De l'esprit des lois*, Montesquieu had argued that the achievement of republican virtue is difficult, even painful, since it requires that the individual repress his native selfishness and develop a spirit of altruism ("... la vertu politique est un renoncement à soi-même, qui est toujours une chose très pénible.").[17] The aesthetic as a special mode of persuasion could turn the exercise of republican virtue from something disagreeable into something pleasing. In Benjamin Rush's report of the Grand Federal Procession, the words "joy" and "pleasure" occur with great frequency. The parade, he argues, exerted powerful "effects" upon "the minds and bodies": "It forced open every heart ... It likewise invigorated the muscles of the body."[18] The procession enabled participants and spectators to experience duty as pleasure; it activated their fellow-feeling and incited them to virtuous activity. In the spectacle of the parade, the nation as a virtuous community came fully alive.[19]

The first section of the parade was not original, nor did it aspire to originality. In order to portray the new American nation that had come into existence through the Constitution, the organizers drew on well-known emblems and allegories.[20] In the European parades, triumphal cars and arches were a familiar sight. In the Philadelphia parade, there was no triumphal arch; it was probably too closely associated with the prowess of military leaders and considered to be unsuitable for the founding celebration of a nation dedicated to republican values and peace. However, there were several ornamental cars such as the Eagle, the "Federal Edifice," and the ship *Union*. The Eagle was modeled on the official seal of the United

States, designed by William Barton and Charles Thomson and adopted by Congress on June 20, 1782, but its use as a political emblem goes back to ancient Rome.[21] Though the ship and the house were not used as political emblems as frequently as the eagle, they were well-known images denoting security and stability.

In the initial section of the parade, the dominant aesthetic principle, as in traditional European spectacles, was that of allegory. Well-known images (the eagle, the ship, the edifice) were presented to evoke the new American nation. The images conveyed desirable qualities (strength, dignity, stability, security, etc.), but they had no intrinsic relationship to the object represented; rather, the connection between sign and referent was vouchsafed by convention and tradition. And yet, as much as the organizers were ambitious to create convincing allegories for the new state, they already must have had some doubts whether the allegorical method would have the desired effect on American spectators. It is striking that many of the allegorical representations in the parade were accompanied by samples of the "real thing." The exhibit commemorating the Declaration of Independence, for example, consisted of a staff and cap of liberty and a silk flag with the words "Fourth of July, 1776" embroidered on it. It was carried by Colonel John Nixon, the very man who had read the text of the Declaration of Independence from a platform at the State House twelve years before.[22] Similarly, the bearer of the flag representing the Franco-American Alliance sat on a horse that had belonged to Comte de Rochambeau, the French lieutenant-general who had joined forces with Washington in the Yorktown campaign. The American Eagle was staffed by members of the political and judicial elite. The organizers thus saw to it that the citizens who manned the exhibits had an authentic connection with the events represented. There seems to have already been a deep skepticism concerning whether the abstract allegorical image would carry conviction and fulfill the parade's educational goals.

The final and most elaborate float in the initial section of the Federal Parade was a wooden structure named "New Roof" or "Grand Federal Edifice." Peale had designed and executed it, but the idea came from Hopkinson. In the *Pennsylvania Packet* of December 29, 1787, the latter had published a satire on the anti-Federalists entitled "The New Roof."[23] In this satire the struggle between the Federalists and anti-Federalists is rendered as a quarrel between the inhabitants of an old house in dire need of repair. The satire castigates those inhabitants who boycott a thorough modernization of the roof and exposes their narrow-mindedness and self-interest. The "Federal Edifice" float in the parade obviously picked up on the "New Roof" satire.

The edifice in the parade had thirteen columns—three were left incomplete, pointing to those states that had not yet ratified the Constitution. Its roof was a dome with a cupola crowned by a figure of the goddess of plenty carrying a cornucopia. Inside the edifice there were ten chairs, which were occupied by ordinary American citizens. During the final celebration on the green, the citizens gave up their chairs to the representatives of the ratifying states. This was to make visible the representational principle espoused by the Constitution.

An image of stability, union, and security, the "New Roof" was a symbol of Federalism and the last exhibit in the official, political section of the parade. However, it also served as a bridge to the displays and floats of the tradesmen and artisans in the second section. Hopkinson planned that the "New Roof" would be followed by 450 architects, carpenters, saw-makers, and file cutters. The rationale for this sequence is made apparent in a poem by Hopkinson entitled "The Raising: A New Song for Federal Mechanics," which had been published in the *Pennsylvania Gazette* on February 6, 1788 and which was reprinted in the same issue of the *American Museum* as Hopkinson's "Account." The first two stanzas run as follows:

> Come muster, my Lads, your mechanical Tools,
> Your Saws and your Axes, your Hammers and Rules;
> Bring your Mallets and Planes, your Level and Line,
> And Plenty of Pins of American Pine;
>   For our Roof we will raise, and our Song still shall be –
>   A Government firm, and our Citizens free.
>
> Come, up with *the Plates*, lay them firm on the Wall,
> Like the People at large, they're the Ground-work of all;
> Examine them well, and see that they're sound;
> Let no rotten Parts in our Building be found;
>   For our Roof we will raise, and our Song still shall be –
>   Our Government firm, and our Citizens free.[24]

In the remaining seven stanzas Hopkinson describes how the federal mechanics, piece by piece, assemble the new "house" of American government. One can read "The Raising: A New Song for Federal Mechanics" in the same allegorical way in which I have interpreted the "New Roof" float in the parade. As the new roof stands for the new Constitution, the federal mechanics stand for the men who drafted the Constitution, i.e., the members of the Constitutional Convention. The very fact, however, that 450 architects and carpenters marched after the "Federal Edifice" changed the meaning of the float and the song, and ultimately also the meaning of the Constitution itself. Hopkinson obviously wanted the "Federal Edifice" float to be understood not merely allegorically, but also literally: the Constitution and, with it, the unity of the United States originated not with the statesmen, but with those who turned the economic wheels of society. The 450 architects and carpenters who marched behind the "New Roof" pageant drastically diminished the significance of the ten citizens sitting under the roof as well as the representatives of the ten states who replaced them later on.[25] The American nation here is thus identified not so much with its political as with its economic forces.

The "New Roof" pageant also beautifully illustrates the "intertextual" character of the parade. Hopkinson invented the allegory in his *Pennsylvania Packet* article, he brought it to life as a float in the parade, and he reinterpreted it in his "New Song for Federal Mechanics." The "New Roof" makes clear that the parade is part of the much larger world of political discourse, and thus supports Waldstreicher's contention that the Federal Processions were not isolated events, but forces at work within a network of political struggles.[26]

The second section of the Federal Parade comprised the displays of the farmers, tradesmen, and artisans. While the floats in the first section had relatively few people (they were staffed largely with members of the political elite), those of the second section were often crowded and drew on a much larger cross-section of American society. Hopkinson tells us that the order in which the trades marched "was determined by lot" (62). Within each segment a certain hierarchy was maintained: prominent senior craftsmen walked at the head of the delegation; they were followed by the younger masters, one of whom usually carried a standard depicting the trade insignia, another one holding a flag with a motto expounding the importance of the particular trade for the commonwealth. Journeymen and apprentices marched at the end of each segment.

The exhibits of the tradesmen and artisans in the Federal Parades are generally traced back by historians to the London Lord Mayor's Shows. In the early thirteenth century, King John granted a mayor to the citizens of London, stipulating that each year the new officer should be presented to him or his justices for approval.[27] From this stipulation originated the Lord Mayor's parades, which set out from the City of London and ended in Westminster. They were conducted and financed by the guild of the mayor-elect and offered the guilds the opportunity to celebrate their achievements and assert their importance for the commonwealth. In the processions' heyday in the sixteenth and seventeenth centuries, the displays were highly elaborate, borrowing elements from other types of festivals such as the medieval morality play and the Midsummer Show as well as the royal entry and the court masque. A poet was generally appointed to design the sets and write the dialogues. The scenes depicted on the floats alluded to classical mythology, the Bible, literature, and history.

Historians have wondered why these guild traditions, which went into a rapid decline in Britain in the early eighteenth century, were revived

Banner carried by the Tobacconists in the Grand Federal Procession, Philadelphia, July 4, 1788. From the Annual Report of the Library Company of Philadelphia, 1988.

towards the end of the century in the United States. Alfred F. Young suggests that urban mechanics, who during the Revolution had participated in various forms of collective action, had acquired a new "consciousness of themselves as citizens, as producers and as a 'mechanic interest.'"[28] Since they could not draw on native traditions to give public expression to their new sense of self-worth, they resorted to the iconographic repertoire of the London guilds. However, the American artisans did not merely copy the traditional images, as Sean Wilentz seems to think;[29] they reinterpreted them and adapted them to a new context. This innovative aspect is evident in the particular use the American craftsmen made of the insignia of the London guilds. The weavers, for example, combined the coat of arms of the London guild ("a rampant lion in a green field, holding a shuttle in his dexter paw") with a new motto: *"May Government Protect Us"* (60). Similarly, the bricklayers added to the sign of their guild an illustration depicting "the federal city rising out of a forest, workmen building it; and the sun illuminating it." Their motto reads: *"Both Buildings and Rulers Are the Works of Our Hands"* (63). The American craftsmen thus blended the traditional trade insignia with American constitutional symbolism and gave them a new, political meaning.

But this overt form of politicizing is not what ultimately accounts for the novelty of the American tradesmen's and artisans' displays. There is a more radical way in which the craftsmen transformed British guild traditions, one which has gone altogether unnoticed by historians. If one compares the London guild pageants and the craft exhibits in the Federal Parades, one realizes that the American artisans did nothing less than revolutionize the aesthetics of the parade. The following two descriptions of guild pageants from the late seventeenth century are taken from Robert Withington's *English Pageantry*. The first describes the Lord Mayor's Show of the year 1685, which celebrated the inauguration of Sir Robert Jeffreys, a member of the guild of the ironmongers. Of the four ornamental cars, only the fourth makes references to the mayor's trade. I will nevertheless quote Withington's description of all four pageants to provide some idea of the elaborate mythological and allegorical designs employed in these shows:

> The first pageant contained eight females, representing Victory, Triumph, Honour, Peace, Plenty, Courage, Vigilance, and Conduct. The next pageant,—a Sea-chariot of cerulean green,—contained Neptune, drawn by Tritons; Amphitrite, attended by Proteus, Glaucus, Thetis, and Galatea. The third was the Arch of Loyalty, surmounted by Fame who was attended by Loyalty, Truth, Union, and Concord; a sea-lion, Tritons, and a negro suggested the 'first commercial city in the world.' Here Loyalty addressed the mayor.
> In the fourth pageant music was combined with a trade appropriateness, in the labor of Vulcan and his attendants. Among the characters on this pageant was 'Polypheme. A Giant of large size, one great Eye in the middle of his Forehead ... standing at the entrance of the Cave with a Crow of Iron in his hand to break the Rocks that hinder the access to the Mines, and a Sword in the other to prevent all others, but the Right Worshipful the Company of *Iron-Mongers* (whose peculiar Prerogatives it is) to enter.' Apollo and Cupids, Vulcan, Brontes, Steropes, and Pyracmon were also on this car; Vulcan addressed the mayor.[30]

From this description one can gain a clear impression of what the Lord Mayor's Shows were like in the late seventeenth century. The pageants provided examples of the advanced skills and talents of the London guildsmen. Out of them speak their professional pride and their sense of self-worth, just as Wilentz has argued.[31] Yet it is obvious that Sir Robert Jeffreys, the ironmonger, can only enter the stage in mythological costume—as the god

Vulcan. The world of work and production would violate the decorum and the dignity that pertained to the world of public spectacle.

The second example comes from the Lord Mayor's Show of 1677. Here the artisans did not figure in the main exhibit, but were part of the side attractions called the "drolls." In the drolls' shows no poems or dialogues were recited, which is why the poets in charge of the Lord Mayor's processions generally looked down upon them. As one of the poets, Thomas Heywood, writes, the drolls' shows consisted merely "of Anticke gesticulations, dances, and other mimicke postures," and were "divised onely for the vulgar, who are better delighted with that which pleaseth the eye, than contenteth the eare."[32] Here is an example of such a drolls' show:

> In 1677, the fourth pageant was a 'Jocular Scene' containing 'a brisk Society of merry Labourers.' Three masculine figures, representing Patience, Labour, and Diligence, occupied the most conspicuous position. At their feet were several workers, spinning, carding, &c., while others, 'more jocose and at liberty sing a Song in Commendation of the *Cloth-workers-Trade*, and at the end of the Song, certain Rusticks, and Shepherd-like persons, Pipe, Dance, and exercise the activity of their limbs, in Gambolling, Tumbling and Capering ... the whole *Pageant* being a piece of ingenious Confusion, or a Comical Scene of delightful disorder.[33]

In this pageant we indeed find representations of work and workers. However, it is no coincidence that they occur in what one might call the "comedy" section of the parade. The Lord Mayor's Show thus seems to have modeled itself on the rules and decorum regulations for tragedy and other serious art. Only elevated characters and subjects were permitted there. The middle and lower classes and the everyday world of work were relegated to comedy. Besides, even in this burlesque part of the Lord Mayor's parade, the scene depicting workers and their work is presented within an allegorical frame: Patience, Labor, and Diligence are juxtaposed with Gambolling, Tumbling, and Disorder.

Witness, in contrast, an artisan pageant from the Federal Parade in Philadelphia. Hopkinson describes the car of the blacksmiths as follows:

> A machine drawn by nine horses, representing the federal blacksmiths', whitesmiths', and nailors' manufactory, being a frame of ten by fifteen feet, and nine feet high, with a real chimney extending three feet above the roof, and furnished for use. In front of the building three master blacksmiths, messrs. Nathaniel Brown, Nicholas Ness and William Perkins, supporting the standard, elegantly ornamented with the smiths' arms.—Motto, 'by hammer in hand, all arts do stand.' The manufactory was in full employ during the procession.—Mr. John Mingler, and his assistant, Christian Keyser, black-smiths, completed a set of plough-irons out of old swords, worked a sword into a sickle, turned several horse-shoes, and performed several jobs on demand. Mr. John Goodman, jun., whitesmith, finished a complete pair of plyers, a knife,

and some machinery, with other work, on demand. Messrs. Andrew Felsinger and Benjamin Brummel forged, finished and sold a considerable number of spikes, nails, and broad tacks. The whole was under the conduct of messrs. Godfrey Gebbler, David Henderson, George Goddard, Jacob Ester, Lewis Prahl and Jacob Eckfelt, and followed by two hundred brother black-smiths, white-smiths and nailors. (64-65)[34]

The American blacksmiths of the early republic no longer feel the need to present themselves in a mythological or allegorical dress. Their workshop and their work have become worthy subjects for aesthetic display. The blacksmiths' and the other craftsmen's pageants in the Federal Parades anticipate the kind of democratic aesthetics propagated by Wordsworth in his preface to *Lyrical Ballads* or, indeed, by Emerson in his famous "American Scholar" address. In the late 1790s Wordsworth turned against the neoclassical idea that poetry should only concern itself with elevated subjects and be written in an elevated style and called for poems that dealt with "incidents of common life" in a "selection of language really used by men."[35] Some forty years later, Emerson prescribed an aesthetic program for the United States that was to 'explore' and 'poeticize' "the near, the low, [and] the common" instead of "the sublime and beautiful."[36] The tradesmen and artisans in the Federal Parades truly invented a new aesthetics—the aesthetics of everyday reality.

Rather than providing a new allegorical rhetoric, this new aesthetics claims to leave allegory behind altogether. In fact, the new aesthetics presents itself as a kind of anti-aesthetics. It makes claims for radical authenticity; it presumes to give unmediated access to truth. The tradesmen and artisans need not engage in an ideological quarrel with the Federalist elite. Their realistic style alone denounces the Federalist allegories as a lie.

In certain ways the realistic style of the tradesmen and craftsmen exhibits seems to square with enlightened liberal notions which assume that the state can forgo the power of spectacle. For modern liberals the state is only a means to an end: it does not need to solicit loyalty actively and dazzle its citizens. There is a joy and an exuberance in the artisans' exhibits which show that they have clearly understood that the everyday world of work and production can be as great a source of aesthetic pleasure as the "artificial" world of mythology and allegory—or, indeed, an even greater one. It is this recognition of the aesthetic potential of their own existence that gives the pageants of the tradesmen and artisans their persuasive power.

The Grand Federal Procession in Philadelphia was a grandiose republican *Gesamtkunstwerk*, even though its character was syncretistic rather than synthetic. In the initial "political" section, the Constitution was celebrated in the old-fashioned allegorical way, although even here one can observe a tendency to connect allegory with an authentic historical object to give it greater authority. In the second section, the artisans and tradesmen celebrated the Constitution in a "realistic" way: they point to what they conceive of as the new nation's basis, namely the people and their economic and occupational activities. The two different aesthetic concepts employed in the parade imply two different ways of conceiving the nation. The Federalists still understand the nation in more traditional republican terms—as being structured by the sphere of politics—whereas the tradesmen see it as largely ordered by the economic realm. If one looks at it from the viewpoint of aesthetic history, the old world of the Federalists seems doomed. Just as Realism displaces Allegory, the new nation of trade and work displaces the old republic of elitist politics.

One should be wary, however, of driving too deep a wedge between the two worlds. Historians agree that the Federalists' success in 1787 and 1788 owed much to their efforts to be inclusive rather than exclusive. Both Hopkinson and Wilson emphasize that the new American government was founded on popular sovereignty. Regardless of whether the populist gestures of the Federalists were only tactics or a matter of conviction, they did give the tradesmen a place in the national parade, and that made all the difference. Thus, the trades and professions could show themselves in their "reality," and by doing so, they asserted themselves as a reality in the new nation.

Certain qualifications also have to be made about the democratic character of the tradesmen's and artisans' exhibits. While it is true that they celebrated the value of work and economic activity, one should not confuse this with a celebration of democracy. The senior tradesmen in the march were definitely part of the elite; and within each individual segment a strict hierarchy was maintained. It also should not be overlooked that in spite of the populist character of the trades and crafts section, large parts of the American population were excluded from marching in the parade: poor white men, women, and members of non-white ethnic groups did not actively participate. The criterion for inclusion in the parade was whether a person had obtained or still had the hope of obtaining what was termed in the eighteenth century an "independent" existence. Although they interpreted it in different ways, it was this ideal of economic independence that the crafts- and tradesmen shared with their Federalist betters. The American nation exhibited in the Grand Federal Procession included many, but it did not include all.

The Grand Federal Procession, viewed from a political perspective, offers no hint of a revolutionary spirit or class struggle. The nation presents itself as being in harmony. Seen from the viewpoint of a history of aesthetics, however, the parade reveals a major rift. The two parties draw on two different aesthetic styles. The allegorical style adopted by the Federalist elite aims at the traditional type of political persuasion. It tries to commit the citizens to the nation by dazzling them with well-known political images. The tradesmen and artisans abstained from such "artificial" rhetoric. They adopt a realist style and show themselves in their everyday sphere of work and production. Their "realism" presents itself as a kind of anti-aesthetics which claims to yield direct access to their essence. This confidence in the power of their reality may explain why there was so little actual strife between the parties: the "realists" do not feel the need to engage in an ideological quarrel with their adversaries, because they assume that "reality itself" produces immediate conviction. Perhaps it was this very conviction in the self-evident power of their reality that allowed the American middle classes to accomplish their revolution in a comparatively peaceful way.

Notes

1. See Whitfield J. Bell, Jr., "The Federal Processions of 1788," *New-York Historical Society Quarterly*, 46 (1962): 4-39.
2. See Bell, "The Federal Processions," 8-10.
3. On Hopkinson see George E. Hastings, *Life and Works of Francis Hopkinson* (Chicago: University of Chicago Press, 1926).
4. See Bell, "The Federal Processions," 11 and 18-19.
5. Most earlier treatments of the Federal Parades appear in the publications of historical societies, and not in scholarly journals. See, for example, Bell, "The Federal Processions," and Sarah H. J. Simpson, "The Federal Procession of the City of New York," *New-York Historical Society Quarterly Bulletin* 9 (1925): 39-58.
6. Kenneth Silverman, *A Cultural History of the American Revolution: Painting, Music, Literature, and the Theatre in the Colonies and the United States from the Treaty of Paris to the Inauguration of George Washington, 1763-1789* (1976; New York: Columbia University Press, 1987). For the federal parades see pp. 578-87; for other festivals see under "Demonstrations" in the Index.
7. See Sean Wilentz, "Artisan Republican Festivals and the Rise of Class Conflict in New York City, 1788-1837," in *Working-Class America: Essays on Labor, Community, and American Society*, eds. Michael H. Frisch and Daniel J. Walkowitz (Urbana: University of Illinois Press, 1983), 37-77; and Alfred F. Young, "English Plebeian Culture and Eighteenth-Century American Radicalism," in *The Origins of Anglo-American Radicalism*, eds. Margaret and James Jacob (London: George Allen and Unwin, 1984), 185-212.
8. Jürgen Heideking, *Die Verfassung vor dem Richterstuhl: Vorgeschichte und Ratifizierung der amerikanischen Verfassung, 1787-1791* (Berlin and New York: Walter de Gruyter, 1988), 709-87. See also Jürgen Heideking, "The Federal Processions of 1788 and the Origins of American Civil Religion," *Soundings* 77 (1994): 367-87, and his contribution to this volume.

9. David Waldstreicher, *In the Midst of Perpetual Fetes: The Making of American Nationalism, 1776-1820* (Chapel Hill: University of North Carolina Press, 1997). See also Susan G. Davis' earlier study *Parades and Power: Street Theatre in Nineteenth-century Philadelphia* (Philadelphia: Temple University Press, 1986). According to Davis, parades represent a kind of theatrical space in which different social groups can communicate their political interests to a larger public; they serve as "tools for building, maintaining, and confronting power relations" (5). However, Davis' analysis of the Grand Federal Procession is somewhat marred by her narrow ideological focus, as she derives her model from nineteenth-century parades, which, to her mind, enact a class struggle between capitalists and workers.
10. Gordon S. Wood, *The Radicalism of the American Revolution* (New York: Alfred A. Knopf, 1992).
11. "Account of the Grand Federal Procession in Philadelphia," *American Museum* (July 1788): 57-75. Page references are given in parentheses in the text.
12. After New Hampshire, Virginia joined the union as the tenth state on June 26.
13. Criticism of pseudo-monarchical display arose a year later during Washington's inauguration; see Silverman, *A Cultural History of the Revolution*, 599. The new vice-president's initiative to introduce grandiose titles for the president and high government officials met with a similar criticism; see James H. Hutson, "John Adams' Title Campaign," *New England Quarterly* 41 (1968): 30-39.
14. See, for example, Philip Freneau and Hugh Henry Brackenridge's well-known *Poem on the Rising Glory of America* (1772).
15. The landmark studies on Republicanism and Civic Humanism are Bernard Bailyn's *The Ideological Origins of the American Revolution* (Cambridge, MA: Harvard University Press, 1967); Gordon S. Wood's *The Creation of the American Republic, 1776-1787* (Chapel Hill: University of North Carolina Press, 1969); and J. G. A. Pocock's *The Machiavellian Moment: Florentine Political Thought and the Atlantic Republican Tradition* (Princeton, NJ: Princeton University Press, 1975).
16. Silverman, *A Cultural History of the American Revolution*, 579.
17. Montesquieu, *Œuvres Complètes*, 2 vols., ed. Roger Caillois (Paris: Gallimard, 1976), 2: 267.
18. "Observations *on the* Fœderal Procession, on the Fourth of July, 1788, in the City of Philadelphia; in a letter from a gentleman in this city to his friend in a neighbouring state," reprinted in *Documentary History of the Ratification of the Constitution*, eds. John P. Kaminski, Richard Leffler, and Gaspare J. Saladino (Madison, WI: State Historical Society of Wisconsin, 1976-), 18: 262-63.
19. Some historians have argued that the Constitution, with its complicated system of representation and checks and balances, sounded the death knell for traditional Republicanism and its idea of a community of virtue (see, for example, Wood, *The Creation of the American Republic*, ch. 14). While this may have been the point of view of political thinkers such as Madison, the vast majority of Americans did not perceive the Constitution as being directed against traditional republican creeds. It is significant in this context that the pageants did not concern themselves with the particulars of the American governmental system. The Federal Parades celebrated the Constitution primarily as an instrument of union rather than as a mechanism for balancing power.
20. The displays of the historical section were probably inspired by transparencies which Peale had created for several peace celebrations between 1781 and 1783 and which depicted scenes and mottoes from Revolutionary history; see Silverman, *A Cultural History of the American Revolution*, 412-14, and 424-26.

21. On the Great Seal, see Silverman, *A Cultural History of the American Revolution*, 416-17, who suggests that the American Eagle may have descended from the "bald eagle" depicted in Joachim Camerarius' *Symbolorum et Emblematum* (Frankfurt: Ammonius, 1654).
22. See Bell, "The Federal Processions," 19.
23. Reprinted in *Documentary History of the Ratification of the Constitution*, 15: 179-88.
24. *Documentary History of the Ratification of the Constitution*, 16: 47.
25. For a different interpretation of "The Raising," see Laura Rigal, "'Raising the Roof': Authors, Spectators, and Artisans in the Grand Federal Procession of 1788," *Theatre Journal* 48 (1996): 253-77; here: 261-64.
26. Waldstreicher, *In the Midst of Perpetual Fetes*, 10-12 and *passim*.
27. On the Lord Mayor's Shows see Robert Withington, *English Pageantry: An Historical Outline*, 2 vols. (1918; New York: Benjamin Blom, 1963), ch. 6; and Frederick W. Fairholt, *Lord Mayors' Pageants: Being Collections towards a History of these Annual Celebrations, with Specimens of the Descriptive Pamphlets Published by the City Poets*, 2 vols. (1843 and 1844; New York: Johnson Reprint, 1965).
28. Young, "English Plebeian Culture," 200.
29. Wilentz, "Artisan Republican Festivals," 47.
30. Withington, *English Pageantry*, 2: 63. Withington quotes here from the original pamphlet describing the show.
31. Wilentz, "Artisan Republican Festivals," 46.
32. Withington, *English Pageantry*, 2: 85.
33. Withington, *English Pageantry*, 2: 84-85n.
34. There were several floats of this kind in the parade. The float of the manufacturing society, for example, contained a workshop equipped with the newest spinning and carding machines and a loom. The spectators could witness the whole process of cotton manufacture and sample different cotton products. There was also a bakery and a print shop. While the bakers distributed bread, the printers handed out a patriotic ode written by Hopkinson; for the German-speaking part of the population, an ode was printed in German.
35. *The Prose Works of William Wordsworth*, 3 vols., eds. W. J. B. Owen and Jane Worthington Smyser (Oxford: Oxford University Press, 1974), 2: 122 and 123.
36. Ralph Waldo Emerson, *Essays and Lectures* (New York: Library of America, 1983), 68.

Chatper 3

REVOLUTIONARY FESTIVALS AND POLITICAL VIOLENCE

The Impact of the French Revolution in America

Marie-Jeanne Rossignol

THE TERM "FESTIVAL" has been variously interpreted by social scientists, as Oliver Ihl notes in his book on republican festivals in France. Linguists, psychologists, sociologists, anthropologists and historians have all tried to constrict the ever-changing configurations of festivals by imposing a general framework onto them.[1] However, my aim here is not putting forward a new theory of festivals but rather at suggesting a number of reflections about certain types of political festivals which took place in America at the time of the French Revolution.[2]

A study of the impact of French Revolutionary events in Charleston, Philadelphia, and San Domingo (later Haiti), reveals the main configurations within which political festivals developed: political festivals as collective commemorations organized by and for the citizens, or political festivals as the total disruption of social and political order as well as of public morality. These configurations help us understand the complex links which connected festivals and political liberation or self-definition in America at the end of the eighteenth century. Political festivals must then be seen as a key component of the public space where private emotions reached a climax over public preoccupations.

Notes for this section begin on page 71.

Needless to say, these configurations hark back to more ancient and encompassing festive conceptions. As collective commemorations, revolutionary festivals borrowed their rituals from religious ceremonies, a traditional framework for festivals;[3] as the total upheaval of the social, political, and moral order, they served as reminders of the Dionysian excesses of antiquity, which one commentator has defined as "encounters with the powers of natural destruction and generation".[4] In this case, festivals are to be associated more with "insurrections" than with rituals.[5]

I will first examine the festivals organized in Charleston and Philadelphia on the arrival of the famous French envoy, Edmond-Charles Genêt; this will lead to a discussion of the complex links between celebrations and political partisanship in the early Republic. Studying the San Domingo slave insurrection will then enable us to analyze another type of political festivals, cruel festivals, which should not be overlooked as they reveal a further dimension of political conflict in that revolutionary period.

"Civic Festivals": Citizen Genêt's Triumphal Journey

On May 18, 1793, Edmond-Charles Genêt, the first minister sent by the French republic to the United States, dispatched the following message to Paris: "My journey [between Charleston and Philadelphia] has been a succession of uninterrupted civic festivals and my entering Philadelphia has been a triumph for liberty. Real Americans have reached the climax of happiness."[6]

Passages from the *Supplément à la Gazette de France Nationale* of July 17, 1793 provide us with a more detailed account of how enthusiastically Genêt was greeted by the American people as he entered Philadelphia, which was then the capital city of the United States: "The committee ... followed by a host of citizens, went to citizen Genêt's house and, when the applause ringing in the streets stopped, they delivered their address, at the end of which applause and cheers started anew."[7]

Thomas Jefferson's biographer describes a banquet held on behalf of Genêt, when the minister made a musical declaration of foreign policy:

> Liberty, liberty, be thy name adored forever!
> Tyrants, beware, your tottering thrones must fall;
> One interest links the free forever,
> And Freedom's sons are Frenchmen all.[8]

However, in the spring of 1793, monarchies were teaming up to attack the regicidal French republic while the United States remained France's only ally. But pro-English influence was so strong in the federal government's upper reaches that it was long debated whether Genêt should be officially received, and thus, whether the new French political regime should be recognized. In the end, it was decided that Genêt would be officially received, but George Washington, the president, delivered a "Neutrality Proclamation" by which the U.S. government declared it would abstain from fulfilling the obligations it had contracted while signing the 1778 Treaty of Alliance with France.[9] Genêt's enthusiastic welcome by the American people was in contrast to his cold reception by the government.

Until May 31, the French minister reveled in this popular glee while being aware of the United States government's reservations towards the new republican regime in France:

> The whole of America has risen up to recognize the minister of the French republic in myself ; the voice of the people keeps neutralizing President Washington's Proclamation of Neutrality. I live here in the midst of perpetual fetes; I receive addresses from all the corners of the continent, I am happy to see that my style agrees with my brothers in the United States, and I am led to believe (…) that my mission will be happy on all accounts.[10]

Genêt's tone and vocabulary ("happy", "fetes" etc.) are of course typical of late eighteenth-century culture with its emphasis on sentiment, but his excitement, as well as the street demonstrations, banquets, toasts and songs offered by his American supporters, genuinely reflect how emotionally involved they all were in the common fate of France, the United States and that of modern political liberty. However, even Genêt's optimism started waning by the end of June 1793. By then, he had realized that his supporters came not from the whole nation, but from Republicans (still probably a majority in 1793), those who favored Thomas Jefferson and believed in the democratic mission of the new nation. By contrast, the federal government's supporters espoused a more conservative approach, which was incompatible with the current activities of the French Republic.

French Historians Look at Civic and Revolutionary Festivals

In order better to understand the meaning of the "civic celebrations" organized in the United States on behalf of Genêt, it may be helpful to rely on the relevant analyses Mona Ozouf provides in her seminal study of French revolutionary festivals.[11] When defining the characteristics of revolutionary festivals, Ozouf uses criteria first expressed by the famous historian of the French Revolution, Jules Michelet:

> A people setting out: this is the first image of a festival, and the first sign that one has occurred. The people set out in some unpremeditated way; no one has ordered them to do so; their movement precedes any call. Their action is subject neither to laws and institutions nor even to concerted direction ... .[12]

In addition to that physical, spontaneous, and joyous popular reaction, Ozouf argues that Michelet added a second dimension, that is the overcoming of individual solitude and the bridging of class differences. Revolutionary festivals had to unify the nation; they celebrated the end of traditional hierarchies and the disappearance of an old world, thus bringing forth a new world free of conflict.[13]

Ozouf shows that existing festivals were indeed transformed during the French revolution. However, she contrasts the authentic, irrational revolutionary festivals described by Michelet with the civic ceremonies and celebrations which French elites deliberately organized after 1789 in order to channel and shackle popular emotional energies in the new national and social order. Understandably these new ceremonies did not meet with much success as they corresponded neither to popular tradition nor to political emotion. In her opinion, "civic" festivals must thus not be confused with "revolutionary" festivals.

The Impact of the French Revolution in the United States: Joy and Anguish over the Future of the American Experiment

Ozouf's findings can hardly be overlooked in any study of the impact of the French Revolution in the United States. She connects concepts such as people, power, public celebrations, and private joy, which are central in any analysis of American political culture at the time; she also rightly stresses the role of new democratic elites, manipulating the people's political emotions in order to strengthen a new regime.

However, the rather rigid and fairly simplistic dichotomy Ozouf establishes between spontaneous, unanimous popular festivals and cold, inauthentic, government-sponsored celebrations is too simplistic. As my own earlier analysis of the Genêt affair suggests, popular festivals could express partisanship, not only unanimity. In addition, spontaneity and joy should not be seen as unalloyed feelings but could also conceal an underlying layer of political anxiety, as will be seen.

The news that France now was a republic, too (September 21, 1792), indeed gave rise to genuine popular enthusiasm in democratic circles in the United States. American citizens started wearing red revolutionary caps, planted liberty poles and waved French tricolors.[14] In December 1792,

Thomas Jefferson wrote: "... the republicans are rejoicing and taking to themselves the name of Jacobins which two months ago was affixed on them by way of stigma."[15] Jefferson, who was then secretary of state, even considered bestowing dual citizenship on nationals of the two republics: in typical 1792 fashion, fraternity was high on the agenda.[16]

Yet these spontaneous outbursts must also be understood as symptoms of deep anguish over the political fate of the new American nation. Democrats were afraid of losing their radical heritage, that of 1776; they believed the ruling Federalists would ally with Great Britain and other monarchies against France, thus jeopardizing their own political institutions. Genêt's arrival relieved Democrats and rekindled their faith in their own Revolution, the survival of which was tacitly confirmed by the existence of another republic, built on similar political principles.

The True Nature of Political Festivals in the Early Republic

Therefore, given the political culture of the early American republic, the festivals organized on behalf of Genêt are not to be seen as substitutes for traditional ceremonies and rituals as much as forerunners of modern political gatherings. The Democratic-Republican leadership, together with its rank-and-file supporters, used Genêt's visit as a pretext for reaffirming its values in the public space. The banquet organizers were neither elite manipulators nor irrational citizens venting their revolutionary joy; they were the political opposition to the federalist government. Through the celebrations on behalf of Genêt and the French Republic, they were supporting their own definition of the nation as well as as laying the ground for future formal opposition politics.[17]

More generally speaking, as David Waldstreicher explains, political festivals in the early Republic can be seen as having occupied a contested political "middle ground" where national feeling and identity were elaborated through rival demonstrations and celebrations. Revolutionary festivals were part of this constant public confrontation: they did not divide the nation so much as create a nation out of many divisions.[18]

The Genêt affair is a case in point: Genêt's coming coincided with the birth of the first Democratic-Republican Societies, which were to serve as active centers for Democratic-Republican party activities for at least the next ten years. Genêt's supporters were to join them and continue the fight for a less conservative version of the American republic within the framework of those societies, which were based as much on fraternal feelings between France and the United States as on the social and political unrest in the United States at the end of the eighteenth century.[19]

Although the societies were joined only by Democratic-Republicans, all social strata were represented. Southern merchants and slave owners, Western land speculators and squatters, as well as small farmers and artisans, all actively defended the spirit of the American Revolution through "civic" festivals, which characterized many of the societies' activities. Thus they somehow reflected Michelet's ideal of a classless revolutionary impulse in the political culture of the early Republic.[20]

'Another Festival': A Cruel Festival

When it is examined from the point of view of African Americans, the distinction between "civic" and "revolutionary" festivals in the aftermath of the French revolution becomes fairly superficial.[21] More significant is the opposition between those who were included in this new political culture and those who were excluded. Indeed, blacks were not allowed to join the societies, which never asked for the abolition of slavery, and whose activities ceased when the slavery debate became more urgent and divisive. However, African-American slaves in America are part of this narrative of popular political culture in the age of the French Revolution, as their own reaction to the Revolution leads us to examine revolutionary festivals from a different yet revealing angle.

French elites believed that providing the revolutionary popular crowds with new types of rituals was necessary if one was to avoid "another" type of festival, which, unlike the euphoric festival described by Michelet, was characterized by licentiousness and cruelty. What they actually meant is spelled out by Ozouf:

> When we read the official accounts stating with such self-satisfaction that the festival took place in order and decency ... we learn, by contradistinction, how the organizers saw that "other" festival. ... the ill-planned festival, the noisy festival, the revelry, the mingling of age groups, classes and sexes, the orgy. Did the festival of the French revolution really manage to avoid completely that image of revolt ? ... At Vic-le-Comte, in Year III, as in so many communes, the Jacobins were chased through the streets. The chase was given the name "festival",

although it probably ended in the death of the Jacobins.[22]

According to Mona Ozouf, the French Revolution was not characterized by happiness and joy, but exhibited "the features of a violence which was the price to pay for the abolition of differences".[23] France thus witnessed another configuration of revolutionary festivals, this time defined as a political bacchanalia which combined blood and happiness.

Power, joy, resentment, anger and cruelty are also closely connected concepts when one studies the master/slave relationships on Southern plantations. Eugene D. Genovese explains that slave festivals on plantations were meant by masters to defuse dissatisfactions of slaves and provided physical and psychic relief. However, masters were well aware of the potential for violence in slave festivals:

> Their more dangerous content remains latent so long as the general conditions of life do not generate a crisis that heightens their critical thrust and points it to political terrain—a crisis that upsets the balance within the bitter-sweet laughter and liberates the anger behind the laughter.[24]

The Joyless Revolutionary Festival in San Domingo

In San Domingo, the greatest island in the Caribbean, masters well understood how much of a threat to their system voodoo ceremonies represented; they could not be controlled because slaves organized them surreptitiously, according to rites which the white elite could not fathom. Although masters denounced voodoo as an "evil religion", their main fear lay in voodoo's capacity to unite the slave population politically. According to Priska Degras, voodoo came to be seen as the symbol of armed resistance to colonial power in the eighteenth century. Legislation was passed to prohibit voodoo meetings (which were also attended by maroon, that is runaway, slaves, who set a bad example).[25]

The French revolution played a key role in the triggering of the "crisis" referred to by Genovese which caused the slaves to vent their pent-up anger. Just as Genêt was landing in Charleston, San Domingo, the richest sugar island in the Caribbean, was being wrecked both by a slave insurrection (which had started in 1791) and a civil war pitting royalists against revolutionaries. In the summer of 1793, Sonthonax, the envoy of the French Convention to San Domingo, abolished slavery on the island in order to benefit from the help of the former slaves in his fight against his royalist opponents.[26] However, although freedom had now been granted to them, the former slaves did not lose sight of their own objectives, keeping on fighting against all colonial powers until they proclaimed their independence.

The United States government was not inclined to consider the San Domingo insurrection as a consequence of the libertarian ideology introduced in the region by the French revolution.[27] But the news of the successful insurrection still spread like wildfire in the other Caribbean islands as well as in the South of the United States: for the slaves, who had always been left out of any revolutionary celebrations, the real revolutionary festival was taking place in San Domingo.

True to the fearful predictions of whites, the events in San Domingo had begun with a voodoo ceremony, which combined singing and dancing with religious rites. Then Boukman, a spiritual guide as well as the first leader of the insurgent slaves, gave the signal for the insurrection.[28] Within days, the rich Northern plain of San Domingo was aflame: contemporaries report that the insurrection was marked by "atrocities, violence, torture and sexual orgy."[29] Still, San Domingo was well known at the time for the harsh treatment masters inflicted on slaves; they may thus themselves have provided their former slaves with the very example of violent behavior which now horrified them.[30] In any case, throughout the long racial war that ensued, whites retaliated with similar and even more imaginative cruelty.[31] The events in San Domingo thus set out the model of a bloody revolution, which negated the pastoral, joyful communion envisioned by early French revolutionaries, by excluding human, or at least racial, reconciliation. They obliterated any possibility of a middle ground, of a public space where different conceptions of the polity could meet and challenge each other. Indeed, when San Domingo became Haiti in 1804, the new constitution prohibited whites from owning land.[32]

Slave insurrections or attempts at insurrections which followed in the United States between 1791 and 1800 drew their inspiration from the San Domingo model. When plans for a slave insurrection were uncovered in Richmond in July 1793, the avowed aim of its instigators was to kill all the whites as blacks had done in the "French island" (San Domingo, of course) a short time before.[33] There were other attempts at insurrection in the United States in the following months and years, one famous rebellion taking place at Pointe Coupée in what was then Spanish Louisiana.[34] The Haitian example was to serve as a model for other insurrectionary projects in the decades to come (one thinks of Nat Turner's rebellion); it was to give rise to constant fears in the master class until the Civil War and may have durably shaped white-black relations in the South of the United States, before, and even after the Civil War, when lynchings and other forms of political cruelty became the ghastly hallmarks of a new political and racial order.[35]

When one examines the celebrations organized on behalf of Genêt in Philadelphia or the slave uprising in San Domingo, the notion of "festival" proves to be a useful tool if one attempts to grasp phenomena which belong both to the emotional realm (spontaneity, joy, friendship, happiness, or anger) and to the domain of politics (revolution, exclusion, oppression and opposition between the elite and the people). However, categories and analyses first devised by Jules Michelet and Mona Ozouf must be reinterpreted in the American context. Political festivals which took place in the United States in the wake of the French revolution retained a measure of genuine revolutionary spirit, although they were mainly organized by the elite in a fractious political environment. By contrast, the revolutionary violence in San Domingo which broke out in the 1790s launched a very somber festival, hardly promoting the values of fraternity so dear to the hearts of early French revolutionaries.

Studying political festivals thus is to be a complex endeavor, yet a necessary one since a combination of thought, action and sentiment was central to late eighteenth-century political culture, in the age of revolutions. In conclusion, I will quote some of Genêt's remarks on his triumphal journey from Charleston to Philadelphia as they are typically characterized by a mixture of emotional and diplomatic language:

> Within the three hundred leagues I have just covered, I have rekindled and personally received the fraternal feelings of the American people for the French people (...) Citizen Minister, I will join to my first despatches a number of very satisfactory pieces of evidence which show the friendships entertained by the American people for the French republic.[36]

Notes

1. Oliver Ihl, *La fête républicaine* (Paris: Gallimard, 1996), 15.
2. "America" here means the Americas, not simply the United States, but my focus will be on the United States and Haiti. I have studied the impact of the French Revolution in both countries in *Le ferment nationaliste. Aux origines de la politique extérieure des Etats-Unis: 1789-1812* (Paris: Belin, 1994). For a full survey of the region see Lester D. Langley, *The Americas in the Age of Revolution 1750-1850* (New Haven, CT, and London: Yale University Press, 1996).
3. Rosemonde Sanson, *Le 14 juillet, fête et conscience nationale, 1789-1975* (Paris: Flammarion, 1976), 9.
4. Paule-Monique Vernes, *La ville, la fête, la démocratie. Rousseau et les illusions de la communauté* (Paris: Payot, 1978), 129.
5. Jean Duvignaud, *Fêtes et civilisations* (1974, Paris: Actes Sud, 1991), 240.
6. Correspondance Politique Etats-Unis/Political Correspondence United States, 37.2: 294 (thereafter CP EU). French Diplomatic Archives. All primary sources translated by M-J Rossignol.
7. CP. EU, 37.2: 297.
8. Merrill Peterson, *Thomas Jefferson and the New Nation* (New York: Oxford University Press, 1970), 487.
9. For details about this complex period, see Rossignol, *Le ferment nationaliste*, 89-90.
10. CP. EU, 37.3: 393.
11. Mona Ozouf, *Festivals and the French Revolution* (Cambridge, MA: Harvard University Press, 1988).

12. Ibid., 16.
13. Ibid., 18.
14. Eugene-Perery Link, *Democratic-Republican Societies, 1790-1800* (New York: Columbia University Press, 1942), 46.
15. Thomas Jefferson, "Letter to John Francis Mercer, Philadelphia, December 19, 1792", *The Writings*, Ford ed., vol. 6 (New York: G. P. Putnam's Sons, 1895). American enthusiasm towards the early stages of the French revolution is also documented and commented upon by David Brion Davis in "American Equality and Foreign Revolutions", *Journal of American History* 76 (December 1989): 729-752.
16. Rossignol, *Le ferment*, 84. Fraternity and friensdhip were terms which belonged both to the realm of sentiment and to the domain of politics, as we shall see. For these very reasons, they also were key concepts in the then very influential network of freemasons in France and the United States, but for lack of space this dimension will not be examined here.
17. My own analysis on this point is very similar to that of Simon P. Newman, in *Parades and the Politics of the Street: Festive Culture in the Early American Republic* (Philadelphia: University of Pennsylvania Press, 1997) which was published after I started researching this topic. See Marie-Jeanne Rossignol, "Modernité de la république: Paine, Jefferson et l'impact de la révolution française en Amérique," in Bernard Vincent, ed., *Thomas Paine ou la République sans Frontières* (Nancy: Presses Universitaires de Nancy, 1993), 121-122.
18. David Waldstreicher, *In the Midst of Perpetual Fetes: The Making of American Nationalism, 1776-1820* (Chapel Hill, NC: University of North Carolina Press, 1997), 173, 352. Also see David Waldstreicher, "Rites of Rebellion, Rites of Assent: Celebrations, Print Culture, and the Origins of American Nationalism," *Journal of American History* 82 (June 1995): 37-62.
19. The first Democratic-Republican society was created in Philadelphia on April 1, 1793, by German immigrants. The Pennsylvania Democratic Society, which was to become the most famous society of all, published its constitution on July 3, thus launching a national movement of similar societies. See Link, *Democratic-Republican Societies*, 6, 20.
20. Link, *Democratic-Republican Societies*, 79, 91, 129, 95, 97.
21. Which of course does not mean African Americans did not have their own festivals. See Shane White, *Somewhat More Independent: The End of Slavery in New York, 1770-1810* (Athens, GA: University of Georgia Press, 1991); also Ramon A. Gutierrez and Geneviève Fabre, eds., *Feasts and Celebrations in North American Ethnic Communities* (Albuquerque, NM: University of New Mexico Press, 1995). But they were not actively associated with partisan politics and festivals in the early Republic. See Waldstreicher, *In the Midst of Perpetual Fetes*, 229-231.
22. Ozouf, *Festivals*, 86, 96.
23. Ibid., 12.
24. Eugene D. Genovese, *Roll, Jordan, Roll. The World the Slaves Made* (New York: Random House, 1974), 584.
25. Priska Degras, "Vaudou et indépendance d'Haïti (1791-1804)," unpublished paper presented at a conference on August 5, 1999 in Lourmarin, 38, 39, 194. Also C.L.R James, *The Black Jacobins. Toussaint L'Ouverture and the San Domingo Revolution* (New York: Random House, 1963), 86.
26. Rossignol, *Le ferment nationaliste*, 211, 214. For an analysis also linking slavery, the United States and the impact of the French revolution, see David Brion Davis, *The Problem of Slavery in the Age of Revolution, 1770-1823* (Ithaca: Cornell University Press, 1975), 73-83.
27. Ibid., 221.
28. James, *Black Jacobins*, 87.

29. For contemporaries' accounts, see Jacques Thibau, *Le temps de Saint-Domingue: l'esclavage et la révolution française* (Paris: J.C Lattès, 1989), 273-330.
30. James, *Black Jacobins*, 11-15.
31. Yves Bénot, *La démence coloniale sous Napoléon* (Paris: La découverte, 1992).
32. Marie-Jeanne Rossignol, "La première Constitution d'Haïti et la presse américaine: étude de cas," *Revue française d'études américaines* 52 (May 1992): 153.
33. Joseph Cephas Carroll, *Slave Insurrections in the United States, 1800-1865* (Boston: Chapman and Grimes, Inc., 1938), 44.
34. Gwendolyn Midlo Hall, *Africans in Colonial Louisiana: The Development of Afro-Creole Culture in the Eighteenth Century* (Baton Rouge: Louisiana State University Press, 1992).
35. Alfred N. Hunt, *Haiti's Influence on Antebellum America: Slumbering Volcano in the Caribbean* (Baton Rouge: Louisiana State University Press, 1988). See Joel Williamson, "Wounds, Not Scars: Lynching, the National Conscience, and the American Historian," *Journal of American History* 83 (March 1997):1221-1254.
36. CP. EU, 37.2: 294.

Chapter 4

FROM CELEBRATING VICTORY TO CELEBRATING THE NATION

The War of 1812 and American National Identity

Michael Wala

THE WAR BETWEEN the United States and Great Britain from June 1812 to December 1814 is often referred to as the "Second War of Independence."[1] It was this conflict that demonstrated to the world that the United States was not likely to again disappear from the international political map. And, it has been maintained, the War of 1812 was the final act in the development of an American national identity,[2] a process marked by the Declaration of Independence in 1776 and the Constitution in 1787.

If we presume that national identity is not something natural and given, but that it is constructed in ritualized processes of communication which use a variety of symbols and artifacts to retrace the past—as a legitimization for the present system of values and an agenda for future developments alike— we should be able to discover changes in these processes as a result of the War of 1812.[3] A general feeling of belonging to an entity elevated above local or regional interests, transgressing party loyalties, should have emerged or been strengthened. If the War of 1812 had an impact on the development of national identity in the United States, this would thus become most pronounced at public celebrations with a national connota-

---

Notes for this section begin on page 87.

tion: Independence Day and Washington's Birthday. By the turn of the century, Independence Day clearly is the more important of these events because it was celebrated in three times as many communities as Washington's Birthday; a factor that increased rapidly after 1800. Washington's name—and thus the anniversary of his birth—soon stood for a form of government contested by members of a political party connected with Thomas Jefferson, the major author of the Declaration of Independence. The celebrations of the Fourth of July re-constructed the War of Independence as a universal experience of all colonists—ignoring the profound divisions among the inhabitants of the thirteen colonies during the conflict—and defined it as a manifestation of a unified and unifying national identity.[4] A large part of the population participated, watched the parades, and listened to orations and toasts on Independence Day. It was not only the social leaders or local heads of political parties that engaged in these celebrations but also members of economic and social groups, artisans, or cultural and social organizations. The choice of historic symbols, speakers, and toasts was often a highly controversial and contested political decision; friends were divided from foes, insiders from outsiders.[5] The large number of people, festive spirit, alcoholic beverages, and nighttime illuminations frequently led to behavior that would otherwise not be tolerated. But more important than chances to overstep social norms was participation in the political process on the local level, which, at the same time, often addressed national or even international problems.[6]

Developments in Europe and the wars of the French Revolution, in which France and Great Britain fought against each other in shifting alliances, had had an impact on the United States and were thus on the minds of many Americans long before the War of 1812 began. During that period, Great Britain established a naval blockade against France and applied a very comprehensive definition of what was supposed to be regarded as contraband. The British practice of not only blockading specified harbors or regions but whole stretches of the European coast cut off the American merchant marine from the European mainland. Having developed into a major trading nation after the American Revolution, the United States had hoped, as a neutral, to supply all nations, whether they were at war or not. The slogan "free ships make free goods" which Americans had favored from the very beginning of national independence, was honored by both the French and the British for some time. However, it prevented the dominant naval power, the British, from using one of its major strategic advantages and was thus ignored as the conflict progressed. Eager to avoid being drawn into the European quarrels, the Americans backed down and sacrificed much of the basis of the nation's growing economic strength.[7]

Less economically damaging but much more insulting, however, were the flagrant and incessant infringements on American sovereignty by the British Navy investigating American ships for contraband or deserters from the Royal Navy. In their eagerness, the British were hardly sensitive to American national pride: British officers did not only check the papers, as the American shipmasters would have liked it, but actually searched American vessels from deck to bottom and ignored American citizens' papers on the principal "once an Englishman, always an Englishman." This was a constant assault on the integrity, pride, and honor of the United States and made all too clear that the British paid little heed to American sovereignty.

The British declaration to blockade the European coast from Brest to the mouth of the Elbe river on May 16, 1806, and Napoleon's Berlin decree of November 21, 1806—declaring a blockade of the British Isles and prohibiting ships from entering French harbors if they had previously anchored in British waters—did not do much to diffuse the tense situation. The subsequent British announcement that all neutral ships coming from France would be seized if they had not visited British harbors before, and, finally, Napoleon's Milan decree of December 17, 1807 that all neutral ships would be seized that had concurred with the British demands left the United States in an untenable position. Neutral shipping had been made impossible and, much to the frustration of the administration, the Americans were in no position to do anything about it short of war.[8]

War with Great Britain seemed almost unavoidable when on June 22, 1807 the U.S. Navy vessel *Chesapeake* was stopped by the British frigate *Leopard* while still being in view of the American coast. When the American shipmaster denied the British captain's request that his ship should be searched for deserters, the *Leopard* shelled the American vessel. Not prepared for a military engagement, the *Chesapeake* suffered ten casualties in almost no time. After firing one shot, the American captain had to allow the British to board his ship. They took four American sailors, supposed to be deserters, prisoner supposedly for desertion and put out to sea again.[9]

After this arrogant provocation of the United States, a declaration of war against Great Britain seemed imminent to many. But President Thomas Jefferson hoped that economic pressure would be enough to persuade the British to discontinue these illegal practices and that the flagrant violation of American sovereignty in the *Chesapeake* case would soften the British government to the American arguments and demands. Jefferson also thought that a conflict with Britain might be able to unite the nation. In 1807, he wrote to the American ambassador in London, James Monroe: The British "have often enough … given us cause for war before, but it has been on points which would not have united the nation. But now they have touched a chord which vibrates in every heart. Now is that time to settle the old and the new."[10]

That Jefferson may have seen cause to lament a lack of national unity among his fellow citizens seems to contradict common understanding of the forces that shaped the American Revolution. What we often perceive as a common, unifying struggle to shake off the shackles of British oppression was much more fragmented. The Declaration of Independence had provided a blueprint for a nation, and the Constitution had cast a legal framework. However, this had not concluded but rather initiated the process of nation-building in the former colonies. At the turn of the century, Americans were not a satisfied, placid people enjoying their hard-won independence from Great Britain, but rather a country in which the political strife that had marked the struggle for the ratification of the Constitution still persisted. It was this necessary discourse about the future development of the political and social system of the young nation, a struggle between members of the Federalist Party and the Democratic-Republican Party, that turned out to be the major obstacle for a trans-partisan, truly national identity.[11]

The most important public battlegrounds in this contest of ideas and ideologies were the national celebrations. The Federalists had already used celebrations, processions, and parades in their struggle for ratification of the Constitution and had celebrated Washington's Birthday and the Fourth of July in that same spirit. The Republicans (later to be called Democratic-Republicans), who had gathered around Thomas Jefferson, soon utilized Independence Day celebrations as a clearly partisan demonstration by putting the Declaration of Independence in the center of high-spirited festivities. By the turn of the century, Republicans in many cities either controlled the festivities, wrestled with Federalist-dominated city councils over control, or staged exuberant festivals of their own.[12] Thus, before long, many Federalists could not bring themselves to celebrate the Fourth of July because that national holiday had been increasingly shaped as an anti-Federalist event. The Republicans clearly had the advantage, simply because it was quite awkward to observe the day without paying tribute to the document that was central to the occasion. But it was precisely this document that Federalists regarded with contempt.

Although many citizens favored keeping party politics out of Fourth of July celebrations—in 1799 a group of as many as 1,000 citizens in Providence, R.I., called for such a separation,[13]—by the end of the eighteenth century party hostilities had made it impossible in some cities to have non partisan celebrations on Independence Day, and, increasingly, the festivities became one-party events. The Philadelphia *Aurora* reported on July 7, 1800:

> Heretofore it was customary with the two parties to vie with each other in the pleasures and congratulations of a day of jubilee and joy. On Friday last [July 4, 1800], no bells were rung in any church on this occasion. ... there was no emulation, no rivalry, no congratulations, no joy seen among those who call themselves Federalists; sorrow and disappointment was marked on their countenance and to them it seems as if their hearts were clothed in sackcloth and ashes as on some day of general mourning. But the day was celebrated by republicans and by them only with their wonted conviviality and gladness. ... It is said that some Federalists begin to think that the celebration of the Fourth of July is not a matter of most importance, that it frequently creates riot and disturbance and that it would be more productive of good order to discontinue in future any particularly attachment to the Anniversary.

Despite these high-strung political emotions, the change of administration to that of Thomas Jefferson in March of 1801 went rather smoothly. It seemed as if a chance for reconciliation still existed. The bells of the Episcopal Church in Philadelphia rang again on the Fourth of July 1801 (and not only on the King's birthday!) after two years of silence—but quite likely only because the Republican Governor of Pennsylvania had issued an order to that effect.[14]

In Boston, separate celebrations were held again in 1803. Here, as in other cities, Republican papers printed the Declaration of Independence, and the document was read at many celebrations of that party, "that our children may know what were the causes which led this country to a separation and to impress on their minds the fallacy of again trusting to their friendship or connecting ourselves in an alliance to oppose a nation [France] who assisted us in our distress." The Federalists, the *Independent Chronicle* also claimed, did not pay adequate tribute to the Fourth of July and the Declaration of Independence. To this, the *Columbian Centinel* reacted with galling contempt. Federalists did not have to learn from Republicans how to celebrate the day. "New emotions," the paper contended, pitching New England aristocracy against recent immigrants, were for "modern patriots" and "Alien-Americans."[15] The Federalists ignored the Declaration, largely because it exhibited language they deemed inappropriate and damaging to the relations with Great Britain, but probably even more so because of the egalitarian language and connotations that were applied by Republicans to the American society. Thus, to provide just one example, the Federalist dominated Common Council in Albany, New York, tried to prevent the reading of the Declaration because it supposedly was disrespectful to the King of England and could lead to tensions between the United States and Great Britain. The members of the Mechanics Society of Albany, fervently disagreed because they stated "Liberty is the equalization of civil privileges." For them, refraining from the ritualized proclamation that "all men are created equal" entailed the possibility that the promise of individual freedom and civil rights, of participation in the political process, might be broken.[16]

The perpetual conflict with Great Britain and, on a smaller scale, with France did not overcome this internal discord and did not lead to unity in face of an external danger but rather provoked an increase in regional dissatisfaction with federal politics. This was the case particularly in New England, which suffered the most from the Embargo and Non-Intercourse Acts of 1807 and 1809 designed to keep the United States out of war. The New England states were particularly hard hit because their economy was based almost exclusively on shipping. But the cotton planters in the South, depending on exports, also suffered a sharp drop in prices because shipping to Europe was impossible.[17] The Embargo Act was repealed in 1809 and replaced under Jefferson's successor, James Madison, with the Non-Intercourse Act that again allowed trade except with France and Great Britain, but this did little to improve the economic situation. In the following year this act was superseded by Macon's Bill No. 2 that turned out to be precisely the opposite of what Jefferson and Madison had tried to achieve earlier: whereas the Embargo Act and Non-Intercourse Act were intended to insulate the United States from the European conflict, Macon's Bill offered an American alliance to either France or Great Britain against its enemy: that nation that was first to repeal the anti-neutrality policies that had made American trade with Europe impossible would find the United States on its side. While these policies were supported by Representatives from the West and the South—often, however, only because of party loyalty—harsh criticism emanated from the New England states.[18]

The animosity between Federalists and Republicans changed little during the years until 1812. Separate celebrations on Independence Day continued in many cities and the toasts made at those occasions—as an important ritual of political expression toasts were reported at length in the papers—bespeak the deep rift between the political parties. In Springfield, New Hampshire, for example, the Federalists, hoping that their candidate for presidency would win the elections in November, toasted "The President of the United States—to ruin a country, govern it by a French Philosopher—we hail the fourth of March 1809."[19] Thus, on June 18, 1812, when the United States declared war on Great Britain, a unifying national identity that transcended regional and party differences was even more elusive than at the end of the eighteenth century.

In Philadelphia, reports of the declaration of war were nonetheless received enthusiastically and the Independence Day celebrations a couple of weeks later turned into city-wide demonstrations of support for the national government and the president. According to the Republican paper *Aurora* "[t]he volunteer associations, composed of the men of the hitherto opposed political sects, were seen united, and rallying around the standard of their country." The following year, with hard times hitting Philadelphia, and in 1814, with an occupation by the British Army seemingly imminent, the celebrations concentrated on military preparedness with martial militia parades.[20] In Charleston, South Carolina, the citizens also reacted with enthusiasm about the news of war. The South may have suffered almost as much as New England from the administration's hapless foreign policy but secessionist ideas were strongly repudiated (as they were in the Northeast). The two opposing political factions agreed to take turns in selecting speakers for Independence Day orations, and the American Revolutionary Society and the '76 Association assembled for a joint parade on the Fourth of July 1812 for the first time in their history. The Declaration of Independence was here, as seemingly everywhere in the South and the West, an integral part of the celebrations. In Wilmington, North Carolina, the day was toasted as "The Fourth of July 1776. The sword of America again drawn from its scabbard in the spirit of that day—May its strokes be directed with such energy as speedily to force the enemy to a just and reasonable peace."[21]

In New England, not surprisingly, opposition to the war was the strongest. Here, sympathies for the country which again had become the enemy of the United States, did not abate after the war was declared. Passive resistance and active verbal opposition to the conflict was based on intense disapproval of the Republican President James Madison and in strong cultural and commercial ties with England, but it resulted also from the Federalists' assumption that the United States was hardly likely to defeat one of the most powerful nations on the globe. What we might assume to be an almost automatic reaction, that every citizen would have put aside political differences in face of a common enemy and rally around the flag, simply did not take place in all parts of the United States after the declaration of war on June 18, 1812.

In Massachusetts, Governor Caleb Strong declared a day of fasting on July 23, 1812 to allow the New Englanders to atone for their sins, among which were as one citizen wrote in his diary, "in electing over them rulers, without Honesty or Knowledge, men neither fearing God or who have any love for their country."[22] Accordingly, Independence Day in Boston—with its dominant Federalist political class—was observed quite differently than in Charleston and Philadelphia. The celebrations in 1812 hardly exceeded the bare minimum.[23] Only a few churches rang their bells and a few cannons were fired to honor the birthday of the nation, but there were none of the otherwise common parades, nor enthusiasm, festive spirit, and hilarity. Speakers fiercely attacked the president's policies and what was soon to be called "Mr. Madison's War." Boston Republicans chose to celebrate in communities in the vicinity where they were welcome; only a small group assembled for a celebration at the Republican meeting place, the Exchange Coffee House.[24]

By the summer of 1813 dissatisfaction had developed into bitterness. Now, even secession from the union was discussed in New England.[25] "Is there any spell which renders the bond of confederacy indissoluble? May not the parties who formed the compact annull it at their option?" the Federalist *Boston Daily Advertiser* asked on July 2, 1813. "We do not say, nay, we do not think, that a separation is desirable—but we consider the subject as much open to discussion, as a question of the division of a parish." And, a few days later, on July 5, 1813, the editor of that same paper almost called for an overthrow of the national government when he wrote that he hoped the

> recurrence to the principles of '76 will kindle a spark of that holy fervor which animated our fathers. ... It would not be amiss to compare the grievances which the sensibility of that day deemed intolerable, and which then, constituted a sufficient motive and justification to resist by any means and at every hazard the encroachment of kingly power, with the flagrant instances of injustice and oppression which we have tamely and stupidly endured from creatures who owe their political existence to our mere volition, from insects that feed upon 'the bounty of an hour,' whom a breath has called into being, and whom a breath can annihilate![26]

In other regions and cities deliberate attempts were made to allow the differing factions to celebrate the national holiday without distinction of party or alliance. Although the Republicans were in the majority in Baltimore, Maryland, and with only one Federalist sitting on the committee organizing the celebration, a well-known Federalist, Lt. Col. William H. Winder, was asked to deliver a speech. The "birth day of freedom" had been celebrated with great splendor and unsurpassing harmony, the *Weekly Register* wrote on July 14, 1812,

> [t]he arrangements made by the general committee were eminently calculated to bring about this happy union, and the *patriot*, resident in any part of our widely extended country, let him be called by what name he may, will rejoice that the *people* of Baltimore, the WHOLE PEOPLE of this prosperous city and neighborhood, have erected a temple to *Concord*.[27]

But 1813, even in parts of New England, such as Dorchester, Massachusetts, the political parties could transcend their differences in 1813 by making an effort to stage a joint Fourth of July celebration. In the South such divisions became a matter of history immediately after June 1812. Independence Day, reported the *Louisiana Courier* on July 5, 1813, was celebrated with "the greatest pomp in this city and it was the first time we had an opportunity to witness here in this feast, a character truely national."[28]

There was little in terms of American successes or victories during the next couple of years that could have made an impression on these political dispositions. However, when news about Napoleon's downfall was received in Boston in the spring of 1814, the Federalist *Boston Spectator* anticipated that the government would finally realize the folly of war and that peace would not be long off. Now, Boston was again willing to celebrate the national holiday. "Welcome, then, welcome once more", the paper wrote on June 18, 1814, "the Anniversary of our Independence." Hopes for a treaty of peace ran high in the summer of 1814 and fireworks were burned in celebration of Independence Day, but the most central document of that day, the Declaration of Independence, was, again, not read in Boston. "The English are *not* our enemy," the *Boston Spectator* had declared in June of 1814, "[t]hey are but instruments in the hands of Mr. Madison, and those who aided him to plunge us into this war ..."[29] Suggestions that some Federalists were still contemplating a secession of New England from the Union, encouraged the Republican *Independent Chronicle* to write on July 4, 1814: "The time calls on us to unite. At this present crisis, UNION is the great objective to be acquired. We cannot but view with indignation the attempts to dissolve this bond of our national security."[30] In other cities, hostility between Federalists and Democrats during the war even increased to the point of violence. The 1814 Independence Day celebrations in Troy, New York, offered a welcome occasion to allow some of the tensions to run their course. Members of the Republican militia fired into the Federal standard, volleys that were returned by members of the Federal rifle corps who brought down the "the democratic standard ... This could not fail to bring on an affray—but it was nothing more than a battle of fisty cuffs in which no lives were lost or limbs broken," a correspondent of the New York *Evening Post* reported.[31]

News about the conclusion of a treaty of peace and information on the American military success in New Orleans reached the East Coast and most other parts of the Union almost simultaneously during the first couple of weeks in February 1815. Whereas information about the successful completion of negotiations in Ghent on December 24, 1814 was enthusiastically and universally greeted, the old divisions along party lines were quite obvious in the reports of Federalist and Republican newspapers about General Andrew Jackson's successful operations in New Orleans on January 8, 1815. *The Albany Argus*, a staunchly Republican paper, was unable to satisfy the demand for "extras" they printed on February 8. The Providence, Rhode Island *Phenix* informed its readers a few days later of the "*Transcendent Triumph*," reporting that "congratulation and glee brightened the countenance, expanded the heart, and exercised the tongue of every inhabitant — save a few confirmed *tories*, whom God forgive!³²

The fervently Federalist *Boston Daily Advertiser* displayed little of that enthusiasm when news finally reached Boston on February 9. "National pride, firmness, dignity and spirit are very laudable qualities, but they are to be controuled and measured by considerations of Prudence and interest," the paper warned. Speculations in the next issue on the impact of the American victory on the negotiations for peace became superfluous when news about the peace settlement reached Boston on February 13. Now, the spontaneity of celebration was almost overwhelming: bells were rung the whole day throughout the city, "mercantile streets and wharfs" were abundantly decorated "with flags, all business was suspended," and in the evening many buildings were illuminated.³³

In New York the news about peace had broken a couple of days earlier, on 11 February, announced by the city's presses in broadsides printed for that occasion. The city, a correspondent for the *Boston Daily Advertiser* wrote in a letter received on February 11, "is in a perfect uproar of shouts, illuminations, &c, &c."³⁴ Similar spontaneous celebrations took place in many other cities, fireworks were displayed, and mayors announced illuminations.³⁵ In Philadelphia the peace treaty was celebrated with an illumination on February 15. Here mayor Robert Wharton made sure to point out that the police would "secure" those in their peaceful rights who did not wish to take part in this occasion.³⁶ In Albany, New York, "at least 130,000 lights, several transparencies, and a display of fireworks from the hills" illuminated the city until 9 o'clock when a signal gun announced that the lights should be extinguished.³⁷ And the Baltimore *Niles' Weekly Register* reported on February 18 the "Glorious News!" and exclaimed: "*Who would not be an American? Long live the Republic! All hail! Last asylum of oppressed humanity! Peace is signed in the arms of victory!*"³⁸

The conflict may have ended on honorable terms and "in the arms of victory" but the division among the American citizens did not cease with the end of hostilities—as it had not ceased with the declaration of war against Great Britain two and one-half years before.³⁹ In Boston, Salem, and Newburyport, the Federalists could not even bring themselves to officially celebrate the peace until the Peace Treaty had been ratified on February 16 by Congress. And then, they combined an official peace celebration and a grand illumination with Washington's Birthday on February 22, thus reinserting a Federalist symbol into the military victory and diplomatic success achieved by the Republicans Jackson and Madison.

But, again, the lack of a unifying national identity was expressed most clearly on Independence Day. The quasi-religious aura that once had surrounded Independence Day celebrations had been sacrificed when the Fourth of July was utilized for party purposes long before 1812. It could not be regained after the war. In many areas, the Fourth of July continued to be observed as it had been before the war. In 1815 the *American Magazine,* in Albany, NY, reported that in New York City

> the spectators were uncommonly numerous, and compromised a great part of the beauty and fashion of the city. The appearance of the militia was splendid. The different societies attached to the two great parties which divide the public, agreeably to the arrangement published in this paper, walked in procession: one to the Washington Hall, and the other to the Circus, to hear the customary oration; and in the evening the public gardens, the theater, and every place of fashionable amusement, were crowded.[40]

Celebrations divided along party lines also continued in other cities and particularly in those of New England, including Boston, Dorchester, and Charlestown.[41] And in Richmond, Virginia, the editor of *The Enquirer* even complained, "the great day, which had ushered the only free nation on earth into light, was not been celebrated ... in a spirit which became the Metropolis of Virginia.—There was no general Association of Citizens, no Oration, no Declaration of Independence read."[42] By now the Republicans clearly had the advantage and used every opportunity to let their adversaries feel the sting of their glee. In that way *The Albany Argus* used the occasion Thanksgiving on December 26, 1815 to attack Federalism: "We have reasons to be grateful for favors of another kind," the paper wrote after mentioning the American victories in the war, "such as the total discomfiture of a mischievous Faction, who had discouraged loans of money, and the enlistment of soldiers, while they encourage the enemy, and prolonged the war; and did all in their power to debase the government and dissolve the union."[43]

The coup de grace, so to say, for the partisan festivities and Federalists' abstentions from Fourth of July celebrations in New England and particularly Boston, came not before the summer of 1817. It was a visit by James Madison's successor and party friend, President James Monroe, that mended much of the rift between the New England Federalists and the Union. Monroe had been opposed to the war but loyally served President Madison as secretary of state until he was elected president in 1816 and, simultaneously, as secretary of war during the latter part of the war with Great Britain.[44] His tour of New England in June and July of 1817—almost like a king visiting an unruly province—did more for reconciliation and to instill a feeling of "national" identity in that part of the nation than the War of 1812. He was applauded in every town he visited along his way and jubilantly welcomed in Boston in a well timed visit a day before the Fourth of July. *The Albany Argus* wrote on July 11:

> The Fourth of July has been observed as a jubilee as generally, and with as much splendor, as at any former period, and with a great deal more national feeling than for some years past. Party asperity seems to have had no seat at the festival; and territorial jealousies and local prejudices appear to have almost totally disappeared. This happy indication in the public temper may in some measure be imputed to the benign effects of the Presidential tour.

In Worcester, Massachusetts, the papers reported, the Fourth of July was celebrated that year "without distinction of party, for the first time in *fifteen* years."[45] In Boston, even the ardently Federalist *Columbian Centinel*, expressed almost unrestrained excitement about the president's visit and provided its readers with lengthy accounts of his reception in the surrounding cities. Preparations for Monroe's visit were extensively reported, orders of processions printed, and the *Centinel* assured its readers, that "though the committee [of arrangements for the president's visit] was composed of gentlemen of opposing sentiments on many political questions—all arrangements were made with perfect unanimity and cheerfulness." The reception, thus well prepared, was a complete success: more than forty thousand Bostonians cheered the president "loud and unanimous." But still, it was not until the Fourth of July, 1820 that the Declaration of Independence was again officially read during the now unified celebrations in the city of Boston.[46]

During this period neither the anniversary of the signing of the Peace Treaty in Ghent on December 24, 1814, nor General Jackson's stunning victory on January 8, 1815 seems to have been observed to any extent aside from occasional veterans' meetings. The Treaty of Ghent may have not been celebrated because it fell on Christmas Eve, but most likely also because there was not much to celebrate. In Ghent, the Americans failed to secure maritime rights and had to give up conquest of Canada, but Native American opposition to American expansion in the Northwest and Southwest was broken. Britain had sought in vain a neutral Native American buffer state in the American Northwest and wanted to revise both the American-Canadian boundary and the 1783 Treaty of Paris that had established the independence of the United States. An honorable peace had been achieved—but not much more; the United States and Great Britain simply returned to the antebellum status quo. The Treaty of Peace was—as one gentlemen pointed out at the Federalist's Fourth of July celebration in 1815 in Cambridge, Massachusetts,—a "*piece* of a Treaty."[47] The Republicans, not surprisingly, valued the treaty much more highly: in Dorchester a toast to the twenty-fourth of December quite overstated the event as "The day which witnessed the acknowledgment of our superior power in arms and in diplomacy." But still, very few accounts of celebrations of that anniversary can be found in the papers.[48]

The American victory in New Orleans, too, was hardly celebrated following the war and before Jackson became a national political figure in the mid-1820s, except in New Orleans. It was a day for the display of "the flag," but only occasionally was the date noted in the papers or the event toasted at festivities. Republicans at times hailed General Jackson during their Fourth of July celebrations (1815 in New York and 1816 in Albany), and in 1816, Jackson's victory was remembered by the Ladies of South Carolina who presented the general with a vase—quite obviously a noteworthy gift because a number of Republican papers carried the information.[49] When the New York *Mercantile Advertiser* reminded its readers on January 8, 1818 that this was the day of the "anniversary of the Battle, and Brilliant Victory achieved by General A. Jackson" it was a rare instant—and even more exceptional was the elegant dinner and the toasts staged by the editors and proprietors of daily New York papers.[50]

In New Orleans, the anniversary of the battle was, quite naturally, a different matter, and was celebrated with pomp equal to Fourth of July celebrations. Both houses of the Louisiana legislature had voted to celebrate the first anniversary in 1816, and the governor of the state led the parades and the church services. "In the evening," the *Louisiana Courier* reported, "all the inhabitants of New Orleans gave themselves up entirely to pleasure—dances, bankets [sic], nothing was spared—It is to be wished that that day be thus celebrated every year."[51] And, the citizens of New Orleans did not fail to include the eighth of January in their Independence Day toasts.[52] However, the most obvious symbols of the War of 1812, the victory at New Orleans and the Treaty of Ghent, did not become commonly used symbols in the rituals of Independence Day celebrations.

An examination of Independence Day celebrations suggests that the War of 1812 has not advanced a common non partisan and unifying national identity as much as we tend to believe. Instead, it became a force supporting regional and non-national (and partially even anti-national) identities. In New England it was the Hartford Convention that instilled a sense of belonging. New Englanders "began to feel their national character, and to cherish a pride, which had been for several years nearly extinct, at being a citizen of New-England," the *Boston Daily Advertiser* claimed on January 21, 1815.[53] When middling people, artisans, shopkeepers, and even laborers replaced the patriarchal "old stock" in Independence Day committees and parades, the liberating connotations of the Fourth of July and the egalitarian language of the Declaration of Independence finally became pillars of American nationalism, a tide that even in New England swept the Federalists aside. The fact that the War of 1812 had left the Federalist Party tainted with an image of disloyalty because of the secessionist ideas during the war, made this all the easier. It was only after the final decline of the Federalists that the Fourth of July became a non partisan national holiday. Only indirectly therefore, through the demise of the Federalist Party resulting partially from the outcome of the War of 1812, did the "Second War of Independence" foster the construction of a national identity in the United States.

Notes

1. The Literature on the War of 1812 is extensive. Bradford Perkins, *Prologue to War: England and the United States, 1805-1812* (Berkeley, CA: University of California Press, 1961), is the classical description, see also Walter Lord's more detailed work *The Dawn's Early Light* (New York: Norton, 1972). Pierre Berton studies the war against Canada and the American internal discourse before the war in *The Invasion of Canada, 1812-1813* (Toronto: McClelland and Steward, 1980), and he provides excellent studies of the major protagonists. Kate Caffrey details the military as well as social and economic aspects of the war for both, the British and the Americans, in *Twilight's Last Gleaming: Britain vs. America, 1812-1815* (New York: Stein & Day, 1977).
2. For the problems connected with a definition of the related term "nationalism" see particularly Benedict Anderson, *Imagined Communities: Reflections on the Origins and Spread of Nationalism* (London: Verso, 1983), Liah Greenfeld, *Nationalism: Five Roads to Modernity* (Cambridge, MA: Harvard University Press 1992), and Eric J. Hobsbawm, *Nations and Nationalism since 1780: Programme, Myth, Reality* (Cambridge: Cambridge University Press, 1992), and more recently Liah Greenfeld, "The Origins and Nature of American Nationalism in Comparative Perspective," paper at 19th Meeting of the Historians of the German Association for American Studies, February 9-11, 1996, Tutzing, Germany. The quite difficult and challenging issue of "national identity" has occupied various academic disciplines. This was the case particularly after World War I in face of the issue of self-determination and has regained prominence after the re-emergence of national identities in the wake of the demise of the Soviet Empire. Raymond Grew provides a good introduction to the topic and furnishes information on a major part of the relevant literature in "The Construction of National Identity" in *Concepts of National Identity: An Interdisciplinary Dialogue—Interdisziplinäre Betrachtungen zur Frage der nationalen Identität*, Peter Boerner, ed. (Baden-Baden: Nomos, 1986), 31-43. The admittedly crude definition of "national identity" I provide below should suffice for the purpose of this paper.
3. For the use of rituals see Robert Middlekauff, "The Ritualization of the American Revolution," in *The Development of an American Culture* (Englewood Cliffs, NJ: Prentice-Hall, 1970), 31-43.
4. Hobsbawm, *Nations and Nationalism since 1780*, 20. Just a few years ago three major studies of Independence Day and other public celebrations and their impact on national identity have been published: David Waldstreicher, *In the Midst of Perpetual Fetes: The Making of American Nationalism, 1776-1820* (Chapel Hill, NC: University of North Carolina Press, 1997); Len Travers, *Celebrating the Fourth: Independence Day and the Rites*

of Nationalism in the Early Republic (Amherst, MA: University of Massachusetts Press, 1997); and Simon P. Newman, *Parades and the Politics of the Street: Festive Culture in the Early American Republic* (Philadelphia: University of Pennsylvania Press, 1997). None of them, however, pays much attention to the impact of the War of 1812 on national identity and its reflection in public celebrations. For the number and location of communities celebrating Washington's Birthday and Independence Day, see Newman, *Parades and the Politics of the Street*, maps pp. 60 and 84.

5. A good case study is Albrecht Koschnik, "Political Conflict and Public Contest: Rituals of National Celebration in Philadelphia, 1788-1815," *The Pennsylvania Magazine of History and Biography* 118 (July 1994): 211-48. However, he provides very little information on the period after 1801.

6. Violence did occur during such celebrations from time to time, but hardly anything more serious was reported in the papers than fistfights or brawls by drunks. The measure of violence Mona Ozouf found in French pre- and post-revolutionary festivals cannot be detected in the United States during the period relevant in this context. See Mona Ozouf, *Festivals and the French Revolution* (Cambridge, MA: Harvard University Press, 1988).

7. That principle was already expressed in the Prussian-American treaty of amity and commerce in 1785. When the treaty was reenacted in 1799, however, the "free ships make free goods" clause was dropped. Samuel F. Bemis, *John Quincy Adams and the Foundations of American Foreign Policy* (1949; Westport, CT: Greenwood Press, 1981), 93-96. See also Charles S. Hyman, "The First American Neutrality: A Study of the American Understanding of Neutral Obligations during the Years 1792 to 1815", *Illinois Study in the Social Sciences* 20.1-2 (1934): 1-178. That promotion of commerce was essential to the new nation and for the development of nationalism is argued in William E. Weeks, "American Nationalism, American Imperialism: An Interpretation of United States Political Economy, 1789-1861," *Journal of the Early Republic* 14 (Winter 1994): 485-95.

8. For a detailed account of the French activities against American shipping (which took part mostly in the Caribbean) see Ulane Bonnel, *La France, les États-Unis et la guerre de course, 1797-1815* (Paris: Nouvelles Editions Latines, 1961). For the impressment of sailors see the unpublished dissertation by Scott T. Jackson, "Impressment and the Anglo-American Discord, 1787-1818," Ph.D. Dissertation, University of Michigan, 1976. A total of about 1,500 American vessels were captured by France or Great Britain.

9. One of the sailors was indeed a deserter from the Royal Navy; three were American citizens. Anthony Steel provides a well-balanced study of the British problems with active U.S. Navy recruiting of British sailors and deserters in "More Light on the Chesapeake," *Mariner's Mirror* 39.4 (1953): 243-65.

10. Quoted in Harry L. Coles, *The War of 1812* (Chicago: University of Chicago Press, 1965), 7.

11. The Democratic-Republicans or Republicans were founded in the early 1790s. See Stanley Elkins and Eric McKitrick, *The Age of Federalism* (New York: Oxford University Press, 1993), and James Roger Sharp, *American Politics in the Early Republic: The New Nation in Crisis* (New Haven, CT: Yale University Press, 1993). Jürgen Heideking gives a short but quite comprehensive overview in "Einheit aus Vielfalt: Die Entstehung eines amerikanischen Nationalbewußtseins in der Revolutionsepoche 1760-1820," in *Volk – Nation – Vaterland*, Ulrich Herrmann, ed. (Hamburg: Meiner, 1996), 101-17.

12. For a study of the celebrations and parades connected with the Constitution see the articles by Jürgen Heideking and Dietmar Schloss in this volume. See also Newman, *Parades and the Politics of the Street*, 81, 85. For information about patterns of Fourth of July celebrations, see Appelbaum, *The Glorious Fourth*, 36-45.

13. Charles Warren, "Fourth of July Myths," *The William and Mary Quarterly* 2.3 (1945): 259.

14. The fact that the capital of the United States was moved from Philadelphia to Washington, D.C., in 1800 may have added to the lack of enthusiasm. *Independent Chronicle*, July 4, 1799; *Aurora* July 7, 1800, *Aurora* July 13, 1801, both quoted in Warren, "Fourth of July Myths," 260-63.
15. *Independent Chronicle*, July 4, 1803; *Columbian Centinel*, July 16, 1803. The political battle, which quite often was most fervently fought in the local papers, led in 1806 even to murder when Thomas J. Selfridge, a prominent Federalist, shot the son of leading Republican Benjamin Austin because of a political dispute; Charles Warren, *Jacobine and Junto, or: Early American Politics as Viewed in the Diary of Dr. Nathaniel Ames, 1758-1822* (1931; New York: AMS Press, [1970]), 183-85. On the role of newspapers in the political controversies of that period see David Paul Nord, "Newspapers and American Nationhood, 1776-1826," in *Three Hundred Years of the American Newspaper*, ed. John B. Hench (Worcester: American Antiquarian Society, 1991), 400-402.
16. *Albany Register*, June 18, 1805; *Albany Register*, July 5, 1805; *Albany Register*, August 10, 1805; quoted in David G. Hackett, "The Social Origins of Nationalism: Albany, New York, 1754-1835," *Journal of Social History* 21.4 (Summer 1988): 668.
17. For the confusion about the possible outcome of the American foreign policy see, for example, the article in the Hudson, NY, paper *The Balance* 7.1 (January 5, 1808): 1.
18. For the drop in prices for cotton and dissatisfaction in the South see George R. Taylor, "Agrarian Discontent in the Mississippi Valley Preceding the War of 1812", *The Journal of Political Economy* 39 (1931): 486-505; and idem, "Prices in the Mississippi Valley Preceding the War of 1812," *Journal of Economic and Business History* 3 (1930-31): 148-63. For the political attitude and discussions of secession James M. Banner, Jr., *To the Hartford Convention: The Federalists and the Origins of Party Politics in Massachusetts, 1789-1815* (New York: Knopf, 1970), is most comprehensive.
19. *Hampshire Federalist*, July 7, 1808. The new president, to be elected in November 1808, was to be sworn into office on March 4, 1809.
20. *Aurora*, July 7, 1812.
21. See A.V. Huff, Jr., "The Eagle and the Vulture: Changing Attitudes Toward Nationalism in the Fourth of July Orations Delivered in Charleston, 1778-1860," *The South Atlantic Quarterly* 73.1 (1974): 14. Raleigh, NC, *Register*, July 17, 1812, Raleigh, NC, *Register*, July 9, 1813; quoted in Fletcher M. Green, "Listen to the Eagle Scream: One Hundred Years of the Fourth of July in North Carolina, 1776-1876," *North Carolina Historical Review* 31 (July and October 1954): 295-320, 529-49, reprinted in J. Isaac Copeland, ed., *Democracy in the Old South and Other Essays by Fletcher Melvin Green* (Nashville, TN: Vanderbilt University Press, 1969), 122.
22. Waldstreicher, *In the Midst of Perpetual Fetes*, 256-57.
23. See, for example, the description of the celebration in 1814 in the *Daily Boston Advertiser*, July 6, 1814.
24. Travers, *Celebrating the Fourth*, 193.
25. This never developed into concrete plans, not even during the Federalists' Hartford Convention, December 14, 1814 to January 5, 1815. However, rumors would not stop and led to the demise of the party. See also Banner, *To the Hartford Convention*.
26. *Boston Daily Advertiser*, July 2, 1813, *Boston Daily Advertiser*, July 5, 1813.
27. *The Weekly Register*, July 14, 1812; "Oration," by Lieut. Colonel William H. Winder in Howard's Park, reprinted in ibid.
28. New Orleans, *Louisiana Courier*, July 5, 1813.
29. *The Boston Spectator*, June 18, 1814; *The Boston Spectator*, June 25, 1814.
30. *Independent Chronicle*, July 4, 1814, *Independent Chronicle*, July 7, 1814, quoted in Travers, *Celebrating the Fourth*, 194-95.

31. The *Boston Daily Advertiser* reprinted this information from the *Evening Post*, July 9, 1814.
32. *The Phenix*, February 11, 1815.
33. *Boston Daily Advertiser*, February 9, 1815: *Boston Daily Advertiser*, February 10, 1815; *Boston Daily Advertiser*, February 11, 1815; *Boston Daily Advertiser*, February 14, 1815.
34. *Boston Daily Advertiser*, February 14, 1815. See, for example, the broadsheet printed by the *Mercantile Advertiser* on February 11, 1815.
35. On illuminations in Baltimore, MD, see *Niles' Weekly Register*, February 7, 1815.
36. New York, *Mercantile Advertiser*, February 16, 1815; *Boston Daily Advertiser*, February 20, 1815.
37. *The Albany Argus*, February 24, 1815.
38. *Niles' Weekly Register*, February 18, 1815. Preceding the text is one of the earlier quotations from "Star-Spangled Banner" by Francis Scott Key: "The star spangled banner in triumph shall wave, o'er the land of the free and the home of the brave."
39. That the United States was "genuinely at peace with itself" after 1815 is based on a rather superficial evaluation; see, for example, George Dangerfield, *The Awakening of American Nationalism, 1815-1828* (New York: Harper & Row, 1965), 2-3. See also idem, *The Era of Good Feeling* (1952; Chicago: Ivan R. Dee, 1989).
40. Albany, NY, *American Magazine* 1 (1815): 91.
41. *Boston Daily Advertiser*, July 6, 1815; *Columbian Centinel*, July 5, 1815. Albrecht Koschnik argues that American national identity remained fragmented in Philadelphia between 1790 and 1815; Koschnik, "Political Conflict and Public Contest," 248.
42. *The Enquirer*, July 5, 1815.
43. *The Albany Argus*, December 26, 1815.
44. A short biography on Monroe is Noble E. Cunningham, *The Presidency of James Monroe* (Lawrence, KS: University Press of Kansas, 1996).
45. *The Albany Argus*, July 11, 1817. In 1817, *The Albany Argus* for the first time reported about a "national feeling" at Independence Day celebrations that had distinguished all public exercises. See *The Albany Argus*, July 8, 1817. Report on Worcester celebration in *Columbian Centinel*, July 12, 1817.
46. *Columbian Centinel*, July 2, 1817; *Columbian Centinel*, July 5, 1817; *Columbian Centinel*, July 9, 1817; *Columbian Centinel*, July 12, 1817; *Boston Daily Advertiser*, July 4, 1820. See also Harry Ammon, *James Monroe: The Quest for National Identity* (Charlottesville, VA: University Press of Virginia, 1990), 371-79.
47. *Columbian Centinel*, July 8, 1815.
48. Boston, *Independent Chronicle*, July 6, 1815. For the lack of enthusiasm for the Peace Treaty and late incorporation of the treaty and Jackson's victory into Fourth of July celebrations in North Carolina during this period, see Green, "Listen to the Eagle Scream," 123.
49. *Mercantile Advertiser*, January 9, 1819; *The Albany Argus*, July 12, 1816; *Independent Chronicle* (Boston), July 8, 1815; for a report about the vase see, for example, *The Phenix*, July 6, 1816.
50. *Mercantile Advertiser*, January 8, 1818. During the following years, the events of January 8, 1815 were reenacted on stage; see theater advertising in *Mercantile Advertiser*, January 8, 1819.
51. *Louisiana Courier*, January 10, 1816.
52. *Louisiana Courier*, January 11, 1819; *Louisiana Courier*, January 7, 1825.
53. *Boston Daily Advertiser*, January 21, 1815.

Chapter 5

PERFORMING FREEDOM

Negro Election Celebrations as Political and Intellectual Resistance in New England, 1740-1850

Geneviève Fabre

IN NEW ENGLAND, from 1750 to 1850 slaves and free blacks held an annual festival to elect their own governors and kings.[1] This celebration developed in the wake of white elections and was at first perceived as mere amusement, an imperfect and wayward imitation of the official festival, a harmless way to use the free time that could prevent restlessness and disorder. Contemporary reports and accounts, descriptions that we find in early histories, have contributed to creating that image. The theory that slaves were unable—or in no position—to create a distinctive intellectual and political culture, to have rituals, institutions, and practices of their own, has informed much research in early African-American history. Negro Election Day offers evidence to the contrary and presents one of the most striking examples of intense creativity, combining styles of performance and artistic expressions with a variety of discursive forms. It also demonstrates the ability of bondsmen and free blacks who had to achieve a measure of autonomy, and to set up a form of self-government that probably had meaningful influence on their daily life, on their status, on their interaction with each other and with whites, and on the structuring of their community.

Notes for this section begin on page 113.

The purpose of this paper is to examine the little acknowledged complexity of this "Negro hallowday," to explore its multifold forms and functions and its far-reaching effects. I would argue that these festive gatherings were ceremonial performances and civic occurrences that conjured a community into existence. Conducted with great seriousness, they created forms of authority and power, and articulated an emerging intellectual and political thought and a will to resist domination. The appearances in public space, and the ensuing engagement in public life were assertive and daring.

African Americans were carving out for themselves a political culture in an order which persistently denied them access to the structures of power. These dimensions have been ignored because these "elections" took place at a level rarely recognized as political: during free and "big" times, when slaves were supposed to entertain and enjoy themselves, and on the periphery of society, "backstage" as it were. I would further argue that this Negro mimicry of white elections was part of a "hidden transcript," that could be revealed only in some form of disguise; it was also part of the "poetics and politics of transgression" that characterize so much of early African-American culture; it included, together with parodic and satiric intent, much reflective criticism and inquiry. This outlook became part of the ethos of the community and was no less cogent and potent for being unofficial and carried out in a playful mode.

This essay will therefore explore the link between festivity, intellectual thought and politics, in an attempt to grasp unheeded or unsuspected aspects of African-American ceremonial life.[2]

On Sources

All the scholars who have been interested in "black coronations" agree that primary sources are scarce. We find passing references in early local histories, in first or secondhand reports, in memoirs, recollections, and diaries. Negro Election is rarely mentioned in travel accounts and even less in the slave narratives themselves.[3] Passing references in different local histories enable us to see how widespread these elections actually were. Initially observed in Connecticut, they are found also in Rhode Island, mostly in Narragansett perhaps because of the colony's special involvement in the slave trade;[4] and reached most of New England towns in the 1760s (Portsmouth, Derby, New Haven, Salem, Lynn, Boston), shifting gradually from cities to smaller geographical sites, mainly along seacoasts and rivers. Some descriptions, such as those collected by Orville Platt, however short, offer a wealth of details and information.[5] They give evidence of the fascination the elections exerted on visitors. But they are often more revealing of the spirit of the time, of the interests and prejudices of the speaker, than of the event and its celebrants. Quite frequently these documents emphasize and deride the childish, ludicrous aspects, or grotesque, slightly farcical and exotic elements, the extravagance and the pomposity. Yet, beyond these cursory statements, they unexpectedly reveal some insight.

A close reading of these accounts suggests ways in which the significance of the festival might be explored. Thus Platt, after having mentioned with some condescension the "curious habit negroes fell into" of "holding elections of their own after the manner of their white masters," offers an interesting perspective: "If we could understand the intense interest in public affairs which characterized our early history, we should not wonder at the origin of a custom which gave the Negro an opportunity to become a politician, an opportunity which, from all that we can learn respecting their elections, *he improved to the utmost*. There was rivalry and electioneering methods surpassing even the political contests of the present."[6] Such a comment invites us to consider the political intent and content of the festival, to examine all the mental skills mustered by those who were not only imitating but trying to outdo their masters.

Descriptions usually do not vary much from one account to the other, but they enable us to build an image of the festival that is fairly consistent even if it remains static. We can have an idea of the main features but are given little information on its origin, its development through a century, and its decline.

Between 1750 and 1850, the colonial and antebellum eras were marked by important events: the war of Independence, the birth of a new nation, the War of 1812, and, as far as slavery is concerned, the manumission laws or restrictions on manumission, the States' emancipations, the abolition of the slave trade (1808) and the abolition of slavery in the British West Indies (1834).[7] It seems important to speculate on the influence these historical moments had on Election Day; conversely, we may wonder if Election Day contributed in any way to the struggle for emancipation and freedom.

The overall question remains: What goals, purposes, and stakes were at hand? What were the interests of the participants, material or symbolic? What functions did Election Day serve both for its black celebrants and slaveowners, for the members of the black and the white communities? And, most importantly, what elementary forms of intellectual and political life did it provide?

In the absence of documents from the actors themselves we must fall back on the only data that are available at this time. From the nature of the performances and the form they assumed we may be able to infer some of the intentions—which could not be revealed with impunity—and try to grasp the meaning behind the act.

White Election: The Official Transcript

White elections usually took place in May or June. On these occasions, slaves accompanied their masters into town and were allowed to participate in the festivities or organize their own amusements. In the mid-eighteenth century, when Election Day became an official holiday in New England, people gathered in great numbers from all the neighboring villages. The day before the votes were cast

> government, state officials, clergy and prominent men marched from the State House, with pomp and military escort, to the congregational church, where a distinguished clergyman preached an election sermon; afterward the 'quality' entertained lavishly and with unusual democracy and congeniality at their houses and taverns, and the populace was regaled at the public expense with the election cake and hard cider ... The custom, serving the purpose of maintaining the clergy and the aristocrats in power, long persisted.[8]

The government of the colonies distributed power among governor, council and assembly. The governor had traditionally been appointed by the King and

> acted as a concept that government existed to protect life, liberty and property. Political authority existed to protect members of the community in free exercise of their just rights -defined over the centuries in England and embodied in the common law carried to the New World. The precepts of government found acceptance in the colonies.[9]

As sacred as the Sabbath, blending religious and political functions ("politics as well as religion absorbed the attention of our forefathers," says Platt[10]), this holiday was observed by more people than Christmas or Easter and was not regulated by the same strict laws.[11] This allowed for much crossing of boundaries, for freer interaction of people of different classes, status and races.

When Negro Election was mentioned at all it was said to have developed from this white custom: "In imitation the negroes developed the African governors";[12] "With his *native fondness* for show ... it was *natural* that the slave imitate his master in political affairs, copying the features of election parade and festivities."[13] These cursory remarks, while acknowledging the existence of Negro Election and its political character, tell little about the circumstances of their emergence or their significance.

There is little doubt that the festival of Negro Election was patterned after white elections. Slaves usually accompanied their masters into town and "these animated sons of Africa" indulged in the sight of the festivities, "several, engaging in the hilarity and dissipation of the day" but also in greetings, gossip, and verbal exchange.[14] In William Bentley's account of celebrations in 1792 and 1794 in Salem, free blacks and whites are presented as enjoying the holiday together.[15] From the early days, "Africans" with their distinctive costumes, languages, musical instruments and demeanor, brought much animation and were among the most visible participants. But for all, slaves or free blacks, the election was more than a mere holiday; their participation as onlookers gave them the opportunity to become keen observers of white practices. They might have resented the limits set on their presence—a presence that was tolerated if it proved to be innocent enough and harmless and if it respected the usual etiquette. On certain occasions, blacks were not allowed to watch the ceremonies. They were barred from the Boston Common on Gunpowder Day in the mid-1760s and no black man was seen on Artillery Election Day, when The Ancient and Honorable Company held its formal parade and selected its new officers who were commissioned by the governor.[16] Desire for a fuller involvement and fear of exclusion, more than "mimicry" or emulation of whites, were the main incentives for creating separate elections.

The New England towns probably had a crucial role in the growth of political consciousness among slaves who came from isolated rural areas. Election Day provided an introduction to city life which to many held promises of action and change.[17] In the urban environment, partly because of its commercial character, political life was more vibrant. In this new educational space blacks heard news, orations and speeches, and were exposed to the debates and rhetoric of the times. They learned to relate their condition to broader issues, and to gather information on the ways of the white world. Furthermore, this moment in the culture of white colonists became an authorized ritual occasion where it was possible to enjoy a break from restraints and taboos; it also gave bondsmen the symbolic tools they needed to assert their political and intellectual claims and interests.

The Site of Negro Election: Time and Space Frame

When the Negroes started organizing their own elections, they followed the same rituals and calendar as the whites. Negro Election usually took place on Saturday, a day that held special significance after a week's labor, either before the white election as in Massachusetts or Rhode Island, or after, as in

Connecticut. Elections often lasted several days and were punctuated by many rituals and ceremonies. The time of the year, spring or early summer, the vernal equinox after the winter season, seemed appropriate for collective renewal and purification. In northern Rhode Island celebrations by agricultural workers in rural areas began as a reward of spring planting. We know that a similar election took place in Africa in the spring and included a famous rite of purification; the Odwira festival of the Yam that has often been compared with the New World festival.[18] Thus slaves could find meaningful connections with their own "African" practices in the calendar imposed by whites.

On the morning of the election, drums were used to summon the crowds and announce the festivities. Slaves who had come on foot or in carriages from distant places assembled. A gunshot was occasionally fired to create more excitement. The mixing of drumbeats and gunfire was another ironic comment on the situation of the slaves, blending the memory of a genuine and cherished African instrument with a reminder of the prohibition on slaves bearing arms. Slaves usually preferred the drum: its rhythm and pulse were truly theirs, its sound had a greater and more secret power.

Horses were also borrowed from well-off landowners. The celebrants mounted the best pacers, adorned with feathers, and flying ribbons, and as a Narragansett witness tells us, "with cues, real or false, head promatumed and powdered, cocked hats" they "pranced to the election, sometimes with their master's sword, gold-headed canes and with their ladies in pillions."[19]

In a slave culture where costuming ranked high and was a symbolic gesture, the appropriation of the emblems of rank and status assumed its full significance and its place in the transcript.[20] This display of finery and adornment, often outdoing white practices, might have had several meanings. It demonstrated not only the capacity to excel in such array, and "the will to adorn," but also the right to do so. It emphasized the fragility, and contingency of rank which could with such ease and rapidity shift from the owners to the owned. Everything could be changed or exchanged: clothes and objects, emblems and symbols. This cross-dressing and code-switching—done with a mixture of ceremonial gravity, irreverence and derision, tacitly acknowledged the arbitrariness of the ascription of social space and identity. If the festival was ephemeral and fragile, so was the social order whose pretensions could be so easily exposed. Election Day combined mild satire and amusement, in a kind of stage play or travesty, with serious intent. On the other hand, there was also much competition and rivalry among blacks themselves and their aspiring governors as to who would make the best appearance; and appearance was no doubt a great asset in any attempt to win the contest and to impress not only the voters but crowds of viewers.[21]

Borrowing, misappropriation and imitation must thus be seen in the general context of the celebration. It was done in an active and creative way and could serve many purposes.

Because Negro Election occurred as a side festival in the margins of the main event, it also often took place in the precincts of the city. Only in Boston were slaves allowed to appear on the Common on that day, "unmolested ... and with an equality of rights and privileges with white people." In most places Negroes were not permitted to appear on the days of formal white parades or to participate in the exercises that usually followed Election Day.[22] These regulations reminded blacks of their marginality, of the constant control to which they had to submit and the limitations, territorial and other, imposed upon their lives.[23] This made their desire to assert their visibility and capacities all the more intense. As was often the case, slaves turned a liability into an asset. In the periphery, in a more secluded and secret place, protected from public gaze, they were able to *assemble* in the strong sense of the term, hold meetings to train themselves and rehearse their performances with more leeway.[24]

The site was always carefully chosen—in open grounds or near a tree—and assumed symbolic significance. In Newport, Rhode Island,[25] the election took place under a large spreading tree, where Liberty Street now stands at the head of the Thames river;[26] in South Kingston, in Potter Wood on Rose Hill, near a burial ground;[27] in Hartford on the Neck. The tree, tree of knowledge, of liberty or of palaver, offered secrecy, complicity, and inspiration; a sacred space, it was reminiscent of many favored sites for African festivals.

Ritualized Form: Processions and Parades

The moment of the festival that was most important to Negro celebrants was the election itself. It was the function they were most anxious to preserve. A procession escorted the aspiring governor, who was fully costumed in red, white and blue, and was accompanied by the honor guard in similar fantastic attire and patriotic colors. The voting session was preceded by harangues: the candidates and their supporters used all their rhetorical powers to convince their audience to cast the right vote. Then usually a line would form behind each candidate and the winner would be the one with the longest line of followers; or a voice vote was used. The counting proceeded, accompanied by comments and encouragements. When the results were proclaimed, a general shout greeted the winner. This particular phase of Election Day set the pattern for a whole series of rituals, which were later to be observed in Freedom Celebrations.[28]

The end of the vote marked a new sequence in the unfolding of the ceremony, described in similar terms in all the accounts. With the parade escorting the elected, the festival took on a different tempo and spirit, with clamor from the crowd, a mingling of many voices in a variety of African languages, and music from an impressive array of instruments—drums, tambourines, banjos, fifes, fiddles, clarinets and brass horns. These parades were different from the inaugural parades of white elections which seemed to have appeared only around 1830; they owed much of their distinctiveness to the skills of the musicians, to the variety of instruments and to a high sense of theatricality and performance, which associated sounds, colors, gestures, pace and adornment. Emblems of majesty and royalty were chosen to enhance this display: crowns and swords or sashes, golden canes with the governor's titles engraved on them. The music may have sounded raucous to white ears, the march may have looked disorderly, "the hustle and carousing" and the tumult raised by "bawdy revelers" disturbing,[29] yet the wealth of the whole ceremonial process, its grand style, and its musical splendor attracted crowds of onlookers, drawn to the scene as to a show whose special quality could not be missed.

These parades were a significant moment. Military style was de rigueur, borrowed from the musters which usually followed white election and from which blacks were excluded.[30] It seemed an appropriate if daring mode to win recognition and to enter the public sphere. It acted as a reminder of the many contributions of blacks in the building of the nation which entitled them to claim full citizenship in a country forgetful of their commitment. Negro celebrants could not fail to notice the close relationship between white Election Day and Training Day. The military escorts of their governors—however awkward and ignorant of proper maneuvers they may have looked to whites who tried to depreciate these exercises and belittle this performance of black leadership—were a major symbolic gesture. The sight of armed bondsmen was considered by some whites a mere diversion or play, a whim on the part of their servants. Loaned weapons could not be dangerous and slaves were just trying to imitate their masters, using borrowed arms and accoutrements. To others, this performance was ominous and a sign of daring insolence which should not be encouraged. Rumor spread that these musters of armed black companies could be used to prepare for insurrection.[31] The adoption of, and predilection for, the military style might have had another meaning, overlooked by the admirers or the deriders of this "Negro Yankee" ritual: blacks were training themselves to become capable soldiers (a title they could justly claim since they had played this role at crucial moments) and were participating in the martial spirit that was then developing in America.[32] We could say that performance and appearance—performing and appearing in style—enabled slaves to rehearse the roles they might one day be called to play. One sees here the complex relation between the military mode and the theatrical; all symbolic acts—training, rehearsal, play and display, appearance and performance—assume a special meaning through this interaction.

Parades, or processions as they were also called,[33] were civic rituals, creating "public ceremonial territory," spelling and acting out "a social vocabulary and syntax" impressing the group's existence, its cohesion and identity upon the minds of participants and observers. They professed loyalty and allegiance to the elected, but also to the values the community was asserting. As such, black parades were less a celebration of the existing order than a *dramatic* performance of an order that was still to be invented in the face of much adversity. In their narrative form and unfolding, they enacted a communal drama and memory; they were also history in the making, stressing the "should" over the "is," challenging cultural practices and rules as well as prevailing misconceptions and misrepresentations, experimenting with new forms and with the idea of power and freedom. This entry into the public sphere, through a ritualized theatrical event, was an act of protest and defiance against rules of exclusion or restriction.[34] Celebrants were rehearsing and performing their own transformation into full citizens.[35]

Governors as Figures of Authority

Of all the images of power and authority which the white ceremony offered, that of the governor was the most compelling.[36] In Negro elections, the choice of the candidate was of primary importance and was preceded by weeks of debate and consultation. It required preliminary deliberations and helped develop political awareness. Slaves trained themselves to have meetings, discussed criteria of eligibility, reached a consensus, judged and ruled over their peers with little interference from whites.

The one to be elected was chosen for his famous royal heritage and was often, in colonial days born in Africa. This insistence on African royal origins not only stressed the ties that the bondsmen wished to keep with their homeland, it also pointed to the irony which kept them enslaved in the New World. This lineage, real or assumed, was considered more prestigious than that of most masters. While expressing their pride in their African roots, celebrants also questioned their masters' claim to superiority and laid bare the injustice of a society where Africans had been imported against their will and with violence by "slavemongers", were kept in bondage and called "niggers." Negro governors or kings were chosen by their peers as both historical and symbolic figures of authority, who could best impress white minds with ideas of dignified leadership and of natural rights, and with the legitimacy of the claims made by all, regardless of their individual background, of their race or color.

The African connection gave a distinct resonance to the title of the elected and set them off from their New England white counterparts. One is tempted to see similarities between Negro governors and African chiefs—notably, as Piersen did, with the Omanhene chief of state in Fanti or Ashanti cultures in Ghana—and to see New World kings as mediators between the enslaved, their ancestors, and their New World rulers.[37] Whether or not the parallel with Africa is justified, the Negro governors were authority figures and became civil rulers and the axis of an emerging political life.

The governor was also chosen for his exceptional physical and moral qualities. The former were most often mentioned by observers: accounts describe their unusual strength, stature and regal bearing. For the Negro celebrants these characteristics were in keeping with the ancestry of the chosen leader. Platt speaks of the "test of wind and muscle."[38] Athletic games and contests, as in Narragansett, often accompanied the election; they were not only mere amusements but also a way to celebrate highly prized values and to emphasize the complementarity between physical and intellectual stature. The elected could be a famous hunter (Quosh Freeman's son, Roswell Quosh of Derby was a noted fox hunter);[39] but he was also praised for his intelligence, wit, readiness of speech, and his education. He had to be a man of courage, worthy of esteem, known for his achievements and his cosmopolitanism.[40]

If a slave, the elected often had a prominent master who occupied positions of high status in the colonies or later in the Republic: congressman, clerk or secretary, member of legislatures, general, or judge. Occasionally, there was much rivalry between slave and master, especially when both happened to be candidates. More often, as was the case after emancipation laws were passed, the black elected was himself a freeman (as his name would often indicate), sometimes a property owner, such as William Lanson of New Haven, or an independent farmer, like Quosh in Derby.[41]

After the Revolutionary War and the War of 1812, Negro governors were frequently chosen from those who had distinguished themselves in a slave regiment. One of the most famous examples is that of Guy Watson—soldiers could also be elected chief marshall—who had valiantly fought under General Greene and captured the British Major General Prescott in Newport in 1777.[42]

Although elections were annual, some governors held offices for several years (Quosh Freeman of Derby is said to have had a longer reign); when they retired they did with grand pomp. Titles were sometimes handed down from father to son, and so were political knowledge and skills. Dynasties were thus created and governors' names appeared in official reports, or were immortalized on grave inscriptions (as was Trow Trow "governor of an African tribe," who died in 1772).[43] Names often associated an official patronym or toponym with nicknames, juxtaposing names borrowed from totally different cultures (Boston Trow Trow of Norwich, King Caesar of Dunham, the last of a dynasty, or the many kings called Pompey). It would be difficult to tell how much was parodic, playful or serious. But name-giving was an important part of the whole ritual; it was history-making and came from a desire to "praise famous (Negro) men" who legitimately belonged to early African-American and American history. There was also certainly, in the deliberate mixing and indication of so many identities (title, place of office, place of origin,) an ironic comment on the "peculiar" situation of slaves or free blacks in the New World. Names were thus definitely part of the hidden transcript, through all the implicit allusions they made; they were also part of the public transcript. In a political culture doomed to be oral, where so few written documents existed, names, inscribed on graves or appearing in local archives, could testify to the existence of Negro Election.

It is interesting to note how, in defining the criteria of selection—signs of status, distinction and prestige—blacks were combining Old and New World values. When the first generation of governors was elected, Africa was still considered the cradle of their native culture; the choice of an African-born governor created a sense of continuity with their home country. For many slaves who came from many different places and tribes, the identification with the place of origin and tribe of the governor restored a sense of common origin which, real or not, was to become symbolically important after the dislocation experienced during the Middle Passage and in the formation of the new African-American community. Leaders and their subjects set themselves under the protection of the same African deities and Old World rituals were incorporated into these new customs.

Slaves saw no harm in associating genuine African qualities—linking physical and spiritual attributes—with certain necessities. They acknowledged the prestige one could derive from the master's status as well as from standards most valued in white society: access to property and formal education, and there was much emulation and rivalry between master and slave, as I noted earlier. The wealthier and better stationed the master of the candidate, the greater the chance of having a grand and successful celebration. Conversely, the greater the display, the stronger the evidence of the master's influence. If slaves made a poor appearance on Election Day, it was a sure sign that the master was not up to the occasion; if a slave governor derived prestige from the fact that he belonged to an affluent master, reciprocally masters prided themselves on having a governor among their slaves.⁴⁴

The result of Negro Election was seldom a matter of contention among the voters. It was loudly proclaimed and usually widely acclaimed and aroused less protest and agitation than white elections. This may have been because slaves knew how to conceal internal divisions from whites, were more careful to reach a consensus, and were concerned not to jeopardize the authority of the elected. Observers have noticed that there was more discipline and dignity among blacks, even when the latter was interpreted as a form of arrogance ill-fitted for a people of an inferior condition. The Negro celebrants knew how to devise the appropriate rituals to reconcile victor and vanquished.

However, incidents did occur, but they seem to have been caused more by external factors and interference than by disagreement or resentment. A few such cases may be quoted here. The revolutionary era brought some confusion and turmoil in the unfolding of Negro Elections. In Newport, the arrival of British troops who took possession of the town put an end to the custom.⁴⁵ In Connecticut the Negro governor, Cuff, who had held office for ten years, resigned in favor of John Anderson, servant of Major Shene, son of a governor who was "suspected by continental Congress of designs inimical to the colonies."⁴⁶ The election of a Tory Negro governor created much alarm. A committee was appointed by the citizens of Hartford to investigate the election; it found out that Cuff had apparently been forced to resign and that Anderson had been appointed by his master without a proper election. This affair is instructive in at least two ways: it shows that occasionally whites were able to manipulate Negro Election; it also gives evidence of the importance of the election in local politics. Much must have been at stake for white rulers if they took the matter so seriously: Negro Election was an important enterprise, involving time and money. The other case occurred around 1800 when a Negro governor had to resign from his office because his master, Mr. Potter of South Kingston, had also been elected in the white election. Apparently the Negro governor was consulted by his master who "stated to him that the one or the other must give up politics or the expense would ruin them both"; the slave governor, the report says, "took the wisest course and resigned to retire to the shades of private life."⁴⁷ We may speculate on the real motivations on both sides. The black man might have feared antagonizing his master by carrying the competition too far, and also feared losing whatever advantage he could get from his resignation. He might even have used the election to negotiate the condition of his own retirement. The white man, on the other hand, probably resented the authority and ascendancy of a slave who had so successfully won the election, and did not wish to carry the rivalry any further. Economics was also a serious issue, and it was difficult for slaves to perform their functions without the financial support of their master.[48]

With the exception of such cases, we usually know little about the relation between white and black governors. Occasionally, white governors lent support to the cause of slave and free blacks—as did lawyer Roger S. Baldwin who, after he became governor in 1844 and after having defended in court the Amistad rebels in 1839, campaigned for the black vote.[49] The renown of the Negro governors was such that they sometimes received official honor and recognition from whites and were even buried with funeral honors—as was Boston Trow Trow, whose cocked hat and sword were laid upon his coffin and whose eulogy was pronounced by a prominent white in an official church.[50]

All these incidents and anecdotes tell much about the extent and limit of the power of Negro governors: they commanded respect among whites as well as among their peers, had authority over many matters, were often consulted, and in some cases inspired both fear and awe (governor Quosh of Derby was as dreaded as many masters and is known to have managed his master's affairs).[51] One is tempted to see their status as very close to that of some overseers on big Southern plantations. One may also wonder if they did not exert excessive sway over other slaves. Abuse, as well as rebelliousness, might have occurred, but is not reported in the sources in which, on the contrary, they are described in terms of mutual respect, deference, reverence and charisma.

As counselors, opinion leaders and rulers, the governors performed many roles, took their tasks and obligations seriously and sometimes extended their authority beyond their local constituency to the whole colony or state, as did the governors of Hartford and Newport. In many ways, one can see them as the early models (although often unacknowledged) of the black leadership that was to develop through the nineteenth century.

With the rise of abolitionism, the emergence of new forms of militancy, the rise to prominence in the public sphere of both religious figures in the developing black church, and former fugitives who became accomplished orators, authors, and consultants—such as William Wells Brown or Frederick Douglass—the image of the black leader changed. Mid-nineteenth-century leaders were considered more as intellectuals in their own right, and, because of the growth of communication, there was a more sophisticated network made available to them for the diffusion of their speeches, testimonies, and ideas on the national level and abroad. Although their narratives and orations seldom mention black governors or Negro Election,[52] one may presume that they were aware of the existence of a tradition of political thinking and action (which in New England was created by this Afro-Yankee elite) and that they, consciously or not, owed much to these forefathers. The great battles of the antebellum era were, one might say, initiated by the governors who promoted citizenship and equality, black suffrage, and participation in civic affairs.

Negro Election was the first symbolic and actual step taken to introduce the idea of a black vote, to demonstrate its necessity, legitimacy or in more pragmatic ways its possibility. Negro voting (at a time when the association of the two terms was inconceivable) was suddenly becoming a reality and could really work.[53]

The most significant institution that grew out of Negro Election was perhaps the court. The election of governor was extended to that of judicial offices: lieutenant governor, sheriffs, deputies, justice of the peace, all received distinct titles and responsibilities for one year or a longer period. Usually these offices could not be held by the governor—only in Portsmouth did a king also take office as judge.[54] These courts heard complaints from whites as well as blacks, settled conflicts and enforced punishment for misbehaviors. As an informant from Rhode Island noted, the punishment was more effective because it was a judgment from their peers ("people of their own rank and color had condemned them") and was executed by the high sheriff or deputy.[55] This Negro jurisprudence met the approbation of masters who "foresaw that a sort of police managed wholly by slaves would be more effectual in keeping them within the bonds of morality and honesty than if the same authority was exercised by whites."[56] The courts probably played a role in creating a common system of values and criteria, of rules and behavior, praising respectability, sobriety, order. One finds already expressed there the ethics that would later become a great concern for the emerging middle class and would be promoted by certain movements and organizations (like the Convention Movement, the Temperance Society of People of Color, or the African Improvement Society) and institutions (the black press and notably the African-American church).[57]

One must bear in mind that in the 1820s and 1830s Negro Election and courts were part of a wider trend, and this was a time when the black community was structuring itself. Sunday schools, churches and lodges appeared everywhere, providing other forums in which one finds echoes of the preoccupations of the courts. Among the most famous institutions were the Hiram Lodge III in Providence created as early as 1799, the African Union School (1819) and the African Union Meeting House (1820).[58] We know that the "procession" after the election often went by certain sites during the ceremony, each providing a different mood and history. Yet we know little about the relation between Negro Election and these newer institutions.

Although they shared common goals, their courses diverged and they became competitive. The Convention Movement had its own election. The Temperance Societies, linked with the fraternal movement, shared some of the rituals of Election, such as pledges, oaths, banners, badges and bands and providing prestige and amusements, but their spirit was different and they preached abstinence, sobriety, reverence and self-improvement, race consciousness and progress. These societies also offered new channels, new forms of participation in community affairs, and emphasized good behavior and formal education. As they grew in numbers and in power, they probably vied for membership and for a role as moral guides. Their rise and growth might have contributed to the demise of Negro Election which developed in the same way as white elections and became wilder, less religious, less orderly. The black middle class adopted the attitudes and prejudices of many whites, seeing the ceremony less as a political event, more as a festival—a secular celebration associated with the less educated classes; as they gave more importance to formal speeches and orations, they grew more critical of theatrical performance and its accompanying entertainments, like dancing and drinking in taverns.[59]

White Response and Perspective

Festivity, which was a welcome and convenient channel to convey intellectual and political meaning, paradoxically was also used as an argument to deny the "serious" intent of the celebration. A closer examination of the perception of the feast by whites and blacks, of their respective strategies and outlooks, may help us reach a deeper understanding of the function Election Day had for all parties involved.

Again, if we rely mostly on descriptions by white observers we are tempted to disregard that dimension; the political import of the Negro Election was seldom acknowledged. James Newhall's or William Bentley's accounts offer striking examples of that denial. The former saw in the event the usual propensity for unlimited jollity and the excess of an ignorant people freed from restraints, who have no reasons to be anxious. On the other hand, in his 1817 account of a 1792 celebration, Bentley speaks of "abuse," of the bewitching influence of a feast, of the most fatiguing dances; he describes the participants as penniless blacks who insisted on going on in spite of their fatigue and who would return "exhausted, dirty, ragged and often hungry and emaciated."[60] When the dignity and seriousness of the ceremony was perceived, it was immediately interpreted as pomposity and arrogance. The election was dismissed either as a popular form of entertainment of the "low other"—a pretentious, preposterous or farcical imitation of white lifestyles by ignorant people, or as harmless fantasies and expressions of suppressed and unconscious desires. When reports emphasized the rejoicings, the dancing and playing, drinking and gambling, and the general license,[61]—they contributed to the discrediting of Election Day and to its perception as mainly an amusement which could be entertaining but could also degenerate and become a threat to law and order. One senses in these attitudes the underlying apprehension that festivity might ultimately affect the social order and should therefore be controlled, and at the same time the belief that it is also a necessity that should not be repressed and could serve many purposes. Hence we find the ambivalent responses which swerved between leniency and surveillance.

From the slaveowners' angle,[62] holidays or any festive time could not be seen as totally harmless and therefore required regulations: the time and place were carefully set (thus contributing to their marginalization) and no trespassing was allowed. If Negro gatherings were less restricted in New England than in the South, they were nevertheless, as we saw, controlled. Even when authorized, any "assembly" was suspect and perceived as potentially seditious. This was true of church services and rituals of worship;[63] and one can imagine that Negro Election could be considered even more threatening, for even if it did not carry the risk of open conflict it could still offer possibilities for revolt or insubordination.

The benign, permissive attitudes of whites were prompted by many motivations and calculations. Festivals were no doubt seen as offering ways of channeling energies, releasing frustrations, of avoiding confrontations and of making amends. They allowed for the return of the usual repressive order, and set the stage for getting back to work, "redirecting .. desire back towards the necessary imperatives of social discipline."[64] Allowing the elections to happen was part of the general policy of granting free time. Participation by whites must also be seen in relation to the complex system of mutual rights and obligations that prevailed under slavery and could be interpreted in different ways. It established a sort of tacit contract—financial and moral support was bartered against the promise that the festival would not be disruptive, that the elected would represent the authority of the master (or that the master was delegating his authority to the elected); and that therefore the loyalty of the governor was not to be questioned.

On the strict level of performance, whites were giving material help to insure the magnificence of the festival and this attitude can be compared to that of Southern masters when they organized entertainments on their plantations.[65] As the custom spread, competition grew, each owner vying to create the most sophisticated event and thus demonstrating his wealth, status, and generosity. One of the functions of the festival was to redistribute the wealth that the servants and slaves had helped to produce. Masters could not fail to give gifts (as they did also at Christmas or at weddings). In turn, blacks were adding to the glamour of white election, and enhancing it with their artistic skills.

Leniency strengthened the reputation of the liberal-minded, philanthropist and "good" masters, and also the image of Northern slavery as opposed to the "peculiar institution" in the South.[66] It was a way of masking nastier aspects of the system: white hegemony and more obscure forms of coercion. By becoming accomplices rather than opponents to the newly emerging Negro leaders, whites could also dissuade them from fomenting rebellion or insurrection. Finally, the existence of Negro Election alongside white election could give the impression of harmony between the two communities, of the existence of common purpose and agreement showing signs of possible integration.

Festivities—mostly carnivals—have often been seen as functioning as a sort of safety valve. This theory serves both to explain and to guide the conduct of elites. From this perspective, whites seem then to be the main instigators and devisers of a performance meant to be a symbolic substitute for the real thing. This interpretation has a variant: the festival helps maintain the status quo and reestablish control; it offers temporary and harmless catharsis and ultimately restores social harmony. This functionalist view holds some truth but is also misleading. It ignores both the actual history and nature of Election Day as a complex event and its meaning for its celebrants. It is based upon evidence yielded by a superficial analysis of attitudes and behaviors and does not take into account the motivations behind strategies that included manipulation, negotiation, and compromise on both sides: political victory, if any, was ambiguous and was not that of the elite alone. This view also serves the purpose of demonstrating—together with the masters' leniency—black compliance and the innocuous nature of these festive activities.

This interpretation is further supported by the very nature of the festival. The political and subversive message was often veiled by necessity. This secrecy and the enigmatic character of Election Day could serve the elite interests, especially when we deal with the oral tradition of verbal and visual performance. Mostly expressed through gestures, music, and dance, never set in written form, any serious purport could easily be disavowed. As James C. Scott has argued, the "ritual modeling of revolt," if less dangerous, does not necessarily diminish the likelihood of actual revolt or is not sufficient to contain it; and ritual may serve as a rehearsal for future action.[67] We could also say that if the festival had been perceived as innocent, there would not have been so much effort to orchestrate and control the authority of the elected, and to accede to certain demands. Fear of the potentially disruptive character of Negro festival—of a transgression which was not just figurative but also literal—was widespread and we have much evidence of the whites' perception of the threat. The claim to sovereignty might not have been taken seriously but the appeal to certain democratic values could not be ignored; after all the reputation of New Englanders was at stake.

After the Revolution, especially for those blacks who had ardently fought for the cause of Independence, Election was an ironic breakthrough: the denial of political rights became more evident and paradoxical in a country which so eloquently committed itself to the defense of freedom and democracy.[68] The power of governors as interlocutors, intercessors, and peacemakers was, as we saw, taken into consideration even if the challenge was not easily accepted.

From the Angle of the Celebrants: The Hidden Transcript

The analysis of the Negro Election from the point of view of the celebrants themselves leads to a very different interpretation, and to a reformulation of some of our questions. Does the evidence of white patronage, the apparent ease with which blacks sought or accepted it, give further support to the "mimicry" theory? Or was it a way of ingratiating themselves with the whites, of convincing them to accept the legitimacy of a new daring custom? Were black celebrants merely reproducing the white hierarchical order to inspire among their peers the same awe and intimidation, or were they using the same symbols of power as a strategic resource to gain access to public life, thus institutionalizing a new site and place of discourse? In order to find further clues beyond those provided by the observers and for lack of information from the participants themselves, one must look at elements in the form and substance of the Negro Election that can be indicative of its truth and supplement descriptions with interpretation.[69]

What is missing in most accounts are the "structures of feeling" that inform these festive activities,[70] the underlying visions, thoughts, and claims to justice and freedom. All these cannot be grasped without reference to the expressive forms—open or disguised—through which these meanings are conveyed.

Black celebrants found the very tools and ideas for a critique of the unjust society they lived in in the official transcript of white election itself and of New England government,[71] political beliefs and principles, their accompanying codes, symbols and images, and they used them to create a utopian anticipation of a new and better order. They reworked them in an arrangement and purpose of their own, "testing their chains" as Michael Craton would say,[72] while calling upon white New Englanders to live up to the reputation they claimed to have established. They appealed not only to white paternalism, or to the principle that the rich and the rulers should provide (food and sustenance) for the less fortunate and be attentive to the needs of the "common people," but also to moral outrage, to the dignity and consideration to which they felt entitled. They insisted on the network of rights and obligations under existing rules, yet maneuvered to alter this set of norms. These "appeals"[73] grew more vibrant after the Revolution which was itself an encouragement to make their claims to authority and self-government more assertive. They were also oriented toward very precise political goals. The election itself imposed, visually as well as mentally, the "idea" of the black vote and participation in civic life. It asserted standards of equity and justice, questioned the existing domination and exclusion and envisioned—if not a radical change—at least an improvement of their condition, a new distribution of status and power. One may speculate as to whether the organization of white election, in which New Englanders were paying tribute to colonial power but also setting forth a form of self-government, was not an incentive for the black population attempting to create institutions which would insure them a degree of independence from their colonial masters and white rulers. We find here the same rhetorical persuasion which was going to prevail in the petitions sent to courts and the local legislature.[74]

For all Afro-Americans, enslaved and free, patriots and Tories, election celebration was a potent symbolic act and a pragmatic experiment; it had a strong message in which one finds "the elementary forms" of political thought and life. The celebrants, behaving as responsible freedmen, were impressing white minds with ideas of full emancipation, showing their capacity while easing the fear whites had of free Negroes. In transferring power from the hands of the masters to those of their fellow slaves, they were taking a definite step towards their access to full citizenship. Election Day was thus, in many ways, a celebration of freedom which combined the memory slaves had enjoyed before their capture with "the memory of the future,"[75] the freedom that was still to come. It demonstrated that celebrants wished to be considered as historical agents in their own right, had something to say about the society they lived in, and could participate in its process of development and change.

Politics and Poetics of Resistance

The very nature of the political outlook constructed in Negro Election was affected by the forms celebrants were compelled to devise to carry it through and these forms, as we saw, affected the way the message was perceived. This may explain the whole range of interpretations these elections gave rise to when they were judged as innocuous or offensive, taken into consideration or ignored. That outlook was also directed at various audiences and encoded differently for each, in signs that were to be understood by some and to remain opaque to others. Furthermore, within the same celebration the message was alternately hidden, revealed, clarified, or obscured as the event moved through its different stages and from one place to another.[76] If we keep in mind the distinctions between offstage and the public sphere, between the hidden and the public transcript, we may be able to grasp the intricacies of the strategies adopted and the poetics and politics of disguise and transgression.

The speech situation varied from one site to the next—open and free here, repressed and veiled there. The choice of site for assembly, marching or rejoicings, was crucial and each assumed meaning in relation to the other. Each site articulated a distinctive mode of discourse, offering possibilities of critical inversion, transgression and displacement of established authority, hierarchy and order in otherwise forbidden domains and across unequal semantic territories. And these discursive modes also played constantly with and against the language and codes of the dominant culture, in and with existing gaps and oppositions.

The site for pleasure and leisure thus becomes a privileged locus for the production of intellectual thought, critical reflection and implicit resistance: a celebration of temporary liberation that is meant to extend beyond the festive moment—a transient moment with long-term consequences—and is certainly more than the mere release of emotions and grievances. The festival site is marked with the intersection and mediation of political and social forces. These displacements, suggesting much overlapping and the blurring of polarities, are important in the invention of a new identity.

One particular example may help illustrate these various processes and the powerful dissonances produced by the intersection of codes and values. The voting requirements for Negro Election stipulate that any owner of a pig and pigsty is entitled to vote.[77] The introduction of the pig image with all its accompanying symbolism creates a complex semantic field and infinite possibilities of transgressions, of oscillation between faked or real oppositions. The image of the pig is in keeping with all the range of animal analogies commonly used to designate blacks. The pig appropriately belongs to the lower order; its filth and fatness are proverbial; its fleshly and carnal, greedy and voracious nature can be read as a synecdoche for sexuality and for the grotesque body. All these characteristics point to the convergence of ideology and fantasy.[78] The pig is also associated with food, with the feasting habits of the lower classes, who like to slay pigs to organize their own rituals of excess, abundance, and rejoicing, replacing moderation with rules of unrestricted consumption; the relationship between consumption and production is thus reconsidered and the claim to participate in both reasserted. Hog killing was a famous "holiday" for slaves, containing all the different stages of metamorphosis of matter: butchering, cooking, eating. Many festivals thus bring the body into the center of the process. Social reality has to be apprehended at this common, down-to-earth level. The humble and abject animal is both living flesh and slaughtered meat and the transition or exchange between life and death and all its transformations is represented.

The pig also belongs to the familiar and rural setting of daily life, as a domestic animal that revels in uncleanness and as a nurturance for an ordinary meal. Finally, in the white imagination, the pigsty is not unlike the places where slaves live their miserable existence, through adverse circumstances or, as whites often assumed, out of their own negligence and sloth. Yet, for the lowly, any animal was a valuable piece of property, whose acquisition required much toil and industry.

The insertion of such an image, so heavily charged with negative stereotypes, in a ceremonial that celebrates kingship and authority, is both appropriate (it evokes the black image in the white mind) and preposterous (when set—displaced—in the dignified context of an election); it creates an interesting intermingling and merging of opposites. In the election, it becomes a sign of eligibility, an asset granting status and power. This interfusion of aesthetic norms and codes, ideological and social constructions—based on distinctions and divisions—undermines existing categorizations and criteria; it is a shrewd and ironic comment on voting rights and the importance of property. The manipulation of this symbolism—of the lowly, trivial, repulsive and grotesque—its transformation through its displacement in a different context, is a recurrent device in African-American culture and folklore.[79] The insignificant, oft-derided animal is transfigured into a valuable piece of property through which political rights may be attained. The inordinate yet legitimate claims are made all the more powerful by this unexpected combination of images of everyday, material and physical existence and its bodily functions with duly sanctioned forms of political or religious authority. We find here two prevailing trends in Negro celebrations: one toward the carnivalesque, in conformity with the elite's image of the "low other," the other toward solemnity and sublimation.[80]

The transcript thus draws upon manifold resources of endless transgressions and symbolic inversions. While it mediates between the official culture and what this culture negates and excludes, it offers suggestions for a more democratic order.

The Political Imagination: Performance and Power

The commingling of holiday and political event, the blending of play and seriousness are key features in Negro Election. The festive ritual was both a vehicle for protest and resistance and a way of disciplining and structuring that protest, of establishing its own logic while creating a rich imaginary repertoire. Subordinate, and assumed to be ignorant, vulgar, and unsophisticated, Negro kings and governors invert the image: they move from the fringes of the society to its center, and occupy this symbolic position precisely because of their marginalization. From their high courts, they contemplate the society which has designated them as low: they question its pretensions, its rules of inclusion and exclusion and point at their arbitrariness in a ritual that both reproduces and dissolves these very rules.

Here lies perhaps the fundamental ambiguity of Negro Election Day, which engaged and also opposed existing white institutions—and its satirical, parodic intent should neither be minimized nor overstressed. On the one hand, it expressed the celebrants' desire to become full citizens and a due respect for a political order of which they wanted to be a part. On the other hand, it showed their critical irreverence for a society which considered them inferior and was not willing to acknowledge the legitimacy of their claims. Simultaneously, whites were slyly invited to see the Negro Election as a mirror of their own life—a life where authority could rest on sham and appearance, on pretense and infatuation, and which was therefore fragile, questionable, and somehow ludicrous.[81]

The festive occasion can be seen as a second culture sustained from one year to the next, a space where skills were trained, weapons whetted, ideas tested, knowledge sought; white mores, customs, and world view, ways of seeing and feeling were challenged in a celebration, which simultaneously aimed at creating a world as structured and coherent as that of white Yankees, at imagining forms of power as awe-inspiring as theirs. It contributed to forging an ideal and a utopia, which were passed on to the following generations. It was a heuristic instrument through which they could define aspirations and imperatives, discover, play, and experiment with possibilities of a better world and of immediate or long-term pragmatic action. Ultimately it may be seen as a *political gestus*, which as such was empowering, intensified their social life, and engaged them publicly in critical reflection. The New England blacks made themselves heard and seen by large and mixed audiences, who no longer kept them at a distance but were attracted to the festival.

Negro Election Day presents characteristics which may help explain why such festivities became so vibrant in African-American culture. One is struck by the artistic expressiveness, the compelling need for "ritualization of life" and by the gift of performance it displays. Once a year, African Americans came out of their quarters and made their invisible culture known to the world; and they did so with much ado and great splendor and emphasis. They proclaimed their right to surpass their masters in glamour and lavishness, to receive high titles, choose their leaders and enthrone them with pomp and ceremony. To the political insistence on the right to vote, to participate fully in civic life and to create their own republican government was added the concern to do so with flourish and deployment, with magnificence and sumptuousness. Negro Election Day became in its own right a *festival*, an occasion for merriment, rejoicing and assembly; an opportunity to exert with a serious purpose their many skills—for oratory, costuming, dance and music, physical excellence—and to "appear" above their station in great stateliness. Symbolic action and celebratory performance were thus not merely play; they carried with them disguised but potent intellectual thought and political meaning.

Notes

1. This is a longer and different version of another essay "Election Day Celebrations" in *Slavery in the Americas*, ed. Wolfgang Binder (Würzburg: Königshausen and Neumann, 1992), 403-20. For this second version I am indebted to some members of the DuBois Institute workgroup on the African-American intellectual, to the discussions that followed my oral presentation at a Bellagio conference in 1993, and to Walter Jackson's careful reading of an earlier draft. I also wish to thank the staff of the American Antiquarian Society and express my gratitude to Leon Litwack and Randall Burkett who kindly gave me access to their private libraries.
2. For the theoretical framework of this essay, I am indebted to several studies; although some have no direct bearing upon African-American culture, they present interesting concepts for the analysis of Negro Election and similar performances: James C. Scott, *Weapons of the Weak: Everyday Forms of Peasant Resistance* (New Haven, CT: Yale University Press, 1925) and *Domination and the Arts of Resistance. Hidden Transcripts* (New Haven, CT: Yale University Press, 1990); Peter Stallybrass and Allon White, *The Politics and Poetics of Transgression* (Ithaca, NY: Cornell University Press, 1986); Michael Bristol, *Carnival and Theater: Plebeian Culture and the Structure of Authority in Renaissance England* (New York: Routledge, 1985).
3. Among the early local histories or annals one may quote: Thomas Bicknell, *The History of the State of Rhode Island and Providence Plantations* (New York: 1920); Frances Caulkins, *History of Norwich, Connecticut* (Norwich, CT: 1845); Alonzo Lewis and James Newhall, *The History of Lynn* (Lynn, MA: 1875); Frederic C. Norton, "Negro Slavery in Connecticut," *Connecticut Magazine 5* (1899); Henry R. Stiles and Sherman W. Adams, *The History of Ancient Weatherfield, Connecticut* (New York, 1914); Jane de F.

Shelton, "The New England Negro: A Remnant," *Harper's Magazine* 88 (March 1894): 536-37; Bernard C. Steiner, "History of Slavery in Connecticut," *Johns Hopkins Studies in Historical and Political Science* 9 (1893): 448-51; S. J. Hammond Trumbull, *The Memorial History of Hartford County, Connecticut: 1633-1884* (Boston, 1886); Wilkins Updike, *The History of the Episcopal Church in Narragansett, Rhode Island* (New York, 1847). Historical proceedings and yearbooks contain interesting descriptions or information: William C. Fowler, "The Historical Status of the Negro in Connecticut" *Charleston, S.C. Yearbook*, 1900, 20-23; William Johnston, "Slavery in Rhode Island 1755-1776, *Publications of the Rhode Island Historical Society* (July 1894): 113-64; on Negro election: Nathaniel B. Shurtleff, "Negro Election Day," *Massachusetts Historical Society Papers* 13 (1873): 45-46; Samuel E. Morison, "A Description of Election Day as Observed in Boston," *Colonial Society of Massachusetts Transactions* 18 (Feb. 1915): 60-61; and most importantly, Orville H. Platt, "Negro Governors," in *Papers of the New Haven Colony Historical Society* 6 (1900): 315-35. Among diaries and memoirs one may consult: William Bentley, *The Diary of William Bentley* (Gloucester, MA, 1914); Charles W. Brewster, *Rambles around Portsmouth* (Portsmouth, NH, 1873); Alice Morse Earle, *Customs and Fashions in Old New England* (New York, 1898); Oliver E. Fich, ed., *The Diary of William Pynchon of Salem* (Boston, 1890); Thomas R. Hazard, *Recollections of Olden Times* (Newport, RI, 1879); Benjamin Lynde, *The Diary of Benjamin Lynde and Benjamin Lynde Jr.* (Boston, 1850). On slave involvement in the political life of Providence, see James William Brown, *The Life of William J. Brown of Providence, R.I.* (Providence, RI: 1883). Travel accounts are informative but rarely mention Negro Election; see for instance: Timothy Dwight, *Travels in New England and New York* (London: W. Baynes, 1823). Among more recent local histories one may quote: Robert Cottrol, *The Afro-Yankee, Providence Black Community in the Antebellum Era* (Westport, CN: Greenwood Press, 1982); Edgar McManus, *Black Bondage in the North* (Syracuse, NY: Cornell University Press, 1973; Lorenzo Greene, *The Negro in Colonial New England* (New York, 1942), William D. Piersen, *Black Yankees: The Development of Afro-American Subculture in Eighteenth-century New England* (Amherst, MA: University of Massachusetts Press, 1988) and Robert Warner, *New Haven Negroes: A Social History* (New Haven, CT: Yale University Press, 1940). More specifically on Election Day, see: Joseph P. Reidy, "Negro Election Day and Black Community Life in New England: 1750-1860," *Marxist Perspectives* (Fall 1978): 102-17; Melvin Wade, "Shining in Borrowed Plumage: Affirmation of Community in the Black Coronation Festivals of New England, c1750-c1850," *Western Folklore* 40, 3 (July 1981): 211-31.

4. "In 1730 there were 1648 Negroes in Rhode Island, 4697 in 1755, chiefly in Newport—the main port of entry for the slave trade from Africa through the West Indies—and in the south county. Narragansett county was most clearly involved in the institution." Well into the nineteenth century Rhode Island was prominent in the trade: of the 40,000 slaves brought into Charleston in 1804-1807 over 8,000 were carried on Rhode Island ships. There were more Negroes in proportion to whites than in any other New England colony. See Irving H. Bartlett, *From Slave to Citizen: The Story of the Negro in Rhode Island* (Providence, RI: Urban League of Greater Providence, 1954), 9; Elizabeth Donnan, *Documents Illustrative of the Slave Trade to America* (Washington, D.C.: Carnegie Inst. Publ., 1935), vol. 3; "The New England Slave Trade after the Revolution," *New England Quarterly* 3 (April 1930): 251-78; William Weeden, "The Early African Slave Trade in New England," *Proceedings of the American Antiquarian Society* (October 1887): 107-28 and idem, *Early Rhode Island, a Social History of the People* (New York, 1910).

5. In this respect, Platt's essay "Negro Governors" is an important document presenting many descriptions but quoting first and secondhand reports without precise references; he

cites Hazard, who is himself citing Updike. He makes allusion to journals and correspondence as well as to interviews with people, mostly blacks, who evoke their own memories of elections or governors.
6. Platt, "Negro Governors," 320. Platt also suggests that "Negroes" might even have invented certain features of the election—the parade—which later were copied by whites in their own rituals.
7. In New Haven, for example, laws and codes were proposed as early as 1717 to hinder the rise of the Negro. In that year, the lower house passed a bill which nearly became law to prohibit slaves from purchasing land. Yet the Negroes advanced to the "definite status of Free People of Color" sharing with whites legal rights and the opportunity for economic and personal freedom. See Warner, *New Haven*, 8, 93. As a result of the American Revolution, manumission laws, then gradual Emancipation Acts were passed, in 1780 in Massachusetts—Massachusetts declared by judicial decision that its slaves had been legally free since Independence—and in 1784 Connecticut stipulated that all persons born of slave parents were to be liberated at the age of twenty-one. By 1805 every New England state had abolished slavery, long before New York (1827). See Arthur Zilversmit, *The First Emancipation: The Abolition of Slavery in the North* (Chicago: Chicago University Press, 1963) and Leon Litwack, *North of Slavery: The Negro in the Free States, 1790-1860* (Chicago: Chicago University Press, 1961). For free Negroes liberty was curtailed; they were often denied access to schools, apprenticeships, the ballot box and jury box. See Jane H. Pease and William H. Pease, *They Who Would Be Free: Blacks' Search for Freedom: 1830-1861* (Urbana: University of Illinois Press, 1990). Laws were designed to control and limit the freedom of former slaves. A slave practice, Negro Election continued to be observed in most places except in Newport, Rhode Island. It was preserved to open the way for victories that were still to come.
8. Warner, *New Haven*, 8.
9. Gary B. Nash, *The Urban Crucible: The Northern Seaports and the Origin of the American Revolution* (Cambridge, MA: Harvard University Press, 1979), 14. Nash analyses the forms of provincial government in the northern colonies and their legislative assemblies. He focuses on Boston politics where the issue of who should manage civil affairs was often raised. He underlines the rise of a popular element in the Massachusetts council, the radicalization of political life in the late seventeenth century, and the more autonomous spirit that reigned in New England in the search for early forms of democracy in New England, ibid., 25-27. Nash also notices that political life operated more vibrantly in the towns than in the country because the urban communities required a greater degree of government given their size and commercial character. For further reading on radicalism see Pauline Maier, *From Resistance to Revolution: Colonial Radicals and the Development of American Opposition to Britain, 1765-1776* (New York: Vintage, 1974) and Alfred Young, ed., *The American Revolution: Explorations in the History of American Radicalism* (DeKalb: Northern Illinois University Press, 1976). See also Sidney Kaplan, *The Black Presence in the Era of the American Revolution, 1770-1800* (New York; Washington, DC: New York Graphic Society; Smithsonian Institution Press, 1973).
10. Platt, "Negro Governors", 318.
11. The Sabbath was not to be profaned by indulgence in sports or games. Regulations were written into the charter (as was the case for the Rhode Island Charter of 1679) or in the colony legislation (in the Rhode Island law of 1679 for example) and whites and blacks could be pursued for Sabbath breaking. More importantly, the Sabbath was meant to keep the clergy and aristocrats in power. On the use of the Sabbath see Christopher Hill, "The Uses of Sabbatarianism," in *Society and Puritanism in Pre-Revolutionary England*, second ed. (New York: Schocken, 1967), 145-218.

12. Platt, "Negro Governors", 317-18.
13. Ibid., 318.
14. Ibid., 324.
15. Bentley, *Diary,* vol.. 1, pp. 368-69; also vol. 2, p. 92.
16. In 1817, a Philadelphia Negro, William Read, enraged because he could not accompany white shipmates, blew up a ship, the *Canton Packet,* in Boston Harbor. Since then a popular rhyme is often used by white boys to taunt the Negroes: "who blew up the ship? / Nigger, why for? / Cause he couldn't go to 'lection / An' shke paw-paw," quoted in Greene, *New England,* 34.
17. See Sylvia Doughty Fries, *Urban Idea in Colonial America* (Philadelphia: Temple University Press, 1977), 97-101 and Raymond Williams, *The Country and the City* (New York: Oxford University Press, 1973).
18. Wade, *Black Coronations,* 220. One could also draw a parallel with another seasonal event, observed in the North but more frequent on Southern plantations, namely corn shucking, and see it as the autumnal counterpart of the spring festival. For an insightful study of corn shucking see Roger Abrahams, *Singing the Master* (New York: Pantheon, Random House, 1992), 21. A captain was elected among the shrewdest slaves and the best singer and he in turn chose his team among the good shuckers. These performances provided "a dramatization of the ways slaves and masters adapted to each other's recreative needs and purposes," 21. Although the purposes could not be conveyed in the same way as in Northern celebrations, the captain played, as did the governors, an important role in the community. Negro Election, a distinctive New England festival, is nevertheless part of a larger network of celebrations in North America and in the diaspora: Pinkster at Whitsuntide in New York and New Jersey, Jonkonnu at Christmas in North Carolina and Jamaica. Royal coronations were also to be found in the West Indies, in Martinique, and in the Spanish islands (El Dia de Los Reyes in Cuba with its John Crayfish leader); in Brazil plays were performed as early as 1706 at the coronations or at the Rei do Congo Kings Day Epiphany festival. Historians have debated whether Negro Elections were more Euro-American or African. For further discussion on "Africanisms" see: Melvin Herskovits, *The Myth of the Negro Past* (Boston, 1941); Daniel J. Crowley, ed., *African Folklore in the New World* (Austin: University of Texas Press, 1977); Hubert H. S. Aimes, "African American Institutions in America," *Journal of American Folklore* 18 (January-March 1905): 15-22; Sidney Mintz and Richard Price, *The Birth of an African American Culture* (Boston: Beacon, 1992); Joseph E. Holloway, *Africanisms in American Culture* (Bloomington: Indiana University Press, 1990). More specifically on the elections see: Piersen, *Black Yankees,* 20-23; Reidy "Negro Election," 108-09; and Wade, "Black Coronations," 217-22.
19. Cited in most sources. See Updike, *Narragansett,* 178; Stuart, *Hartford,* 39; Platt, "Negro Governors," 330-32.
20. Costuming was even more extravagant in the South, where a festival like Jonkonnu—a festival mostly observed in Key West and North Carolina (it was canceled in Virginia after the Nat Turner rebellion)—almost matched the magnificence of some Caribbean celebrations. Slaves, who always looked for opportunities to dress up, appeared in great style. The borrowed clothes were transformed according to the occasion, in striking and symbolic associations of colors and material. We also know that runaway slaves often used their masters' costumes as disguise in their escape. Jonkonnu is part of a network of "coronations" which existed in both South and North (Election Day in New England, Pinkster in New York and New Jersey). If the rituals in all these celebrations present common features—they were more exuberant and carnivalesque in the South—there were significant differences in the way they were perceived, and in the functions they held. See

Geneviève Fabre, "Festive Moments in Antebellum African American Culture: Jonkonnu," in *The Black Columbiad*, ed. Werner Sollors and Maria Diedrich (Cambridge: Harvard University Press, 1995); and idem, "Pinkster Festival," in *Feasts and Celebrations in North American Ethnic Celebrations*, ed. Geneviève Fabre and Ramon Gutierrez (Albuquerque: New Mexico University Press, 1995), 13-29. The Pinkster festival establishes an interesting link between the more carnivalesque Jonkonnu, and the civil performances of Negro Election. All occurred in secret and in public areas—near the quarters, near the master's house, and in the streets. All three festivals were centered on a major figure, all made statements on power relations or claims to social justice, but there was more exuberance and parodic travesty, more devilment and derisive use of masks in the Southern celebration.

21. Riding horses, and racing as they went when they were not seen, were favorite sports among slaves which created much disturbance, see *Rhode Island Historical Tracts*, No. 15, p. 57. As coachmen—a much desired and gratifying position—Negroes enjoyed high hat and livery. Horses granted status, but the ownership of horses was often denied to free Negroes. Riding on special occasions—allowed or forbidden—in mock-serious fashion could be seen as a subversive act.

22. In Boston, Negroes celebrated Election Day but probably did not elect officials as they did in Lynn. Reidy, "Negro Election," 103. In the nineteenth century, on days of huge national parades, blacks would be invited to march, mostly as musical performers and to enhance the event. On the role and the use of blacks—their participation in and exclusion from the great national parades, see Alessandra Lorini "Festivals and Celebrations among Afro-Americans in New York City: Cultural Conflict over the Creation of Public Space," unpublished paper presented at a conference in Paris in December 1989.

23. Slaves' and free blacks' activities and gatherings were strictly limited and controlled by legislation. Participation in forbidden meetings was severely punished, especially in Rhode Island where there were more Negroes in proportion to whites than in any other New England colony. Petitions were often sent by Negroes to request permission to hold meetings and conduct their worship independently. As in the South, any gatherings aroused fears of plots or rebellion. See Johnston, *Rhode Island*, 21-33. The fact that surveillance was much stricter in the South—the first laws were enforced in 1740, 1800 and 1839 in South Carolina—and became more stringent after the Nat Turner rebellion may explain why the custom of holding elections could not be maintained in the South. See H. M. Henry, *The Police Control of the Slave in South Carolina* (Emory, VA, 1914) 14, "Gathering of Negroes," 133-46. Laws were not always enforced in spite of the vigilance of militia, and the masters' attitudes in both North and South were more ambivalent; they could act as intercessors between the law and the slaves. As the number of free blacks grew in the North, whites became more apprehensive of their activities, see Greene, *New England*, 290-315. This accounts for the subtle system of surveillance they set up around Negro Election.

24. One is reminded here of the role the "hush arbor" and similar hidden places played in the development of slave religion and slave culture. Albert J. Raboteau, *Slave Religion: The "Invisible Institution" in the Antebellum South* (Oxford: Oxford University Press, 1978); Sterling Stuckey, *Slave Culture: Nationalist Theory and the Foundation of Black America* (Oxford: Oxford University Press, 1987).

25. In 1756 the negro population there was estimated at 1,300, of which most were slaves.

26. Platt, "Negro Governors", 324.

27. In New York, the Pinkster festival was also held near a burial ground. For a more precise analysis of the symbolic importance of African-American ceremonial sites, see my article on "Pinkster Festival."

28. In many respects Freedom Celebrations continued the tradition set by Election Day but they were more commemorative. They followed a distinct calendar in memory of various events: Independence on the Fourth or Fifth of July, then from 1808 to the 1830s the abolition of the foreign slave trade (January 1); after 1834, the abolition of slavery in the British West Indies (August 1). For a more detailed analysis, see G. Fabre, "Freedom Celebrations in Ante Bellum America," in *History and Memory in African-American Culture*, eds. Robert O'Meally and Geneviève Fabre (New York: Oxford University Press, 1995). Leaders developed their oratorical skills. Frequent references were made to decisive historical events and official documents were read.
29. Such are the terms that recur in all reports. See Platt, "Negro Governors."
30. For a precise description of musters see Trumbull, *Hartford*, 1: 359-60; Caulkins, *Norwich*, 330. On Muster Day in the Middle colonies see Susan Davis, *Parades and Power* (Berkeley: California University Press, 1986), 38-62.
31. Fear of conspiracy seems to have been a minor concern among New Englanders who viewed the parades as slightly farcical and burlesque and were contemptuous of a people ignorant of infantry, incapable of issuing orders or having them executed. Piersen, *Black Yankees*, 123, n. 29. In New York, where a conspiracy was discovered after a muster in 1741, the fear was much greater. Paradoxically, blacks were welcome in the militia in the eighteenth century as essential musicians. They enlisted as drummers, trumpeters (as Nero Benson did in Captain Isaac's troops in 1725); they served as musicians in both French and Indian Wars and in the 22nd Regiment of the Continental Army. See Dena J. Epstein, *Sinful Tunes and Spirituals* (Urbana: University of Illinois Press, 1977), 119.
32. See Marcus Cunliffe, *Soldier and Citizen: The Martial Spirit in America, 1715-1865* (Boston: Little Brown, 1968). Rhode Island had one of the most famous black regiments and Negro troops played an important role in the Revolution. On Negro soldiers see William Nell, *Services of Colored Americans in the Wars of 1776 and 1812* (Boston, 1852) and idem, *Colored Patriots of The Revolution* (Boston, 1865). In 1831, the African Greys, a colored military society, marched through the streets of Providence to celebrate the opening of the African Meeting House. See Bartlett, *Rhode Island*, 35.
33. The latter term could be seen as more religious but also emphasized movement, as the march proceeded from one place to another and along a specific itinerary; it was also often used in early American history for processional performances that constructed communal bonds (see "Historic Processions in Boston," *Bostonian Society Publications* 5 [1908]: 65-119); one also spoke of the Grand Federal Procession of July 4, 1788, as well as of funeral processions. The term *parade* was increasingly used in the nineteenth century, stressing the civic and sometimes military character of the ritual. White celebrants marched past official buildings, churches and government or state buildings. Black marches were not allowed to use the same route but also chose highly symbolic places, honoring new sites—black churches, community houses, meeting places—as the community structured itself and became more and more visible. For further analysis of parades, although none deals with the black parading tradition, see Susan G. Davis, *Parades and Power*; Mary Ryan, "The American Parade. Representation of the Nineteenth-century Social Order" in *The New Cultural History*, ed. Lynn Hunt (Berkeley: University of California Press, 1989); David Glassberg, *American Historical Pageantry: The Uses of Tradition in the Early Twentieth Century* (Chapel Hill: University of North Carolina Press, 1990).
34. On the notion of public sphere, see Jurgen Habermas, "The Public Sphere: An Encyclopedia Article," *New German Critique* 2 (1974): 49-55 and Osker Negt and Alexander Kluge, "The Public Sphere and Political Experience," *New German Critique* 2 (1975): 51-75.
35. Performing power or freedom does not necessarily yield freedom or power, yet performance—as Herbert Blau has demonstrated in his book *The Eye of Prey* (Bloomington:

Indiana University Press, 1987)—has an empowering force. For further analysis see Davis, *Parades and Power*.

36. The elected were called governors in the colonies where the whites chose their governors, kings in the colonies, like New Hampshire and Massachusetts, where white governors were appointed. Piersen, *Black Yankees*, 118.
37. There are remarkable differences also; in Ashanti culture the queen mother had a role to play and publicly nominated the successor of the king. One can understand why mothers could not in New England perform such a function. In most New World coronations, with the exception of the islands (Jamaica, for example, where Jonkonnu was celebrated and where women could even be elected), women never had important roles. However, their presence at the side of the elected, on horses, in parades, or at the official banquet, was always noted in the descriptions. The first known African-American political woman was probably Maria Stewart who in 1831 published a pamphlet—a decade before Douglass—and campaigned for women's rights. See Marilyn Richardson, ed., *Maria W. Steward: America's First Woman Political Writer* (Bloomington, IN: Indiana University Press, 1987). There is much debate on whether any comparison with Africa is grounded. Historians of Negro Election, like Piersen or Wade, have seen many instances of Africanisms in that festival. The memory of Africa was certainly very much present at a time when the slave trade was bringing many Africans to American shores, and this may explain why it became such an important symbol. Although for a long time much speculation has been based upon the assumption that most slaves arriving at a certain period and a certain place might have had the same geographical origin, this hypothesis does not seem to be grounded on enough evidence, and scholars now think that even if slaves came from the same area, West Africa, the cultures and tribal identities were very diverse. For further discussion see Sidney Mintz and Richard Price, *The Birth of an African-American Culture* (Boston: Beacon, 1992); Hubert H. S. Aimes, "African Institutions in the New World," in *Journal of American Folklore* 18 (January-March 1905): 15-32; J. E. Holloway, ed., *Africanisms in American Culture* (Bloomington: Indiana University Press, 1990). For further study of a possible analogy between the authority of African chiefs and Negro governors see Georges Balandier, "Le Corps B corps politique," 21-56, in *Le Detour* (Paris: Fayard, 1985); Claude Meillassoux, *The Anthropology of Slavery: The Womb of Iron and Gold* (Chicago: University of Chicago Press,): 169-72 and 180-84.
38. Platt, "Negro Governors", 330.
39. See ibid., 331.
40. "The person selected for office was usually of much note among themselves, of imposing presence, strength, firmness and volubility, who was quick to decide, ready to command and able to flog. If he was inclined to be arbitrary, belonged to a master of distinction, and was ready to pay freely for diversion—these were circumstances in his favor—still he should be an honest Negro or appear to be wise above his fellows." I. W. Stuart, *Hartford*, 38-39.
41. Property was not always acquired by honest means. In New Haven, Lawson created the residential middle-class sections, called significantly by African names—New Guinea, New Liberia—but he also owned the disreputable vice district. Nevertheless his affluence won him much respect. Warner, *New Haven*, 28-29. For a more precise description of the personalities of Negro governors see Platt, "Negro Governors," 320, 326, 330-31, and Wade, "Coronation Festivals," 219. Negro Election throws an interesting light on the relation between free blacks and slaves, often wrongly perceived as two separate communities. Slaves lent their support to the cause of freedmen whose status was still precarious and free blacks expressed their concern for their enslaved sisters and brothers. Election Day demonstrates the strength of the ties—family ties but also the shared commitment to advance the cause of complete emancipation and freedom.

42. On former black soldiers see Nell, *Colored Patriots* (Boston: 1855), 27-28. The habit of electing a king could spread to more unpredictable places. Thus Nell (op. cit. 27-28) quotes the case of a Salem-born soldier who was elected king in a British prison during the 1812 war and exerted much authority among black prisoners. He had, at sixteen, joined the British navy; when the war broke out, he chose to go to prison rather than fight against his country. There he was appointed king by 450 fellow prisoners.
43. Caulkins, *Norwich*, 330.
44. Significantly, slaves were given more chance to participate in elections than poor whites who did not secure such help and sponsorship. In that respect, elections probably increased the antagonism that existed between the two groups: in spite of their alleged racial inferiority, slaves had access to certain privileges denied to poor whites.
45. Rhode Island sources are quoted by Platt, "Negro Governors," 324.
46. Bartlett, *From Slave to Citizen*, 14.
47. Ibid.
48. Other incidents of a different nature occurred; for example, when whites disrupted the escort of a black governor in Woodlidge around 1838-39 and pulled him off his horse; eventually the governor had the upper hand and threw his attackers into a nearby pigpen. Platt, "Negro Governors", 324.
49. See Warner, *New Haven*, 58-60.
50. Caulkins, *Norwich*, 330.
51. Wade, *Black Coronations*, 226. Many anecdotes are quoted by chroniclers and observers, who often tell about the striking looks, high deeds and feats of governors. One may quote here the portrait of Quosh Freeman: "He was a man of herculean strength, a giant six footer, and it is said that he could take a bull by the horns and the nose and at once prostrate it to the ground. No one dared to molest or try to make him afraid, and when he was approaching from a distance, he awakened the sense of a coming thundercloud." Samuel Orcutt, *Henry Tomlinson and His Descendant* (New Haven, 1891), 549. The terms used in this description show how the governors could enter African-American and also American folklore. Similar accounts are to be found in other recollections: Bradford Kingman, *The History of North Bridgewater, Plymouth County, Mass.* (Boston, 1866), 317; C. H. Webber, *Old Naumkeag* (Salem, 1877), 200.
52. William Wells Brown's narrative is an exception, *The Life of W. W. Brown*, 12-16. On abolitionist leaders, see Benjamin Quarles, *Black Abolitionists* (New York: Oxford University Press, 1969).
53. It would be interesting here to know more about the way governors might have been instrumental in furthering the cause of Negro suffrage (given the fact that they existed and that their legitimacy was founded on an election). Until 1754 in colonial New England, there is no evidence that free Negroes enjoyed the franchise (whereas in some plantation colonies they did); yet there was no prohibition except in Connecticut, where they were excluded until after the Civil War. Negro suffrage became a matter of considerable concern, and was connected to the anti-slavery movement and the ideal of Christian Brotherhood. It created much agitation in the 1820s and 1840s, especially in Rhode Island with the Morr rebellion of 1841. Bartlett, *Rhode Island*, 38-39. On Negro suffrage see Albert McKinley, *Suffrage, Franchise in the Thirteen English Colonies* (Philadelphia, 1905); James Truslow Adams, "Disfranchisement of Negroes in New England," *American Historical Review* 30 (1925): 544; Kirk Porter, *History of Suffrage in the United States* (Chicago, 1918); Emil Olbrich, "The Development of Sentiment on Negro Suffrage to 1861," *Bulletin of the University of Wisconsin*, No 4, History Series 3, no. 1 (1912). One may also wonder if another debate, the colonization movement—which started in 1787 and began officially in 1816 with the creation of the American Colonization Society—had

some influence on Negro Election and vice versa. We know that colonization created much dissension among the more official leaders. Conceived by Granville Sharpe, founder of Sierra Leone in 1783, and advocated by Paul Cuffe, it was strongly attacked in the 1830s by the American Society of Free Persons of Color (ASFPC). It had its pros and cons: those who thought Africa was still the homeland fought to promote the idea, others saw it as a device to get rid of the free black population. For many whites, free blacks were placing a heavy burden on society, making inordinate claims and setting a bad example for the slaves. Hostility towards free blacks was at its height from 1830—1850. In Providence, in 1824 a mob of 2,500 descended on the Negro settlement of Hard Scrabble. The ASFPC fought back as it held its first Convention in 1830; it passed vigorous attacks and resolutions and tried to repeal discriminatory laws. Warner, *New Haven*, 47. Freedom had brought more insecurity than equality. At this point in the history of black militancy, the initial impetus created by the Negro Election was lost; the last Negro governors, like Lanson who was mainly addressing local constituency and interests, were replaced by the new abolitionist leaders or by church leaders, like Breman of the Temple Church of Philadelphia, who became prominent on the national scene.

54. Platt, "Negro Governors", 331.
55. This informant is quoted in ibid., 324.
56. Ibid., 324.
57. The *Freedom Journal*, founded in 1927, soon called *Rights of All*, which was the first Negro journal, and along with *The Colored American* became the main organs of the black press. There, intellectual and ethical debates were held to define not only the issues and the strategies but also to defend certain values. It is in these journals that the propriety of public celebrations was discussed—mainly in relation to the Fourth of July (*Freedom Journal*, June 22 and July 13 issues) and other freedom celebrations. Public appearances often met with objections and this general feeling may have been partly responsible for the decline of Negro Election. The press became a major network and replaced word—of mouth communication. This written and printed culture grew out of the needs for expression that Negro Election had created, but departed from the earlier oral and visual tradition.
58. For an analysis of an emerging community, one may consult Cottrol, *The Afro-Yankee*; Julian Rammelkamp, "The Providence Negro Community, 1820-1842," *Rhode Island History* 7 (Jan. 1948): 26-27.
59. This change in outlook taking place in the nineteenth century is evidenced in the press which became the organ of these middle-class values and in which celebrative life was often discussed, and the opportunity of parades and marches debated. The press thus played an ambiguous role: on the one hand it supported ceremonial life by announcing and reporting ceremonial events, on the other hand it tried to control them and criticized any license and excess.
60. James Newhall, *History of Lynn, Massachusetts, 1864-1890* (Lynn, 1890): 236. Bentley, *Diary* I, 368-369 (May 30,1792); II, 92 (May, 28, 1794).
61. *Customs and Fashions*, 226.
62. Observers' comments were often in line with masters' attitudes; yet one may assume that the latter knew better, hence their more complex responses. Without being aware of the full meaning of the election they sensed some of its implications; this expression of autonomous collective action from "below" was certainly troubling to them.
63. In many ways the "hush arbors" where slaves held their secret religious meetings were comparable to some of the sites where the elections were prepared.

64. Bristol, *Carnival*, 32. For a further discussion of the safety valve theory and its variant see also 27-39, Scott, *Domination*, 177-79; and more specifically on Negro Election, Reidy, "Negro Election," 109.
65. Such as corn shuckings. See Roger Abrahams, *Singing the Master*. Corn huskings also happened in the North. See Earle, *Fashions And Customs*, 331-32.
66. It is not a mere coincidence that it is in the states where Negro Election was observed that slavery was first abolished. One may speculate on whether New Englanders were driven to these measures because they were more liberal or whether they were more inclined to be liberal by the persistence and persuasiveness with which slaves proved that their claims were legitimate.
67. Scott, *Domination*, 178. For further discussion see also p. 187. On the conjunction of festivity and revolt, see Emmanuel Le Roy-Ladurie, *Carnival in Romans*, trans. Mary Feeney (New York: Braziller, 1979).
68. This contradiction was to be emphasized by black orators in many Fourth or Fifth of July orations, especially in Frederick Douglass' famous 1852 speech.
69. Clifford Geertz has discussed this issue in *Interpretation of Cultures* (New York: Basic Books, 1973). See also Scott, *Weapons of the Weak*, 138.
70. This expression is borrowed from Raymond Williams, *The Long Revolution* (New York: Columbia University Press, 1961), 48-78.
71. There are interesting comments on New England government in Thomas Hamilton, *Men and Manners in America* (London: W. Blackwood and Sons, 1843), 123.
72. In *Testing the Chains* (Ithaca, NY: Cornell University Press, 1982).
73. These appeals were much less revolutionary or incendiary than the famous Walker's Appeal, less articulate and organized than the petitions constantly brought into court, but they are nevertheless implicitly present in the Negro Election. Or we might say that the rhetorical tradition of black jeremiad that developed throughout the nineteenth century grew out of a spirit that existed in the Negro Election.
74. On petitions and black involvement in the American Revolution, see G. Fabre "L'autre revolution americaine: Les acteurs oubliés de la Guerre d'Independance," in *Les Oubliés de la Revolution Americaine*, eds. Bernard Vincent and Elise Marienstras (Nancy: Presses Universitaires de Nancy, 1990), 55-99.
75. The expression is borrowed from the French historian, Pierre Nora. *Les Lieux de Mémoire* (Paris: Gallimard, 1987).
76. After the procession, parts of the festivities honoring the new governor were held alternately in the master's home and in the slaves' quarters. In the Big House, dinner was served—paid for by the master but prepared by the slaves. Indoors and with the more official presence of whites, celebration proceeded with greater order. During the banquet toasts were given and everyone received the appropriate seat and a proper salute, according to appointed functions and titles; ministers, counselors, and deputies were placed at the right of the governor and his aides. The defeated candidate was hailed and took part in the ceremonial. In due pomp official appointments were made. All these rituals were followed by much feasting in the quarters, in more liberty away from white surveillance. The activities for the rest of the week are less known; they were seldom mentioned in chronicles. One may surmise that they were similar to other holidays. Some rejoicings became the affair of the community and were less visible and more private; others preserved the same public character and were staged and performed to be seen and enjoyed by all. They contributed to create these rare moments where conviviality prevailed, bringing together, as the Pinkster Festival also did, "high, low, rich and poor" Negroes, whites and squaws (according to a poem quoted in Piersen, *Black Yankees*, p. 123, n. 29). Food and dance played an important part; contests, jumping and wrestling, stick fighting, and races

brought much excitement. Certain occupations were borrowed from white culture—like throwing quilts and pitching pennies—others were derived from African customs, like paw paw and wrestling.

77. Platt, "Negro Governors", 324.
78. One is tempted to draw a parallel with another animal, the mule, and to think of the interesting analysis suggested by Zora Neale Hurston in *Mules and Men* (New York: Harper, 1935). The most common analogy however was to the raccoon, and the word coon was used as both adjective and noun.
79. See Lawrence W. Levine, *Black Culture and Black Consciousness: Afro-American Folk Thought from Slavery to Freedom* (New York: Oxford University Press, 1977).
80. On the carnivalesque the most often quoted reference is to Mikhail Bakhtin, *Rabelais and His World* (Cambridge, MA: MIT Press, 1968). On inversion see Barbara Babcock, ed., *The Reversible World: Symbolic Inversion in Art and Society* (Ithaca, NY: Cornell University Press, 1978) and Robert C. Elliott, "Saturnalia, Satire, and Utopia," *Yale Review* 55 (1965-66): 521-36.
81. If we have indications that white authority was implicitly challenged—in the sly, innocuous way that was part of the politics and poetics of transgression—we have no evidence that male authority was questioned. Women were more actively present than in white election and parades (where they were often mere allegorical figures, representing Freedom or Liberty). Just as in white society, the issue of power and the vote was considered a male issue. It is only in the later part of the nineteenth century that women made their claims known and that black women became very prominent in most crusades.

Chapter 6

ITALIAN-AMERICANS AND COLUMBUS DAY

A Quest for Consensus between National and Group Identities, 1840-1910[1]

Bénédicte Deschamps

ACCORDING TO ROGER Caillois, celebrations are "accompanying myths."[2] They are "a time outside of time that recreates, purifies and rejuvenates society."[3] This seems to be particularly true of ethnic festivals and ceremonies when minority groups are given the opportunity to temporarily reshape society not only by reversing social roles, but also by elaborating their own mythology and rewriting their common history vis-a-vis the dominant group. At the turn of the century, Italian-Americans participated actively in the making of the Columbus myth. They initiated and sponsored commemorations honoring the Genoan sailor all over the United States, thus glorifying not just any Italian hero but a man who they were convinced had changed the course of world history, a man they thought every American was indebted to for the part he had played in the birth of their nation. Therefore, the fight for the recognition of Columbus Day as a legal holiday led by the Italian-American leaders was above all a fight for legitimating the Italian presence in the United States and a quest to achieve consensus[4] with their country of adoption.

Notes for this section begin on page 137.

Early Celebrations of Columbus Day : From Oblivion to Private Initiatives

Americans, not Italians, were, as Giovanni Schiavo emphatically put it, "the first in the world to express their gratitude to the Discoverer of [America]."[5] Indeed, the first celebration dedicated to Christopher Columbus was organized in 1792 by the Tammany Society or Columbian Order, an association which had chosen for patrons both the Italian navigator and the legendary Indian chief Tammany and which aimed to "connect in the insoluble bonds of patriotic friendship American Brethren of known attachment to the political rights of human nature and the liberties of their country."[6] The *Diary or Loudon's Register*, published in New York City, praised the order for observing "the commencement of the IVth COLUMBIAN CENTURY as a Century Festival" and celebrating it "in that style of sentiment which distinguishes this social and patriotic institution."[7] The ceremony included the erection of an obelisk "in memory to the Discoverer of a New World," an oration "pathetically" describing the life of "this remarkable man,"[8] and even a procession. All those elements, as Claudia Bushman has noted, would later become part of the Columbus Day rituals and be adapted to the needs of the different groups claiming Columbus as their hero.

Even though other ceremonies were performed the same year in Baltimore and Boston, Americans thereafter showed so little interest in the anniversary that there were no official festivities observed at all until 1892. The first recorded Italian-American celebration, however, dates back to the 1840s. In fact, an old Italian immigrant remembered the commemoration of October 12 as the "oldest celebration of the colony of Chicago." According to him: "When from 1840 to 1857, Chicago was nothing but a simple town, and there were neither theaters nor auditoriums, the few Italians of that time never failed to pay tribute to the great Italian, the Discoverer of America, on this memorable day."[9] Nevertheless, the celebration was then still part of the private sphere and no public space was yet devoted to it. "As there was nothing else we could do," complained the old man, "we met in our homes and we just had a party." It was not until the first Italian society of Chicago, Unione e Fratellanza[10], was established in the early 1860s that they were able to celebrate Columbus "properly."

Festa di Colombo: Staging a Positive Identity

As Italian immigration increased,[11] so did the desire of immigrants from the Peninsula to assert themselves in America, to become visible. They sought to organize and defend their ethnic pride by establishing various institutions such as newspapers or mutual aid societies, and by exhibiting their *italianità* with statues and festivals dedicated to Dante Alighieri and other great Italians. More popular than any other figure was Christopher Columbus whose reputation had spread beyond the narrow limits of their homeland. As was the case with other ethnic festivals such as the West Indian Carnival in Brooklyn,[12] the commemoration of the discovery of America hence proved to be the occasion for the emerging Italian associations to "display their banners, count their numbers and test their influence in the community as well as in the larger society."[13] At the end of 1866, the Compagnia del Tiro al Bersaglio[14] organized in New York City the first public Italian-American celebration of the Festa di Colombo, setting an example which would then be followed by the "colonies"[15] of San Francisco, St. Louis, New Orleans, Boston and Philadelphia. By 1869, most of the ceremonies included a ball, a dinner with officials from both Italy and America, and sometimes a parade.[16] In New York City, a painting showing Columbus's landing was also exhibited, a first step toward the later ritualization of the landing reenacted in the port of Manhattan and at the Aquatic Park in San Francisco.[17]

The first aim of the celebration was to construct a positive image of the Italian community. At the end of the eighteenth century, as eugenic theories permeated American society[18] and the population feared that mingling with "Mediterranean races" would "mongrelize" their "native stock," the massive influx of immigrants from Italy was regarded as a growing "problem."[19] In that context of intolerance toward southern and eastern Europeans, Italian-American leaders or *prominenti* tried to prove to local authorities that their countrymen were not just illiterate peasants but the worthy heirs of a highly civilized people. Columbus represented, therefore, the perfect hero for immigrants not only to identify with but *to be* identified with. Not yet viewed as a controversial figure, he was for many historians the man who "had planted the flag of civilization in the New World."[20] To the nativist movements that used the rural origins and lack of education of many Italian immigrants as an argument for demanding a stricter selection of immigrants at the gates of the United States, the Italian ethnic press responded indirectly with articles emphasizing the qualities of "one of Italy's noblest sons,"[21] who embodied "Knowledge and Virtue,"[22] and whose discovery of America had supposedly marked "the chronological passage from the history of the Middle Ages to Modern History."[23] *L'Eco d'Italia*'s enthusiastic comments on the 1869 New York celebration provide an insight into the Italian periodicals' efforts to use Columbus's image for the promotion of Italian qualities in the United States:

> The glorious commemoration which our colonies celebrated last Tuesday in the United States is one of those lavish occasions which inspire respect and a feeling of affinity for the Italian name. Americans who gratefully acknowledge everything dealing with the origin of their national life, their social progress and development keep in their souls a strong feeling of affection for the name of the Ligurian sailor, a feeling which translates into admiration for the land which gave birth to this amazing Genius of the Sea.[24]

By associating words such as "affinity," "affection" and "admiration" with Christopher Columbus, *L'Eco d'Italia* tried to create a sentimental connection between Americans and Italians. The admiration felt for the "Ligurian sailor," who also happened to be an American mythical figure, was therefore to be transferred to the Italian immigrants. In other words, Italians appropriated Columbus, claiming credit for his past achievements, and also claiming respect for the hero's proud descendants who had then migrated to America.

Italians Celebrate Columbus as the "Founding Father" of America

Respect, however, was not the only thing at stake for Italian-Americans. It was also essential for them to create with the United States a link that no other ethnic group could ever claim to have established and which would render their presence in America if not natural, at least legitimate. The Columbus festival was then an opportunity for reminding Americans of the indissoluble and everlasting bonds uniting American and Italian histories. Carlo Barsotti, the editor of the most famous Italian-American newspaper *Il Progresso Italo-Americano*, expressed this feeling quite clearly in the address he gave at the laying of the foundation stone of the Columbus monument erected in 1892 by the New York community:

> The name of Columbus can never be dissociated from any American celebration because without Columbus there would have been no America. And it is for us and no one else to unite the sacred names of Italy and America, of Columbus and Washington.[25]

The elaboration of the myth of Columbus as the Founding Father of America—which Washington Irving had largely contributed to with the publication of his biography of the Genoan sailor in 1831—was the key to the rehabilitation of Italian immigrants.[26] In the 1890s, while congressman Henry Cabot Lodge defended the Literacy Test project on the ground that southern Europeans belonged to those "races whose traditions and inheritances, whose thoughts and whose beliefs are wholly alien to ours and with whom we have never assimilated or even been associated in the past,"[27] C. A. Barattoni, the vice president of the Executive Committee of the Christopher Columbus Monument, praised the common heritage of Italians and Americans:

> [T]he Italians of this City have thought it appropriate ... to perpetuate the memory of that great genius, CHRISTOPHER COLUMBUS, a humble son of Italy, but to whom America owes its discovery, and we might say the primary foundation of its existence as a Nation, which although comparatively young is, nevertheless, ranked foremost in the World for Civilization and progress; and if George Washington is rightly and reverently called the father of this Country, Columbus, who encountered so many obstacles, and underwent enormous personal sacrifices and risks to achieve his discovery, ought justly and rightly to lay claim to the title of Grand father of this Great Continent, where millions of people of all nationalities are now dwelling in peace and happiness.[28]

Whoever tried to challenge that precious link that allowed Italians to claim a part in the birth of America, and consequently of the United States, was severely criticized. Thus, when in 1873 Professor Waddell from South Carolina professed he had found evidences that a Caucasian colony had been established in North Carolina two thousand years before Columbus was born, *L'Eco d'Italia* urged Italians "not to pay attention to this nonsense, because if Columbus did not create America, it is true without any doubt that this continent owes him exclusively its civil existence."[29] Questioning the discovery of America by Columbus meant depriving Italian-Americans of a privilege that marked their very difference from other ethnic groups and their uniqueness with regard to American history. Columbus was therefore not to be celebrated "only because he had discovered America, but rather because he was an auxiliary of the famous 'Pilgrims.'"[30] Interestingly enough, the same process was observed in Canada, when "the urge to own a respectable North American pedigree"[31] led the local Italian community to revisit Canadian history in the 1920s, so as to present Italian sailor John Cabot[32] (instead of Jacques Cartier) as the first discoverer of Canada. Again, the use of a "glorious past" was of no little consequence, because it was supposed to legitimate the Italian immigrants' presence and enabled them to lay claim to the same status as the French and English Charter groups.

The Catholicization of Columbus Day: Italian-Americans Both Supportive and Reluctant

In 1882, the Irish priest Michael McGivney created the Knights of Columbus, a fraternal society which was meant to organize Catholic men, provide "mutual aid and assistance to its members and families"[33] and promote Catholic values in a predominantly Protestant environment. In that regard, the birth of the order significantly influenced the fate of what was not yet called Columbus Day. In July 1892, President Benjamin Harrison declared Friday, October 21, of that year "the four hundredth anniversary of the discovery of America by Columbus, as a general holiday" and recommended that "schools be made by the people the center of the day's demonstrations" while Americans were asked to express their "gratitude to divine Providence for the devout faith of the discoverer, and for the divine care and guidance which [had] directed [their] history, and so abundantly blessed [their] people."[34] The educational and religious meaning of the commemoration was thus emphasized and the Knights of Columbus proceeded to give it a Catholic flavor it did not have before. The magnificent festivities and parades organized in the whole country in 1892, as well as the opening of the Columbian International Exhibition one year later, were largely based on their efforts, which were displayed in the New York, Chicago, and San Francisco processions.

The Catholicization of the event did not go unnoticed by American newspapers. The *New York Times,* favorably impressed by the one thousand Knights parading on horsebacks, could not help mentioning the statue of Columbus whose "hand pointed ahead ... held the flag with a cross."[35] But more remarkable were the clergy's blatant efforts to use the press as a forum for Catholic propaganda. In the *New York Herald,* for example, Reverend E. S. Halloway succumbed to quite daring comparisons:

> Without a parallel in history, the name of Christopher Columbus stands alone, like some great oak towering in the forest trees, so does he stand far in advance of his age with a work which is the most important since the birth of the Saviour of Mankind. He was chosen by God (like Moses) to reveal the marvels of the New World.[36]

A few years later, Bishop D. J. O'Connell was to formulate even more plainly what most Catholic societies believed, stating that: "without the church, the world could not have had Columbus."[37]

As is well-known, the Knights of Columbus was not an Italian association. It seems that the Catholicization of the celebration was primarily an Irish movement aimed at giving this despised ethnic and religious minority a widely esteemed American symbol while promoting at the same time Catholic unity among the various immigrant groups. In an article comparing the celebration of St Patrick's and Columbus Day in Worcester, Massachusetts, Timothy Meagher shows how the Irish community gradually abandoned the observance of St. Patrick's Day for Columbus Day because the latter permitted the involvement of the new Lithuanian, French, Polish, and Italian Catholic immigrants pouring into the city at the turn of the century. The Knights of Columbus wanted, in Meagher's words, "to speed up the melting process and thus hasten the forging of the American Catholic community in Worcester."[38] Nevertheless the process was not necessarily successful as some communities rebelled against "the Knights' attempt to depict Columbus as an exclusively Catholic figure rather than a hero for all Americans."[39] In fact, Italians were not active supporters of the Catholicization of Columbus Day. Even though their societies joined the Knights in the New York processions, "relieving the monotony"[40] of the parade with their "New World" float, they didn't show the same enthusiasm for Catholic propaganda as the Irish community. Two main reasons justified the Italians' mixed feelings in that regard. First, Columbus was *their* hero. He was an Italian before he was a Catholic, and if they were more than willing to share him with Americans, they were not ready to share their "glorious" heritage with other ethnic groups. Second, Italians were trying to draw a line between their religious festivities and the celebration of Columbus Day, hoping to gain wider American support. The Chicago Italian daily *L'Italia* was quite explicit in that respect:

> We turn to the distinguished officials of the Chicago Italian societies, ... so that they make people understand it is not necessary to organize religious *feste* and processions to be good Catholics. Let's pay tribute to our great men and then we'll be respected and esteemed.[41]

Columbus Day: The Difficult Art of Displaying Order and Control

In their quest for consensus with their American environment, Italians wanted to stage a new identity which would be more acceptable to Anglo-Saxon Americans. The religious *feste* dedicated to San Gennaro, or even more remote regional saints, always gave way to displays of unchecked emotion, sometimes ending in absolute chaos. Robert Orsi's essay on the celebration of the Lady of Mount Carmel, one of the most important *feste* in Harlem, is quite revealing of the emotional aspect of such religious festivals. The event brought thousands of Italians onto 115th Street and as the procession made its way to the Church of "Monte Carmelo," beer and wax amulets were sold on the sidewalks, while "penitents crawled up the steps on their hands and knees, some of them dragging their tongues along the stone."[42] Feeling these uncontrolled outbreaks of "pagan" faith were hardly tolerated by the natives, the important members of Italian-American institutions tried to induce their fellow citizens into adopting more "American" ways into their behavior in order to blot out their image of unpolished "Mediterraneans." Therefore, the Columbus Day celebration also implied the elaboration of a new concept of festivity. As it was a ceremony in the making which, unlike national or religious commemorations, had not been codified by centuries of tradition, Italian immigrants were given the opportunity to model a new kind of festival which was to bear the same characteristics as that of the hero it celebrated. Italian immigrants believed Christopher Columbus was almost the only Italian yet universal figure who was dignified enough to restore American faith in the qualities of the Italian population, but on the condition their community proved worthy of such a noble figure. For that purpose, Columbus Day was to take place in very delimited time and space, and display Italian dignity, control, and order.

Most Italian-American editors disapproved of the parade that always accompanied the celebration because it was too close to the Italian festive tradition, too ethnic, and too difficult to organize in an orderly manner. Moreover, they felt Americans highly disliked it as they presumed "the American spirit [was] hardly keen on festivities."[43] Italian immigrants though would not give up their fascination for a form of celebration that evoked pleasant nostalgic memories of their mother country. Italian-American newspapers assigned themselves the role of educating their fellow countrymen, tutoring them in American dignity. In an article published in Chicago in 1910, after the first celebration of Columbus Day as an Illinois state holiday, the editor lectured Italian immigrants in a very patronizing way:

> While the parade proceeded through Green Street, Jackson Boulevard and Michigan Avenue, our reporters posted in different places along the way gathered data for their articles, noting details which were not really favorable to some of the marchers. Shoes covered with mud up to the ankles seemed to be a common thing this day, which is quite unbelievable when we think that all the shoe shiners in Chicago are Italian! Many faces with week-old beards could be seen, and that certainly did not contribute to making them attractive, while a little washing and shaving would have given their owners a more decent aspect.... There was even one person who was seen inside a gaudy car transporting in the most noisy way chinking bottles of beer as if the point of the commemoration was to celebrate Bacchus instead of Columbus.[44]

Although a significant part of the Italian-American crowd seemed to consider Columbus Day as a moment of unrestrained joy and release, Italian leaders tried their best to make it, above all, a time for representation. It was as if the entire community was to impersonate Christopher Columbus by appropriating his admitted virtues. With that perspective, Italians had to act as potential heroes, and could not afford to be associated with filth, noise, and bad taste any longer. The *prominenti*'s obsession with conforming to what they thought was American solemnity could reach extreme forms, as was the case in 1909 when the Italian societies of Boston organized a celebration featuring a dinner, a reading of poetry by the most elegant ladies of the Italian upper class, and ending with the supreme delight of a Chopin concerto.[45] The American celebrities invited to this brilliant party could then be convinced that those well educated people had nothing to do with the threatening Italian reds or Black Hand gangsters depicted in the American press.

In the Shadow of Columbus: Celebrating Unity

Columbus Day did not only serve as a means for the Italian communities to enhance their image or to seek a consensus with their American environment. At a time when Italian Unification (1861) had just been achieved, celebrating Columbus Day was also viewed as a contribution to the shaping of Italian national identity. A main concern for Italian-American leaders was to try and organize a heterogeneous community into a national force, for, as *L'Italia* deplored in 1897:

> It is unfortunately painful to confess that 37 years after the unification of our homeland, we still find ourselves in the condition which drove the Italian statesman Massimo d'Azeglio[46] to say : "Italy has been created, and now we need to create Italians."[47]

Neither the anniversary of the Italian Constitution, nor the commemoration of the Proclamation of Rome as the capital of Italy on September 20, were celebrations which succeeded in bringing Italians together because the very events they referred to generated numerous political, religious, and regional controversies.[48] By contrast, Columbus was seen as a universal symbol, and October 12 as a date that could unite all Italians whatever their geographical or ideological backgrounds. Columbus Day was meant to be a time for harmony not only with Americans but also within the boundaries of the Italian community itself. For that reason, Italian-American editors never failed to call for the mobilization of all components of the colony and praised their fellow countrymen each time they showed "that whenever the Italian name [was] at stake, Italians [were] all united and so demonstrated that [the journalists'] exhortations in favor of union were not wasted."[49]

The *prominenti*'s efforts to reconcile, on Columbus Day, the major conflicting regional and political forces of the Little Italies were shown in scores of apparently insignificant yet very symbolic details in the organization of the celebration. For example, as early as 1869, *L'Eco d'Italia* depicted with satisfaction the presence, in the ballroom where the Festa di Colombo took place, of numerous women who formed "a bouquet of flowers quite representative of the diversity of the different Italian types, from the blond-haired and blue-eyed girls of the North to the black-haired and black-eyed ones of the South."[50] A few years later, the Chicago Columbus Day dinner menu was proudly reproduced in the newspapers, and it was no coincidence that it carried both *"maccaroni alla genovese"* and *"maccaroni alla napoletana,"*[51] thus pleasing both northern and southern Italians. The quest for unity became all the more intense as the *prominenti*, in their endeavor to play the role of spokesmen for a cohesive ethnic community, decided to lobby for the passage of a state bill which would make Columbus Day an official holiday. In Boston, as in other cities, Italian newspapers joined the fight, and entreated the antagonistic factions to stop quarrelling:

> The aim of the commemoration is to initiate an efficient movement leading the state to declare Columbus Day an official state holiday. Politics, religion, regionalism have nothing to do with it. In this solemn occasion we must all unite and show we are both sensitive and sensible.[52]

Sociologist John Williams noted the celebration fulfilled this "bridge-building" function not only in the Little Italies of the greater areas but also in the smaller communities of Walla Walla, Washington, and Pueblo, Colorado, where the Columbus tradition "helped unite a community that was sharply divided between Northerners and Southerners and so helped pave the way for the community's achievements."[53] Even though the ceremony sometimes created competition between the main Italian-American associations, it undoubtedly proved to be, as *L'Italia* described it, "a powerful magnet which attracted all the elements of the colony."[54] It was so instrumental in the cementing of the different Italian-American components, that even *Il Proletario*'s radical editors rallied to the cause.[55] Of course they also seized the opportunity to emphasize the ambiguous role of the Church, and explained "how priests, the eternal enemies of progress, largely contributed to harming Columbus and his ideas."[56] Nevertheless, they supported Columbus Day because "the great Genoan belongs to the whole humanity" and "October 12 is dedicated to navigation science and not to a stingy feeling of patriotism."[57]

Columbus Day: In Praise of the First Immigrant

Unlike Dante Alighieri, whose figure appealed to the intellectual elite, Christopher Columbus was a hero to whom every Italian immigrant could feel close. In fact, if Italian-Americans admired and claimed respect for the "discoverer of the New World", the "Catholic conqueror," and the "herald of European civilization," what they cherished most about Columbus was the similarities they saw between his experience and theirs. Like Columbus, Italian immigrants had crossed the ocean, like Columbus they had chosen to leave their mother country in order to start a new life, and like Columbus they had gone through an ordeal. In other words, he was one of them, not only because of his nationality, but also because of his sufferings. They resented the Spanish Crown's ingratitude toward him as much as they condemned the American indifference with regard to the Columbus Day celebration. They empathized so completely with him that they felt the very neglect shown by American authorities was yet another expression of the discrimination to which Italians were subject in the United States. In 1909, *L'Italia* commented bitterly: "[P]eople here in the United States are trying to conceal that Columbus discovered America because he does not belong to the races which have their preference."[58]

Christopher Columbus was somehow seen as the "Italian Pilgrim Father" who had overcome every possible hardship in order to open the way for European immigration and whose torments had been ultimately rewarded. While lobbying for the recognition of Columbus Day as a legal state holiday, Italians were thus fighting for the recognition of an Italian-American "success story," the first of many to come. In their opinion, "had Columbus not discovered America, they would not be now the prosperous citizens of this free and independent republic, but would be submitted instead to hard work, earning little money in their overpopulated motherland."[59] To some extent, by reenacting the landing of Columbus, Italian immigrants therefore staged in reality their own arrival in America, with the difference that, in the parade, they were promoted from steerage to the *Santa Maria*'s deck. In 1962, poet Joseph Tusiani captured the particular spirit of this celebration:

> ... This is *gente mia*,[60]
> for I can see (is there a lump in my throat?)
> dear Christopher Columbus on a float
> called for all time to come Santa Maria.
>   How beautiful he beams! He has the eyes
> of my Grandfather, and his callous hand;
> he is the immigrant of every land,
> unhappy in his happy paradise,
>   misunderstood in all this misunderstanding
>
>   Look closer! There's Grandfather, come this year
> to represent Columbus on his float.
> A hero and the worthiest of note,
> he is the very one no crowd will cheer
>   tomorrow when the town goes back to work;

but look at him today, today at last,
in all the greatness of his humble past—
the new Columbus conquering New York. ... [61]

In this long poem dedicated to the tradition of Columbus Day, Tusiani analyses how the pageant allowed Italian participants to reverse their roles, from despised immigrants "no crowd will cheer" to American heroes "conquering New York", while at the same time yielding the opportunity for a complete fusion of Italians with the experience of Columbus. As a matter of fact, during the festival the Ligurian sailor and the immigrant were nothing but two sides of the same person.

At the end of the nineteenth century, as American authorities were beginning to consider the Italians' plea for an official Columbus holiday, the Genoan navigator's adventures were getting more and more emblematic of the immigrant experience in general. Christopher Columbus was gradually becoming the symbol not only of the birth of a new continent, but of America's diversity. From that perspective, some politicians were ready to support the celebration of the first "stranger", whose positive image every immigrant, whatever his nationality, could identify with. When the New York legislature finally passed the bill legalizing Columbus Day in the state (1910), the *Independent Magazine* praised the initiative with the following words:

> Columbus was the first immigrant to America. He was an Italian; he was a Catholic. There have been efforts made, and some progress in them, to have him canonized as a saint in the Roman Catholic church. ... Let him be the favored saint of our Italian immigrants, of our Spanish citizens, and let our Irish Catholics honor him next to St. Patrick.[62]

Similar considerations must have led Congress to approve, in 1934, a Proclamation which designated the twelfth of October of each year as Columbus Day.[63] Felix Frankfurter's interpretation of Columbus's enterprise (which was later expressed in a memorandum to be used for one of Roosevelt's speeches) was in fact gaining more and more supporters among American legislators:

> The destiny that fate had in store for the Americas was symbolized by the enterprise which founded the Continent. It was led by an Italian of vision of will. It was made possible by the imagination and faith of Spain. And it was achieved by the hardihood and devotion of a crew which at various times was composed of Spaniards, an Irishman, an Englishman, and a Jew. The cooperative nature of the discovery of the New World has been reflected in its development.[64]

For progressive American politicians of the twentieth century the celebration of Columbus Day thus became a way of acknowledging the immigrants' contribution to the American nation, without referring to other heroes who might have been seen as too ethnic.

Whether they wanted to "institutionalize themselves"[65], reaffirm their American identity, claim their rights, exhibit their ethnic pride or express their resentment, minority groups have always used celebrations as a means of communication with American society. In 1968, when President Lyndon B. Johnson finally made Columbus Day a federal holiday, he gave the nation's respect to the most famous Genoan navigator, but also crowned a century of Italian-American efforts to establish a special bond with the United States. Other communities have tried to accomplish the same feat, inventing festivals that emphasized both their group and national loyalties. Such is the case of the Poles, for example, who on October 11 celebrate General Kazimierz Pulaski, who fought in the American Army during the Revolution, thus becoming the "hero of the two continents."[66] Nonetheless, very few ethnic groups proved as successful in their struggle for the recognition of their contribution to the American past as Italians were with their defense of Christopher Columbus.[67] In the 1930s, Columbus Day was depicted in the Works Progress Administration New York guide as "at once the most Italian and the most American of holidays," as "the real national *festa* of all Italian immigrants."[68] What gave Columbus Day such a particular significance with respect to other ceremonies was that it allowed Italian-Americans to celebrate at the same time their Italian identity, their Italian-American group specificity, and their allegiance to America.

Notes

1. Some of the material collected for this research paper was provided by Professor Rudolph J. Vecoli (Immigration History Research Center, University of Minnesota) to whom I am most grateful for sharing his private file on Columbus.
2. Roger Caillois, *Man and the Sacred*, trans. Meyer Barash (Glencoe, IL:The Free Press of Glencoe, 1959), 163.
3. Ibid., 164.
4. The term "consensus" is used here in reference to Werner Sollors's essay: *Beyond Ethnicity, Consent and Descent in American Culture* (New York: Oxford University Press, 1986), 6. Sollors explains: "Descent relations are those defined by anthropologists as relations of 'substance' (by blood or nature); consent relations describe those of "law" or "marriage". Descent language emphasizes our positions as heirs, our hereditary qualities, liabilities, and entitlements; consent stresses our abilities as mature free agents and 'architects of our fates' to choose our spouses, our destinies, and our political systems. ... We could rephrase Tocqueville's question and ask : How can consent (and **consensus**) be achieved in a country whose citizens are of such heterogeneous descent?"
5. Giovanni Schiavo, *Four Centuries of Italian American History* (New York: The Vigo Press, 1958), 35.
6. Quoted by Claudia Bushman in *America Discovers Columbus, How an American Explorer Became an American Hero* (Hanover: University Press of New England, 1992), 82. For a detailed description of the first celebration of Columbus Day, see the whole chapter 5, 81-97.
7. *The Diary or Loudon's Register*, October 19, 1792, 1.
8. Idem.
9. "Il Ballo delle società unite per la scoperta d'America," *L'Italia*, October 15, 1887.
10. Union and Brotherhood.
11. Between 1821 and 1830 only 409 Italian arrivals were registered, while between 1841 and 1860 over 11,000 Italians entered the United States (Bureau of the Census, *Historical Statistics of the U.S.*, Washington, 1960).
12. See Remco van Capelleveen, "The 'Caribbeanization' of New York City: West Indian Carnival in Brooklyn," *Revue Française d'Etudes Américaines*, 16.51 (February 1992): 27-34.
13. Ramón A. Gutiérrez and Geneviève Fabre, eds., *Feasts and Celebrations in North American Ethnic Communities* (Albuquerque: University of New Mexico Press, 1995), 4.
14. The Sharpshooters Society.
15. The word "colony" was used at the time to define the Italian "community."
16. "Festa Colombo," *L'Eco d'Italia*, October 6, 1869.
17. For more details about Columbus Day rituals in San Francisco, see Charles Speroni, "The Development of the Columbus Day Pageant of San Francisco," *Western Folklore*, 7. 4, (October 1948): 325-335, and John B. Molinari, "The History of San Francisco's Columbus Day Celebration," in 1977 Columbus Day Committee, ed., *Columbus*, (San Francisco: Columbus Day Committee, 1977), 29-33.
18. Eugenic theories, which supported the idea of racial inequality, developed in the United States under the initiative of such biologists as Charles B. Davenport at the turn of the century. Eugenicists thus paved the way for the Nativists who found in "science" the justification for the passage of the quota laws. For more details see: John Higham, *Strangers in the Land, Patterns of American Nativism, 1860-1925* (New Brunswick: Rutgers University Press, 1988). As for eugenic literature, see : Madison Grant, *The Passing of the Great*

Race, (New York: Charles Scribner's Sons, 1919), and Henry Pratt Fairchild's *The Melting-Pot Mistake*, (1926; New York: Arno Press, 1977).
19. See Gino Speranza's analysis of the difficult integration of Italians in American society in "How it Feels to Be a Problem: A Consideration of Certain Causes Which Prevent or Retard Assimilation," *Charities*, 12 (1904): 457-463.
20. "Cristoforo Colombo e il 12 Ottobre," *Il Progresso Italo-Americano*, October 12, 1881.
21. Philip Roach, *Address of the Hon. Philip A. Roach on the Three Hundred and Eighty-Fifth Anniversary of the Discovery of America by Columbus, delivered October 14, 1877, at South San Francisco Park*, (San Francisco: W.M. Hinton and Company, 1877), 1.
22. "Le ceneri di Cristoforo Colombo," *L'Eco d'Italia*, October 11, 1879.
23. "Cristoforo Colombo e il 12 Ottobre," op. cit.
24. "Anniversario della Festa di Colombo," *L'Eco d'Italia*, October 15, 1869.
25. "Per Cristoforo Colombo," *Il Progresso Italo-Americano*, July 6, 1892.
26. See Rosella Mamoli Zorzi, "The Celebration of Columbus in Nineteenth-century American Art and Washington Irving's *Life of Columbus*," in Mario Materassi and Maria Irene Ramalho de Sousa Santos, eds., *The American Columbiad: "Discovering" America, Inventing the United States* (Amsterdam: VU University Press, 1996), 61-78; Washington Irving, *The Life and Voyages of Christopher Columbus*, (New York: G. & C. & H. Carvill, 1828).
27. Henry C. Lodge, *Congressional Record*, 54th Congress, 1st Session, March 16, 1896.
28. "Per Cristoforo Colombo," op. cit.. Unlike Barsotti's, Barattoni's speech was presented in English and was meant for the American press, as was clearly explained in the article.
29. "La Scoperta d'America," *L'Eco d'Italia*, October 15, 1873.
30. "Per il Columbus Day," *La Fiaccola*, August 21, 1909.
31. Cf. Robert F. Harney, "Caboto and Other Parentela: The Uses of the Italian-Canadian Past," in *Arrangiarsi: The Italian Immigration Experience in Canada*, Robert Perin and Franc Sturino, eds. (Montreal: Guernica, 1989), 41.
32. Originally named Giovanni Caboto.
33. Quoted by Alvin J. Schmidt in *The Greenwood Encyclopedia of American Institutions* (Westport: Greenwood Press, 1980), 176.
34. "The Columbus Quarto Centenary," in *Public Papers and Addresses of Benjamin Harrison, Twenty-Third President of the United States, March 4, 1889, to March 4, 1893* (Washington: Government Printing Office), 244-245.
35. "The Triumph of America," *The New York Times*, October 13, 1892.
36. *New York Herald*, October 10, 1892, quoted by Lionel B. Davis, in *1892: A Time for Myth–Making*, unpublished term paper, University of Minnesota, Immigration History Research Center files, 1967, 4.
37. "Columbus Forms Text of Talks," *San Francisco Chronicle*, October 13, 1909.
38. Timothy Meagher, "'Why Should We Care for a Little Trouble or a Walk Through the Mud': St Patrick's and Columbus Day Parades in Worcester, Massachusetts, 1845-1915," *The New England Quarterly* 58 (March 1985): 23.
39. Ibid., p.24.
40. "The Triumph of America," op. cit.
41. "La scoperta dell'America," *L'Italia*, October 14, 1897.
42. Robert Anthony Orsi, *The Madonna of 115th Street: Faith and Community in Italian Harlem, 1880-1950* (New Haven: Yale University Press, 1986), 4.
43. *L'Italia*, October 16, 1909.
44. "Il Columbus Day festeggiato dagl'Italiani con parata e carri allegorici – 25,000 in marcia," *L'Italia*, October 15, 1910.
45. "'Colombeide' a Boston," *La Gazzetta del Massachusetts*, October 16,1904.

46. As a statesman and a writer, Massimo Taparelli D'Azeglio (1798-1866) fought for the Italian national resurrection, and therefore strongly supported the new Italian Republic which was at last free from the Austrian yoke.
47. "La scoperta dell'America," op. cit.
48. The proclamation of Rome as the capital of Italy in 1870 was made possible after the seizure of the papal states, which many Catholics resented and would therefore refuse to celebrate. See for example "Commemorazione del XX settembre", *La Parola dei Socialisti*, September 27, 1913.
49. "I festeggiamenti per il quarto centenario colombiano in tutti gli Stati Uniti," *L'Italia*, October 15, 1892.
50. "Anniversario della Festa di Colombo," *L'Eco d'Italia*, October 15, 1869.
51. "Il Ballo delle Società Unite per la Scoperta d'America," op. cit.
52. "La festa a Colombo," *La Gazzetta del Massachusetts*, October 12, 1907.
53. John Alexander Williams, "The Columbus Complex" in *Old Ties, New Attachments, Italian American Folklife in the West*, David A. Taylor and John A. Williams, eds. (Washington: Library of Congress, 1992), 204.
54. "Il Columbus Day affratella in un solo fascio tutta la nostra colonia," *L'Italia*, October 16, 1909.
55. In the 1930's, *Il Proletario*'s position changed radically, as the Fascists took over the celebration, appropriating Columbus as their hero. See for instance : "XII Ottobre, La festa della Marmaglia," *Il Proletario*, October 15, 1935.
56. "Echi del Columbus Day," *Il Proletario*, October 21, 1910.
57. "Columbus Day," *Il Proletario*, October 27, 1907.
58. "Il debito dell'America a Cristoforo Colombo," *L'Italia*, October 9, 1909.
59. "La fontana di Colombo e le parole della Tribune," *L'Italia*, October 10, 1908.
60. *Gente mia* means "my people."
61. Joseph Tusiani, "Columbus Day in New York," *Gente Mia and Other Poems* (Stone Park, IL: Italian Cultural Center, 1978).
62. "The Significance of Columbus Day to New Americans," *The Independent Magazine*, October 20, 1910, quoted by Hilah Paulmier and Robert Schauffler, *Columbus Day*, (New York: Dodd, Mead and Company, 1938), 270.
63. Columbus Day Proclamation, Public Resolution No 2101, signed by Franklin Roosevelt on September 30, 1934.
64. Felix Frankfurter to Judge Sam Rosenman, 7 October 1940, in Roosevelt and Frankfurter, *Their Correspondence 1928-1945*, Max Freedman ed. (Boston: Little Brown and Company, 1967), 545.
65. Roland L. Guyotte and Barbara M. Posadas, "José Rizal and the Changing Nature of Filipino Identity in the American Setting: Filipinos in Twentieth-Century Chicago," *Revue Française d'Etudes Américaines* 16.51 (February 1992): 50.
66. Anthony F. Zaleski, *Hero of the Two Continents*, (Chicago: Polish Daily Zgcda, n.d.).
67. The consensus reached by Italian-Americans in that respect was shattered in the sixties and has been now largely affected by the polemical debate about Christopher Columbus. In fact, a study of the Columbus Day celebration today would show that in the 1990s, the Italian-American attitude towards the navigator evolved as some Italian groups expressed publicly their disapproval of a figure they held responsible for one of the greatest massacres in world history.
68. Works Progress Administration in the City of New York, *The Italians of New York: A Survey Prepared by Workers of the Federal Writers' Project* (1938; New York: Arno, 1969), 216.

Chapter 7

"... TO DIVIDE THEIR LOVE"

Celebrating Frenchness and Americanization in San Francisco, 1850-1909

Annick Foucrier

IN A SPEECH given during the celebration of Bastille Day in San Francisco, on July 14, 1909, the consul general of France "advised the French people present to divide their love, giving half to their birthplace and the other half to their adopted country."[1] Both the *Marseillaise* and the Star-Spangled Banner were sung by singers dressed in the costume of the Goddess of Liberty and both flags were waved side by side. The French community celebrated the long history of its presence in California and its distinctive character.[2] Answering the nativist objections to immigration and the pressures for Americanization, the French reaffirmed their loyalty to the United States as well as to France.

Immigrants played a very important part in the formation of American culture, whether they were included or excluded. Studies have been devoted to the experience of Irish, Italian, Chinese, and Mexican immigrants. Very rarely, however, can we find studies about the French way of adapting to the American society. Considering the definition given by Andrew Greeley of an ethnic group—"a combination of European cultural background, American acculturation experience, and political, social and economic common interest,"[3]—this essay will explore French ethnicity in San Francisco through

---

Notes for this section begin on page 155.

patriotic celebrations. Its objective is to understand the political assimilation of immigrants under the influence both of inner factors and the pressure of outside actors. Based on articles from the three major San Francisco newspapers (the *Alta California*, the *Examiner*,[4] and the *San Francisco Chronicle*) as a source for images, descriptions, and reports of speeches, it will analyze how Americans considered what the French brought from France and how these immigrants dealt with the American official culture.[5]

San Francisco has been called an "instant city." At the time of the Gold Rush, gold seekers arrived from all over the planet. More than in most states, the population of California was a mix of many origins. The majority planned to stay only long enough to become rich. But others, especially those who came from the East—New England, New York—or the South, came to occupy a land only recently purchased from defeated Mexico. Each group was anxious to install their political traditions while confronting the practices and the convictions of other immigrants and earlier inhabitants. The forms of civic culture developing in San Francisco were the result of these compromises. As historian Roger Lotchin has remarked, parades were occasions for multinational gatherings, and the public space was a place of confrontations and unification as historians Philip J. Ethington and Mary P. Ryan have shown, although they differ in their appreciation of the moment of construction in the public sphere of categories of race, class, and gender.[6]

The French were among the first to reach the coasts of California, and, at the time of the Gold Rush, they contributed to the growth of San Francisco where they gathered in a French quarter. Like other immigrants, they remained involved in the affairs of their native country and could be considered as being between two worlds. Those who left after the political conflicts of 1848 transported French-related political differences, primarily between those who were in favor of the Republic and those who, after 1852, sided with the Second Empire of Napoleon III. Even among the former, differing interpretations of the fall of the Second Republic led to opposing attitudes. These groups expressed their divisions in separate celebrations: the twenty-fourth of February for the Republicans, the fifteenth of August for the Bonapartists. But contrary to what has been often claimed, the French did not have their eyes exclusively turned toward France. Their participation in Independence Day parades bore testimony to their desire for integration, even though their naturalization rate remained low. In 1853, the *Daily Alta California* stated: "There are 30,000 French in California. They are industrious, intelligent and respected; and if they should become citizens they would be astonished at their influence."[7]

The Naturalization Act of 1802 had set the requirements for becoming an American citizen: "Residence of five years with a declaration of intent three years before admission; oaths or declarations abjuring titles and foreign allegiance and swearing attachment to the principles of the Constitution; and satisfactory proof of good character and behavior."[8] Later in the century, starting with the Chinese Exclusion Act in 1882, Asian immigrants were barred from citizenship, on the argument that the first naturalization law of the United States, on March 26, 1790, was for "free white persons". The only exception was an addition to the Fifteenth Amendment in 1870, that authorized the naturalization of immigrants from Africa or of African origin. Their European origin allowed the French to be eligible for citizenship, but becoming American required more than naturalization. Even as American citizens, the French retained important parts of their French identity and culture. When in 1880, the fourteenth of July became the national anniversary in France, this set a new pattern. In years to come, more and more French residents in San Francisco united in this patriotic celebration.

The French in the Celebrations of the Fourth of July

The first Independence Day celebrations in San Francisco displayed the diversity of its inhabitants. On July 4, 1852, a journalist of the *Daily Alta California* noticed the presence of Brazilians, Chinese (whom he called "singular beings"), *Californios*,[9] and French in the parade. The members of the French benevolent society—the Société française de bienfaisance—were, as a journalist of the *Alta California* wrote, "preceded by veteran drummers, who had seen several revolutions in 'La Belle France' and who aroused many of our citizens in the morning by beating the *rappel* as they marched through the streets." They displayed a banner "on which were pictures of Washington and Lafayette, and also a beautiful painting of the Angel of Charity relieving a distressed wayfarer." The portraits of Washington and Lafayette were obviously intended to recall the help given by the French to the independence of America and to celebrate the friendship between the two peoples. And the "Angel of Charity" underlined the Catholic traditions of the French. The most striking feature of this American celebration was that the hymn of the French Republic, the *Marseillaise*, was sung right after the prayer and before the reading of the Declaration of Independence and even before the singing of American hymns, *Hail Columbia* and *The Star Spangled Banner*.[10]

Future participation of the French followed this pattern: a display of both militarism and benevolence. The French voluntary firefighters, the "Lafayette Hook and Ladder Company n°2", appeared in their bright uniforms. Acting as a firefighter was a social opportunity for ambitious young men who enjoyed the prestige of a useful corps and the admiration raised by their sparkling uniforms. When the Fire Department was founded in 1866 and the voluntary companies were dissolved or absorbed, the Lafayettes transformed their company into a musical society, and kept on parading on appropriate occasions, such as national celebrations or official receptions of French navy vessels. In 1862, there were fifty-five (including thirty-five in uniform) to march for the reception in honor of the French corvette *Bayonnaise*.[11]

In 1870, another society was created, the French Zouaves, which was more military oriented. The French Californian population was very fond of these military societies since, as Daniel Lévy wrote, "through their military aspect, they contribute to give us the kind and dear illusion of our missing fatherland during our national celebrations."[12] This martial attitude grew among the French population after the defeat of 1870 during the Franco-Prussian War. The hope to recover the lost territories of Alsace-Lorraine was quite intense among the French population in California because many among them were born in these provinces.

Year after year, the French renewed a civic compact with their adopted land. The military societies marched, and the elite of the community, rich bankers and entrepreneurs, gave money for the ceremonies of Independence Day (in 1867, for example, the firms of Lazard brothers gave $50, Pioche and Robinson $25). The French residents mingled with the rest of the population in the crowded streets and applauded the parades. In 1876, the centennial of the Declaration of Independence was an opportunity to assert their identity as French Californians, and their loyalty toward the United States and its government. On Kearny Street, near Post Street, they erected a giant arch, beautifully decorated and dedicated to "the memory of these two illustrious representatives of the French and American nationalities, Washington and Lafayette" whose portraits hung on top. A large banner announced: "The French residents commemorate a century of Liberty."

After 1893, the French disappeared from the Fourth of July parades, which became more of a display of American military might. They returned only in 1917, when the United States entered World War I on the side of England and France.

The Celebrations of February 24 Versus Those of August 15

In addition to participating in the celebration of the national anniversary of the United States, the French had their own dates of commemoration. After the revolution of 1848, February 24 became the national anniversary in France, at least until 1852, when the overthrow of the republic by Louis Napoleon in 1851 resulted in the installation of a new imperial government

The French Residents Commemorate a Century of Liberty.
Courtesy of the California Historical Society.

one year later. But in California, the French republicans kept commemorating the revolution. In 1852, Louise Clapp (Dame Shirley), the wife of a doctor, in a letter to her sister who had stayed in New England, described how their torchlight procession to Rich Bar wound up "the hill, each one carrying a tiny pine tree, the top of which was encircled with a diadem of flame, beautifully lighting up the darker verdure beneath, and gleaming like a spectral crown through the moonless, misty evening." She quoted their watchwords phonetically: "Shorge Washingtone, James K. Polk, Napoleon Bonaparte! Liberte, Egalite, Fraternite! Andrew Jackson, President Filmore and Lafayette!"[13] What was to her the subject of mild irony, is an interesting indication of the addition of American heroes to the pantheon of the French residents in California.

More often than in parades, at banquets French republicans would recall the memory of the revolution and express their hopes for a French republic, making toasts in honor of France and of the republic, thus recalling the practice of political banquets by which they used to protest during the Monarchy of July. It was a welcome opportunity to gather and reaffirm their love of liberty and democracy. Such a demonstration was aimed at their countrymen as well as at their foreign neighbors. The description of a banquet in 1854 is a good example of their festivities:

> A large party, numbering more than two hundred persons, collected last evening at the Hotel d'Europe to celebrate the anniversary of the French Revolution of the 24th February, 1848 .... After a well served repast had received deserved attention, the Union Band struck up the Marseillaise Hymn, the favorite air of the French Republicans. It was answered with thunders of applause. The toasts followed. The President arose and made a short address, and was succeeded by the different vice-presidents present; by ... many others who, in short and vigorous addresses, spoke their various views in regard to the benefits, causes, effects, and causes of the downfall of the Revolution, and attachment to the cause of Liberty. The meeting was very enthusiastic, and the company did not separate until a late hour.[14]

The French consul, instructed by the French ministry of Foreign Affairs, did his best to promote the August 15 as the national day of France, and the anniversary of the Bonaparte dynasty. This date coincided with a traditional religious feast in France. For peasants, it was a welcome moment of rest after the hard work of harvesting and before the exhausting labor of grape-cutting. The consul wanted to gather as many French residents as possible around this celebration to present an image of unity and prestige to the French as well as to the Americans.

After the end of the Civil War, such a show was emphasized for a different reason: to minimize the hostility that had erupted after the French military intervention in Mexico. During the celebration in 1867 people could admire the elegant uniforms of the diplomatic corps, those of the Lafayette company, the former voluntary firefighters and of the Irish guards, longtime close friends to the Lafayette company.

> The Fete Napoleon was celebrated yesterday in San Francisco with considerable eclat. Lafayette Company, N°2, escorted by the McMahon Grenadier Guard, of the Independent Irish Battalion, and accompanied by Kidd's Band, marched from the house of the former, on Broadway, to the Church of Notre Dame, on Bush street, where high mass was celebrated. The church was profusely decorated with flags. On the floor of the altar, during the services, the American and French banners were entwined, forming something like an arch over the heads of the officiating priests. The soldiers, uncovered, occupied the aisles, and at the Elevation presented arms.
> The banquet at Platt's Hall was a very fine affair, M. de Cazotte, the French Consul, presided, and at the head table a number of prominent citizens occupied seats. The McMahon Guard and the French firemen, in brilliant uniforms, were a striking feature in the Hall. The French, American, Italian and Irish flags were to be seen on every side.[15]

The religious dimension is a reminder that many French residents were Catholics. And the association of the consul, the military companies, and the church reflected the structure of power in France (the state, the army, and the church) and proves that it was transplanted into the French community. But it led to the absence of those among the French residents who were not Catholic or in favor of the political regime.

At the end of the banquet, toasts to "The Emperor Napoleon," "The President of the United States," and "The Foreign Consuls," testified to the integration of the French in San Francisco and to the social preoccupations of the elites assembled. "Lafayette Company, N°2," mentioned the Lafayette Hook and Ladder Company of French firefighters (in 1866, the company was dissolved when the San Francisco Fire Department was created, a group which also was toasted). Toasts to "Colonel Cazneau" of the Irish guards, "The McMahon Grenadier Guard," and to "Ireland" and "Italy" emphasized the presence of societies from two other Catholic European populations, the Irish and the Italians. Emile Marque, from the French newspaper *Courrier de San Francisco*, responded to a last toast to "The Press." "The tricolor was visible in every part of the city," the *Daily Alta California* wrote, "and the number of French residents who took part in the celebration was quite large. The house of Lafayette Company was handsomely ornamented with flags. The McMahon Grenadier Guard, numbering fifty-six rank and file, presented their usual fine appearance, and the firemen with brass helmets attracted a good deal of attention. The interior of the Church of Notre Dame was decorated with American, French, Italian and Irish ensigns, and, surmounting all, an Imperial crown. In the evening there was a grand ball at Platt's Hall, which was largely attended."[16] With the fall of the Second Empire, however, this celebration was abandoned.

Bastille Day, a Republican Celebration

As early as 1857, a French newspaper published in San Francisco, *Le Phare*, tried to organize a celebration on July 14. According to the *Daily Alta California*, there was a dinner at a French restaurant on Commercial street, and it was a very enthusiastic and interesting gathering. But it was not before 1869 that a large banquet for the fourteenth of July was again mentioned in the papers. Now, the toasts had a clear socialist undertone: "to the United States," " to the fall of all the Bastilles," "to the members of the Republican Party recently elected in France," "to the Memory of Lincoln, the Martyr President," "to Babeuf, the Apostle of the Socialists," "to the Federation of the People," and "to Rochefort, Editor of the *Lanterne*."[17]

In 1870, when the Second Empire came to an end, many French Republican residents had already returned to France. But after the failure of the Commune uprising and the repression that followed, some returned to the United States and to California. Together with those who had elected to stay in California, they kept celebrating, year after year, the fall of the Bastille with a banquet, as it was done in France. In 1880, the new republican regime in France seemed securely enough established for the Chamber of Deputies to pass, on June 8, 1880, a resolution that "the Republic adopts the 14th of July as an annual national holiday," which became a law on July 6, 1880. This was not without debate, some other dates having been suggested, such as the February 24 (the anniversary of the Second Republic in 1848) or the September 21 (the date of the proclamation of the First Republic in 1792). July 14 also had the advantage of referring to the Fete of the Federation in 1790, a symbol of national unity.[18]

Reacting immediately, the French residents of San Francisco elected a committee to organize a big celebration which incorporated French and American elements. Downtown stores were beautifully decorated with French and American flags. People proudly wore blue, white, and red ribbons, gathered in a powerful symbol of national unity, just like in France in 1789. Behind sappers and a detachment of the American Guards, the French military societies (Lafayette Guards, French Zouaves) departed from the Lafayette Hall, followed by the Swiss Carabineers, the organization committee and Swiss citizens. They marched toward the consulate where they saluted the French tricolor. The consuls of France, Belgium, and Switzerland were part of the procession to the Opera House, where the French "Declaration of the Rights of Man and the Citizen" was read. Orations in English and in French followed, and the national anthems. The pedagogical intention was obvious in the addresses, stressing the fight for liberty that had been conducted in both countries. Festivities were then continued well into the night at parks: Woodward's gardens first, and in later years the Chutes, with concerts, fireworks and a ball.[19] The highlight of the fireworks each year was the reenactment in burning glory of the destruction of the Bastille as the symbol of tyranny; in 1896, the reporter of the *Examiner* called it "a monster representation of the burning of the Great Bastille." In the years to follow, French, Swiss, and Americans were joined in the procession by military and civil societies of other ethnic groups: Mexicans (Juarez Guards), Italians (Italian Bersaglieri), and Belgians. In 1893, this led a journalist of the *Examiner* to give his article the subtitle: "How the Latin Quarter Dazzled all San Francisco."[20]

For the second such parade, in 1881, the French displayed another daring innovation. "One noticeable feature of the procession was that of a woman who marched with the civil societies," the *Examiner* reported, "evidently considering it her right, and enjoying the comment which was bandied on all sides."[21] From there on, women marched with military societies as "daughters of the regiment" or on floats as representations of the Goddess of Liberty, an allegorical embodiment that was more of a traditional role for women, like Reason, Virtue, or Peace.

In 1889, the French population enthusiastically celebrated the centennial of the French Revolution for three days. However, two celebrations took place. In both, orators referred to the fall of the Bastille, recalled "the aid given by liberty-loving Frenchmen to the struggling American patriots of 1778," and saluted America, who has "done so much for liberty and for the emancipation of the human mind." *La Marseillaise* and songs to Alsace-Lorraine were vigorously applauded. But political differences were noticeable. In one speech, the orator glorified "the Voltaires, the Diderots, the Rousseaus, the D'Alemberts and the Montesquieus, these prophets and precursors of the Revolution," while the other orator spoke of "Marat, Robespierre and Danton, the triumvirate who had started the Revolution, and of the noble patriots Generals Marceau, Kléber and Hoche," expressing a more nationalistic attitude. The same opposition can be detected in the fact that while the former saluted the government of President Carnot, the latter denounced in a more socialist tone "the new Bastilles that had risen in its place, and the money lords and mercantile lords who have supplanted the aristocratic lords."[22]

A minor newspaper, the *San Francisco Newsletter and California Advertiser*, took the opportunity of the celebration to express nativist ideas against the recent French immigrants who were portrayed as a foreign element unable to assimilate and become Americans. "More than half the French in this city cling to their own language, read only French newspapers and regard San Francisco as a kind of purgatory, residence in which for a term of years will fit them for the heaven of Paris," the paper stated with regret, "they consequently never come within touch of American interests, and are as alien to all our life and customs as though they lived in Tonquin." Probably conscious of the harshness of such a description, he added: "In strong contrast to these are the small body of enterprising Frenchmen of this city who possess all true American traits, and are valuable citizens."[23]

The *San Francisco Chronicle*, one of the city's major newspapers, gave a slightly different and more tolerant picture than the *Advertiser*:

> The prominent members of the community are among the most respected of our citizens; liberal, philanthropic, enlightened, they have readily coalesced with the native population, gone side by side with them in public enterprise, and adopted all worthy American ideas. It is only in his home or club circle that the Franco-American of California is a Frenchman still. Not unnaturally, he is unwilling to forget entirely the language and domestic customs of his native land, and to do this he is forced to unite with his compatriots in social gatherings, circles, lodges, etc., where French is exclusively spoken. Otherwise the affiliation between the French colony and the American people is complete, even to the ready adoption of the ties of citizenship.[24]

But in light of a growing self-consciousness and fear of some American citizens of revolutionary ideas among some American citizens, the *Daily Alta California* felt it had to defend the right of the French to celebrate their fight for liberty. Against those who stressed "excesses" committed during the French Revolution (such as the massacres enacted by the Parisian crowd in September 1792), it declared:

> It is not wrong that her sons who seek here that which she [France] has tried to establish, should—without seeking to involve our Government, without trying to influence our politics to an alien purpose, respecting like good citizens our laws and in love for our institutions—emphasize their devotion to liberty by this observance of the anniversary of an incident that marks the fall of old oppressions and the rise of modern institutions in their own country.[25]

Obviously, the issue was the acceptance and assimilation of immigrants, were they French or from any other country, and the fear of radical ideas. On July 14, 1888, General Barnes, the speaker chosen by the French committee of organization for the English-language oration, still exhibited an attitude of inclusion, beginning his address in French, and stating: "I come before you therefore as an American, as we all are, without regard to our place of birth or the words that brought to us our first ideas."[26] But a few years later, on July 4, 1891, Merton C. Allen, then a young journalist, gave his American audience a different kind of oration that met with great appreciation. "The orator reviewed the history of the country and then went to more interesting things," the *Examiner* reported. "The keynote of it is found in the sentence, 'The naturalization laws of the United States should be more carefully amended without delay, and the immigration of foreign citizens to this country should be placed under greatly increased restrictions.' That sentiment was applauded to the echo, and around it was built the best of the story which the young orator had to tell."[27] This revealed the beginnings of a new wave of nationalism among Americans.[28]

The speeches had always stressed the similarities between the two "liberty-loving" peoples. However, some competition had existed over which revolution was the true model for the future. In his address as president of the day, on July 14, 1884, M. de Jouffroy d'Abbans stated: "The 14th of July is not only a French fete, but a fete that belongs to the universe." This assertion was echoed by Irish-American nationalists. In 1885, the representatives of the Irish National League, during a convention at Irish-American Hall, sent a letter of congratulation to the organizers of the French celebration: "The 14th of July is a day which must be remembered by every one having aspirations for liberty."[29] In announcing the celebration of 1887, the *Examiner* repeated such an appreciation: "Not only Frenchmen, but liberty-loving people of all lands can enter into the spirit of the occasion." Some orations even presented the Fourth of July as mainly significant to the United States only, for its independence, while July 14 celebrated universal values. Against such a pretension, American politicians began to emphasize the antecedence of the American fight for liberty. On July 14, 1897, Mayor Phelan expressed a renewed feeling of Manifest Destiny when he explained the philosophy of successive celebrations:

> This is the French national holiday, and its significance is in full accord with the principles that underlie the structure of the American Government. America celebrates the Fourth of July; France a few days after, the 14th. The one following the other is more than a coincidence—it is a consequence. The example of America in 1776 was closely followed by the French people in 1789, and the success of Freedom's cause in this country was the inspiration of French patriotism, which overthrew that frowning emblem of despotic rule, the Bastille.[30]

The question of American identity, which was at the core of this discourse, was an important issue in the 1890s, as the Independence Day oration by Merton C. Allen in 1899 testified. Commenting on the Spanish-American War of 1898-99, he said: "The Glory that has come to American arms on land

and on sea has been the glory of a united American people. We are to-day, as never before, one nation and one people, marching under one flag, possessing but one impulse." He was still being applauded even after he had taken his seat.[31]

The French adapted quickly to the growing nativism in San Francisco. They used the opportunity of the July 14 to reaffirm each year their gratitude for the hospitality they received in the United States, and their loyalty to both countries. In 1899, the consul-general for France, A. de Trobriand, referring to the Oregon Volunteers coming home after the Spanish-American War, declared that "the French of the city felt just as much interested in their return as native Americans." He added, that he was sure of the friendship of the two republics. The English-language orator, City and County Attorney F.K. Lane, recalled what the French had brought to California: "What you have done toward the developing of our State, considerable as is our debt in this regard, it is to my mind of less moment than the color, the vivacity, the sparkle and the artistic elements you have added to our life. For the Frenchman is pre-eminently an artist, whether he is making a poem, a picture or a ragout." In a paraphrase of Napoleon the First (who had claimed: "It is Europe's destiny to be either French or Cossack,") he turned to European politics and added: "The United States of Europe may be a dream .... Nevertheless, it is true that Europe must become Cossack or Republican. And France stands practically alone upon the continent to show forth the advantages of republican institutions."[32] This unique characteristic of France among the nations of the world, earned the French the sympathy of Americans who shared republican feelings.

Still, the question of assimilation versus visible ethnic identity remained. Already in 1893, a journalist of *The Examiner* gave an interesting view of the French solution when he reported with some surprise that on July 14 "the Frenchmen were radiant with the red, white, and blue ..., and men who would have been passed unnoticed on the street the day before suddenly blossomed into national distinctiveness."[33] The celebration made the French visible, drawing into the streets a Frenchness that they still nurtured in their private lives.

In 1895 a new law forbade independent military companies from parading with arms in the state without the license of the governor, a decision that visibly affected French participation in the annual celebration. This decision came at a time when the urban-industrial depression that had struck the United States in 1893 led to much social violence, and when the discontent of farmers was expressed in populist demands for reforms. It was also a moment of political realignment, just prior to the advent of what has been called the Fourth Party system, which was characterized by the hegemony of

San Francisco Cronicle, July 15, 1899.

the Republican party.[34] By measure of exception, and for the last time, the French companies were granted permission to carry arms by the Governor in 1895. The Lafayette Guards, the French Zouaves and the French Legion stopped marching in the streets of San Francisco. But even after the end of the military processions, July 14 was still brilliantly celebrated by the French, with military reviews, orations, concerts, fireworks, balls, and games. However, with an audience that was less politically and more popularly minded, entertainment became more and more important in the celebration: July 14 became the day of the most popular picnic in the community. At the end of the century, the parades were abandoned altogether, the celebration of July 14 disappeared from the streets, and the festivities took place in a park. And while the French and American flags were usually hung side by side, in 1900, a journalist of *The Examiner* noticed with obvious satisfaction that the Chutes, a San Francisco park where the French celebrated the fall of the Bastille, was decorated "with ropes and festoons of the tricolor of France swung from every available point. But on the tall flag staff, high above all, floated the stars and stripes."[35] This display was quite obviously meant to reassure those who might have had doubts about the assimilating capacity of American society.

Leaders in the French Celebration. San Francisco Examiner, July 14, 1896.

The establishment of the Lafayette Club by the French in 1916, a political club which was designed to help French immigrants to apply for naturalization, was the logical outcome of their adaptation to the customs of their country of residence.[36] But in contradiction to the sociological theories of the School of Chicago, they were French *and* American, dividing their love and their loyalty.

Conclusion

Since the French were European immigrants, they did not suffer racial exclusion, like Asians or Blacks, but being predominantly Catholics, they might face religious bigotry.[37] As was the case with other immigrants, the celebration of their national anniversary was for the French a means to display their inner identity, allowing them to act as Americans for the rest of the year. Stressing their Republican tradition served a strategy of accommodation and was a way to find a common ground with American official culture by asserting values of liberty.

Some of them found an opportunity to exercise leadership, acting as elites: they organized festivities and participated in committees; others gathered and gave money, displaying their wealth; still others presented orations composed with the purpose of political education. Businessmen, journalists, officers of military societies, they originated from inside the community and made themselves known and appreciated during those ceremonies. The orations were especially important, since they formulated the references and the symbols that could help French immigrants to become an ethnic group which shared a common public memory. Other leaders gained their legitimacy from powers outside the group, although they could not be considered as being at the periphery. As the representative of the French government, the consul was the major personality in the celebrations, but it took time, after the fall of the Second Empire, for some of these diplomats to accept the Republic. Between 1856 and 1870, the Catholic priest of Notre-Dame des Victoires was also a major component of the ceremonies. After that, however, the religious dimension of the ceremonies was less pronounced, and conflicts that broke out between the state and the church in France at the end of the century set him, for a time, apart from the patriotic celebrations in San Francisco.

There was no perfect unity within the French community in San Francisco. The celebrations reflected the composition and the evolution of the group, its regional origins, its religious and political characteristics. In the 1850s, the French immigrants in San Francisco had come from all over France, they were largely urban in origin and quite politicized by the recent revolution of 1848. At the end of the century, their origins were mainly rural, they came from a limited number of places in France, and their interests were more regionalist than national. The rival commemorations of the centennial of the Fall of the Bastille in 1889 point to conflicts, be they political or social, or both.

Because they kept feeling an intense pride for the cultural achievements of France, the French Californians reaffirmed their loyalty to their "adopted land," but they also expressed a rivalry between the "Sister Republics"[38] about the issue of which of the two revolutions, the French or the American, would serve as the model for universal values. The participation of other immigrants in the French celebrations of August 15 and July 14 also revealed associations with other nationalities along religious lines (with Catholic Irish and Italians); linguistic lines (French-speaking Swiss and Belgians); and ethnic lines (some kind of common 'latinity' with Italians and Mexicans). These associations complicated and, at the same time, fostered the assimilation of an ethnic group that, for the longest time, "divided its love" between France and the United States.

Notes

1. "Divide Love, Says Consul to French," *Daily Examiner*, July 15, 1909.
2. Annick Foucrier, *Le rêve californien. Migrants français sur la côte Pacifique, XVIIIe-XXe siècles* (Paris: Belin, 1999).
3. Andrew A. Greeley, *Why Can't They Be Like Us? America's White Ethnic Groups* (New York: Dutton & Co, 1971), 33.
4. This newspaper's title has changed several times during the period studied: *The Daily Examiner* from 1881 to 1889, *The Examiner* from 1890 to 1901, *The San Francisco Examiner* from 1902.
5. Dirk Hoerder and Leslie P. Moch, eds., *European Migrants: Global and Local Perspectives* (Boston: Northeastern University Press, 1996); John Higham, ed., *Ethnic Leadership in America* (Baltimore: The Johns Hopkins University Press, 1978); Victor R. Greene, *American Immigrant Leaders, 1800-1910. Marginality and Identity* (Baltimore: The Johns Hopkins University Press, 1987); Jürgen Habermas, *The Theory of Communicative Action* (Boston: Beacon Press, 2 vols. 1987); John Bodnar, *Remaking America: Public Memory, Commemoration, and Patriotism in the Twentieth Century* (Princeton: Princeton University Press, 1992).
6. Gunther Barth, *Instant Cities: Urbanization and the Rise of San Francisco and Denver* (New York: Oxford University Press, 1975); William Issel and Robert W. Cherny, *San Francisco, 1865-1932. Politics, Power, and Urban Development* (Berkeley: University of California Press, 1986); Roger W. Lotchin, *San Francisco, 1846-1856: From Hamlet to City* (1974; Chicago: University of Illinois Press, 1997); Philip J. Ethington, *The Public City. The Political Construction of Urban Life in San Francisco, 1850-1900* (New York: Cambridge University Press, 1994); Mary P. Ryan, *Civic Wars: Democracy and Public Life in the American City during the Nineteenth Century* (Berkeley: University of California Press, 1997).
7. "The French in California," *Daily Alta California*, November 30, 1853.
8. James H. Kettner, *The Development of American Citizenship, 1608-1870* (Chapel Hill: University of North Carolina Press, 1978), 245-46; Annick Foucrier, "Immigration et citoyenneté aux Etats-Unis: la dialectique de l'inclusion et de l'exclusion," *Revue Française d'Etudes Américaines* 75 (January 1998): 4-21.

9. The *Californios* were the inhabitants of Spanish and Mexican descent who lived in California prior to the treaty of annexation of 1848.
10. "Celebration of the Anniversary of our National Independence," *Daily Alta California*, July 7, 1852.
11. *Daily Alta California*, July 21, 1862. Annick Foucrier, "La compagnie Lafayette d'échelles et de crochets : Les pompiers volontaires français à San Francisco (1853-1866)," *Le Sapeur-Pompier* 899 (February 1999): 74-76.
12. Daniel Lévy, *Les Français en Californie* (San Francisco: Grégoire, Tauzy & Co, 1884).
13. Louise A.K.S. Clappe (Dame Shirley), *The Shirley Letters* (1922; Salt Lake City: Peregrine Books, 1983), 101-102.
14. *Daily Alta California*, February 25, 1854.
15. *Daily Alta California*, August 16, 1867.
16. *Daily Alta California*, August 16, 1867.
17. *Daily Alta California*, July 14, 857; "Banquet in Honor of the Anniversary of the Fall of the Bastille," *Daily Alta California*, July 15, 1869. *La Lanterne* was a radical newspaper.
18. "The French National Anniversary," *Daily Alta California*, July 14, 1880.
19. Advertisement in the *San Francisco Chronicle*, July 13, 1880; "Vive la République," *Daily Alta California*, July 15, 1880; "The French Republic. Magnificent Display of the French Citizens of San Francisco," *The Daily Examiner*, July 15, 1880; "Vive la République," *San Francisco Chronicle*, July 15, 1880.
20. "Gaul's Great Day," *The Examiner*, July 15, 1893.
21. "Freedom of France—How the City Celebrated the Fall of the Bastille," *Daily Examiner*, July 14, 1881.
22. *Daily Alta California*, July 16, 1889; *The Daily Examiner*, July 15, 1889.
23. *San Francisco News Letter and California Advertiser*, July 13, 1889.
24. *San Francisco Chronicle*, July 13, 1889.
25. *Daily Alta California*, July 16, 1889.
26. "Rejoicing Frenchmen. Exultant Patriotism. General W.H.L. Barnes' Speech," *The Daily Examiner*, July 15, 1888.
27. "The Nation's Birthday. An American Ovation and an Appreciative Audience," *The Examiner*, July 5, 1891.
28. John Higham, *Strangers in the Land: The Patterns of American Nativism, 1860-1925* (1955; New Brunswick, NJ: Rutgers University Press, 1992).
29. "The Irish National League Meets in Convention," *The Daily Examiner*, July 15, 1885.
30. "Liberté, Egalité, Fraternité," *The Examiner*, July 16, 1897.
31. "The Exercises in Metropolitan Hall," *San Francisco Chronicle*, July 5, 1899.
32. "Prise de la Bastille," *The Examiner*, July 15, 1899.
33. "Gaul's Great Day," *The Examiner*, July 15, 1893.
34. Paul Kleppner, *Who Voted? The Dynamics of Electoral Turnout, 1870-1980* (New York: Praeger Publishers, 1982), 74-77.
35. "French Colony Remembers, in Oratory and Songs of Joy, the Fall of the Bastille," *The Examiner*, July 15, 1900.
36. Annick Foucrier, "Des identités régionales à l'unification nationale par l'intégration politique. Les Français à San Francisco au tournant du siècle et le club Lafayette (1916)," *Des modèles en question. Villes, culture, citoyenneté en Amérique du Nord*, J. Portes and C. Pouzoulet, eds. (Lille: Presses Universitaires de Lille, 1998): 147-60.
37. John Higham, *Strangers in the Land*.
38. Patrice Higonnet, *Sister Republics. The Origins of French and American Republicanisms* (Cambridge, MA: Harvard University Press, 1988).

Chapter 8

CHARITY ON PARADE

Chicago's Jews and the Construction of Ethnic and Civic "Gemeinschaft" in the 1860s

Tobias Brinkmann

IT IS GENERALLY assumed that the cohesion of Jewish immigrants in nineteenth-century America was much stronger than that of other immigrant groups—notably of the large and heterogeneous group of German-speaking immigrants. But while European Jews—who for centuries had been forced to live isolated on the fringes of societies—had a strong tradition of community life, the clear-cut separation of church and state in the United States presented a challenge for Jewish immigrants. In Chicago, Jews were separated by so many internal divisions in the 1860s that one can hardly speak of a "community."[1]

The term "community" is often used by scholars of American immigration-history but is rarely questioned. An ethnic community can be defined as an institutionally organized network of associations and congregations of an ethnic group at a given locality that extends over a period of several years or longer. While the meaning of the term community in a general sense goes much further, an ethnic community of shared ethnic identities at a given place extends beyond any ethnic institutional network, and is almost impossible to define for a historical analysis which has to deal with a limited number of sources. More importantly, a "Gemeinschaft" is only as strong as its

---

Notes for this section begin on page 171.

weakest members. The existence of collective relief societies is a reliable litmus test for an institutionally organized community in the making. Most immigrant communities provided a social network for poor and sick immigrants, for recent arrivals, and for widows with children. In the Jewish case, associations for the payment and organization of burials were often forerunners of charitable associations or congregations.[2]

This essay places the complexities of the concept "community" within the context of American Jewish history prior to the large increase of Jewish immigration from Eastern Europe in the 1880s. It attempts to explain why Jewish immigrant leaders in Chicago put "Charity on Parade" in 1867.

Between 1850 and 1890 roughly fifty percent of Chicago's population was made up of foreign-born immigrants. Even for urban America this was an unusually high proportion. The numbers are even more impressive if one adds the American-born children of immigrants.[3] However, a look at the rather small Jewish group in Chicago—which numbered roughly three thousand in the mid-1860s, itself torn by social, religious, political, and in particular regional ("Landsmannschaft"-related) differences, shows that even the ethnicization of immigrants who, according to popular belief, were already 'ethnic' and formed a homogeneous group when they arrived in America, was a complex matter.[4] And even more importantly, even this small case study shows that the processes of ethnicization, assimilation and community-building were intertwined.

The second day of September 1867 was a remarkable day for the Jews of Chicago. On this day all five congregations, the Jewish fraternal lodges and the philanthropic societies formed a parade led by the Jewish Civil War hero General Edward Salomon, Chicago's mayor, and the Great Western Light Guard Band. The parade, made up of carriages and marching columns, moved from the business district up to Chicago's North Side toward the building site of the future Jewish Hospital that promised to open its doors to every distressed person "without distinction of nationality, race, religion or color." After the cornerstone for the hospital was laid, Chicago's mayor gave a short address praising the Jews of Chicago and their work for the poor in the city. He was followed by businessman Godfrey Snydacker who spoke to the large crowd in German. He pointed out that this event reminded him of his "dear old [German] home country, the beloved Fatherland" (*theure alte Heimath*), where Jews used to live in close-knit communities. In America, he lamented, Jews formed separate groups, driven apart by different religious orientations, conflicting political affiliations, and social differences. But one platform remained, Snydacker claimed, where Jews "from the North Sea, the Baltic, from the Rhine and Danube" could meet and unite as "true brothers and sisters:" "Charity" *(Wohlthätigkeit)*. "Charity" was the "true" source of "unity" for all Jews in Chicago and, he concluded, "unity makes us strong." Banker Henry Greenebaum described in his speech, which he delivered in English, the importance of philanthropy as a Jewish tradition. Using a classical stereotype of his day, he addressed a 'taboo' topic: anti-Jewish stereotypes. The Rothschilds were, Greenebaum emphasized, unjustly targeted by countless anti-Jewish attacks. Yes, this family was extremely wealthy but the Rothschilds were also among the most active benefactors of charitable and philanthropic endeavors worldwide. His Jewish listeners, he concluded his speech, should follow the Rothschilds' example and contribute generously to Catholic charities in Chicago and attend the upcoming German "Turner-Fair," a big fundraiser for the "German Aid Society."[5]

Parades, researchers have suggested more recently, were "invented" in the first half of the nineteenth century as unifying "rituals" in times of rapid urban growth and social disorder. Parades were, in other words, a show of civic unity transcending social differences in the cities. After 1850, however, when the related processes of immigration and industrialization boosted city growth, urban parades became more "ethnic"—eventually exclusively so—as ethnic groups staged their own parades. Civic unity in the city was thus replaced by difference, as Mary Ryan has argued. In the following paragraphs the parade described above will be analyzed from two perspectives: Its meaning in the general context of parades in nineteenth-century Chicago and, more specifically, its function for the Jewish community itself.[6]

Superficially the Jewish parade of 1867 fits into the pattern described by Ryan. During the 1860s, the large immigrant-groups in Chicago increasingly staged their own parades. These ethnic parades, as Kathleen Conzen and others have demonstrated, brought immigrants with often diverse backgrounds together and served as important symbolic displays of a group's ethnicization and unity both for members of the group and for non-members. The research done by Kathleen Conzen and others in this respect has been ignored by Ryan, who does not look at the immigrants themselves but rather at their impact on the public discourse in the city. However, the issue of unity and difference was as important for immigrants as it was in the city on a more general level.[7]

The Fourth of July parade of 1862 in Chicago marks an intermediary stage in this process between the earlier inclusive civic parade to the later exclusive ethnic parade. Two large cohorts of this parade were made up exclusively of German and Irish immigrants. The German cohort was led by Henry Greenebaum and Edward Salomon, both of whom were active in Jewish congregations and associations but also belonged to the German ethnic leadership in Chicago.[8] The giant German parade of 1871, celebrating German unification, quite clearly marked the end of the traditional civic parade in Chicago. In fact, this was the first time that almost all German Americans in Chicago were mobilized in large numbers across the board. Again, individual Jews could be found among the leading organizers of the German "community" project in Chicago: the parade of 1871 was planned in the office of the respected Jewish lawyer Julius Rosenthal and led by Henry Greenebaum. But Jewish congregations and associations did not participate in this parade. However, the 1871 parade was the first *and* last inclusive German parade. In later years German immigrants, notably Socialist German-American workers, would continue to organize large public events, but only for clearly defined subsegments of the German-American group.[9] If there ever was an organized German community in Chicago, it existed only for very limited periods of time, during the parade of 1871, and before that during the Civil War when immigrants from Germany organized their own regiments. This raises an interesting question in regard to Mary Ryan's interpretation: the disintegration of civic unity within the transforming city was followed by the increasing disintegration of ethnic unity within large and heterogeneous immigrant groups.

The Jewish parade of 1867 was certainly an ethnic parade strengthening the cohesion of the small Jewish immigrant group in Chicago. Godfrey Snydacker justly emphasized in his speech that the meeting of most of the Jewish congregations and associations could not have been expected and therefore marked a special event. And yet this Jewish parade was not primarily a demonstration of ethnic difference. The very object of the parade—the construction of the Jewish hospital that was to be open to everybody but financed almost exclusively by Jews—was a powerful statement of civic unity and duty transcending all religious, social, ethnic, and racial boundaries. The directors of Chicago's United Hebrew Relief Association, the Jewish umbrella organization for philanthropy in the city, expressed this vision of unity in the annual report of 1867, praising the donation by the (non-Jewish) male choir *Germania* to the Jewish Hospital:

> They [the non-Jewish and Jewish donors] set thereby an example, most worthy of imitation, of the duty of mankind to work together irrespective of religious creed for the common good, the best means of fighting the prejudices and narrow-mindness of illiberal, shallow brains, not worthy of our age or country.[10]

Greenebaum had also linked this idea of an universal and open society symbolized by the inclusive Jewish hospital in his speech with his arguments against anti-Jewish stereotypes by calling on his Jewish listeners to contribute to non-Jewish charities. This was more than a polite reminder: Jews in Chicago and other American cities invested much time and energy in charitable efforts beyond the confines of the Jewish group.

If there was one German association where Jews were disproportionally active (in relation to other immigrants from Germany) then it was the "Deutsche Gesellschaft" or "German Aid Society," the German philanthropic association for poor and needy immigrants from Germany.[11] Lawyer Julius Rosenthal was the only immigrant (and German-American and American Jew) who belonged to the board of the Chicago Relief and Aid Society in 1871, which was directed by the elite businessmen of the city.[12] Thus the parade and the hospital became important public symbols of Jewish civic engagement for Chicago. They were supposed to strengthen the acceptance of Jews in American society—and at the same time to foster the cohesion of the Jewish community. That Snydacker appealed to the Jewish crowd in German—calling for a stronger community—and that Greenebaum addressed non-Jewish listeners in particular in English to remind them of Jewish civic engagement—and to condemn anti-Jewish stereotypes—served these ends.

The vision of an universal society free of racial hatred and social barriers echoes the theology of the radical Jewish Reform movement and the program of the Jewish fraternal order B'nai B'rith. Both Jewish reformers and B'nai B'rith brethren wanted to open Judaism to the world. They distanced themselves, sometimes vigorously, from the not too distant ghetto and from traditional Judaism. Radical Reform Judaism was hardly recognizable as Judaism for traditional Jewish immigrants from eastern Europe. As early as the 1860s, established Jews in Chicago were embarrassed by Jewish immigrants from Lithuania who (as Orthodox Jews) were visibly Jewish. The Reform movement, which was particularly strong in Chicago, tried to adapt the theology of Judaism to modern society and scientific progress. The essence of Reform Judaism was strongly influenced by the German ideal of *Bildung*, which can be defined as constant spiritual self-education with a strong emphasis on universal principles such as freedom, equality, and openness. The subsequent success of Reform Judaism made (on the Jewish side at least) contacts between Jews and Gentiles easier.[13]

Of course, not all the Jews in Chicago were radical Reformers, and not all Jews came from the same region in Germany. The differences Snydacker alluded to in his speech were real: there were numerous secular associations which had little contact with each other. Bavarian Jews excluded *Ostjuden* from the Prussian province of Posen from their congregation, some Jews were Democrats, others Republicans. And while most were well off, some were poor. A few Jews lived in a small area in the southern part of the Loop, but most were dispersed all over the city—class being more important than ethnicity in choosing a neighborhood. Many Jews were active in the German *Vereine*—Greenebaum, Salomon and others belonged to the ethnic leadership of the Germans in Chicago—and some Jews were active in Czech associations.[14]

During the 1850s, another serious rift had opened when the rise of the German-oriented radical Reform movement split the leading Jewish congregation, Kehilat Anshe Maarab (Men of the West), into two hostile camps. The congregation had been founded in the late 1840s by Jews coming from Franconia and the Palatinate. They excluded Jews from the Prussian province of Posen who in turn organized their own congregation, B'nai Sholom (Sons of Peace).[15] Thus, within a few years, there were already two separate congregations in Chicago, a "German" and a "Polish" congregation. This pattern repeated itself in other cities where Jewish immigrants established congregations according to their regional origins. St. Louis and Milwaukee had by the 1850s "German", "Polish" and even "Bohemian" congregations.[16]

For Jewish immigrants these institutional divisions were a new experience: In Germany all Jews at a given locality belonged, even after the emancipation in 1871, to one Jewish congregation, the so called *Einheitsgemeinde*, which was supervised by the state. Beyond the religious sphere this congregation directed a wide range of social and philanthropic tasks, from providing education to building hospitals. The *Einheitsgemeinde* was *the* given Jewish institution, the center of a Jewish community, defined from the outside.[17] The clear-cut separation of church and state created an altogether different pattern for Jewish life in the United States. Jews could experiment with new forms of community life that were hardly imaginable within the German *Einheitsgemeinden*. Reform Judaism, for instance, was developed in Germany, but Reformers had only limited success there since they had to compromise with more traditionally minded Jews within the *Einheitsgemeinden*. In America, however, Reform Judaism made tremendous progress within a few years.[18]

In Chicago, the arrival of better educated and acculturated Jews from Germany in the early 1850s triggered discussions within the older "Bavarian" congregation about Reforms. The new arrivals clashed with older members who opposed any changes. The Reformers accused the traditionalists of hypocrisy. Reforms, they argued, were an obvious choice because many of the traditionally minded members ignored the strict Jewish laws by not attending the services and keeping their shops open on Saturdays. Soon, serious conflicts rocked the congregation. The outcome of the annual elections of the congregation board reflected the gradually growing influence of the Reform faction. The longtime president, an opponent of Reform had to resign in 1856. His successor, a compromiser who supported modest changes, soon came under intense pressure himself. In 1857, the Reformers managed to elect their candidate into the top position and packed the board with their men. But the heated election of 1857 was not only fought on theological turf. The original president, who continued to oppose any changes, complained in an open letter to the leading Jewish weekly, *American Israelite*: "... our election was not reform but proscription ... ." The Reformers were "a party, ... mostly from Rhinisch Bavaria," the principle of the election for the board was, "... it must be a man from a [*sic*, the] Pfalz."[19] And indeed, most Reformers came from the Palatinate. They were part of a migration network that helped Jews to move from a number of villages west of Worms, through villages and small towns in northern Illinois and Indiana, to Chicago. Most Reformers belonged to this network.

Theological issues were closely intertwined with divisions related to *Landsmannschaft* when it came to the distribution of power within Jewish communities. The power struggle within the congregation, the wooing of congregation members for the campaign of candidates, and regular democratic elections were all new experiences for Jewish immigrants who were used to a traditional religious leadership not democratically elected. Democracy within Jewish congregations and secular associations became an important element of the emerging American-Jewish ethnicity.[20] In 1861 the Constitutional Grand Lodge of the B'nai B'rith abolished its board, the "Council of Skenim," whose members hitherto had been appointed (not elected) for unlimited terms. Rabbi Isaac Mayer Wise and other members, many from Chicago, called for a democratically elected board "believing that a life aristocracy is contrary to the idea of government entertained in this democratic community."[21]

However, even with their man in the presidency, the Chicago reformers could not steer the congregation immediately onto a new course. Their demands for a German-language sermon, mixed seating of the sexes, a choir and an organ, met fierce opposition from the anti-Reform camp, still a powerful minority. In the mid-1850s an attempt to organize an independent Reform congregation had failed, since too few reformers were willing to leave the old congregation which, after all, owned a small synagogue with rooms for a school. The biggest drawback for the reformers was the lack of a clear theological agenda. Eventually, they lured Bernhard Felsenthal, a Jewish theologian from a small congregation in Southern Indiana, to Chicago, providing him with a job in a bank owned jointly by two of the leading reformers. Although Felsenthal also belonged to the network from the Palatinate, he took a different approach to the conflict by developing a thorough theological agenda.

In the religious sphere, Felsenthal was an advocate of Germanization. Germany as a cultural center was important for him because the emergence of modern Judaism and the Reform movement in the first half of the nineteenth century were closely linked with the spiritual revolution, the emergence of critical and rational *Wissenschaft* in Germany. Felsenthal emphasized in 1865:

> We must not distance ourselves from German Judaism and its influences. As in the medieval times the sun of Jewish 'Wissenschaft' was shining on the Spanish sky, this sun is now shining on the German sky sending out its lightrays to all Jews and Jewish communities, which live under the modern cultured peoples. Germany has replaced Sefard.[22]

In 1859 he stressed: "The German people are still the first among the cultured peoples of the world, and we bow our heads in reverence before its spirit, its literature, its language ... We American-German Jews want to keep German in our Synagogues."[23]

For Felsenthal German Reform Judaism had to serve as the model for American Reform Judaism. The "Germanization" of Jewish theology was synonymous with the thorough modernization of Judaism. Felsenthal argued that external Reforms of the service, such as the introduction of an organ, were useless unless Judaism was not redefined as a modern religion consistent with intellectual progress in the sciences and humanities. Judaism was in his conception a progressive religion centered around monotheism. Traditional religious practices that did not convey the essential religious truths were to be abandoned, new elements had to be added, especially a sermon in the German language which would be understood by all congregates. It did not make sense, Felsenthal argued, to introduce copied versions of the Christian service using external reforms or by turning the Jewish service into *Schaugepränge* (a show) with choirs and music. Radical Reform was a matter of spiritual *Bildung* rather than superficial accommodation to the "present age." Felsenthal did not oppose music as such in the service, but the congregates had to be affected in their inner spirit and "religious feelings" rationally rather than emotionally.[24] Another example for *Bildung* is the Sabbath: it was wrong to rush to the service from the store for one hour on Saturday, or not to attend the service at all, Felsenthal declared. But it was also wrong for Jews to obey the talmudical rules without intellectually recognizing the important religious truths behind them. Yes, one could smoke a cigar on the Sabbath, or even better, attend a drama by Schiller, or walk in the park, to listen to a symphony by Beethoven. To educate oneself in this way was better than to obey robot-like hollow laws without recognizing their inner spirit.[25]

It was very characteristic for "radical Reformers" like Felsenthal to question the notion of authority as such, the authority of "holy" texts like the Talmud, that had regulated religious observance and the daily lives of

Jews for centuries, the authority of religious elites, who had controlled religious affairs in the old ghetto, and the authority of the state which had interfered with religious affairs of the Jewish communities. In America there was no state interference in religious affairs and Felsenthal often praised the religious freedom in the United States.

Numerous quotes on the importance of spiritual Germany could be added. But the hymns Felsenthal and other radical Reformers sung to "Germany" can only be understood in their very American context. In the United States (as opposed to Europe), Felsenthal argued convincingly, every individual Jew was "free" to evaluate Judaism and opt for Reforms. The Constitution guaranteed the separation of state and church, there were no old, established religious elites, and religious factions within a congregation could split from each other and form new congregations. Felsenthal called for a split of the congregation to prevent long lasting conflicts. Addressing the reformers, he wrote, "do you want to push them [the traditionalists] out? ... Do you—and I am addressing American Israelites—do you want to dictate consciousnesses of others how they have to praise their Lord? ... Let us not fight each other, we are brothers. Let us separate."[26] The last words read like a paradox, but his arguing for separation illustrates that the call for "Germanization" was American in its very roots. Only in America could Jews split peacefully over religious matters and form their own congregations and remain united as Jews on a higher level, in secular and philanthropic associations. For Felsenthal America was a cultural desert, a land of spiritual superficiality, and he praised Germany on a spiritual and cultural level, but politically, he emphasized, Germany was *elend* (miserable).[27]

In 1861 the Reformers, led now by Felsenthal, split from the Kehilath Anshe Maarab congregation and founded what was to become one of America's leading radical Reform- congregations of the nineteenth century, Sinai Congregation. Some of the measures introduced at Sinai show that the Reformers were inspired by the German model, but that they were American Jews when it came to take the reforms to their logical end. From the beginning mixed seating of men and women was introduced at Sinai. Later, in 1873, Sinai became the first Jewish congregation to introduce Sunday services on a long-term basis. And in the mid-1880s Sinai was one of very few Jewish congregations to abolish Saturday services completely. Leading Jewish Reformers in Germany were alienated by these measures, an indication of the Americanization of German Reform Judaism in America.[28]

Felsenthal became Sinai's first rabbi, but after only three years he left the congregation. The conflict over his pay and contract illustrated that rabbis in America were much weaker than their European colleagues. The power within the congregation rested with the members and the democratically elected board. Several members followed Felsenthal and started a new Reform congregation on Chicago's Westside in 1864. In 1867 there were already five established congregations and at least two proto-congregations, separated by religious and "Landsmannschaft"-related differences.[29] After the long struggle of the 1850s there was little doubt that there was no basis for a Jewish community in Chicago within the religious sphere. It is hardly surprising, then, that the parade in 1867 was led not by a rabbi, but by prominent and successful businessmen.

Organized Jewish communities did not exist in America. Jews had to define a community on their own and obviously, divisive issues such as religion and "Landsmannschaft" were "off limits" within an organized community. The founding of B'nai B'rith, the most prominent Jewish fraternal order, in 1841 was an early response to the new diversity of Jewish life in America. B'nai B'rith leaders called for a new union of Jews from all over Europe in the new "homeland." The most promising way to achieve this union was to promote social justice *(tzedakah)*, one of the fundamental principles of Judaism. *Tzedakah* obliges every pious Jew to care for every distressed person irrespective of his or her creed. It is hardly surprising that in Chicago B'nai B'rith leaders such as Henry Greenebaum were the leading promoters of a strong Jewish community and of *tzedakah*.[30]

Thus the theme of unity and difference played an important role for Chicago's Jews in 1867. The parade and the *Festreden* (orations) highlight the attempt of Jewish leaders to foster a collective identity and to build a community centered around *tzedakah*—in order to unite the participating Jews of diverse backgrounds and, at the same time, to demonstrate to Chicagoans that Jews were not a marginal group but rather a civic-minded and patriotic Jewish community who contributed to the city's well-being. *Tzedakah* was the most important but not the only force uniting Chicago's Jews. Closely connected with *tzedakah* were patriotism and the threat of anti-Jewish stereotypes. Communal charity was primarily an inter-Jewish affair, although, particularly when the hospital project developed, Jews began to reach out to other charities. Patriotic acts or speeches were to prove to the public that Jews were not "foreigners" but Americans who owed their freedom and success to the United States and that they would defend the principles America stood for. Anti-Jewish stereotypes were beyond the control of Jews in Chicago. Yet the promotion of welfare and patriotic statements or festivities served as effective counterforces against anti-Jewish agitation, attitudes, and statements.

Partly to refute anti-Jewish attacks but primarily driven by a strong sense of obligation toward their new home country where Jews enjoyed full civil equality (still denied to Jewish subjects in the German states), Chicago's

Jews met for the first time as a group during the Civil War in August 1862—more than twenty years after the first Jews had settled in Chicago. All differences were put aside for the time being and an all-Jewish company was raised. This patriotic act earned Chicago's Jews much praise in Chicago and beyond the city's limits, because the company's soldiers fought bravely in the Civil War, and some returned as highly decorated officers. This would not even have been imaginable in Germany at the time. Among the Union troops, only one other all-Jewish company was organized—in Syracuse, New York.[31]

These meetings were the first sign of an ethnicization of Jewish immigrants in Chicago. Although Jewish leaders insisted that Judaism constituted only a religion, the serious religious differences had to be postponed, in order to attract most Jews to the war meetings. All speeches at the war meetings were given in German and the Jewish company became part of the 82nd Illinois Volunteer Regiment, led by the famous Forty-eighter Friedrich Hecker who, together with other German ethnic leaders, was present at the meetings. Among them was Lorenz Brentano, another famous Forty-eighter, who edited Chicago's leading German-language paper, the *Illinois Staatszeitung*. Before the revolution of 1848, Hecker and Brentano had been the leading promoters of Jewish emancipation in the southern German Duchy of Baden. In his speech during the last meeting, Hecker recalled this struggle for the emancipation of Jews and stressed the need to emancipate the black slaves in the Confederate States. Political refugees from Germany and Jewish immigrants had found freedom in the United States, therefore they were obliged, Hecker emphasized, to fight together for the emancipation of blacks in the South.[32]

And yet, although Chicago's Jews were closely involved with other immigrants from Germany, they began to form a separate ethnic group. Jewish leaders insisted that they owed their freedom to America since most Jews in the German states (not to mention eastern Europe) were still not emancipated in the 1860s. This distinguished them from other (non-Jewish) immigrants who had had citizens' rights in their home countries. Among the many non-Jewish immigrants from Germany only the few but influential Forty-eighters were in a comparable situation. After the failed revolution of 1848-49 they had sought and found political asylum in the United States. Therefore, Forty-eighters such as Friedrich Hecker and Brentano could act as middlemen during the meetings recruiting the Jewish company for the German regiment. The swift and successful organization of the Jewish meetings impressed leading Germans in Chicago. Forty-eighter Wilhelm Rapp declared that "the Germans of Chicago should follow the example of Jewish men and women in Chicago, who had found strength in unity."[33] Rapp's words indicate that there was no strong and organized German community in Chicago, not even during the war.

Chicago's Jews went to war to defend rights of themselves and others to equal citizenship of a free and democratic republic. This is illustrated by one of the most impressive sources on Chicago Jewish history, five sermons that Rabbi Liebman Adler gave to the congregation Kehilat Anshe Maarab in the spring of 1865. Adler reminded the members of his congregation that the success story of American Jewry presented a new chapter in the long and often unhappy history of the Jewish diaspora. But he warned his listeners not to take wealth and happiness for granted. The rights that American citizens enjoyed entailed the duty to defend and protect them. Adler praised the American republic and democracy by comparing it with the European monarchies where Jews did not enjoy civil equality.[34] The Jews of Chicago may have spoken German in their service, they were inspired by the Jewish Reform movement in Germany and by Germany on a cultural level, but they emphasized from the early beginning that they were free Americans and that they were proud of it. On the occasion of Lincoln's second inauguration, Adler declared: "Thank you, o God, for saving this free land. ... Do you, o you people, want to love a country and do what you can to support it with all available means, when this country gives you such an unlimited degree of power?"[35] Adler addressed not the Jewish people in this paragraph, but rather he addressed the American people. The persecution of Jews in Germany and Eastern Europe and their special duty to defend the freedom of America were not an issue in these sermons; Adler spoke as an American to Americans, and he praised the democratic republic of the United States while condemning the monarchies of Europe.

The organization of the Jewish company during the Civil War illustrates that the processes of assimilation, ethnicization and community-building were closely related with each other. The war effort provided an opportunity for Jews to bridge all differences, to unify Jews as a group, but it also served as a means of bringing different immigrant groups together in the Union Army to fight for their adopted country.

With the war over, however, and with the immediate threat of anti-Jewish agitation gone, all hopes for Jewish unity rested on an institution that had been founded in 1859 to coordinate the work of the different Jewish philanthropic societies in the city, the United Hebrew Relief Association (UHRA). To rally around communal charity was attractive for most Jews in Chicago, especially since patriotism and the fear of anti-Jewish stereotypes were not powerful enough to sustain a communal "Gemeinschaft" in the long run. The UHRA had grown out of a network of collective insurance societies. Most Jewish congregations and other associations became institutional members of UHRA and sent representatives to its annual meeting. The UHRA quickly became the center of the loose institutional Jewish network in Chicago. Other ethnic groups, notably the Germans, Poles, and Swedes formed similar institutions, but they either collapsed after a few years or never played a role comparable to the UHRA with its unique organizational structure bringing all Jewish associations and congregations in constant contact with each other.[36] Jewish communities were built around centralized philanthropic societies all over the United States, sometimes successfully as in Chicago and Boston, sometimes rather late and with limited success as in Detroit. The large impact communal welfare had on Jewish community building, rooted in the Jewish tradition, had been reinforced in the European ghettos where Jews were forced by the authorities to take care of their own poor. After the emancipation, Jews in Europe kept their philanthropic networks to preserve the tradition and strengthen Jewish "Gemeinschaft" but also to counter anti-Jewish stereotypes and to win a higher degree of acceptance in the larger society.[37]

Patriotism had brought Chicago's Jews (and other immigrants such as the Swedes, the Irish, and the Germans) together in 1861-62, and as the prominent role of Civil War General Edward Salomon as "Festmarschall" of the Jewish parade shows, it was an important part of their ethnic identity. Ethnic leaders emphasized especially two aspects of what patriotism meant to them as Jews: in the United States Jews enjoyed full civil equality and the government did not interfere with religious affairs as in the German states—even after full emancipation in 1871.[38]

Anti-Jewish stereotypes were rampant in the public discourse in the 1850s and especially during the Civil War, but in Chicago and other Western cities, everybody was a newcomer. Jews were accepted early on in the political and gradually in the economic spheres as equals, and were rarely used as scapegoats for the costs connected with the rapid transformation of the United States to an urban industrial society. Only the upper classes excluded Jews, to some extent, but in the late 1860s even here the social barriers began to erode—at least on an official level. In 1867, several of Chicago's elite businessmen joined their Jewish colleagues in a boycott of a number of New York-based insurance companies which discriminated against Jews. This act of solidarity created a lot of publicity and, even more importantly, trust between Jews and non-Jews, which helps to explain why Greenebaum could address the touchy subject of anti-Jewish stereotypes in his public speech.[39]

Reformers and Orthodox Jews, even members of secular Jewish associations, could accept *tzedakah* as a central element of their Jewishness. Active charity work reinforced a feeling of "belonging together" among the

Jews active in such work and with the Jewish poor, thus continuously recreating Jewish "Gemeinschaft." The Jewish activities on behalf of the public good guided by the principle of *tzedakah* was also a rebuttal of hostile images of Jews as "Shylocks," acting only in their own interest. And finally, *tzedakah* demanded organization, and—in the face of rapid growth and technological change—modernization. The Jewish hospital of Chicago offered the latest technological standard available, as Jewish leaders repeatedly stressed. Chicago's Jews therefore rivaled the Jews of other cities (and other ethnic groups in Chicago) who had not yet produced such a monument of public virtue.

In the long run *tzedakah* and thus the UHRA became the focal point of the organized Jewish community in Chicago. In 1874 Rabbi Liebman Adler addressed the Jews of Chicago:

> Scarce two decades have elapsed since all the Israelites of this city were living as in the bonds of one family circle. Each knew the other. All worshipped harmoniously in one temple and shared others' woes and joys. How great is the change! Thousands scattered over a space of thirty miles, in hundreds of streets, divided by pecuniary, intellectual and social distinctions and differences. Separation, division, dissolution, estrangement, repeated and continual, are the words which characterize the history of our brothers in faith until now. Dissolved in the mass of our population, we are losing the consciousness of homogeneity and the strength gained for each by concerted action. Praise upon you: The U.H.R.A.! You provided Chicago's Israelites with a common platform. Here come our Israelites through their representatives together.[40]

The construction of ethnic "Gemeinschaft" in America was hardly limited to the Jews of Chicago. Ethnic leaders of other immigrant groups with diverse backgrounds, notably German Americans, developed comparable rituals to foster a sense of belonging. The Jewish parade, however, highlights the intention of Jewish leaders to foster Jewish "Gemeinschaft" and, at the same time, civic "Gemeinschaft" transcending all religious, ethnic, and social barriers, thus showing how closely the themes of difference and unity were intertwined. The Jewish parade was a significant stepping-stone on this path because it was visibly displayed in the urban public space. All Chicago papers reported extensively and very positively on the Jewish effort for Chicago at large. *Tzedakah* thus had a double function: it strengthened the cohesion of the Jewish community and, at the same time, of the urban society. Mary Ryan's argument thus needs to be refined by paying closer attention to the subtext of ethnic parades. Although these parades were important demonstrations of ethnicization, their function for the ethnic community in relation to the community at large cannot be ignored. Immigrants were not only making themselves visible and heard in the urban public, they were also striving for acceptance and inclusion into the larger community. The themes of difference and unity cannot be separated, and the Jewish parade of 1867 proves that difference could in fact strengthen unity in the city.

Notes

1. Little research has been done on Jewish immigrants from the German states and Eastern Europe who arrived before the surge of Jewish immigration from Eastern Europe in the 1880s. Hardly any of the few works on American Jewish history covering the period before 1881 have included the analysis of German-language sources. Useful general studies are: Avraham Barkai, *Branching Out: German-Jewish Immigration to the United States 1820-1914* (New York: Holmes and Meier, 1994); Hasia Diner, *A Time for Gathering: The Second Migration 1820-1880* (Baltimore: Johns Hopkins University Press, 1992). Stanley Nadel is one of the few authors on the subject of German migration to the United States who looks at Jewish participation in German-American community life before 1880. See Stanley Nadel, *Little Germany: Ethnicity, Religion and Class in New York City 1845-80* (Urbana, Chicago: University of Illinois Press, 1990).
2. The so-called Chevra Kadisha (burial societies) have a long tradition in Judaism. Maximilian Gerstley, one of the first Jews who settled in Chicago in the 1840s, remembered in 1877 the origins of Jewish life in Chicago: "The first necessity which impressed itself on their [the early Jewish settlers'] minds—however limited their number—was the propriety—agreeable to a long cherished custom practiced amongst Jewish communities—of providing a place of burial ... " (M. M. Gerstley, Preface to the list of burials at the cemetery of Kehilat Anshe Mayriv (20 April 1877, manuscript [Chicago Jewish Archives, Kehilath Anshe Maarab-file]).
3. It is not possible in this article to describe the larger context of the complex and intertwined processes of assimilation, ethnicization, and class-formation in Chicago for the 1860s along the lines of David Gerber's important study on Buffalo. David Gerber, *The Making of an American Pluralism: Buffalo, New York 1825—60* (Urbana, IL: University of Illinois Press, 1989). For statistics on immigration to Chicago see Thomas L. Philpott, *The Slum and the Ghetto: Neighborhood Deterioration and Middle-Class Reform, Chicago, 1880-1930* (New York: Oxford University Press, 1978) 7-8.
4. For the estimate of three thousand compare: *Sinai*, Sept. 1862, 232. The *Sinai* was a German-language monthly on Jewish theological issues published between the mid-1850s and 1860s by Rabbi David Einhorn, a prominent leader of the Jewish Reform movement in Germany and (after 1855) in the United States. Bernhard Felsenthal, "A Contribution to the History of the Israelites in Chicago," manuscript 1863, Col. Felsenthal, Bernhard. Box 130, Chicago Historical Society.
5. *Illinois Staatszeitung*, September 4, 1867; hereafter *ISZ*. See also: *Allgemeine Zeitung des Judenthums*, October 15, 1867. *American Israelite* (Cincinnati), September 13, 1867.
6. Ryan's thesis is strongly influenced by Jürgen Habermas' book on the transformation of the public sphere which was only translated into English in 1989. Mary Ryan, "The American Parade: Representations of the Nineteenth-century Social Order," in *The New*

Cultural History, ed. Lynn Hunt (Los Angeles and Berkeley: University of California Press, 1989), 131-153. The general argument is developed in Mary Ryan, *Civic Wars: Democracy and Public Life in the American City during the Nineteenth Century* (Berkeley and Los Angeles: University of California Press, 1997). See also Jürgen Habermas, *The Structural Transformation of the Public Sphere*, transl. by Thomas Berger (Cambridge: MIT Press, 1989).

7. Kathleen Conzen, "Ethnicity as Festive Culture: Nineteenth-Century German America on Parade," in *Invention of Ethnicity*, ed. Werner Sollors (New York, Oxford: Oxford University Press, 1989), 44-76.
8. *ISZ*, July 4, 1862.
9. *ISZ*, January 31, March 3, May 26, 1871. Eugen Seeger, *Chicago: Die Geschichte einer Wunderstadt* (Chicago: privately published, 1892), 131-32. Hartmut Keil, Introduction, in *Deutsche Arbeiterkultur in Chicago von 1850 bis zum Ersten Weltkrieg: Eine Anthologie*, ed. Hartmut Keil (Ostfildern: Scripta Mercaturae Verlag, 1984), 6.
10. *Eighth Annual Report of the United Hebrew Relief Association of Chicago* (Chicago: Illinois Staatszeitung, 1867).
11. Article taken from *Der Westen* (Sunday edition of the ISZ), November 1909 (day not known), in Folder 129, German Aid Society, Historical Collections, Library of the University of Illinois at Chicago. Obituary of Julius Rosenthal, *Chicago Legal News*, May 21, 1905. Emil Dietzsch, *Chicago's deutsche Männer* (Chicago: privately published, 1885), 36, 129, 193. *Cooke's City Directory for Chicago, 1859-60* (Chicago, 1860). Julius Rosenthal was president of the German Aid Society in 1860, compare *D. B. Cooke & Co's Chicago City Directory for the Year 1860-61* (Chicago, 1860). See also for the names of known Jewish families in all annual reports of the German Aid Society before 1900; see for example *Fünfundzwanzigster Jahresbericht der Deutschen Gesellschaft von Chicago, Illinois—1878/79* (Chicago, 1879).
12. Kathleen D. McCarthy, *Noblesse Oblige: Charity & Cultural Philanthropy in Chicago, 1849-1929* (Chicago: University of Chicago Press, 1982), 66. Other board members were elite businessmen such as George Pullman.
13. This aspect is a central topic of my dissertation, titled "'We American-German Jews': Jewish Immigrants in Chicago 1840-1900—Acculturation, Ethnicization, and Community-Building" which will be published in German in 2000. While the general history of the Reform movement has been covered, particularly by Michael Meyer, see especially his *Response to Modernity: A History of the Reform Movement in Judaism* (New York and Oxford: Oxford University Press, 1988), the history of the large Jewish fraternal order B'nai B'rith remains largely unwritten. I cover its history in Chicago in my dissertation. For an introduction see Deborah Dash Moore, *B'nai B'rith and the Challenge of Ethnic Leadership* (Albany, NY: SUNY Press, 1981). Cornelia Wilhelm, a German scholar, is currently working on a larger study of the B'nai B'rith.
14. For an overview see Hyman L. Meites, *History of the Jews of Chicago* (Chicago: Jewish Historical Society of Illinois, 1924), 47-118. For Jewish involvement with Czech immigrants see the memoirs of the longtime president of the B'nai B'rith Adolf Kraus, *Reminiscences and Comments, the Immigrant, the Citizen, a Public Office, the Jew* (Chicago: Rubovits, 1925).
15. Meites, *History of the Jews of Chicago*, 53. Posen was one of the most important sources of Jewish immigration to North America before 1880. On Jewish emigrants from Posen see Cornelia Östreich, *"Des rauhen Winters ungeachtet ...": Die Auswanderung Posener Juden nach Amerika im 19. Jahrhundert* (Hamburg: Dölling und Gallitz Verlag, 1997). Unfortunately, Östreich concentrates on the causes of emigration and does not look at the migration of Jews from Posen within the United States.

16. On St Louis: Walter Ehrlich, *Zion in the Valley: The Jewish Community of St. Louis* (Columbia, MO: University of Missouri Press, 1997), 63-64, 89-90. *The Occident*, June 1852, 136. The monthly *Occident*, edited by Philadelphia Rabbi Isaac Leeser (who was born in Neuenkirchen, Westphalia), was America's first national Jewish newspaper. On Milwaukee: Kathleen Conzen, *Immigrant Milwaukee: Accommodation and Community in a Frontier City* (Cambridge: Harvard University Press, 1976), 167.
17. For a recent comparative analysis of the Jewish "Gemeinde" in Germany and in England see Rainer Liedtke, "Jewish Welfare in Hamburg and Manchester, c. 1850-1914," Ph.D. diss., Oxford University, 1995.
18. For this see especially Meyer, *Response to Modernity*.
19. *American Israelite*, October 16, 1857.
20. These developments are covered extensively in my dissertation.
21. *Report of the Annual Meeting of the District Grand Lodge No. 2 Independent Order B'nai B'rith* (Philadelphia, 1863), 25.
22. Bernhard Felsenthal, *Jüdisches Schulwesen in Amerika: Ein Vortrag gehalten am 13. Dezember 1865 in der 'Ramah-Loge' zu Chicago von Bernhard Felsenthal Prediger der Zionsgemeinde daselbst* (Chicago: Albert Heunisch, 1866), 37. Original German version: "Wehe uns, wenn wir jetzt von deutschem Judenthum und seinen Einflüssen uns frei machen würden! Wie im Mittelalter die Sonne jüdischer Wissenschaft erhaben und herrlich in Spanien leuchtete, ..., so steht nun diese Sonne am deutschen Himmel und sendet von da aus ihr wohlthätiges Licht zu allen Juden und jüdischen Gemeinschaften, die unter den modernen Culturvölkern zu finden sind. Deutschland ist an die Stelle Sefard's getreten."
23. Bernhard Felsenthal, *Kol Kore Bamidbar. Ueber jüdische Reform. Ein Wort an die Freunde derselben* (Chicago: Chas. Heß, 1859), 25. Original German version: "Das deutsche Volk ist immer noch das erste Kulturvolk der Welt und wir beugen uns mit Ehrfurcht vor seinem Geiste, seiner Literatur, seiner Sprache ... Wir amerikanisch-deutsche Juden wollen daher das Deutsche in unseren Synagogen beibehalten haben."
24. Ibid., 19-20. David Einhorn, "Felsenthal's Kol Kore Bamidbar," in *Sinai*, May 1859, 115. *American Israelite*, September 30, 1859.
25. Felsenthal, *Kol Kore Bamidbar*, 22-23.
26. Ibid., 14. Original German version: "Wollt ihr sie [die Reformgegner] hinaustreiben? [...] Wollt ihr – wir reden zu amerikanischen Israeliten – wollt ihr den Gewissen Anderer dictieren, wie sie ihren Gott verehren sollen? [...] Lasset keinen Streit sein zwischen uns, wir sind ja Brüder! Trennen wir uns."
27. Ibid., 25.
28. Ibid., 26. The history of the Sinai congregation is treated in my dissertation. On the alienation of German reformers (notably Abraham Geiger): Michael Meyer, "German-Jewish Identity in Nineteenth-Century America," in *Toward Modernity: The European Jewish Model*, ed. Jacob Katz (New Brunswick, NJ: Rutgers University Press, 1987), 259-61.
29. One important work, that covers the origins of Chicago's first Reform congregation is Bernhard Felsenthal, *The Beginnings of the Chicago Sinai Congregation: A Contribution to the Inner History of American Judaism* (Chicago: Sinai Congregation, 1898). For a general treatment see especially Meyer, "German-Jewish Identity in Nineteenth-Century America," 247-67.
30. *Constitution des Unabhängigen Ordens B'nai B'rith—Constitution of the Independent Order B'nai B'rith* (New York, 1851). *First Annual Report of the District Grand Lodge No. 6 Independent Order B'nai B'rith and Constitution and By-Laws and Rules* (Chicago, 1869), 8-10.

31. *Sinai*, September 1862, 231-33. On Syracuse: Bertram Korn, *American Jewry and the Civil War* (Philadelphia: Jewish Publication Society, 1951), 117-18.
32. *ISZ*, August 15, 1862. *Sinai*, September 1862, 231-33 (Hecker's speech). *Allgemeine Zeitung für das Judenthum*, October 7, 1862. Alfred Theodore Andreas, *History of Chicago* (Chicago: A. T. Andreas and Co., 1884-86) 2: 231-33.
33. *ISZ*, August 20, 1862.
34. Liebmann Adler, *Fünf Reden: Gehalten in der Israelitischen Gemeinde Kehilas Anshe Maarab hierselbst an wichtigen nationalen Gedenktagen der Ver. Staaten* (Chicago: Illinois Staatszeitung, 1866).
35. Adler, *Fünf Reden*, 6. Original German version: "Dank dir, o Gott, für die Rettung dieses freien Landes vor dem Untergang. ... Willst du, o Volk, nicht ein Land lieben, für dessen Erhaltung Alles einsetzen, in dem du so viel gilst? in dem du mit einer so unbegränzten [sic] Macht bekleidet bist?"
36. For this aspect the annual reports of the UHRA are the main source, see especially *First Annual Report of the UHRA* (Chicago, 1860). For the other ethnic charity-organizations mentioned see Bessie Louise Pierce, *A History of Chicago* (New York: Knopf, 1937, 1940, 1957), 2: 20-23. Ibid., 3: 30.
37. Jews in Boston set up an institution comparable to Chicago's UHRA in 1864; Susan Ebert, "Community and Philanthropy," in *The Jews of Boston*, ed. Jonathan Sarna and Ellen Smith (Boston: Northeastern University Press, 1995), 211-37. Detroit's Jews only did so in 1899—with limited success; Robert Rockaway, "Ethnic Conflict in an Urban Environment: The German and the Russian Jew in Detroit, 1881-1914," *American Jewish Historical Quarterly* 60 (1970/71): 133-50. For the tradition of Jewish welfare and its impact on Jewish communities in Germany and England see Liedtke, "Jewish Welfare in Hamburg and Manchester."
38. For this argument see especially Adler, *Fünf Reden*.
39. On the insurance boycott see: *Chicago Tribune*, April 12, 1867. For a general treatment see Frederic Cople Jaher, *Scapegoat in the New Wilderness: The Origins and the Rise of Anti-Semitism in America* (Cambridge: Harvard University Press, 1994).
40. Executive Board of the United Hebrew Relief Society of Chicago, ed., *15th Annual Report to the Delegates of the UHRA for the Year 1873-1874* (Chicago: Max Stern, 1874). Adler's speech was printed in (the original) German and an English translation.

Chapter 9

DEMONSTRATING THE VALUES OF 'GEMÜTHLICHKEIT' AND 'CULTUR'

The Festivals of German Americans in Milwaukee, 1870-1910

Heike Bungert

"THIS AFFAIR IS nothing less than a social gathering ... where lager is drunk ad infinitum and tobacco smoked ad nauseam, while songs are sung and comic performances indulged in from an impromptu stage."[1] Such was the image many contemporaries had of celebrations organized by German immigrants in the United States. Obviously, this is not all there was to the phenomenon of German-American festivities.

Festivals[2] are an important subject for study, since their staged symbols,[3] myths,[4] and rituals[5] reflect the mentality of specific, often otherwise inarticulate groups.[6] As forms of collective representation and regeneration[7] or cultural memory,[8] festivals reveal expectations and wishful thoughts, as well as collective fears. Being dense forms of communication, celebrations have polyvalent meaning.[9] All researchers agree that festivals, as a necessary temporary release from everyday life,[10] build up a sense of community and give meaning to life.[11] Celebrations, Eric Hobsbawm has shown, are essential as "invented traditions."[12] They are particularly important for transplanted people, as Geneviève Fabre has noted.[13] They connect the individual with

---

Notes for this section begin on page 185.

the group, the past with the future.[14] Whether one views celebrations as an orderly tranquil affirmation of the existing order,[15] or as a regenerative excess and escape from reality,[16] or, what seems most appropriate, as a mixture of both,[17] they mirror, on the one hand, the existing social structure and, on the other hand, contribute to the formation of social, political, and cultural conditions.[18]

With the increased interest in cultural history, festivals have become a popular subject of study. Whereas historians—as compared to sociologists and anthropologists—are latecomers in this field, some work has already been done on national and regional festivities in nineteenth century Germany,[19] on festivals during the American Revolution and the early American republic,[20] and on American pageantry.[21] Yet, apart from an excellent essay by Kathleen Conzen,[22] there is no literature on the intersecting point between both nationalities, on the festive culture of German Americans.

Taking Milwaukee as a case in point and looking at four festivals spaced over a period of thirty years, the present article seeks to answer the following questions.[23] How did German Americans view themselves and their past? Which perception of the United States do the celebrations reveal? What values were emphasized in the discourse on German contributions to the emerging American national character? How did a sense of common ethnicity[24] develop among immigrants with diverse regional origins? How did the festivals change over time?

For a long time, Milwaukee, called the "German Athens," was considered the most German of all American towns. Settlement began in the 1830s, and Milwaukee received its first city charter in 1846. After the failed European revolution of 1848, Germans poured into the city. Other settlers came from the Northeastern United States, England, and Ireland; from the 1880s onwards, they were joined by Poles and Italians. The Germans, though, until the late 1890s represented more than a third of the total population.[25] Even in 1910, three quarters of the population were of foreign white stock, 53.5 percent of Teutonic background.[26]

Milwaukee was to be the backdrop of four big festivals. In 1871, German Americans all over the United States rejoiced over the German victory in the Franco-Prussian War. They organized huge celebrations that put German-American festivals of the 1840s and 1850s on a new plane. Being able to draw on the strength of a newly unified Germany, the immigrants for the first time consciously used social symbols—or in Pierre Bourdieu's words symbolic capital—to put an end to their being derided as "Dutchmen."[27] At the same time, they endeavored to use the festivities to bind together the local German-American community and to instill self-respect in it.[28] Before, different associations had participated in each other's celebrations; also, singers and gymnasts had staged national festivals. Yet the German peace jubilee was on a different scale: English-language newspapers across the country admitted that this was one of the biggest parades they had ever witnessed.[29]

The official celebration in Milwaukee took place on Whitmonday, May 29, 1871. A uniform celebration all across the United States had been prevented by weather conditions.[30] On Saturday, a rather tedious festival play and the reading of a congratulatory address to the German parliament opened the celebration.[31] On Whitsunday, only two private picnics were held to avoid offending Puritan America. On the following day, more than 100,000 people from all walks of life and all trades, including many Anglo-Americans, crammed the streets to make the jubilee into a real popular festival *(Volksfest)*. Many businesses closed, stores, taverns and private residences were amply decorated, and municipal authorities officially recognized the German festival by greeting the day with cannon fire and by riding in the parade. Only women were excluded: they were barred from marching in the procession but were celebrated in speeches and images as republican mothers of valiant sons and as faithful brides tending to hearth and home while waiting for the return of the successful soldiers. They were also asked to decorate the windows of their homes.[32]

The main event of the day, the procession, strung out for six miles[33] and consisted of 170 wagons in six divisions, each preceded by a musical band to mark the requisition of public space[34] not only visibly but also audibly. The very precise movement of these bands was noted as a German characteristic. Militia companies, including German Civil War veterans, gymnastic clubs, and sharpshooters were followed by fraternal orders, singing societies, mutual benefit associations, and church clubs. In a manner reminiscent of the Federal Processions of 1787-88 and of early modern guild processions in Germany,[35] German artisans demonstrated their skills and distributed their produce: the butchers roasted an oxen; the printers made copies of the patriotic German songs "Watch on the Rhine", "What is the German's Fatherland?" as well as of a festive song composed by themselves; the locksmiths proudly produced the key to unity. The artisans were followed by floats of firms in related trades that had made Milwaukee famous, such as breweries, machine shops, and corn mills: among them could be seen even a few Anglo-Americans businesses, who participated for advertising reasons.[36] The parade also included some topical floats; their semi-fictitious or invented symbols[37] were to become staple fare for German-American festivities in decades to come: the Kyffhäuser mountain with King Barbarossa; the Watch on the Rhine; Germania; Arminius the Cheruskean; Gambrinus, the king of beer; and finally, particular to the 1871 celebration, twenty-five white-clad "virgins" representing the twenty-five German states. Values stressed as typically German—as in many festivals to come—were loyalty (*Treue*), both to the old and the new home country, discipline, industry, German customs, culture, and German intellectual and cultural achievements (*der deutsche Geist*). After the parade, emotional orators delivered patriotic speeches that enlarged upon the triple purpose of the celebration: to evince sympathy with the German Empire, to demonstrate strength vis-à-vis other national groups in the United States, and to achieve unity among the German Americans.[38]

The plea for unity was a leitmotif of the celebration, thus revealing the actual lack of ethnic identity. Speakers stressed the parallelism between the strength Germany had gained by unification and the potential power German Americans might attain if they declared union among the German-American community to be their historic mission in America.[39] The second striking feature of the celebration was the frequent use of martial and nationalistic vocabulary. Former revolutionary Friedrich Hecker sent a letter extolling Germany as the most powerful country in Europe. Even the formerly socialistic gymnasts talked about having squashed the French enemy by iron force, and the Catholic *Seebote* proclaimed: "The highest good is the sword!"[40] Banners advised of the necessity to redeem the Germans yet outside the new empire. Only a handful of critical voices could be heard: with most of the former forty-eighters and freethinkers among the gymnasts wishfully stating that unity was the immediate precursor of freedom,[41] it fell to the predominantly working-class South Side gymnasts to carry a banner: "Break the despotic yoke; liberty is still missing."[42] As to its outreaching effect, the peace jubilee of 1871 was considered quite successful. It "forced Anglo-Americans to take cognizance" of the increased political weight of the German Empire and of the importance of German Americans as an ethnic group.[43]

The appeals to unity in 1871, however, did not bear fruit. Twelve years later, parts of the German-American press and the North American Gymnastic Union attempted to motivate German communities outside of Philadelphia to celebrate an event that seemed to be a natural rallying point for all German Americans: the two hundredth anniversary of the first German settlement in the United States.[44] Only after constant prodding by the *Milwaukee Freie Presse* did the Swabian mutual benefit society on September 12 publish a call for a bicentennial celebration on October 7.[45] While the German-American press in general did not report extensively on the festival, attendance seems to have been satisfactory. The German clubs managed to set up a parade of reportedly five thousand marchers. In contrast to 1871, the parade contained an entire division of Catholic societies who apparently felt more at ease celebrating German-American history than the German Empire. Once again, some businessmen used the parade for advertising purposes, which was frowned upon by the English-language newspapers. The historical scenes depicted on floats were chosen rather randomly and incoherently, probably due to the lack of time to prepare. Thus, George Washington with the two German generals DeKalb and Steuben strangely preceded the ship Concord with the first German immigrants of 1683.[46] Afterwards, the Germans celebrated informally in parks. In the evening, they met for poems, singing, and tableaux vivants.[47]

The festival focused on three motifs: unity of the immigrant community, pride in their achievements, and their specific German-American identity. All three themes, nevertheless, were idealized concepts rather than reality. They were used by established upper middle class German Americans to forge a common bond connecting the new massive immigration from Germany, which was mainly economically motivated, with the older group of emigrés that had left Germany mostly for political reasons.

Unity evidently had not yet been forged within the past twelve years. The press and German-American organizations constantly had to admonish their compatriots to forget differences of religion, politics, and social standing and some associations declared their participation but one day before the festival.[48] In the parade, no trade associations and only few mutual benefit associations and members of the Knights of Labor participated, while several of the historical floats depicted local or individual rather than German-American symbols; thus, a float with the founder of Württemberg, The Swabian duke Eberhard im Bart, seemed slightly out of place." The admission fee for the afternoon's "popular fest" and the evening's official celebration largely barred low-income Germans from attending, leading to vociferous complaints and preventing unity across class lines.[49] Furthermore, the freethinkers and gymnasts were somewhat reluctant to celebrate before all of their ideals had been firmly established in the American republic. Finally, despite several admonitions by the press and the festival committee, the majority of Milwaukee's Germans did not decorate their houses for the occasion, thus disclosing their lack of interest in the bicentennial.[50]

The nationwide celebration was also intended to boost the immigrants' self-confidence. Thus, the organizers demanded that German-American achievements be recognized in United States history books. By making their fellow Germans aware of the contributions of "German America" to the development of the American nation, the self-proclaimed spokesmen of the immigrants wanted their compatriots to stand up to Anglo-Americans, to maintain their native language, and to pass on German traditions and culture to their children. But again, the constant repetition of German-American achievements indicates that self-confidence among the German immigrants was still lacking.[51]

Finally, the festival was intended to establish the German immigrants' right to an identity of their own. The specific German-American ethnicity was illustrated in a simile that would recur time and again while Germany was the immigrants' mother, the United States was their bride.[52] Proud of their heritage, the organizers emphasized the courage, diligence, and perseverance of the German pioneers, their love of freedom and struggle against slavery and oppression, their contributions to culture, music, and science, and, lastly, their sociability, heartfelt emotions *(Gemüt),* and aestheticism as a corrective to crass American materialism.[53] Yet, the festival organizers had to tread carefully. Continually stressing their patriotism and loyalty to the United States, they voted against inviting the German consul.[54] The propaganda directed at native-born Americans, however, did not accomplish its goal. While the mayor in his speech praised the quick assimilation of the immigrants, Milwaukee's English-language press demanded a final end to German "clannishness."[55]

Ten years later, the immigrants had grown more self-confident. This was particularly true for the subgroup of German-American gymnasts in Milwaukee, who organized the twenty-second national festival of the North American Gymnastic Union in Milwaukee in July 1893.[56] The Union, formed in 1850, worked for social and political reforms, intellectual and political liberty, and the conservation of German mores and virtues.[57] It held national festivals every two or four years. The growth of the movement as well as the attraction of German-American festivals were demonstrated when more gymnasts than ever before attended the celebration in Milwaukee.[58] Two big processions and smaller bands of gymnasts parading through town with musical instruments throughout the festival assured that Milwaukee's population stayed aware of the ongoing celebration.[59]

The two parades as well as the gymnasts' mass exercises were to demonstrate the virtues the gymnast, or *Turner,* movement had brought to the United States: unity, equality, manliness, and discipline. The competitions between individual gymnasts and gymnastic clubs in the eyes of both German and American observers in addition proved the dexterity, athleticism, endurance, and team spirit of the active gymnasts making them ideal soldiers for the American republic. In their banners, floats, and performances, the gymnasts showed their attachment to their country of immigration but also their pride in their achievements and their place of origin thus underlining their pride in their dual identity. [60]

Although Milwaukee's English-speaking population was conspicuously absent from the festival,[61] the English-language press devoted considerable space to the celebration and public officials greeted the gymnasts whose role in boosting Milwaukee's economy was clearly recognized.[62] An afternoon gymnastic performance by three thousand boys and girls from Milwaukee's public schools, a novel feature in a gymnastic festival, demonstrated the inclusion of German gymnastic ideals into the American curriculum.[63]

For the gymnasts themselves, the festival also served to renew their impetus to strive for their goals. During the social get-togethers, the gymnasts played pranks and performed funny carnivalesque parades,[64] i.e. indulged in the excessive elements necessary for celebrations to provide real regeneration. The merrymaking[65] was an important ingredient of the celebration for the organizers because it was seen as a typically German trait and provided *Vergemeinschaftung* (creating community).[66] Accordingly, one morning was reserved for excursions or *Turnerfahrten*, which sought to make the immigrants familiar with their new home country. Additionally, the excursions provided the open space necessary for ritual or symbolic activities.[67] Finally, the excursions catered to the German romantic attachment to nature.[68]

Even women gymnasts were allowed to participate in an unprecedented way. Their marching in the parade aroused much curiosity and admiration from both English- and German-speaking spectators. Women in the female mass exercises were praised for their dainty yet precise performances as well as for their endurance and self-confidence.[69] Furthermore, women helped raise money, prepared food, and welcomed the guests. They presented the winning gymnastic clubs with laurel wreaths and demonstrated their supportive roles as wives and daughters as well as the unity of German Americans. In a standardized rite, they presented a flag to the male gymnasts; in their accompanying poem, they used the same ideological vocabulary as their male counterparts, thus trying to assert their right to an equal role.[70]

Whereas the festival demonstrated the self-confidence of the gymnasts, it still revealed some rifts in the German-American community.[71] Conflict broke out over the location of the festival grounds.[72] In addition, each gymnast group proudly showed its local pride with every club wearing differently colored hatbands, and the *Turners* from Denver and Rochester even brought their own beer.[73] The adaptation[74] of the second generation of German-Americans was demonstrated by the fact that most of the younger participants spoke English off the athletic grounds and assembled for baseball games.[75] Because of the Columbian World Exposition in Chicago, which took place simultaneously, general interest in the festival was somewhat less than expected,[76] and in the end, the organizers were left with a deficit of nearly 21,000 dollars.[77]

German-American festivals reached their height and most nationalistic phase at the turn of the century. This is demonstrated by the spirit in which German Americans greeted Admiral Prince Henry of Prussia, the brother of Emperor William II, in February and March 1902. For the Emperor and the

Foreign Office, Henry's goodwill tour was to improve German-American relations. They were primarily interested in his meeting influential Americans and speaking to the American population in general. For diplomatic reasons, Henry was to avoid any impression that he was visiting his German compatriots. In addition, German Americans did not present an important target group for the German government, who considered them too Americanized and mostly lower class.[78]

Germania Abendpost, March 1, 1902.

Henry's tour included half a day in Milwaukee.[79] Weeks in advance, Milwaukee Germans discussed possibilities to entertain the royal guest. Despite pleas for unity, a dispute erupted between the Musical Society, who had scheduled a concert for the evening of Henry's visit, the German theater, and the organizing committee.[80] In the end, the committee, consisting of prominent citizens, many German-born, decided on two long drives through the city, showing the prince Milwaukee's public, commercial, and private buildings. In addition, the festival was to be popular and democratic *(volkstümlich)* with people being admitted to the official reception for the prince on a first come first serve basis.[81] German-American endeavors to point out to Milwaukeeans that a grand celebration for the visiting royalty was required out of courtesy proved successful, as thousands of spectators lined the streets.[82]

The prince was welcomed at the train station by a reception committee and state and city officials. Outside the station, Henry was greeted by the salute of 1,200 members of German warriors' clubs from all over Wisconsin. That Milwaukee's German-American population chose to be represented by former soldiers is indicative of their adherence to the German Empire's growing nationalistic and militaristic spirit. German newspapers even praised those veterans, who in 1848 had helped suppress the revolution.[83] The prince's visit sparked the foundation of two new veterans' associations pledging to uphold the Hohenzollern tradition.[84] At the official reception at Milwaukee's exhibition hall, attended by 15,000 Milwaukeeans, the two German-American speakers were a former member of Congress and, once again, a representative of the German veterans' clubs. In his speech, the latter stressed that many of the recent German immigrants had fought in the German Wars of Unification and that most immigrants were still profiting from the soldierly virtues they had learned in the German army, "the best school of life." The mayor and the governor in their speeches underlined the impact of German immigrants in shaping American commerce, agriculture, industry, science, literature, and art, and praised the harmonizing influence of the German on the Puritan, commercial Yankee character. Both speakers recognized the right of German Americans to feel attached to Germany *and* the United States. After watching a show demonstration by Milwaukee's fire department, Henry attended a banquet at Milwaukee's best hotel with 300 invited guests, where he emphasized the important role of German Americans in ensuring harmonious relations between the two countries. He also praised the beauty of Milwaukee's women, though he was only briefly introduced to the wives of some prominent citizens because the rest of Milwaukee's female population was barred from official functions.[85]

According to the press, the visit was a resounding success, despite Milwaukee's cold weather which caused the prince to alter some of the arrangements.[86] Only the freethinkers and some of the gymnasts voiced criticism and derided their compatriots for their subservience to the monarch they had fled in Germany;[87] and Polish-Americans for obvious reasons abstained from the festival.[88] For many German Americans, the prince's visit had one important result: for the very first time, their role in defending the American republic, educating its citizens, and contributing to its culture and customs had been officially recognized. German-American journalists took great care to underline that all of their English-language colleagues stressed the German Americans' part in American nation-building.

With even Anglophile newspapers running pro-German comments, prospects for the future looked bright.[89]

In conclusion, some characteristics of German-American festivals stand out. First, since commemorations consist of only few elements and are by nature conservative, as Duvignaud has shown,[90] there was a fixed canon of topoi, which was recognized both by the immigrants themselves and by their American compatriots.[91] This canon can be interpreted, following Jan Assmann, as a new form of cultural coherence providing individual and collective identity in times of stress.[92] It consisted of: the compatibility of love for Germany with loyalty to the United States; the cultural contributions of German Americans to the development of the United States, i.e. their right to participate in American nationalism; the orderliness of their celebrations; the specific German talent for celebrating, socializing, having fun, and providing companionship as contrasted with American bigotry and so-called muckerism; and finally the frequency of German-American festivities.

The festivals mentioned as well as the myriads of smaller German-American celebrations[93] all adhered to a common schedule: visiting guests were marched from their points of arrival to the festival hall in little parades, marking the separation of the celebrants from ordinary life and resembling the medieval *adventus* of the king in town.[94] After a welcome by municipal authorities, which represented some token recognition of German-American identity, the liminal phase of the festivities began, which included speeches, singing, tableaux vivants, often gymnastic performances, and carousing. The main feature was usually a parade to some picnic ground to alert American compatriots to the German-American celebration and to foster community. The participants were reincorporated into their daily routine by a closing gala ball.[95]

Second, although festivals especially in the early stages of German mass immigration revealed underlying divisions of the German-American community, they served as the primary vehicle to create a specific German-American identity. German-Americans established a whole inventory of festivals; they equally participated in American festivals and stayed in contact with Germany by inviting German clubs to their festivals and by visiting national festivals in Germany.[96] In their own celebrations, German Americans tried to merge German and American national traits, symbolically represented by the German and the American flags and the figures of Germania and Columbia. With growing self-assertiveness, German Americans believed that they combined the best of both worlds and were the only ethnic group on a par or even superior to the Anglo-Americans. By constructing their own specific cultural memory, which proved that they were a distinct group, and by displaying it publicly, German Americans managed to preserve their ethnicity even if they increasingly had to include English speeches and American pastimes into their festivals. Their specific dual German and American identity also explains why in the end despite some differences in their celebrations, the workers and the middle classes, the Catholics and the Protestants, the Swabians, Bavarians, and Low Germans, men and women, all shared a basic common festive culture.[97]

Third, there was a significant change over time. German-American festivities became bigger, more numerous, and increasingly commercialized.[98] Festival cigars and beer, lotteries and souvenirs increasingly gave way to professional amusement park stands. In the history of German-American festivals, 1871 can be regarded as a first turning point with German Americans starting to become prouder of their ethnicity. The 1890s served as a second watershed, when German Americans, though still mainly defining their ethnicity culturally, as stated by Kathleen Conzen,[99] began to adopt more nationalistic symbols and discourses.[100] Yet, the pull towards a separate German identity was constantly offset by the immigrants' emphasis on having made important contributions to the development of the American nation, which paradoxically partly rendered their festivals vehicles to integrate German Americans into mainstream America. Thus, German Americans with the help of their festivals were able first of all to create a however tenuous German-American community and, second, to maintain it as a separate, both German and American, identity.

Notes

1. *New York Times*, September 15, 1864, 8/3.
2. The terms "festival" and "celebration" will be used interchangeably throughout the article.
3. Symbols give life its meaning, Clifford Geertz, *Dichte Beschreibung* (Frankfurt/Main: Suhrkamp, 1983), 136, and filter the permanent from the passing, Hans-Georg Gadamer, *Die Aktualität des Schönen* (Stuttgart: Reclam, 1977), 62.
4. Myths can be seen as collectively transmitted and remembered forms of expressions, compare Robert David Sack, *Conceptions of Space in Social Thought: A Geographic Perspective* (Minneapolis: University of Minnesota Press, 1980), 144; Dietrich Harth, "Revolution und Mythos: Sieben Thesen zur Genesis und Geltung zweier Grundbegriffe historischen Denkens," in idem and Jan Assmann, eds., *Revolution und Mythos* (Frankfurt/Main: Fischer, 1992), 29; they reduce complexity, represent the most important medium of imagining community, and function as an essential part of cultural memory, Jan Assmann, "Frühe Formen politischer Mythomotorik: Fundierende, kontrapräsentische und revolutionäre Mythen," in Harth and Assmann, *Revolution und Mythos*, 39, 42.

5. Rituals can be seen as either cultural representations of fixed social reality, Harry Pross, "Ritualisierung des Nationalen," in Jürgen Link and Wulf Wülfing, eds., *Nationale Mythen und Symbole in der zweiten Hälfte des 19. Jahrhunderts: Strukturen und Funktionen von Konzepten nationaler Identität* (Stuttgart: Klett-Cotta, 1991), 101, or as oscillating between structure and antistructure, cp. John J. MacAloon, "Introduction: Cultural Performances, Culture Theory," in idem, ed., *Rite, Drama, Festival, Spectacle: Rehearsals toward a Theory of Cultural Performance* (Philadelphia: Institute for the Study of Human Issues, 1984), 3; both positions, however, agree that rituals bring order to culture, serve social continuity and establish collectivity, ibid.; Sally Falk Moore, "Epilogue: Uncertainties in Situations, Indeterminacies in Culture," in Barbara Myerhoff and idem, eds., *Symbol and Politics in Communal Ideology: Cases and Questions* (Ithaca, NY: Cornell University Press, 1975), 221; David Chaney, "A Symbolic Mirror of Ourselves: Civic Ritual in Mass Society," *Media, Culture, and Society* 5 (1983): 120. Rituals humanize space while myths humanize time, cp. Harvey Cox, *The Feast of Fools: A Theological Essay on Festivity and Fantasy* (Cambridge: Harvard University Press, 1969), 71.
6. Frank-Michael Kuhlemann, "Mentalitätsgeschichte," in Wolfgang Hardtwig and Hans-Ulrich Wehler, eds., *Kulturgeschichte Heute* (Göttingen: Vandenhoeck & Ruprecht, 1996), 208; Heinz-Gerhard Haupt and Charlotte Tacke, "Die Kultur des Nationalen," in Hardtwig and Wehler, eds., *Kulturgeschichte Heute*, 264.
7. Emile Durkheim, *Die elementaren Formen des religiösen Lebens*, trans. Ludwig Schmidts (Frankfurt a.M.: Suhrkamp, 1981), 471, 509.
8. For Assmann, cultural memory is socially constructed and embraces, but is not equivalent to, tradition and communication; its function is to reproduce group identity via circulation and repetition especially in the form of festivals, Jan Assmann, *Das kulturelle Gedächtnis: Schrift, Erinnerung und politische Identität in frühen Hochkulturen* (Munich: Beck, 1992), 23, 35; Jan Assmann, "Der zweidimensionale Mensch: das Fest als Medium des kollektiven Gedächtnisses," in idem, ed., *Das Fest und das Heilige. Religiöse Kontrapunkte zur Alltagswelt* (Gütersloh: Verlag Hans Mohn, 1991), 23-24.
9. Don Handelman, *Models and Mirrors: Towards and Anthropology of Public Events* (Cambridge: Cambridge University Press, 1990), 9; Hermann Bausinger, "'Ein Abwerfen der grossen Last ...': Gedanken zur städtischen Festkultur," in Paul Hugger et al., eds., *Stadt und Fest* (Stuttgart: Metzler, 1987), 252. For Bausinger, festivals include order and chaos, organization and spontaneity, tradition and innovation, the construction of sense and sensualness, separation and harmony, partialness and totality, ibid., 254-66.
10. E.g. Assmann, "Der zweidimensionale Mensch," 13-17; Odo Marquard, "Moratorium des Alltags: Eine kleine Philosophie des Festes," in Walter Haug and Rainer Warning, eds., *Das Fest* (Munich: Fink, 1989), 684-91.
11. Winfried Gebhardt, *Fest, Feier und Alltag. Über die gesellschaftliche Wirklichkeit des Menschen und ihre Deutung* (Frankfurt a.M.: Lang, 1987), 12; Gadamer, *Die Aktualität*, 31; Geertz, *Dichte Beschreibung*, 96. If one follows Johan Huizinga, who posits that the community of a festival or play has the tendency to become permanent, one could even argue that associations and clubs, so characteristic for German-American life, grew out of festivals, not vice versa, compare idem, *Homo Ludens: Versuch einer Bestimmung des Spielelementes der Kultur* (1938; Amsterdam: Pantheon 1940, 21.
12. Eric Hobsbawm, "Introduction: Inventing Traditions," in idem and Terence Ranger, eds., *The Invention of Tradition* (Cambridge: Cambridge University Press, 1983), 1-7.
13. Geneviève Fabre, "Essai introductif: Lieux de fête et de commémoration," *Revue française d'Etudes Américaines* 51 (1992): 9.
14. Durkheim, *Die elementaren Formen*, 509.
15. Josef Pieper, *Zustimmung zur Welt: Ein Theorie des Festes* (Munich: Kösel, 1963).

16. Roger Caillois, *L'homme et le sacré* (1938; Paris: Gallimard, 1950); Jean Duvignaud, *Fêtes et civilisations* (Paris: Librairie Weber, 1973); Durkheim, *Die elementaren Formen*.
17. Assmann, "Der zweidimensionale Mensch," 17; Cox, *The Feast of Fools*, 22; Gerhard M. Martin, *Fest und Alltag: Bausteine zu einer Theorie des Festes* (Stuttgart: Kohlhammer, 1973), 29. For good, albeit differing summaries of festive theories compare Gebhardt, *Fest, Feier und Alltag*; Hugger, "Einleitung: Das Fest," in idem et al., eds., *Stadt und Fest*, 9-24. Thus, festivals are basically ambivalent, cp. Bruce Willems-Braun, "Situating Cultural Politics: Fringe Festivals and the Production of Spaces of Intersubjectivity," *Environment and Planning D: Society and Space* 12 (1994): 78.
18. Max Weber, *Gesammelte Aufsätze zur Religionssoziologie*, vol. 1 (Tübingen: Mohr, 1978), 252; Geertz, *Dichte Beschreibung*, 123; Susan G. Davis, *Parades and Power: Street Theatre in Nineteenth-Century Philadelphia* (Philadelphia: Temple University Press, 1986), 6. Thus, I am not convinced by Don Handelman's argument that most festivals are events that "present the lived-in world" and have no impact on the lived-in worlds of peoples, compare Handelman, *Models and Mirrors*, 41-42.
19. Cf. e.g. Manfred Hettling and Paul Nolte, eds., *Bürgerliche Feste* (Göttingen: Vandenhoeck & Ruprecht, 1993); Dieter Düding, Peter Friedemann, and Paul Münch, eds., *Öffentliche Festkultur. Politische Feste in Deutschland von der Aufklärung bis zum Ersten Weltkrieg* (Reinbek: Rowohlt, 1988); Ute Schneider, *Politische Festkultur im 19. Jahrhundert: Die Rheinprovinz von der französischen Zeit bis zum Ende des Ersten Weltkrieges (1806-1918)* (Essen; Klartext, 1995).
20. Jürgen Heideking, "Die Verfassungsfeiern von 1788," *Der Staat* 34/3 (1995): 391-413; Simon P. Newman, *Parades and the Politics of the Street: Festive Culture in the Early American Republic* (Philadelphia: University of Pennsylvania Press, 1997); David Waldstreicher, *In the Midst of Perpetual Fetes: The Making of American Nationalism* (Chapel Hill, NC: University of North Carolina Press, 1997); Sean Wilentz, *Chants Democratic: New York City and the Rise of the American Working Class, 1788-1850* (New York: Oxford University Press, 1984).
21. Susan G. Davis, *Parades and Power: Street Theatre in Nineteenth-Century Philadelphia* (Philadelphia: Temple University Press, 1986); David Glassberg, *American Historical Pageantry: The Uses of Tradition in the Early Twentieth Century* (Chapel Hill, NC: University of North Carolina Press, 1990); Mary Ryan, "The American Parade: Representations of the Nineteenth-Century Social Order," in Lynn Hunt, ed., *The New Cultural History* (Berkeley: University of California Press, 1989), 131-53.
22. Kathleen N. Conzen, "Ethnicity as Festive Culture: Nineteenth-Century German America on Parade," in Werner Sollors, ed., *The Invention of Ethnicity* (New York: Oxford University Press, 1989), 44-76.
23. This paper forms part of a book-length project to investigate the extent, forms, and transformations of German-American festivities from 1848 to 1925.
24. I am using Kantowicz's definition of ethnicity as "a collective, inherited, cultural identity, buttressed by social structures and social networks, and often formulated in opposition to competing social groups". Edward R. Kantowicz, "Ethnicity," in Mary Kupiec Cayton, Elliott J. Gorn, and Peter W. Williams, eds., *Encyclopedia of American Social History* (New York: Scribner, 1993), 454. The *Harvard Encyclopedia of American Ethnic Groups* names six criteria for ethnicity: common historical origin, some conception of cultural and social distinctiveness, a role as a unit in a larger and diverse system of social relations, a manifest or latent network of associations, some acknowledgment of one's own diversity, and some attachment to a set of historically derived group symbols, Harold J. Abramson, "Assimilation and Pluralism," in Stephan Thernstrom et al., eds., *The Harvard Encyclo-*

pedia of American Ethnic Groups (Cambridge: Belknap Press of Harvard University, 1980), 151.
25. There were 71,000 in 1870 and 115,000 in 1880. Bayrd Still, *Milwaukee: The History of a City* (Madison, WI: State Historical Society of Wisconsin, 1948), 112, 329, 572-75.
26. Ibid., 258-59, 453, 572-75.
27. Cp. Pierre Bourdieu, *Zur Soziologie der symbolischen Formen* (Frankfurt a.M.: Suhrkamp, 1991), 60; Ingrid Gilcher-Holtey, "Kulturelle und symbolische Praktiken: das Unternehmen Pierre Bourdieu," in Hardtwig and Wehler, eds., *Kulturgeschichte Heute*, 120; *Banner und Volksfreund*, March 2, 1871, 3/1; March 19, 1871, 3/1; *Milwaukee Seebote*, June 5, 1871, 1/1.
28. *Banner und Volksfreund*, March 19, 1871, 3/1; April 30, 1871, 3/1; *Milwaukee Seebote*, June 5, 1871, 1/1.
29. *Milwaukee Sentinel*, May 2, 1871, 1/5; May 30, 1871, 4/2-3; *New York Times*, April 11, 1871, 1/7; *Evening Post*, April 10, 1871, 4/1-2.
30. It is interesting to note that in many places victory was celebrated either on Easter Monday (New York, Baltimore) or on Whitmonday (Milwaukee, Chicago, Manitowoc, Kenosha); the German communities evidently were looking for a religious connotation and at the same time trying to avoid angering their compatriots by celebrating on a Sunday, compare *Milwaukee Sentinel*, March 21, 1871, 4/1; *Banner und Volksfreund*, March 2, 1871, 3/1; March 17, 1871, 3/3; May 13, 1871, 3/5; June 4, 1871, 3/1-2; *New York Times*, April 11, 1871, 1/7, 2/1-4; *Evening Post*, New York, April 10, 1871, 4/1-2.
31. *Milwaukee Sentinel*, May 15, 1871, 4/3; May 29, 1871, 4/1.
32. *Milwaukee Seebote*, June 5, 1871, 1/1-3; *Banner und Volksfreund*, May 23, 1871, 3/4-6; May 18, 1871, 3/5; May 25, 1871, 3/4; May 26, 1871, 3/1; May 28, 1871, 1/2; May 31, 1871, 2/2-7, 3/1-5.
33. According to the *Sentinel*, it was only three miles long, *Milwaukee Sentinel*, May 30, 1871, 4/2-3.
34. I define public space following Stephen Carr as the common ground where people carry out the functional and ritual activities that bind a community together both in daily life and in periodic festivities, Stephen Carr et al., *Public Space* (Cambridge: Cambridge University Press, 1992), xi. For Habermas' more discursive concept of public sphere and recent criticism of it, compare Jürgen Habermas, *Strukturwandel der Öffentlichkeit: Untersuchungen zu einer Kategorie der bürgerlichen Gesellschaft* (Neuwied: Luchterhand, 1971); Craig Calhoun, ed., *Habermas and the Public Sphere* (Cambridge, MA: MIT Press, 1992). Geographers emphasize especially that the public sphere can only exist via material space, cp. Don Mitchell, "The End of Public Space? People's Park, Definitions of the Public, and Democracy," *Annals of the Association of American Geography* 85 (1995): 108-33. Access to public space is highly contested, compare e.g. Peter Goheen, "Negotiating Access to Public Space in Mid-Nineteenth-Century Toronto," *Journal of Historical Geography* 20 (1994): 430-49.
35. Cp. Heideking, "Die Verfassungsfeiern," 391-413; Gisela Jaacks, *Festzüge in Hamburg 1696-1913: Bürgerliche Selbstdarstellung und Geschichtsbewußtsein* (Hamburg: Hamburger Museums-Verein, 1972), 1-12.
36. *Banner und Volksfreund*, May 16, 1871, 3/2; May 31, 1871, 2/2-7, 3/1-5. Some American firms had also decorated their buildings, *Milwaukee Seebote*, June 5, 1871, 1/3, or put advertisements in the newspaper that their goods had become cheaper with the end of the war, *Banner und Volksfreund*, May 26, 1871, 3/6.
37. Hobsbawm, "Introduction," 7.
38. *Milwaukee Seebote*, June 5, 1871, 1/1-7; *Milwaukee Sentinel*, May 30, 1871, 4/2-3; *Banner und Volksfreund*, May 28, 1871, 2/2-4, 3/2-5; May 31, 1871, 2/2-7; June 1, 1871, 2/2-3.

39. *Milwaukee Seebote*, May 29, 1871, 1/4; *Banner und Volksfreund*, May 10, 1871, 3/2; May 21, 1871, 2/2; May 31, 1871, 3/1-5.
40. *Milwaukee Seebote*, 1 January 1871, 1/9; *Banner und Volksfreund*, 28 May 1871, 2/2-4; 31 May 1871, 2/2-7, 3/1-5.
41. *Milwaukee Seebote*, June 5, 1871, 1/1-7; Horst Ueberhorst, *Turner unterm Sternenbanner* (Munich: Heinz Moos, 1978), 121; the same happened in Germany, cp. Dieter Langewiesche, "'... für Volk und Vaterland zu würken ...': Zur politischen und gesellschaftlichen Rolle der Turner zwischen 1811 und 1871," in Ommo Grupe, ed., *Kulturgut oder Körperkult? Sport und Sportwissenschaft im Wandel* (Tübingen: Attempto, 1990), 58; *Gedenk-Blatt an das Deutsche Friedens-Fest in Milwaukee, Wisc., vom 27. bis 29. Mai 1871 und an den Deutsch-Französischen Krieg* (Milwaukee: Herold, 1871), Pamphlet 57-542, 2, State Historical Society Wisconsin, Madison, WI.
42. *Milwaukee Seebote*, June 5, 1871, 1/4.
43. E.g. *Milwaukee Sentinel*, May 30, 1871, 4/2-3; *Gedenk-Blatt*, 1; *Banner und Volksfreund*, June 8, 1871, 3/2.
44. *Milwaukee Freie Presse*, March 22, 1883, 4/4; June 15, 1883, 4/1-2; August 29, 1883, 4/3; August 31, 1883, 4/2-3.
45. In later years, most German communities would celebrate German day on October 6.
46. *Milwaukee Freie Presse*, October 3, 1883, 5/2-3; October 8, 1883, 4/2-3.
47. *Milwaukee Freie Presse*, October 3, 1883, 5/2-3; October 8, 1883, 4/2-3; *Sentinel*, October 8, 1883, 1/1-2.
48. *Milwaukee Freie Presse*, October 6, 1883, 5/2-3.
49. *Milwaukee Freie Presse*, August 23, 1883, 2/2; September 11, 1883, 4/2; September 13, 1883, 4/2; October 3, 1883, 5/2-3; October 6, 1883, 5/2-3; October 8, 1883, 4/2-3; *Seebote*, October 4, 1883, 4/2; *Sentinel*, October 8, 1883, 1/1-2. There were a lot of complaints about the admission fee charged in the afternoon as well, *Sentinel*, October 8, 1883, 1/1-2.
50. *Freidenker*, October 14, 1883, 1/1-3; *Milwaukee Freie Presse*, September 24, 1883, 5/3; October 4, 1883, 1/3; October 8, 1883, 4/2-3.
51. *Milwaukee Freie Presse*, March 22, 1883, 4/2; May 29, 1883, 4/1-2; June 15, 1883, 4/1-2; August 31, 1883, /2-3; October 8, 1883, 1/3-6, 2/1-2; *Freidenker*, October 7, 1883, 1/1-2; *Seebote*, October 11, 1883, 4/2-3.
52. *Milwaukee Freie Presse*, October 8, 1883, 1/5; *Freidenker*, October 7, 1883, 1/1; *Seebote*, October 11, 1883, 4/2-3. This image supposedly was first used by Carl Schurz, Philip V. Bohlman, "Music in the Culture of German Americans in North-Central Wisconsin," Ph.D. diss., University of Illinois, Urbana, 1979, 70.
53. *Milwaukee Freie Presse*, March 22, 1883, 4/2; May 29, 1883, 4/1-2; August 31, 1883, 2-3; September 1, 1883, 4/1-2; October 8, 1883, 1/3-6, 2/1-2; *Freidenker*, October 7, 1883, 1/1-2; *Seebote*, October 11, 1883, 4/2-3.
54. *Milwaukee Freie Presse*, May 29, 1883, 4/1-2; October 6, 1883, 5/2-3; October 8, 1883, 1/3-6, 2/1-2.
55. *Milwaukee Freie Presse*, October 8, 1883, 1/3; October 9, 1883, 5/2; *Sentinel*, October 8, 1883, 1/1-2; October 9, 1883, 6/2.
56. Milwaukee had already hosted the seventh and seventeenth festivals in 1857 and 1877, cp. Heinrich Metzner, *Geschichte des Turnerbundes* (Indianapolis: Verlag Zukunft, 1874), 52; *Jahrbücher der Deutsch-Amerikanischen Turnerei* III/6 (1894), 272-73. The program for the 1893 festival is described in detail in *1893 Nord Amerikanischer Turner-Bund, 26tes Bundes Turn Fest Milwaukee-Wisc.* (Milwaukee: Evening Wisconsin Co., 1893), in *The Immigrant in America*, Unit 5, Reel 148, Item 6, 17-23.

57. Klaus Zieschang, *Vom Schützenfest zum Turnfest: Die Entstehung des Deutschen Turnfestes unter besonderer Berücksichtigung der Einflüsse von F.L. Jahn* (Ahrensberg: Czwalina, 1977), 182-95; Ralf Wagner, "Zwischen Tradition und Fortschritt: Zur gesellschaftlichen und kulturellen Entwicklung der Deutsch-amerikanischen Turnbewegung am Beispiel Milwaukees und Chicagos, 1850-1920," Ph.D. diss., University of Munich, 1988, 4-50.
58. *Freidenker*, July 30, 1893, 4; *Sentinel*, July 21, 1893, 1/3-4; for the size of the other festivals compare *Jahrbücher der Deutsch-Amerikanischen Turnerei* I to III (1892-1894).
59. *1893 Nord Amerikanischer Turner-Bund, 26tes Bundes Turn Fest Milwaukee-Wisc.*, 17; *Freidenker*, July 30, 1893, 4; August 6, 1893, 4/3-4; *Sentinel*, July 21, 1893, 1/3-4; July 22, 1893, 1/2-3; July 25, 1893, 1/1-2. For the second and bigger parade, The *Sentinel* spoke of ten thousand marchers, but admitted these numbers to be exaggerated, July 23, 1893, 1/7.
60. *Berichte des Beobachtungs-Ausschusses beim 28. Bundesturnfest des Nordamerikanischen Turnerbundes abgehalten in Philadelphia, Pa., in den Tagen vom 21. bis 24. Juni 1900* (Milwaukee: Freidenker Publishing Co., 1900), in *The Immigrant in America*, Unit 5, Reel 148, Item 4, 18; *1893 Nord Amerikanischer Turner-Bund, 26tes Bundes Turn Fest Milwaukee-Wisc.*, 31; *Milwaukee'r Abend-Post*, April 12, 1893, 2/2; July 13, 1893, 2/3; July 15, 1893, 2/2, July 18, 1893, 2/2; July 25, 1893, 1/4, 8/4-5; *Freidenker*, July 30, 1893, 4; *Sentinel*, July 21, 1893, 3/3; July 23, 1893, 1/1; July 24, 1893, 1/1-2; July 25, 1893, 1/1-2; Ueberhorst, *Turner*, 142.
61. *Sentinel*, July 26, 1893, 2/3-4. Two days earlier, the *Sentinel* had still underlined the cosmopolitan makeup of the audience, specifically mentioning Americans and Bohemians, cp. July 24, 1893, 1/1.
62. *1893 Nord Amerikanischer Turner-Bund, 26tes Bundes Turn Fest Milwaukee-Wisc.*, 17; *Freidenker*, July 30, 1893, 4; *Sentinel*, July 22, 1893, 2/1; July 26, 1893, 2/3-4.
63. *Milwaukee'r Abend-Post*, July 25, 1893, 8/4-5; Nordamerikanischer Turnerbund, *Offizielle Festzeitung für das 26. Bundesturnfest in Milwaukee, Juli 1893* 5 (March 1, 1893), 3; *Freidenker*, July 30, 1893, 4.
64. *Milwaukee'r Abend-Post*, July 25, 1893, 8/4-5; *Freidenker*, July 30, 1893, 2/1; *Sentinel*, July 24, 1893, 1/3; July 25, 1893, 1/1-2.
65. The active gymnasts mainly drank non-alcoholic beverages, cp. *Sentinel*, July 25, 1893, 1/1.
66. *Freidenker*, July 23, 1893, 1/1; August 6, 1893, 4/3; *Sentinel*, July 23, 1893, 1/3; for *Vergemeinschaftung* and *Vergesellschaftung* cp. Ferdinand Tönnies, *Gemeinschaft und Gesellschaft: Grundbegriffe der reinen Soziologie* (1887; Darmstadt: Wissenschaftliche Buchgesellschaft, 1969).
67. Duvignaud, *Fêtes et civilisations*, 15-16.
68. Conzen, "Ethnicity as Festive Culture," 69. At later gymnastic festivals, the lack of opportunity to socialize was to evoke severe criticism, Ueberhorst, *Turner*, 143.
69. *Milwaukee'r Abend-Post*, July 22, 1893, II/1/6; July 24, 1893, 8/2-3; November 3, 1893, 5/3; *Freidenker*, July 30, 1893, 5/1; August 6, 1893, 4/1-2; *Sentinel*, July 22, 1893, 1/7, 2/1; July 23, 1893, 2/1; July 24, 1893, 1/3; July 25, 1893, 1/3. Officially, women were not allowed to participate in national gymnastic festivals before 1901, Ueberhorst, *Turner*, 143. They did not become equal partners until 1923, Gisela Bentz, "Vom Fischbein-Korsett zum Gymnastik-Anzug: Die Rolle der Frau in der Turnbewegung," in *Deutsche Turnfeste* (Homburg: Lippert, 1985), 36. Despite their professed belief in equality, the gymnasts had only admitted women into female sections of gymnastic clubs in the 1870s; they did not grant them full membership rights until after World War I, compare Wagner, "Zwischen Tradition und Fortschritt," 258-60.

70. *Milwaukee'r Abend-Post*, July 21, 1893, 2/4, 8/3; July 22, 1893, 2/4-5; *Freidenker*, July 30, 1893, 4; August 6, 1893, 4/2; *Sentinel*, July 26, 1893, 2/3-4; for women's roles in parades cp. Mary P. Ryan, *Women in Public: Between Banners and Ballots, 1825-1880* (Baltimore: Johns Hopkins University Press, 1990), 48.
71. *Nordamerikanischer Turnerbund: Offizielle Festzeitung für das 26. Bundesturnfest in Milwaukee, Juli 1893*, No. 6, March 1893, 8.
72. *Milwaukee'r Abend-Post*, March 31, 1893, 2/3; *Freidenker*, July 30, 1893, 4.
73. *Sentinel*, July 22, 1893, 1/2-3, 2/1; July 24, 1893, 1/3; July 25, 1893, 1/1.
74. Adaption is one of the steps in Barkan's model, Elliott R. Barkan, "Forum: Race, Religion, and Nationality in American Society. A Model of Ethnicity—From Contact to Assimilation," in *Journal of American Ethnic History* 14/2 (1995): 55-56.
75. *Sentinel*, July 21, 1893, 3/3; July 24, 1893, 1/1; July 25, 1893, 1/2; July 26, 1893, 2/4.
76. Ueberhorst, *Turner*, 142, n. 592; *Freidenker*, July 30, 1893, 5/1. The press reported between 15,000 and 20,000 spectators, *Sentinel*, July 22, 1893, 1/1; July 26, 1893, 2/3-4; *Milwaukee'r Abend-Post*, July 24, 1893, 8/2-3. This does not square with the sale of 13,000 tickets, even if one considers that Milwaukee's Turners and their families went in for free. The same newspaper report announced a lowering of the entrance fees, which is indicative of slack attendance, see *Milwaukee'r Abend-Post*, July 27, 1893, 2/2. Nevertheless, correspondents from several Eastern and Midwestern German-American papers attended the festival, *Sentinel*, 22 July 1893, 1/3-4.
77. *Milwaukee'r Abend-Post*, July 27, 1893, 2/2; July 31, 1893, 5/2; September 29, 1893, 5/4. In 1898, the North American Gymnastic Union offered to pay for the remaining 3,500 dollars, ibid., July 11, 1898, 5/2.
78. No direct political results were expected, compare Chancellor Bernhard v. Bülow to Henry, January 30, 1902, ad A 207, R #3868, IA: Preußen, Acten betreffend Seine Königliche Hoheit Prinz Heinrich, Politisches Archiv (PA), Auswärtiges Amt, Bonn (AA); cp. also Reiner Pommerin, *Der Kaiser und Amerika* (Köln: Böhlau, 1986), 107-110; Alfred Vagts, *Deutschland und die Vereinigten Staaten in der Weltpolitik*, vol. 1 (New York: Macmillan, 1935), 149-50, 558; Ambassador Th.v. Holleben to Bülow, January 8, 1902, RM3/2368, Reise nach Amerika, 1902-1903, Papers of Admiral Tirpitz, Bundesarchiv, Militärarchiv.
79. Holleben to Bülow, January 16, 1902, A 821, vol. R 3868, IA, PA AA; Note Chancellor Bülow, January 19, 1902, 946, ibid.; Pommerin, *Der Kaiser*, 107-109.
80. *Milwaukee Herold und Seebote*, February 11, 1902, 1/1-2; February 14, 1902, 1/7; *Germania-Abendpost*, January 26, 1902, 1/1-2; February 12, 1902, 3/1-7; *Milwaukee Free Press*, February 21, 1902, 9/1.
81. *Germania-Abendpost*, January 24, 1902, 6/2-3; March 3, 1902, 4/2-3; *Milwaukee Herold und Seebote*, March 5, 1902, 1/1; *Milwaukee Herold und Seebote*, February 18, 1902, 5/4-5; *Milwaukee Free Press*, February 20, 1902, 9/3; *Sentinel*, March 5, 1902, 6/1.
82. *Germania-Abendpost*, January 15, 1902, 1/2-4; January 16, 1902, 1/1-2; January 19, 1902, 1/4; January 20, 1902, 1/1-2; March 4, 1902, 1/2-6; *Milwaukee Herold und Seebote*, March 2, 1902, 7/2-3; *Sentinel*, March 5, 1902, 1/1-7.
83. *Germania-Abendpost*, March 5, 1902, 1/7; *Milwaukee Herold und Seebote*, March 6, 1902, 6/3; *Sentinel*, February 26, 1902, 8/3-5; February 27, 1902, 8/2-4; March 1, 1902, 7/3-5; March 2, 1902, 7/2-6. Of course, the German Americans also wished to demonstrate to the Emperor's representative that they were still good Germans at heart and had been rendering services to their German fatherland.
84. *Germania-Abendpost*, March 3, 1902, 2/1; *Milwaukee Herold und Seebote*, February 28, 1902, 5/1; March 1, 1902, 4/6-7; March 17, 1902, 5/4.

85. *Seebote*, March 4, 1902, 1/2-3; March 7, 1902, 1/1-3; *Germania-Abendpost*, March 5, 1902, 1/5-7, 2/1-7; *Milwaukee Herold und Seebote*, February 25, 1902, 5/2-5; March 5, 1902, 1, 5/1-2, 7/3-6, 8/2-5; *Sentinel*, March 5, 1902, 1/1-7, 4/4-7; *Milwaukee Free Press*, March 5, 1902, 1, 2, 4, 5/1-3. Milwaukee's African Americans were also marginalized, but nonetheless able to present the prince with an aquarium of goldfish, *Milwaukee Herold und Seebote*, March 5, 1902, 7/5. Interestingly enough, the visitors from Germany interpreted the speeches very despondently as funeral orations for the German way of life in the United States (*Grabreden auf das Deutschthum*), cp. Admiral Fritz Graf von Baudissin, Zusammenstellung von Tagebuch-Aufzeichnungen über den Aufenthalt in den Vereinigten Staaten, 1902, manuscript graciously placed at my disposal by Baudissin's granddaughter, Christa Dempf-Dulckeit.
86. *Sentinel*, March 6, 1902, 2/4; *Milwaukee Free Press*, March 5, 1902, 4/4-5; *Germania-Abendpost*, March 5, 1902, 4/2.
87. *Freidenker*, January 26, 1902, 4/2-4; March 9, 1902, 5/2; *Germania-Abendpost*, January 16, 1902, 1/1-2, 3/2; January 17, 1902, 1/1-2. In the end, however, the Northside and the Southside Gymnastic Clubs both participated, whereas the Turnverein Milwaukee apparently abstained, cp. *Germania-Abendpost*, February 2, 1902, 1/3-4.
88. *Milwaukee Free Press*, March 5, 1902, 5/3.
89. *Germania-Abendpost*, March 9, 1902, 6/5 (copy from the *Baltimore Correspondent*); March 17, 1902, 4/4; March 22, 1902, II/6/3; *Seebote*, March 4, 1902, 1/2; *Milwaukee Herold und Seebote*, March 3, 1902, 4/2-3; March 11, 1902, 4/2-3; *Sentinel*, March 5, 1902, 6/1; *Milwaukee Free Press*, March 5, 1902, 4/4-5.
90. Jean Duvignaud, "La fête. Essai de sociologie," *Cultures* 3.1 (1976): 22.
91. E.g. *New York Times*, July 1, 1871, 4/2-3; August 10, 1871, 8/3. Many of these stereotypes were evaluated positively by Anglo-Americans, who from time to time praised the Germans for adding these characteristics to the American national character, *New York Evening Post*, August 5, 1871, 4/3; *New York Times*, October 9, 1883, 4/4-5.
92. Assmann, *Das kulturelle Gedächtnis*, 127.
93. For a description of the different festivals German-Americans celebrated see my forthcoming *habilitationsschrift* "Die Festkultur der Deutsch-Amerikaner im Spannungsfeld zwischen deutscher und amerikanischer Identität, 1848-1925."
94. Klaus Tenfelde, "Adventus: Zur historischen Ikonologie des Festzugs," *Historische Zeitschrift* 235 (1982): 45-84.
95. For liminality and the three major phases of rituals compare Arnold van Gennep, *Les rites de passage* (Paris: Emile Nourry, 1909), 14; Victor Turner, *The Ritual Process: Structure and Anti-Structure* (London: Routledge, 1969), esp. chs. 3 and 5; compare also Conzen, "Ethnicity as Festive Culture," 60-61.
96. Thus, the Milwaukee *Turners* attended the first gymnastic festival in Frankfurt in 1880, and the Milwaukee *Männerchor* toured Germany in 1913, see *Offizielle Festzeitung für das 5te allgemeine deutsche Turnfest zu Frankfurt a/M 1880*, No. 5, July 26; No. 8, July 29; No. 9, July 30, 1880; *Germania-Herold*, August 21, 1880, 6/1-6; April 29, 1913, 1/5-6; May 5, 4/3-4; June 2 to 24, 1913.
97. This was already recognized by Conzen, "Ethnicity as Festive Culture," 48. Workers celebrated in separate associations, used some different symbols and songs, and included more lectures; celebrations by parishes and church choirs always contained a service, a sermon, and some hymns. In Germany as well, the workers' celebrations borrowed from the middle classes, see Wolfgang Hardtwig, "Nationsbildung und politische Mentalität: Denkmal und Fest im Kaiserreich," in idem, *Geschichtskultur und Wissenschaft* (Munich: dtv, 1990), 297.

98. Even the prince's visit was used by businesses for publicity stints, *Germania-Abendpost*, 5 March 1902, 8; *Milwaukee Herold und Seebote*, 5 March 1902, 10; *Milwaukee Free Press*, 4 March 1902, 2/2-4, 3; cp. also Davis, *Parades and Power*, 17.
99. Conzen, "Ethnicity as Festive Culture," 60.
100. This may owe both to a growing American nationalism, which stimulated the ethnic Germans to make their contribution to nation-building known, and to the fact that the more recent immigrants had left a united country, served in its army, and experienced Germany's growing economic and political power.

Chapter 10

HALLOWEEN— A "REINVENTED" HOLIDAY

Celebrating White Anglo-Saxon Protestant Middle-Class America[1]

Adrien Lherm

HALLOWEEN SEEMS TO be deeply rooted in the American culture. Yet, originally, it was not an American tradition. A major date in the Celtic calendar, it celebrated the temporary return of the dead and the opening of winter before it was turned into an early modern British and rather joyful observance. Until the nineteenth century in the United Kingdom it was both a propitiatory rite observed by male farmers and a pretext for merriments attended by other members of the local community. In nineteenth-century America, when country people settled in booming cities, the festive custom soon attracted attention: actually, its old licentious revelries and masqueraded parades did not fit in with the capitalist setting. Disrupting the new urban order, it soon became a social problem. Middle-class editors, journalists, social workers, and educators decided to rid poor young people of their Halloween carnivalesque tendencies by "domesticating" the celebration—i.e. bringing it off the streets into the homes as a respectable part of the new Victorian domestic and civil religion. In booklets and articles published in women's magazines or juvenile literature, the long history of the holiday was

---

Notes for this section begin on page 210.

stressed in order to impose as immemorial a selection of rites picked up in the works of British antiquarians, adapted to the new context and made into games, stunts and plays. They provided an oversimplified, mythological and ideological point of view, emphasizing such leitmotifs as Celtic origins, Anglo-Saxon traditional folklore and continuity between the Old and the New Worlds. This was a way to make sure that the United States, in a context of massive immigration, was of British stock and that it would remain so. The images and practices which the "new Halloween" conveyed nurtured the white Anglo-Saxon Protestant values and norms of behavior. As for the reinvention and refurbishing of Christmas which took place in the 1820s and 1830s, the "new Halloween tradition" helped reinforce the image that members of the white middle class had of their country and of themselves. However, the populations targeted by the reshaping of the holiday resisted this effort and continued to celebrate the event their own way.

The Old British Halloween: A Cohesive Holiday

Until the end of the eighteenth century Halloween[2] was a major festival in British rural and urban communities. The dead and creatures from beyond who people believed to be released for the night, had either to be ritually welcomed or driven away. To compensate for the decline of the sun and make sure it would rise again, people used to light bonfires and dance around them.[3] Before community merriments took place, male heads of families would wander down the streets or through the fields, "beating the bounds"[4] with flaming pitchforks in order to get rid of evil spirits for the year to come, and thus protect crops and protect cattle. They would return to the community center where they would gather with the family and neighbors for a good cheer and a good time.

Consecrating the end of the main farm works Halloween introduced the more relaxed period of time, the twelve days of Christmas and winter.[5] This was a time of frequent social gatherings and visits, especially from house to house. The occasion enabled people to reinforce emotional ties and express concern and friendship for their acquaintances. It also stressed both status differences within the village and common belonging to the community. At this time male adults were able to get inside the houses of the wealthy and powerful. In many places underprivileged adults gathered, performing processions, dance and masquerade plays[6] as pretexts to enter these premises and obtain something in return: "We've come here to claim our right ... And if you don't open your door, We will lay you flat upon the floor," was one of the rhymes. Then marchers would spend the night eating and drinking up their loot. Villagers' social distinctions, structures of power as well as community membership were thus reasserted and turned into dramatic, festive and joyful realities.

Halloween provided an opportunity to express not only the emotional ties but also the functional bonds that turned the community into an organic unity. The rituals used ordinary objects linked to the group's daily activities—food, salt, ashes, stones, wood, straw, yarn—or activities performed at this time of the year, such as the collecting and picking of fruits and vegetables, the sheltering of crops and cattle etc. They were also held at those places where life and work took place—the fields and meadows, the more distant woods (where fuel for bonfires was collected), the hills, graveyards, squares (where bonfires were set), the homes, barns, and gardens. The activities reflected hierarchical community structures. Yet, they also stressed its cohesive organization. The main actors were male heads of families, but wives, children, and servants also participated during the preparations, observances, and merriments. Even the deceased took part, as they were believed to come back and help the living, usually females, to perform divination rites. Women gathered on church porches or in churchyards and tried to see the ghosts of those who were to die in the year to come, and the disguised males had to be properly welcomed with food that was left out for them for the night. In short, these customs made the cohesion of the community visible symbolically—gentry and peasants, masters and servants, family heads and the homeless, males and females, the elderly and the young, the living and the dead, almost all members were involved.

On the other hand, Halloween was not such a good time for the outcasts of the local community because it could also serve as an occasion for direct popular justice. Woman's divinations about those who were to die soon might have been a way to get rid of, or at least to warn those who were not very much appreciated. Moreover, outsiders had to face shivarees, tricks, or exclusion from the community's merriments. Halloween was an expression of a search for solidarity and unanimity, an attempt to reactivate—ritually and festively—the ordinarily invisible ties that pervaded the group every day.

As any other holiday ritual, Halloween also provided a safety valve for releasing community pressures. Entering homes and begging functioned as inversion rites. Yet, their "victims" -usually members of the local elite—had nothing to fear for status differences and authority were as unquestionable as God's will, hence strong enough to be loosened up and reversed for a night.[7] Furthermore, it was an indirect way for the former to reassert their leadership over the other members of the local community. The elite's acceptance of, and submission to, popular misrule and to inversion rituals was actually taken by common people as a proof of their benevolence to them. These inversion practices were considered as a gift as well as a right bestowed temporarily, which presented and thus reinforced the elite's power. Halloween practices were not subversive. In a hierarchical social and cultural context they did not challenge the authority or the position of the gentry. However, by the mid-eighteenth-century support of the traditional holidays was reconsidered by the elites.

With the growth of individualism and capitalism, social bonds—or at least their definitions—shifted from submission to authority to negotiation between contracting parties. New values came to the foreground and clashed with those pertaining to the old holidays. This clash of values was at the core of the foundation of the British American colonies: the building of "a city upon a hill"[8] juxtaposed "old, corrupted Europe" with the "New World," tradition to future, heritage with progress. In Britain, a century after Cromwell's ban on holidays, dissenters' ideas began to triumph even among the gentry who had sustained the restoration of their own leadership over local communities through supporting the revival of old customs. Moreover, a new work ethic as well as a cult of property and privacy, thrift and self-control began to flourish. In the new individualistic and progress-oriented society, tradition and hierarchy were no longer much praised and leadership took on new forms.

By the late seventeenth century, and especially in the second half of the eighteenth century, the rise of the middle classes and the process of social and cultural differentiation[9] prompted the gentry to detach itself from community life and festivities and thus cut most of the paternalistic bonds that had allowed "misrule" rituals to work as safety valves. The established church had also progressively disengaged itself from the supervision of popular red-letter days.[10] The traditional celebrations and merriments thus became more plebeian and merged with radical movements, thus becoming a means of airing protests. Riots such as those of the Luddists borrowed some of their forms (transvestitism and disguise) from the repertories of the old red-letter days. The distinction between demonstrations and celebrations blurred—at least in those reports which expressed establishment and middle class disapproval. Halloween license became considered as sheer rowdiness and sometimes actually led to petty mischief or crimes.[11]

With industrialization and urbanization the old community fell apart and so did the festivals which used to strengthen its cohesion. Cottagers, tenants, and the poor migrated to the booming towns; social status no longer depended on birth. In this rather "fluid" and unstable social environment, inversion rites and their festive atmosphere of license became much more subversive and were increasingly despised by the new middle class and gentry who were cut off from the traditional holiday spirit and were elaborating new ways to distinguish themselves and maintain their dominant positions.

The national celebration of Guy Fawkes' Day, first celebrated on November 5, 1606, gradually replaced many Halloween rituals on the calendar.[12] Bonfire Night, on the eve of Guy Fawkes' Day, offered common people fire rituals, masqueraded processions, collections, and an occasion to "let off steam", and designate scapegoats (the "Guy" meaning the effigy to be burnt) as had been the case on Halloween. Many of Guy Fawkes' Day's observances were based on those of Halloween, and its social and cultural meanings—the denouncing of deviancies and the celebration of cohesion—were judged by the political elite to be more appropriate than those of Halloween. The "imagined community"[13] highlighted on Bonfire Night was no longer the village but the whole country. Even though Bonfire Night reproduced and eventually replaced many Halloween practices, its purpose was more in harmony with the elite's objective to create disciplined individuals and workers.[14] The emergence of individualism and its supposed social impact—the formation of a relatively homogenous population—actually turned against the old parochial community bodies and their entire sets of particular celebrations.[15] Patriotic holidays could provide citizens with a common identity without jeopardizing this process. Unlike most of the red-letter days, the celebration of November 5 was thus encouraged by the authorities. This caused Halloween to fall into oblivion. By the second half of the nineteenth century, Halloween celebrations were left to children and people living in remote parts of the kingdom (Ireland, Wales, the Highlands). Yet, while it disappeared in England, it was being recreated or "reinvented" in America where it was adapted to the new urban individualistic environment and filled with middle class values.

What Happened to Christmas in America

In America Halloween was not transplanted onto a barren soil, devoid of any festive tradition. However, there were very few celebrations in the New World.[16] Most had been modernized—that is to say adapted to an individualistic, modern society—by the end of the nineteenth century. In colonial America the strength of social order could hardly temper the holiday license and inversion because local authorities were not as powerful as in England, and within rather homogeneous communities there were not as many differences to express and accept.[17] In addition reasons and goals—actually the very values which were to prevail a bit later in industrializing Britain—came into play that had led to the American struggle for independence, utilitarianism, capitalism, individual rights, and personal autonomy. Prescribed status and compulsory behavior were never and nowhere—among whites—as rigid, secure, and praised as in Europe. The culture of authority and hierarchy was not so deeply rooted, and society was thought to be more fluid. Lines between emerging social classes were not—at least theoretically—as difficult to transcend as those between feudal ranks. The new environment and agricultural rhythms were no longer directly connected with the traditional festive calendar. Besides, in places where the Puritan spirit had been dominant, revelries met with objections. Colonial towns had developed a tradition of prohibiting demonstrations for the sake of law, order, and work.[18] Holidays had been observed nonetheless, most of the time informally, privately, among the poor, young and the sailors, more openly and generally in the South where social and cultural structures had developed more in line with the English pattern. But the War of Independence led to the rejection of the remaining old British customs which were not to be replaced by new ones for a long time. As a consequence, there were few traditional holidays in the early nineteenth century, and those few were even more plebeian than in Britain at the same time. Hence they were more likely to either disappear or be reshaped. Most of the local American elites actually not only dissociated themselves from popular culture but also debunked it.

Accordingly, there is no mention of Halloween in the documents before 1849. The frugal Federal culture, heritage of the above-mentioned trends, a reaction to British aristocratic lavishness, and Protestant opposition to any Catholic or pseudo-Catholic, "pagan" demonstration of collective fervor and joy all dominated the period.[19] Besides, people were actually busy building the new nation—or just making money—and they did not consider spending time in leisure. Emerging middle classes tried to distinguish themselves from ways of life of the lower classes with their particular use and "waste" of time and money. They also sustained the revival movements and held that American "manifest destiny" was to lead to the millenium.

Among the lower classes, old revelries continued to exist—providing opportunities to have fun and to forget about poor living conditions. But in strained economic and social contexts, they could lead to demonstrations of public anger, such as noisy parades alongside the fights, damage, and robberies depicted by the newspapers of the time. Thus, for newspaper editors and their readers primarily the social urban elite, these popular celebrations became synonymous with rowdiness and crime. In the new industrial and urban context, they soon emerged as a social problem with which the elite tried to cope with. They gradually considered reshaping a few red-letter days as safety valves which reaffirmed their ideas of social conduct and which could be used as rituals to celebrate and impose their domestic religion. Christmas was first on the list.[20]

"Customary Christmas license combined with seasonal unemployment made the winter holiday a noisy, drunken, threatening period in the eyes of the respectable,"[21] Susan Davis wrote about early nineteenth-century Philadelphia. Paul Gilje agreed: "Callithumpian" or "Fantastical" gangs, noisy and rowdy bands of urban poor young, apprentices and unemployed who roamed New York City's streets during the season, could be considered as "a bridge between the traditional youth group misrule of the English village ... and a more direct challenge to authority."[22] Confronted with drastic demographic change, American cities in the early nineteenth century faced poverty, vagrancy, homelessness and unemployment. There could be an outburst of public anger during the winter season, which was a time of hardship for the poor and a period of scarce jobs: harmless traditional gatherings and masqueraded parades would possibly degenerate into demonstrations of protest and grievances eventually leading to mob riots. While the upper classes increasingly sheltered themselves from the social mixing of the old walking city in more distant new elegant neighborhoods and the poor and immigrants left middle-class business downtowns to settle in close slum areas, bands of roaming lower-class male youth reminded the members of upper- and middle-classes of their existence when reveling freely outside of their own districts.[23] Callithumpian gangs used traditional forms of celebrating holidays to visit the homes of the wealthy, and they made much noise and paraded in costumes down the main streets. For most of the local establishment and middle classes this "made night hideous,"[24] was threatening and became synonymous with misbehavior, drinks in taverns, fights on the streets, outrageous extortions, robberies and petty damage, racial tensions and potential riots.

Fearful reports flourished in newspapers from the 1820s to the 1850s.[25] In 1826, for instance, paraders stopped in front of the mayor's house on Broadway in New York City where they enacted "a scene of disgraceful rage."[26] The next year, another newspaper described these gangs as "a number of ill-bred boys, chimney sweeps, and other illustrious and aspiring persons" longing "to perambulate the streets all night, disturbing the slumbers of the weary ... by thumping upon tin kettles, sounding penny(whistles) and other martial trumpets."[27] In 1828, a violent parade started along the working-class Bowery and went to an upper-class ball in a fancy hotel on Broadway, then marched to a black neighborhood church where they "demolished all the windows, broke the doors and seats", and thrashed African-American congregates, before they went back to the main commercial district, looted shops, and eventually headed to the Battery where they broke the windows of several of the city's wealthiest residences.[28] During the first decades of the century, the upper classes, quickly followed by the middle classes, shifted from either acceptance, tolerance, or even benign neglect to strong disapproval of these public revelries. They planned either to get rid of them or to control them and turn their main actors into what they thought could be good Christians and Americans. The emerging "domestic religion" could help them reach this goal since it was largely spread and reinforced by new rituals. By filling the new Christmas with a culture of family, privacy, sobriety, and gift-giving—actually their own values and their conceptions of America—they attempted to promote their own leadership.[29]

In the early part of the nineteenth century, John Pintard, a wealthy New York City merchant, lamented the lack of holidays in America and the disappearance of old festivals which enabled common people to release their energies in orderly parades. His letters to his daughter are filled with nostalgia for old customs and usages of the Christmas season, when rich and poor folks, old and young, would be together in harmony.[30] He was an antiquarian and the founder of the New York Historical Society; he helped to establish Washington's Birthday and the Fourth of July as national holidays, and fostered the transplantation of St. Nicholas as the patron saint of both New York City and his Society.[31] On St. Nicholas' Day, December 6, 1810, he published a poem, "Sancte Claus goed heylig man," in a broadside that he paid for and which the Historical Society sponsored, accompanied by a picture of St. Nicholas bringing gifts to children. The following years he held banquets in honor of St. Nicholas. He then went on supporting formal calls on New Year's Day's among New York City's establishment: houses were to be opened as usual to friends and relatives. In 1828, however, he acknowledged that "the joyous phenomenon had declined gradually." But, by then, Pintard's efforts had actually been relayed and his focus had gone to a new holiday, a reinvented Christmas, celebrated by both Washington Irving and Clement Moore.[32]

His friend Washington Irving also regretted America's lack of tradition and social harmony, and he thought that an old revived paternalistic

St. Nicholas, 1810. From Stephen Nissenbaum, The Battle for Christmas, 1997.
(Just illustration, not the poem.)

Christmas could help to soothe the violence of modern society. The drastic social and economic changes of the early century created a search for stability and nourished a nostalgia both for the old, supposedly stronger social system and for Christmas's past. In his *Sketchbook of Geoffrey Crayon, Gentleman*, Irving depicted an old British hierarchical order (recreated by the local squire on the pattern of what he thought had been practiced in the past) where, unlike what happened at the time in America (as well as in Britain), all classes joined in harmony.[33] The occasion "seemed to throw open every door, and unlock every heart. It brought the peasant and the peer together, and blended all ranks in a warm generous flow of joy and kindness."[34] Charles Dickens in his *Sketches by Boz*[35] regretted the lack of tradition, too: "Some people will tell you that Christmas is not to them what it used to be … when good old customs were thought more of than at present, and Christmas kept up with greater hospitality."[36] Fear of social unrest, criticism of the new capitalistic setting, nostalgia and idealization of the past merged to forge a "reinvented" tradition.

The theologian Clement Moore, a wealthy New York City landlord and an acquaintance of both Pintard and Irving, did much to support this craving for tradition and social learning by writing an account of a visit from Saint Nicholas ("The Night Before Christmas") in 1822. It was anonymously published the following year in the *Troy Sentinel*, with such success that very soon it was reproduced and illustrated. In his Christmas setting, the binding ties were no longer among different social or status categories of people but among family members. The recipients of the gifts were no longer poor adults but children. Instead of being a public ritualistic exchange between distant adults, Christmas gift-giving became a private happening at home.

> Such a child-centered event was new. Before, children were merely dependents, miniature adults who occupied the bottom of the hierarchy within the family. But perhaps that was exactly the point. Making children the center of joyous attention marked an inversion of the social hierarchy. In essence, the structure of an older Christmas ritual was being precisely preserved: People in position of social and economic authority were offering gifts to their dependents. The ritual of inversion was now based on age and family status alone.[37]

In order to feel comfortable at Christmas time, patricians needed a class of dependents—children—who through their good will would assure them to have fulfilled what they conceived as their paternalistic obligations. The creation of Santa Claus balanced the contemporary common bustle and democratic "misrule". As Nissenbaum remarked, Clement Moore's Old Nick looked like a peddler, precisely the kind of man who might have come to "visit" a wealthy New York patrician on Christmas or New Year's Eve, noisily and uninvited. But in a different, more respectable way—single, old, silent, not with demands but with treats—he was the ideal version of the callithumpian visitor.

A generation later, Santa Claus was taken over by the middle class (and even by a fraction of the poor themselves), who during the seventeenth and eighteenth centuries had objected to the festival, but now became its most ardent champions, imitating the English establishment depicted by Irving and Dickens in the works mentioned above. They also were filled with new concerns such as the problems of increased wealth and leisure time and a growing belief in the importance of home and family unity. In spite of the material benefits that industrialization gave them, they reacted to the ugliness of some of its consequences (poverty, unemployment, social conflict) without questioning it. For a day Santa Claus's generosity albeit balanced the new capitalist materialism and social harshness, while giving manufactured toys as gifts romanticized the emerging consumerism.[38] Urban upper and middle classes installed the belief that Christmas was a time for the celebration of family values and, with Santa Claus presenting a Christ-like figure demanding moral behavior, involving prayer, public ritual, and faith. Fir trees, sitting imposingly in parlors by the 1850s, embodied the new centrality of the home, as illustrated in popular middle-class magazines.[39]

Revisiting, "A Visit from St. Nicholas". From Stephen Nissenbaum, The Battle for Christmas, 1997. (Just illustration, no text.)

Christmas also fostered civil religion and national identity since it soon became both an American icon shared by most people and a joyous duty fulfilled by many. Merchants perceived the benefits they could get in supporting the holiday and of course they did advertise it. The celebration of Christmas as an expression of the new domestic and consumerist way of life came to be regarded as proof of the acceptance of American mainstream values. Half a century after Christmas had been redesigned and its reinvention had contributed to the emergence of a middle-class culture, Halloween underwent a similar process.

Halloween: The Reinvention of a Tradition and the Staging of Middle-Class Values and Identities

> I have often regretted that so many of the diversions which formerly enlivened the leisure hours of very young people should long since have become obsolete, or only be found in circles which are yet untouched with the folly and the affectation of what is called fashion. And also that in families where the children are over-educated ... parents, forgetting that they themselves once were young, allow no recreations, but those of so grave a character, that play becomes more difficult and fatiguing than study.[40]

At the time when Christmas was being reshaped as a child-centered holiday, a new need for play and recreation for youth was identified.

> The more trivial our recreations the more accurately they often reveal the qualities of the mind, as the lightest feather we can toss up will best determine the direction of the wind. If this be true of an individual, it will be equally applicable to a nation, whose family and domestic character we may much better ascertain from their sports, pastimes, and amusements, than from those more prominent and important features to which historians have usually restricted themselves in their delineations: Laws, institutions, empires, pass away and are forgotten.[41]

This link between a nation and its sports would be clearly emphasized in the second part of the century after editors, journalists, educators and social workers took this concern into account and supported holidays and recreation: "Nothing shows the character of a people more truly than the manner in which it observes its holidays, and the kind of amusement followed by a nation is a fairly true index to its degree of moral development."[42] By the 1870s, Halloween appeared as one of the best holidays to turn children into good Americans.

After "reinventing" Christmas, the middle class actually reshaped other red-letter days: St Valentine's Day in the 1840s to 1850s, Thanksgiving and Easter by the 1860s. Halloween appeared a decade later in magazines and newspapers, as well as in calendars and entertaining guidebooks.[43] Burns' and Gay's poetic depictions of the ritualistic community evening were well known to the educated and Christmas nourished a whole nostalgia about what was thought to be the old celebration. A *New York Times* journalist expressed regret that

> the glory of this once popular festival [had] departed. Its triumph and rough jollities, festive and marriage rites are a matter of history, and live only in the

immortal verse of Burns and traditional folklore ... The old Halloween revelries are gone. Even in New York, among the Scotch-Irish inhabitants, they live in the memory only as tradition—a pleasant tradition it is true, but never to be revived or reenacted on this early stage. That last night passed over the heads of many who did not even recollect that it was Halloween we doubt not, and in a few years, when the older generation gives way to the new, when modern social customs have effectively worked out of existence the antique pleasantries of older condition of societies the 'heirs of civilization' will laugh at the absurdities of 'the old folks' and be laughed at their tune hereafter.[44]

Indeed, Gaelic clubs and Caledonian societies were reported to be the only places where the holiday was still observed.[45]

Yet Halloween might have been celebrated elsewhere, especially in rural communities in the Alleghenies or in Canada.[46] There it would have taken on old-fashioned carnivalesque forms: disguised beggars collecting food, and pranks performed by the young (e.g. inversion practices or mischievous pranks as carts on roofs, pieces of outdoor furniture on trees, soaped windows, turned-over outhouses, painted cows unleashed in the meadows). Adults usually agreed treating teenagers whose victims were usually recruited among the old, single, non-integrated members and whose pranks were very much appreciated by the other adults.[47] However, by the 1870s, Halloween was surely not popular throughout the continent.

In newspapers such as *The New York Times*, Halloween was reported to exist in the cities: immigrants, poor, and rural people coming to towns celebrated the day in their own way. In the cities the traditional rural misrule was regarded as as a "carnival of lawlessness."[48] For the newcomers to the urban setting, it provided a picturesque way to discover their new world. They accompanied their peers and neighbors, met people and visited the city. Parading through its streets, along monuments and public institutions, they became accustomed to their new geographic and social environment. In this regard the students especially looked forward to Halloween: not long after their first encounter with their peers and new environment, they used to make a spectacle of themselves and parade through the streets. The festive event provided them with fun, a guided tour of their new world and a very appropriate rite of integration. They played the pranks they could have played before in their rural native places and mocked the local elite.[49] But the first few reports of city-wide Halloweens in newspapers strongly opposed the demonstrations:[50] honorable passers-by were said to have been insulted or assaulted (with flour, bags of feathers), even injured, traffic was interrupted and signs torn down. Halloween observances became thus synonymous with damaged property and juvenile rowdiness. Among the paraders were many blacks, unemployed and poor people. Frowning members of the middle class thus linked Halloween merriments with the outcast.

> Before darkness bands of boys, in which negroes predominated, paraded the streets, hooting and shouting and leaving behind them a trail of flour ... About three o'clock a crowd of fully 200 hoodlums rushed down Newspaper Row, yelling and whistling and flinging flour at every one they met. At the Corner of 14th Str. and the Avenue they surrounded a man and woman who were on their way to a theater when the two broke away from this unwelcome company, covered with flour ...[51]

Halloween could be a way to air grievances and fears,[52] but the line between revelry and riot was, once again, very loose. It had thus to be given a new, more appropriate Victorian flavor.[53]

By the 1870s middle-class periodicals and women's magazines brought Halloween home as a respectable part of the domestic and civil religion.[54] Children, teenagers, and young adults were their targets. Practices were reshaped to be supervised by mothers and educators. In many booklets and articles, Celtic beliefs in the supernatural were used to create the gothic atmosphere and new ghoulish decor which soon became a characteristic of this time of the year. A selection of rites picked up in the works of British antiquarians were made into games, stunts, races, plays, love divinations, and pantomimes.[55] The new celebration was to take place inside, in the parlor, kitchen, cellar, attic, and sometimes even in the garden. The sacred sphere of home was to counter the corrupting dreaded public sphere—a pattern similar to that of Christmas.

Women's magazines[56] provided mothers with the different steps to spend an entertaining evening and keep guests inside: First the invitations, then the introductions (usually ghostly), stunts (about Halloween gothic themes), games, refreshments and dinners, playlets, visits to horror chambers, sometimes bonfires and camp story tellings. A series of norms were taught playfully: respect for property and order, compliance with supervising adults who were in charge of the ritual, even though the children were told it was their celebration. The holiday was being used not only to teach children what was valued by mainstream society, but also to orient their gender identities, roles, and expectations. In the playlets, stunts and games designed or reshaped for the evening, girls had to forecast through special divination rites who their future husbands would be and they were taught to become "perfect wives." Or, as their mothers tried to do, they had to discipline mischievous and tough boys and get them off the streets back into the sacred domestic sphere. The latter had to listen to girls and eventually be "converted" and "saved."[57] Halloween helped to reinforce the images that white Anglo-Saxon Protestant middle classes had of themselves—of female and male roles and positions, social expectations—and also those of their country.

Stunts and games provided by juvenile literature,[58] women's magazines and booklets of games written especially for Halloween stressed challenges, individual records, and skills, developed originality and spontaneity (for which editors and journalists gave instructions[59]). Prizes were recommended to be given for the most original, ugliest, funniest costumes, as well as to the most skillful players. Stunts were believed to foster a spirit of competition which in the "age of the self-made man" was thought to be very much American. The holiday's (hi)story was underlined in order to impose as immutable a whole series of British rites.[60] If Irish immigrants may have added some stamina to the custom in America, they were not much referred to, compared to Northern English and Scottish or Scotch-Irish immigrants. While immigration became more and more important, established middle classes praised all the more their Anglo-Saxon identities and thus preferred to emphasize this very English Protestant heritage rather than the Irish Catholic one.[61] Besides, American figures, such as the ghost of George Washington, were called to visit.[62] Performances could provide a lesson of Anglo-Saxon identity. Halloween worked as a way to Americanize children and make sure that the United States, in the context of massive immigration, was and would remain an Anglo-Saxon culture.

Yet, this normative effort faced strong resistance. For both ways of celebrating, the public, lower class and the private, middle class were in conflict. The reinvented tradition was too prescriptive and too compulsory. The targeted populations could not be reached by the ways and references that this reshaping wanted to develop. Booklets and magazines addressed only middle class people. Poor people, immigrants' children, teenagers and students went on celebrating Halloween the old way and parading and rowdiness remained a means to air grievances and claims as well as to reaffirm identities and differences.

In response to the question of how to get Halloween under control, the celebration had to take place at home. This program was applied with some success to private middle-class Halloweens and to some public ones: university administrations, for example, managed to control their own students' festivities. To get them off the streets and back to the alma mater, balls were organized on campuses. For social workers and educators, this was the proof that this approach could be adapted to neighborhoods and even whole cities and turned into large-scale supervised community events. By the early twentieth century, new devices were found to control public carnivalesque revelries and to deal with what was now called the "Halloween problem" (its pranks, "mischief", and the actual reluctance of the poor and teenagers to celebrate at home).[63] Social workers and educators tried to involve community clubs, schools, YMCAs, parent-teacher associations, Kiwanis Clubs, as well as Chambers of Commerce and City Halls to organize huge community events with floats, parades, costume contests, plays, sport tournaments,[64] dances, and merriments. To keep kids and teenagers busy, to make them play and have fun under adult supervision,[65] and to keep them away from soaping windows, throwing eggs, playing with fire and from generally misbehaving, organizers set up local events such as downtown window-painting contests, neighborhood chambers of horrors or witches' dens, and public theatricals.

This change in the celebration of the holiday went along with the emergence of child and adolescence studies.[66] On October 31, 1916, in Fort Worth, Texas, four thousand schoolchildren took part in an afternoon masquerade and pageant. At night, scenes were staged on floats which passed along the streets. The subject was *Preparedness for Peace* (!), and included scenes from American history in which peace played an honorable part, the conference of William Penn and the Quakers with the Indians, and the opening of the East to American trade. This was not a subject limited to performances at Hallowtide, and yet, Halloween offered a joyful opportunity to stage topics and teach students. The students had to do research on Halloweenish themes to become familiar with Anglo-Saxon identity and American history, and they had to set up committees and develop initiatives.[67] At a time when America was entering an age of organization and recoining its social goals from the production of self-made men to that of good team workers,[68] these tasks were supposed to arouse comradeship and to support the habit of working in a group.

> The festival provides the only way in which the vast masses of our enormous city can find any adequate expression of the great ideas of freedom, equality, fraternity, duty, loyalty, service, which ought to be fixed stars in the firmament of popular imagination in a democratic society.[69]

Other initiatives were elaborated to get rid of teenagers' Halloween mischief and develop their civic conscience:

> An attempt to make the teaching of citizenship function in a practical way is being made this week in Chicago, according to a plan sponsored by Dr. William McAndrew, Superintendent of Schools. The objective is to lead boys and girls to change their attitude towards Halloween pranks which are said to have deteriorated into extreme rudeness, disregard for the comfort of others, trespass upon private property, displacement of it, sometimes into misdemeanor and criminality. Chicago principals and superintendents have united to try a practical test of citizenship teaching. Every teacher is making a series of enquiries of all her children as to who is paying for their education and as to what each child owes in return. An effort is being made to impress upon the young people that every citizen of Chicago, whether he has children in school or not, is paying good money

... and that they are obtaining the benefits. The question is being put to them: 'how, therefore, should you behave on Halloween?' The Flag salute: 'I pledge allegiance to the American flag and to the republic for which it stands,' is being interpreted by the chicks 'what does it mean to pledge allegiance?' 'Who is the republic?' ... 'If I promise to protect all these people within 24 hours of making my promise I annoy them (the republic, everybody) and injure them ...; I am a liar and a traitor.'[70]

Yet these diverse attempts to discipline poor and young people did not completely succeed. In many periodicals from the 1920s to the 1950s Halloween was reported to have lost its "good old spirit" and degenerated into mere juvenile vandalism; the youth kept resisting and asserting another identity, which they thought was their very own. Halloween was no longer a unanimous rite (if it had ever been), but a battlefield of competing rites, norms, values and representations of the self (as far as youths were concerned). It offered middle class normative celebration, along with expectations about youth and America, which the lower classes challenged licentiously.

Halloween (as well as other holidays) in the United States had been redesigned to fit in with the capitalist urban environment as an American tradition supposed to teach lower-class and immigrant children the norms and values of the white Anglo-Saxon Protestant middle-classes. They were considered part of the national culture which had to be reinforced in a context of massive immigration. Rituals were redefined to be performed by youths so that the references and images that they put into practice might inspire their daily behavior. But this attempt to make Halloween part of the process of the "Americanization" of the newcomers, the poor and their children, did not really succeed. Those who were targeted resisted and invented—or kept their own traditional—ways of celebrating. It induced a competition of rites and of claims and representations of what America meant to participants. This was the first step towards today's multiple reappropriations and celebrations of a diverse holiday. For the past twenty years, Halloween has been extremely popular and its celebration has spread to new places and categories of people. In America, it has lately been turned into a community and adult event. Furthermore, for the past five years its party spirit has come to France and Germany where until then Halloween had been completely unknown. And, one is compelled to admit, so far the event has been a great commercial success.

Notes

1. The notion of a reinvented holiday is borrowed from Eric Hobsbawm and Terence Ranger, eds., *The Invention of Tradition* (1983; Cambridge, MA: Cambridge University Press, 1994).
2. Halloween is the contraction of All Hallows' Eve, the English word for Samhain, the Celtic end of the year and beginning of winter. All Hallows' Day was established in 837 by Pope Gregory IV to christianize the day, after many fruitless attempts to eradicate its "heathenish" practices and beliefs.
3. According to travel narratives, ministers' pamphlets against "pagan" observances, and early nineteenth-century records of antiquities, such as H. Bourne, *Antiquitates Vulgares* ... (Newcastle, 1725); J. Brand, *Observations on Popular Antiquities* (1776; London: Vernor, Hood & Shapes, 1810); T. Pennant, *A Tour in Scotland* (Chester: Monk, 1771); C. Vallancey, *Collectanea de Rebus Hibernicis* (Dublin: White, 1781); C.S. Burne, *The Handbook of Folklore* (London: Sidwick & Jackson, 1914); the volumes of *The Folklore Record* (London: Nutt, William Glaisher, Sidwick & Jackson, especially those published between 1878 and 1930); the periodical *Folklore* (London—especially the issues between 1888 and 1939).
4. As mentioned in the documents quoted above.
5. This was the social season in many places according to the sources mentioned above.
6. They were called mummers' plays and practiced at other moments in the year, such as the twelve days of Christmas, Candlemas, Eastertime, or even Ascension Day. In the sources used, the ministers, travelers, and antiquarians stressed the link between these practices and dates.
7. Louis Dumont's *Homo hierarchicus. Le système des castes et ses implications* (1966; Paris: Gallimard, 1978)—referring not to old Britain or other Ancien Régime society but to contemporary India—presents this cultural cult of hierarchy with its stable and rigid social organization.
8. The Puritan and Congregationalist colonists' ("Pilgrims") project was to cross the ocean and build "a new Jerusalem" in the "Promised Land."
9. Broadly and brilliantly first analyzed by Norbert Elias in *La Civilisation des moeurs* (1939; Paris: Calmann-Lévy, 1969).
10. David Cressy analyzed this particular trend in *Bonfires and Bells: National Memories and the Protestant Calendar in Elizabethan and Stuart England* (London: Weidenfield and Nicolson, 1983), 170. For a general history of the ancient British holidays, see Robert W. Malcolmson, *Popular Recreations in English Society 1700-1850* (Cambridge, MA: Cambridge University Press, 1973), especially 68, 130.
11. E.P. Thompson, "'Rough music': le charivari anglais", *Annales ESC* (March-April 1972): 285-312; "Patrician Society, Plebeian Culture," *Journal of Social History* 7 (1974): 382-405.
12. This tendency was particularly obvious to antiquarians, who reported it in their folk collections: see M. Banks, *British Calendar Customs*, Scotland, v. II (London: L. Glaisher, 1939); "Brand Material," *Folklore* (March 1912): 10-170; C.S. Burne, *The Handbook of Folklore* (London: The Folklore Society, 1914); R. Chambers, *The Book of Days: A Miscellany of Popular Antiquities* (London: Tegg, 1864); Thyselton Dyer, *English Folklore* (London: Hardwicks and Bogue, 1878); *British Calendar Customs* (London: Bells and Sons, 1876); R. T. Hampson, *Medii Aevi Kalendarium* (London: Kent Carston, 1841); Mrs Gutch, *County Folklore*, vol. 6 (London: Bells and Sons, 1876); W. Hone, *The Year Book* (London: Tegg, 1832); *The Every-Day Book, or the Guide to the Year* ... (London: Tegg, 1827); J. E. Simpkins, *County Folklore*, vol. 7 (London: The Folklore Society, 1914);

J. Strutt, *The Sports and Pastimes of the People of England* ... (London: Tegg, 1834); N. W. Thomas, *County Folklore* (London: Nutt, 1903).
13. See Benedict Anderson, *Imagined Communities. Reflections on the Origins and Spread of Nationalism* (London: Verso, 1991).
14. Depicted by Karl Polanyi, *La Grande transformation* (1944: Paris: Gallimard, 1983). This sociologist focused on the process of turning craftsmen and peasants into "good" workers. According to Polanyi this "great transformation" first took place in England, from where it spread to the whole of the Western hemisphere.
15. At the same time as the "great transformation" took place, the concept of citizenship evolved. Community members gradually became individuals whose common identity was based on the growing importance of national origin; cf. Ernest Gellner, *Nations et nationalismes* (Paris: Payot, 1989).
16. Eighteenth-century and early nineteenth-century American calendars as well as travel narratives scarcely mentioned holidays. This lack of attention reflects a predominant resentment against traditional merriments.
17. See, for instance, Bernard Bailyn, *The Peopling of British North America* (New York: Harper, 1986), 1-35.
18. See Cressy, *Bells and Bonfires*, 190-206.
19. The first North American document mentioning Halloween is a Canadian almanac published in Halifax, Nova Scotia: *The Belcher's Farmer Almanack for the Year 1849*; the first reference in print in the United States appeared in 1861 in *The Fireman's Almanach and Reference Book for the Year 1861* published in Brooklyn. By the late 1870s the mentioning of Halloween was becoming commonplace in calendars—an indication of its spreading throughout the country.
20. See Stephen Nissenbaum, *The Battle for Christmas* (New York: Knopf, 1996). Various essays on Christmas in America appeared in nineteenth-century literature, diaries, newspapers and periodicals demonstrating how the members of the New York City establishment succeeded in turning old Christmas celebrations and potential riots into a private and safe festival centered around families and homes; Penne Restad, *Christmas in America* (New York: Oxford University Press, 1995), depicts how the modern Christmas, soon after it was designed, spread both to the whole of the United States and from top (of society) to bottom; it also shows how merchants turned it into a commercial bonanza, a process which supported its broad diffusion as well as its "mainstream" new touch; J.M. Golbie and A.W. Purdue, *The Making of the Modern Christmas* (Athens: University of Georgia Press, 1986), illustrates this particular reinvention of Christmas and its Victorianization through popular culture; Susan Davis, *Parades and Power: Street Theatre in 19th-Century Philadelphia* (Philadelphia: Temple University Press, 1986), proves that according to local diaries and newspapers the season proved to be a time for rowdy demonstrations in early nineteenth-century Philadelphia, in which craftsmen and workers, young and poor people could air their grievances. Soon this outburst of emotions was resented by middle-class and upper-class citizens. Therefore, spontaneous street shivarees were gradually replaced by more organized and socially-controlled parades.
21. Davis, *Parades and Power*, 108.
22. Paul Gilje, *The Road To Mobocracy: Popular Disorder in New York City, 1763-1834* (Chapel Hill, NC: North Carolina University Press, 1989), 130-33, 253-60, cited in Nissenbaum, *The Battle for Christmas*, 55.
23. As David Nissenbaum notes in *The Battle for Christmas*, 52-57.
24. Susan Davis, "'Making Night Hideous': Christmas Revelry and Public Order in nineteenth-Century Philadelphia," *American Quarterly* 34 (Summer 1982): 185-99, based on diaries and articles from local newspapers.

25. As David Nissenbaum states in *The Battle for Christmas*, 52-55; *New York Advertiser*, January 4, 1828; *New York American*, January 4, 1822; December 28, 1827; *New York Morning Herald*, December 25, 1839; *New York Daily Herald*, December 23, 1839; *New York Tribune*, January 3, 1850.
26. Gilje, *The Road to Mobocracy*, 253-54, cited in Nissenbaum, *The Battle for Christmas*, 54.
27. Ibid.
28. *New York Advertiser*, January 4, 1828; Gilje, *The Road to Mobocracy*, 257-59—references cited in Nissenbaum, *The Battle for Christmas*, 255.
29. This use or reinvention of a holiday by the elites to reassert their leadership is particularly well illustrated in Restad, *Christmas in America*, 42-57; Nissenbaum, *The Battle For Christmas*, 90-130.
30. *Letters from John Pintard to his Daughter 1816-1833*. 4 vols. (New York: New York Historical Society, 1940), vol. 1: 44, 151, 156, 161, 358-59; vol. 2: 117, 320, 324, 382; vol. 3: 51-52, 117, analyzed by Nissenbaum, *The Battle for Christmas*, 49.
31. Nissenbaum, *The Battle for Christmas*, 55.
32. Ibid., 57; Restad, *Christmas in America*, 46; Golbie and Purdue, *The Making of the Modern Christmas*, 75.
33. Washington Irving, "Christmas", "Christmas Eve", "Christmas Day", "The Christmas Dinner", in *The Sketch Book of Geoffrey Crayon, Gent.* (1818-1819; New York: The Heritage Press, 1939), 194-200, 209-21, 222-37, 238-54.
34. Irving, "Christmas day", 222-37.
35. Charles Dickens wrote his *Sketches by Boz* in 1833 and his *Christmas Carol* in 1842. These references are taken from Restad, *Christmas in America*, 136-140.
36. References cited in Nissenbaum, *The Battle For Christmas*, 58.
37. Nissenbaum, *The Battle For Christmas*, 62.
38. Restad, *Christmas in America*, 57-74; Leigh Eric Schmidt, "Christmas Bazaar", in *Consumer Rites: The Buying and Selling of American Holidays* (Princeton, NJ: Princeton University Press, 1995), 105-95; William Waist, *The Modern Christmas in America* (New York: New York University Press, 1993), 50.
39. Such as *Godey's Magazine and Lady's Book* (December 1850, January 1851); Schmidt, *Consumer Rites*, 120, 125; *Harper's Weekly* (December 25, 1858); Thomas Nast's drawings and sketches for the same magazine, December 29, 1866, did much to spread these "traditional" representations, Restad, *Christmas in America*: 118.
40. Miss Leslie, *American Girl Book of Occupations for Play Hours* (Boston: Munrose & Francis, 1831), 11 (introduction).
41. Horatio Smith et al., *Festivals, Games & Amusements: Ancient & Modern* (1832; New York: Harper, 1844), 13.
42. Helen Patten, *The Year's Festival* (Boston: Este, 1903).
43. "Hallow Eve", *Frank Leslie's Chimney Corner* (a special publication for children from *Frank Leslie's Magazine*) (November 11, 1865); "Hallowe'en", *Scribner's Monthly* (November 1871); "Hallowe'en", *Godey's Lady's Book*, (November 1872); "All Hallow Eve", *The New York Times* (November 1, 1872); "The Decadence of Halloween", *New York Times* (November 1, 1876); Annie Frost and Henry Williams, *Evening Amusements* (New York: Williams, 1878).
44. "The Decadence of Halloween", *New York Times*, November 1, 1876: 8.
45. In Toronto, Montreal, Boston, and New York, the Gaelic and Caledonian societies were social clubs. They arranged meetings and banquets for prominent local Anglo-Saxon personalities. During these events poems and speeches about the Old Country's folklore and traditions were delivered and common roots emphasized. These very activities were sometimes published in special books and booklets. See Alexander Dick, *Splores of a Hal-*

loween Twenty Years Ago (Woodstock: W. Warwick, 1867). Or they were reported in newspapers: "Celebration of Halloween by the Gaelic Club," *New York Times*, November 2, 1891: 6.
46. Especially in Scottish, Scotch-Irish, and Welsh communities, because immigration to the New World was often a way to strengthen community structures, when these were disrupted in the Old World: Bernard Bailyn, *The Peopling of British North America* (New York: Harper, 1986); Timothy Smith, "Religion and Ethnicity in America", *American Historical Review*, 83 (December 1978): 1155-85.
47. For the remainder of Halloween practices in remote places, see lore collections such as Wayland D. Hand, ed., *The Franck C. Brown Collection of North Carolina Folklore* (Durham, NC: Duke University Press, 1961), vols. 6 and 7; Harry M. Hyatt, *Folklore from Adams County, Ill.* (Memoirs of the Alma Hyatt Foundation, 1935); and of course the *Journal of American Folklore* (Arlington, VA, 1888-), the first issues (1888-1913) provide the reader with many short references to Halloween or other similar festive events.
48. "Halloween in Washington: Harmless Sports of the Past Have Given Way to Rowdyism," *New York Times*, November 4,1894: 19.
49. Keith Walden, "Respectable Hooligans: Male Toronto College Students Celebrate Halloween 1884-1910," *Canadian Historical Review* 68 (March 1987): 1-34.
50. There would be many more articles later, by the 1890s, when Halloween began to become worth mentioning as part of a new American folklore, and as source of increasing juvenile misbehavior.
51. "Halloween in Washington," *New York Times*, November 4, 1894, 15.
52. This was the case for students whose status and future remained unstable in an environment of rapid social and economic change: Walden, "Respectable Hooligans," 25-33.
53. Karen S. Hybertsen, "'The Return of Chaos': The Uses and Interpretations of Halloween from the Victorian Era to the Present," Ph.D. diss., Drew University, 1993.
54. "Hallow Eve," *Frank Leslie's Chimney Corner* (November 11, 1865), 377 is a depiction of traditional Halloween practices and its nature as a cheerful family event; "Hallowe'en," *Scribner's Monthly* (November 1871); *Godey's Ladies' Magazine* published stories of young ladies who ritually found their true loves.
55. *Harper's Monthly, Harper's Bazar, Harper's Weekly, Colliers* etc. See also Mary Barse, *Games for Halloween* (New York: Barse & Hopkins, 1912); A.H. Burnett, *Halloween at Merryvale* (New York: New York Book Co., 1914); Edna Guptill, *The Complete Halloween Book* (Lebanon: March Brothers, 1912); E.G. Koogle, *Halloween Adventure* (Lebanon: March Brothers, 1906).
56. *Godey's Lady's Magazine*, and then by the 1890s the *Woman's Home Companion, Ladies' Home Journal, The Delineator.*
57. For example M. Schell, *Halloween Festivities* (New York: Denton, 1900); E. Guptill, *Bright Ideas for Halloween* (Lebanon: March Brothers, 1915) published stunts and plays for special Halloween parties and even presented a dialogue for a mischievous boy and a wise girl, who told the boy the meaning of the holy eve and explained how to behave properly. This topic and kind of play would later become widespread.
58. *Harper's Round Table, St Nicholas.*
59. Mrs. Hamilton Mott, *Home Games and Parties* (Phildadelphia: Curtis Publishing, 1891), 147, recommended innocent, not too elaborate merriments, barn-like decorations, the "pairing of lads and lassies," divinations, recipes for supper (simple meals, such as caviar sandwiches!), gift-giving, recitations of poems: "Burns' 'Halloween' is especially appropriate and "Tam O' Shanter" will help produce the sensation of thrilling excitement which is true Halloween spirit;" Martha Orne, *Halloween and How To Celebrate It* (Boston: Baker, 1898), gave advice on how to play games in the kitchen and invite unmarried

friends ("married couples are rather de trop on such occasion"), "and especially avoid all formality."

60. This aspect frequently appears in articles of the general magazines: *Harper's Monthly, Harper's Bazar, Harper's Weekly, Colliers* etc. It is also developed in the parlor theatricals.
61. "All Hallow Eve", *New York Times*, November 1, 1872: 8; Annie Frost and Henry Williams, *Evening Amusements* ... (New York: Williams, 1878), 83; the book presented a series of old Scottish Halloween divinations and games; D.C. Beard, *The American Girl Handybook* (1887; New York: Charles Scribner's Sons, 1898), 187, staged plays about druids, their harvest rites and great fires and listed "superstitions made into games now." Burton Kingsland, *In and Outdoor Games* (New York: Doubleday, 1904), 27, maintained Scotland was "Halloween home."
62. For instance E. Glover, *"Dame Curtsey's" Book of Guessing Contests* (Chicago: McCleng, 1908).
63. See magazines such as *Playground* (later entitled *Recreation*), *The Rotarian* or *The American Home*.
64. Robert Meyer Jr., *Festivals USA* (New York: Warbush, 1950); see also "Keep Halloween in Park," *The New York Times*, November 1, 1913: iv, 4, "To Make Halloween Safe and Sane", *The Survey* (October 1917): 30-31; *Playground*, ibid. (October 1921): 432-33; February 1922: 578-79.
65. A.M. Chesley, *Social Activities for Young Men and Boys* (New York: Arno Press, 1913), advised YMCA leaders to "secure a leader for 6 boys (Six boys being the right number for a country farm Halloween party)."
66. As Dominick Carvalho remarked in *Morals and Muscles: Organized Playgrounds and Urban Reform, 1880-1920* (Philadelphia: University of Pennsylvania Press, 1981).
67. R.E. Kelley, *The Book of Halloween* (Boston: Lothrop, 1919), 170-71.
68. William H. Whyte, Jr., *L'Homme de l'organisation* (1847; Paris: 1977); Daniel Riesman *La Foule solitaire* (Paris, New York: 1962).
69. Percival Chubb, *Festivals and Plays in Schools and Elsewhere* (New York: Harper & Brothers, 1912), 118; see also Mrs Needham, *Folk Festivals*, (Cleveland, OH: 1912), 5.
70. "The teaching of Citizenship and Halloween Pranks in Chicago," *School and Society*, November 7, 1925: 585-86.

Chapter 11

CLIMATE, IDENTITY, AND WINTER CARNIVALS IN NORTH AMERICA

Bernard Mergen

WHAT HAPPENS WHEN members of a community decide to hold a public celebration to commemorate some feature or accomplishment of their community? Who are the organizers? How do they decide when, where, and how to hold the festival? What activities are officially sponsored? What unofficial behavior is prohibited? These are some of the questions that must be addressed when considering the relation of festivals and ceremonies to group and national identities. Historians and anthropologists agree that festivals—whether arising more or less spontaneously in response to a specific event such as a political victory, or ritualized in periodic celebrations that adhere to rigid formulas such as religious holidays—reveal deeply held attitudes and values. When a community or part of a community celebrates in public it displays its character, but in its presentation it may ridicule as well as reaffirm its identity. It may simultaneously flout and flaunt its sense of self, as individual participants interpret and improvise their performances within the structure of the festival. Above all, as Johan Huizinga observed, festivals are a form of play.[1]

This paper looks at the first organized winter carnival in the United States, which was held in St. Paul, Minnesota, February 1 to 13, 1886. Its origins, its specific activities and events, and the explicit and implicit pur-

---

Notes for this section begin on page 226.

poses of its sponsors tell a familiar story of civic pride and boosterism, competition for trade and tourism, and conflicts among participating groups. A celebration based on natural phenomena such as winter, however, raises several questions about the ways in which festivals grow out of and help to shape a regional identity. Moreover, it raises questions about the relation of regional to national identities. What part does gender, ethnicity, and class play in organizing and maintaining rituals? Does the celebration of winter, in St. Paul and other places, tell us anything about American attitudes toward nature? By placing the St. Paul Winter Carnival of 1886 in the context of the meanings of winter weather in nineteenth-century North America and by examining closely the parades and events of the festival, I hope to show that what began as an effort by the city's businessmen to promote investment and tourism became a polysemic event in which various and sometimes conflicting interests were expressed.

Freezing temperatures and deep snows were hallmarks of winter weather in the area that became St. Paul. Minnesota acquired an image as America's Siberia, but in the 1850s a pioneer newspaper editor proclaimed that the state's climate was a source of the robustness and longevity of its citizens. The cold was healthful, invigorating, and fun. By the 1880s the state had a number of sanatoriums for patients suffering from tuberculosis and other diseases.[2] Minnesota's climate was, of course, not unique. To the north, Canadians experienced long, cold winters and sought ways to turn them to their advantage. In 1883 the city of Montreal organized its first winter carnival and succeeded in attracting tourists from all over the world.[3] Its carnival grew over the next two years, but a smallpox epidemic late in 1885 forced officials to cancel plans for the 1886 celebration.

St. Paul, in economic competition with its neighbor Minneapolis and anxious to promote its position as the railroad center of the northwest, saw the cancellation of Montreal's carnival as an opportunity to sponsor its own. The choice of a winter carnival to promote the city of St. Paul was therefore partly inspired by nature—climate was a determinant of St. Paul's culture—and partly the result of Montreal's temporary misfortune—an unpredictable event that had nothing to do with the identity that St. Paul sought to create. Indeed, significant differences between American and Canadian attitudes toward winter and toward carnivals are obscured by the use of the phrase "winter carnival" for both festivals, but it is beyond the scope of this paper to make detailed comparisons.[4]

American attitudes toward winter originate in what Karen Ordahl Kupperman has called "the puzzle of the American climate in the early colonial period."[5] European expectations about North American weather were based on the assumption that climates would be similar along the lines of latitude, warmer toward the equator, colder toward the poles. English writers, Kupperman points out, usually used the words "climate" and "latitude" synonymously and promoters of colonization maintained that English culture was a product of England's temperate climate. Therefore, they were more concerned that New England, sharing the latitudes of northern Spain and Portugal, would be too hot, not too cold. When experience demonstrated that summers were warmer than in England, but that winters were much harsher, colonists and their financial backers became concerned, lest the colonial effort fail because of cold and snow.

As they searched for explanations of New England's freezing temperatures, promoters also sought to reassure colonists that they were strong enough to overcome the hardships and that the abundance of food and fuel in the New World more than compensated for temporary discomfort. Failure to thrive, they argued, was a sign of laziness, ignorance, or moral weakness. Finally, they reasoned, settlement would ultimately improve the climate. Cutting forests would allow more sunlight to warm the land, and the fires of the hearths of Boston and other towns would remove the chill from the air.

Weather modification and climate improvement through human activity remained a powerful belief—that "rain follows the plow" was its most familiar expression in the nineteenth century—but many residents of New England and New France enjoyed snow and winter and did not wish to modify their climate. For them, cold and snow were a measure of their physical, mental, and moral strength; and the contest between man and nature, an emblem of their identity. St. Paul storekeeper and railroad developer James J. Hill, who was born near Guelph, Ontario, in 1838, summed up their creed: "No man on whom the snow does not fall ever amounts to a tinker's damn."[6]

Generations of New England poets, beginning with Timothy Dwight, Philip Freneau, and William Cullen Bryant, and continuing with Ralph Waldo Emerson, John Greenleaf Whittier, and Emily Dickinson, extolled the benefits, beauty, and pleasures of cold winters. The painter George Henry Durrie and countless illustrators for Currier and Ives and other lithographers depicted winter scenes of family reunions, promenades in graceful sleighs, and carefree children sledding. These images of winter were carried throughout the nation in schoolbooks and Christmas cards. Like an expanding glacier, winter snow grew from a regional icon to a seasonal symbol of the nation even where it seldom fell.[7]

The joys of winter and childhood were closely linked. Snow invited play—building snowmen, snowball fights, sledding—spontaneous activities that by the 1880s were receiving increased attention from adults. Magazines for children such as *The Child at Home, Golden Days for Boys and Girls,* and *St. Nicholas,* featured stories on winter recreation, and in 1880 the illustrator and author Daniel Beard offered instructions on "Snowball Warfare," the building of "Snow-Houses and Statuary," and the construction of "Sleds, Chair-Sleighs, and Snow-Shoes" in magazine articles. Inventors took out more than sixteen patents for children's sleds before 1886, and by 1883 the Paris Manufacturing Company in Maine was selling 200,000 of its sleds annually. The discovery of children's play contributed directly to the emerging leisure ethic that Herbert Spencer labeled the "gospel of relaxation." This gospel was preached by supporters of the St. Paul Winter Carnival.[8]

The most popular recreational activity of the Montreal Winter Carnival of 1883 was snowshoeing, but the Canadian pastime that appealed most to Americans was tobogganing. Reporting on the Montreal toboggan slides, *American Agriculturist,* a popular magazine of rural life, claimed that tobogganing and other winter amusements made "a strong and healthful race, which rises superior to the hard conditions of climate." Moreover, the toboggan was seen as the perfect adult alternative to the reckless and dangerous sledding by children on their small cutters. It is not a coincidence that the city of St. Paul banned sledding on a popular hill just weeks before the 1886 carnival and that a newspaper published a maudlin story about an Italian immigrant whose wood carvings were destroyed when a reckless boy struck him with a sled.[9]

When plans for the St. Paul Winter Carnival began to take shape in October 1885, its citizens organized clubs to promote winter sports. The St. George's Snow Shoe Club of Montreal chartered a St. Paul chapter and recruited members from the city's social elite. Five additional snowshoe clubs were formed with 1,400 participants, and 2,800 tobogganists joined forty-seven clubs to practice their sport. Some of the most prominent organizations, namely Wacouta, Nushka and Windsor, encouraged both snowshoeing and tobogganing, and built elaborate slides for the exclusive use of their members. Following the Canadian example, women were generally excluded from snowshoeing, an activity equated with manly virtues and male camaraderie, but tobogganing allowed women an opportunity to participate and in a sense to control the outcome of the slide.[10]

Paul Larson, in his well-illustrated book on Minnesota winter carnivals, quotes a tongue-in-cheek newspaper article of 1886 that conveys covert messages in a list of "rules":

1. When a gentleman takes a lady down the slide and she, by her swaying from side to side, upsets him in the snow, the practice of picking up the toboggan and thumping her over the head with it is now obsolete in good society. ...

3. After a gentleman has broken a leg or his neck he is expected to make his apologies to his companion and withdraw for the evening. It is regarded as bad form to go on sliding unless particularly requested to do so by the lady. ...

6. When steering it is unadvisable to seek to get extra purchase by planting your unemployed foot in the small of the back of the lady in front of you.[11]

Such playful advice, Larson notes, shows that tobogganing was a challenge to the social codes of the day, but the "rules" are similar to the commentary accompanying the croquet fad of the 1860s and 70s. Croquet permitted young men and women close physical contact that was otherwise prohibited. In the game, middle-class women were allowed to be aggressive, and flirtation was encouraged. As Mayne Reid, better known as the author of *The Octoroon* and other thrilling adventures, put it in his *Croquet: A Treatise, with Notes and Commentaries*, "She whom he came to croquet, croquets him."[12]

Winter offered various alternatives to croquet coquetry. Young men often intentionally upset their horse-drawn sleighs for a chance to cuddle their sweethearts, while tobogganing was a somewhat less dangerous, but still socially sanctioned, option. Both he and she could tumble happily in the snow at the end of a toboggan slide. A St. Paul newspaper, obviously eager to demonstrate that Minnesotans were as sophisticated as New Yorkers, quoted a reporter from Tuxedo Park on why women like tobogganing:

A man's arm about the waist of his passenger was a necessity, after all, to hold the proper lady upright, and 'when the toboggan begins to slew around and there is some danger of completing the slide in an undignified and distressing attitude,' she naturally implores him to hold tighter. He in turn, assuming he is not altogether devoid of wit or a misanthrope, must respond at once by taking away what little breath she may have left in her.[13]

While tobogganing was the most popular winter activity as measured by the number of clubs and members, and snowshoeing the second, St. Paul's six ice skating clubs claimed 400 members, and there were two clubs with over a hundred members that represented sports limited to recent immigrant communities. The Auld Scotia Curling Club was relegated to the end of the Carnival's opening parade on January 15, 1886, but its members competed with clubs from other towns at each of the subsequent carnivals, keeping an element of Scottish identity alive. More significant in terms of its later impact on winter recreation was the Scandinavian sport of skiing.

The St. Paul Ski Club, often identified in the press as the Norwegian Snow *Shoe* Club because of confusion over the pronunciation of the work "ski" as "she," reported thirty-five members. Scandinavian immigrants brought skiing to the mining camps of the Sierra Nevada in the 1850s and races were held in California in the 1860s, but it was the Norwegian clubs of Michigan, Wisconsin, and Minnesota that organized the sport in the 1880s and introduced the concept of *idraet*, meaning, as John Allen has written, "out-door physical exercise in which 'strength, manliness, and toughness' were the goal." The term also conveyed Norwegian and Swedish national pride.[14] Since the 1886 carnival was hastily organized and emphasized pageantry and demonstration of winter sports rather than serious athletic competition, the most dramatic of the ski events, jumping, was not part of the St. Paul celebration until a few years later.

The role of social class, ethnicity, gender, and generation can all be seen in the organization of the 1886 and subsequent St. Paul Winter Carnivals, and each of these shapers of identity ultimately served other interests as well. In modeling their festival on Montreal's carnival, the organizers sought to demonstrate that cold and snow were causes for celebration; that winter sports were healthful and fun; and that tourists would travel from warmer climates, attracted by the novelty.

Lithograph of 1888 St. Paul, Minnesota, Winter Carnival, showing the ice palace, ice skaters, toboggan slide (men riding behind women), and, in the inset, members of a uniformed snow shoe club. Not the Indian camp next to the ice palace.
From the Collections of the Minnesota Historical Society.

The primary attraction was the ice palace. Designed by Alexander and J. H. Hutchinson of Montreal, the 1886 palace was 160 by 180 feet (forty-nine by fifty-four meters) with a central tower over 100 feet (thirty meters), more than twice the size of the largest Montreal structure. It took more than 100 workmen two weeks to put the 20,000 blocks of ice each of which measured 44 x 22 x 20 inches in place (112 x 56 x 51 cm).[15] Although most of the ice was quarried from the Mississippi River and nearby lakes, communities as far away as Fargo, Dakota Territory, sent blocks to emphasize the importance of recently opened rail routes that linked the northwestern United States and Canada to St. Paul.

The parades of the 1886 Winter Carnival were in many ways repetitions of the parade that celebrated the completion of the Northern Pacific Railway in September 1883. That parade also featured military units; Union Army veterans; police and fire departments; ethnic organizations such as the Ancient Order of Hiberians, the Union Française, both Bohemian and German Turner societies; occupational groups and labor unions; and, always last and least, Sioux Indians. The St. Paul Chamber of Commerce invited Henry Villard, President of the Northern Pacific, to a lavish celebration with 300 guests including Villard's British and German business associates; diplomats from Germany, England, Denmark, and Sweden; President Chester Arthur and several members of his cabinet, former President Ulysses Grant, and former Illinois governor Carl Schurz.[16]

The German-American businessmen of St. Paul were especially prominent because of Villard's participation. Born into an important Bavarian family, Ferdinand Heinrich Gustav Hilgard immigrated to the United States in 1853 at the age of eighteen because of political differences with his father. He changed his name to Henry Villard and became a journalist for both German and English language newspapers. As a journalist he studied the public and private financing of banks and railroads, which led to his membership in a committee to build railroads in the Pacific Northwest. By 1881 Villard had risen to the presidency of the Northern Pacific Railroad and oversaw the completion of the line. The strength of German ethnic feeling in St. Paul can be seen in Villard's remarks at the banquet. Responding in German to a toast by the editor of *Die Volkszeitung*, Villard said, "I consider it a great fortune to me that I, a German, was permitted to complete the great Northern Pacific Railroad which was begun and started more than ten years ago by enterprising citizens of my adopted country."[17]

German names predominate in the parade that celebrated the opening of the railroad—Mrs. Joseph Geisen was costumed as Columbia, Mrs. Charles Schmidt as Germania, Miss Pauline Faber as Britannia, Miss Julia Winter as the goddess of the Northern Pacific Railroad, and Miss Mary

Schnitzius was Portland, the west coast terminal of the line—but most of the men on the executive committee of the Chamber of Commerce bore English, Irish, and old New York Dutch names. A key link between the 1883 and 1886 celebrations is W.A. Van Slyke, a former resident of New York State who had been a resident of St. Paul since 1854, the year the capital was established. He owned a dry goods business, organized a company of volunteers in the Civil War and participated in the Mississippi and Tennessee campaigns. Returning to his business, Captain Van Slyke, as he was henceforth addressed, was active in the Chamber of Commerce and the Grand Army of the Republic and became the city's commissioner of parks.[18]

The St. Paul Winter Carnival officially opened Monday, February 1, 1886, although the first parade had taken place two weeks earlier when construction of the ice palace began. The first two days were filled with receptions held by the various sport and social clubs and the opening of ice skating rinks and toboggan slides. On the third day the city welcomed the arrival of King Borealis, played by General R. W. Johnson, who was carried through the streets of the city in a sleigh shaped like a boat. Johnson was a 1849 graduate of the U.S. Military Academy and a career officer who rose to the rank of brigadier general during the Civil War. He settled in St. Paul where he taught military science at the University of Minnesota until 1870.[19] The Fire King, also an army veteran, arrived on Thursday the fourth and led an unsuccessful assault on the ice palace amid a fireworks display. A week of sporting events, costume balls, Indian performances, and concerts followed. The carnival was suspended on Sunday, despite the protest of one Congregational minister who preached a sermon on "The Relation of Amusements to the Church of Christ," concluding that "the man who has no play in him is only a part man … [sic]" On the twelfth day of the carnival, units of the Grand Army of the Republic (GAR), the organization of veterans of the Union Army, gathered from all over Minnesota and marched through the city. That night, with more fireworks, the veterans captured the ice palace and dethroned winter.[20]

The prominent participation of the GAR in the parades and in the storming of the ice palace to dethrone the Ice King (King Borealis) seems a curious reversal of Civil War symbolism that depicted the North in terms of arctic vigor and the South as "languid and dissipated" by heat. Nevertheless, it is reasonable when considering that the purpose of such public rituals in post-Reconstruction America was reconciliation of the formerly divided nation—and, for St. Paul, a desire to attract southern tourists.[21] Whatever the outcome of the battles between the Fire King and the Ice King, the struggle represented the national identity as established by the climate of the United States, the cycle of seasons, and the creative tension of frost belt and sun belt.[22]

Decorated parade float by the entrance of the ice palace at the 1888 St. Paul Winter Carnival. The three young women on the float are identified as the "Duchess of Minnesota and the Countesses of Rochester and Mankato" [Minnesota]. Photo by Ingersoll, collections of the Minnesota Historical Society.

The parades of the carnival also reveal the complex interplay of local and national identities emerging in St. Paul in 1886. The first parade, on January 15, preceded the opening of the festival by two weeks. It was led by the police department in winter uniforms, followed by the parade marshal and his aides. Next was the Great Western Railroad band, a sleigh with Miss Clemmie Finch, carnival queen and daughter of George Finch, the Carnival Association President, dressed in the red wool jacket of the Nushka Toboggan Club. She was followed by a carriage containing the governor of the state and several mayors. One hundred and twenty-five members of the St. George Snowshoe Club with snowshoes strapped to their backs were jeered, according to the *Daily Pioneer Press*, by spectators who shouted: "Take off those Mother Hubbards. Take those bladders off your feet." Fifty members of the Wacouta Toboggan Club escorted twenty members of the Minneapolis club. They were followed by the Windsor Club, which was congratulated by the press for having "the gallantry to bring ladies along." Next came the Nushka Toboggan Club, thirty-five men carrying Chinese lanterns and chanting the club's name in a kind of cheer: "N-U-S-H-K-A, Nushka," to which the crowd responded: "R-A-T-S, Rats."

Other clubs followed, including the Ice Bears, dressed in white duck and firing shotguns every few minutes. The Scandinavian Ski Club, a sleigh from Boston in the form of a ship held forty passengers and required a team of eight horses; firemen, postmen, militia, and the GAR, were important units in the parade. No Native Americans brought up the rear. Instead, the symbolic end of the parade consisted of thirty-five horseshoers, identified in the newspaper as "the only contingent from the working class," and the Auld Scotia Curling Club.

There were parades almost every day of the two-week celebration. These included King Borealis and his court on February 3, the Fire King and his entourage the following day, Indians and dogsled teams on the sixth, and on the ninth of February, a large parade consisting chiefly of floats sponsored by local merchants, including the German language newspaper *Die Volkszeitung* that had a wagon with figures of Germania and Concordia, and the Bohn Manufacturing Company's entry, a logger on a logging sled. "A fact worthy of notice in connection with the parade," the *St. Paul and Minneapolis Pioneer Press* observed,

> was the large number of women and girls who occupied sleighs or walked with their respective clubs. It is probable that not less than 500 females were in the line, the number being the largest ever known in any festival parade, and especially remarkable as being in connection with a midwinter street display.[23]

Such remarks reflect the cultural convention of separate spheres for men and women. Larson writes that women were excluded from the first parade by the carnival organizers, but also suggest that the women of St. Paul took advantage of the carnival spirit to challenge patriarchal authority. Many businesses organized clubs and entertainment for children. Finally, the prominence given Native American sports is another indication that the organizers of the first winter carnival were emphasizing leisure over work. Women, children, and Native Americans—three relatively powerless groups—were encouraged, within limits, to teach the white male elite of St. Paul how to play.[24]

The St. Paul Winter Carnival of 1886, as well as subsequent carnivals, was also, of course, about markets, marketing, and the creation of a marketable identity. In its carnival, St. Paul used its climate in a positive way to distinguish itself from its "twin city" of Minneapolis. It encouraged its citizens to maintain their ethnic, gender, and generational identities in the construction of a distinct metropolitan identity, which in turn was subordinate to a regional and even national identity created by railroad routes, historical events, and modernization.

A day after the carnival closed on February 13, 1886, an editorial writer commented:

> One of the good things which the carnival has brought to St. Paul is a beginning of attention to the conditions of some of the principal streets. Along the route traversed by the numerous parades gangs of men were set to work and their labor produced in a short time a very passable thoroughfare. The experience, limited and not wholly satisfactory though it was, has in it a valuable hint for other than carnival times. There is no excuse whatever in a city of this size for permitting the streets to become obstacles to locomotion as they are here in any winter when the snows are numerous and heavy.[25]

The carnival was, in the final analysis, about modern efficiency of organization, whether for snow removal or festival management, and the citizens of St. Paul, perhaps even those who shouted, "rats," and "take those bladders off your feet," were proud to earn the respect that the thousands of tourists bestowed on them for those qualities.

St. Paul's Winter Carnival was held off and on, depending on the weather, until 1946, and annually ever since. Each year brought greater organization and stratification. Skiing, skating, and other sports became more professionalized. Fewer and fewer GAR veterans survived. By 1916, when F. Scott Fitzgerald immortalized the carnival in his short story "The Ice Palace," the carnival was already largely "deseasonalized." By 1982 when a record storm buried St. Paul under more than fifty centimeters of snow, most of the events were held indoors and had nothing to do with winter. In 1984, the ice palace was eliminated, partly because insurance companies refused to write liability policies at affordable rates. The restructuring of the city's economic base in the 1980s and 1990s—the decline of locally owned businesses and their replacement by multinational corporations with no ties to the community—may finally force the carnival's organizers, members of the snowshoe and toboggan clubs founded by their wealthy forefathers, to broaden the base of support in order to survive. But once ritualized, festivals are hard to change.[26]

Throughout its history, the St. Paul Winter Carnival has functioned to perpetuate the status of social and economic elites, to give marginalized groups a measure of legitimacy, and to allow both groups to play with the symbols of power in the context of historical and environmental myths. Snow may erase the boundaries between public street and private shops, make all citizens equal before the Ice King, but according to one humorist "the snowshovel will find the boundary line between two lots more accurately than the best surveyor."[27] The final paradox of festivals is that they contain the seeds of their own destruction. They are ephemeral, liminal, welcome interruptions whose conclusion is also welcome. After offering a glimpse of a different order, carnivals, like parades, must end. Costumes are put away, the streets swept clean, and planning for next year begun.

Notes

1. The literature on festivals, carnivals, and rituals is vast. Some of the work that informs this paper may be found in Victor Turner, *The Ritual Process: Structure and Anti-Structure* (New York: Aldine Publishing Company, 1969); James Fernandez, *Persuasions and Performances: The Play of Tropes in Culture* (Bloomington, IN: Indiana University Press, 1986); Susan G. Davis, *Parades and Power: Street Theatre in Nineteenth-Century Philadelphia* (Philadelphia, PA: Temple University Press, 1986); Don Handelman, *Models and Mirrors:Towards an Anthropology of Public Events* (New York: Cambridge University Press, 1990); Ramón A. Gutiérrez and Geneviève Fabre, eds., *Feasts and Celebrations in North American Ethnic Communities* (Albuquerque, NM: University of New Mexico Press, 1995) and, *nonpareil*, Johan Huizinga, *Homo Ludens: A Study of the Play Element in Culture* (Boston: Beacon Press, 1955).
2. William Lass, "Minnesota: An American Siberia?" *Minnesota History* 49 (1984): 149-155; Paul Clifford Larson, *Icy Pleasures: Minnesota Celebrates Winter* (Afton, MN: Afton Historical Society Press, 1998).
3. Sylvie Dufresne, "Le Carnaval d'hiver de Montréal 1803-1889," *Urban History Review/ Revue d'histoire urbaine* 11 (February 1983): 25-46.
4. I comment briefly on some of the differences between Canadian and American attitudes toward winter in *Snow in America* (Washington, D.C.: Smithsonian Institution Press, 1997). For insights into Canadian attitudes, see Margaret Atwood, *Survival: A Thematic Guide to Canadian Literature* (Toronto: Anansi, 1972); idem, *Strange Things: The Malevolent North in Canadian Literature* (Toronto: Oxford University Press, 1995); Glen Norcliffe and Paul Simpson-Housley, eds., *A Few Acres of Snow: Literary and Artistic Images of Canada* (Toronto: Dundurn, 1992); and Michael Dorland, "A Thoroughly Hidden Country: *Ressentiment*, Canadian Nationalism, Canadian Culture," *Canadian Journal of Political and Social Theory/Revue canadienne de théorie politique et sociale* 12 (1988): 130-64.
5. *American Historical Review* 87 (1982): 1262-89.
6. Hill's comment is cited without a source in J. Russell Smith, *North America, Its People and the Resources, Development, and Prospects of the Continent as an Agricultural, Industrial, and Commercial Area* (New York: Harcourt, Brace and Company, 1925), 8.
7. Mergen, *Snow in America*, passim.
8. Beard, "Snow-Ball Warfare," *St. Nicholas* (January 1880): 263-66; "A Snow Battle," *St. Nicholas* (January 1881): 235-36; *The American Boys Handy Book* (Boston: David R. Godine, 1983): 257-79; Emma Stiles, "Children's Sleds and Sleighs," *Spinning Wheel* (January/February 1980): 18; Mergen, *Play and Playthings* (Westport, CT: Greenwood Publishing, 1982).
9. *American Agriculturist* 42 (March 1883): 114-15; *The St. Paul and Minneapolis Pioneer Press*, December 20, 1885, 10; Larson, *Icy Pleasures*, 30-31.
10. St. Paul had a population of about 120,000 in 1886, so the participation of 4,700 club members in the carnival represents a substantial percentage of the adult male population. The festival drew tens of thousands of tourists. Larson estimates that 150,000 paid twenty-five cents each for admission to various events, some of them more than once. On Canadian snowshoe clubs, see Don Morrow, "The Knights of the Snowshoe: A Study of the Evolution of Sport in Nineteenth-century Montreal," *Journal of Sport History* 15 (Spring 1988): 5-40.
11. Larson, *Icy Pleasures*, 32-33.
12. David Park Curry, *Winslow Homer: The Croquet Game* (New Haven, CT: Yale University Art Gallery, 1984), np.

13. Larson, *Icy Pleasures*, 32.
14. E. John B. Allen, *From Skisport to Skiing: One Hundred Years of an American Sport, 1840-1949* (Amherst, MA: University of Massachusetts Press, 1993), 11.
15. The dimensions are given in Jean Spraker, "'Come to the Carnival at Old St. Paul': Souvenirs from a Civic Ritual Interpreted," *Prospects* 11 (1987): 243. Larson gives the dimensions as 140 by 175 feet (forty-three by fifty-three meters), and believes the size was exaggerated in later reports, but acknowledges that communities vied with each other to send blocks of ice which allowed the construction of additional towers during the celebration. Larson, *Icy Pleasures*, 48 and 152 fn. 20.
16. C. C. Andrews, *History of St. Paul, Minn.* (Syracuse, NY: D. Mason & Co., 1890), 553-60.
17. Andrews, *History of St. Paul, Minn.*, 552. Incredibly, there is no recent biography of Villard.
18. Andrews, *History of St. Paul, Minn.*, 201, 549, 554-55.
19. "Johnson, Richard W.," *The National Cyclopedia of American Biography* (New York: James T. White & Co., 1916), 391-92.
20. *St.Paul and Minneapolis Pioneer Press*, February 1-12, 1886.
21. On the use of meteorological metaphors in the Civil War era, see Eduardo Cadava, *Emerson and the Climates of History* (Stanford, CA: Stanford University Press, 1997), 39.
22. Bernard Mergen, "Climates of Opinion: Regional and National Identity and the Weather," unpublished paper read at the 1997 annual meeting of the Organization of American Historians, San Francisco, California.
23. *St.Paul and Minneapolis Pioneer Press*, February 4, 1886, 3.
24. On the appropriation of the Native American into American ideas of playfulness, see Philip J. De Loria, *Playing Indian* (New Haven, CT: Yale University Press, 1998).
25. *The St. Paul and Minneapolis Pioneer Press*, February 14, 1886, 3.
26. Larson, *Icy Pleasures*; F. Scott Fitzgerald, *Flappers and Philosophers* (New York: Scribner's, 1920), 47-71; Robert H. Lavenda, "Festivals and the Creation of Public Culture: Whose Voice(s)?" *Museums and Communities: The Politics of Public Culture*, ed. Ivan Karp, Christine Mullen Kreamer and Steven D. Lavine (Washington, DC: Smithsonian Institution Press, 1992), 76-104. On the deseasonalization of cities since the nineteenth century, see André Guillerme, "The Disappearance of Seasons in the City," paper read at the American Society for Environmental History meeting, Pittsburgh, PA, March 7, 1993; and the papers in *Annales de la Recherche Urbaine* (Spring 1994).
27. Don Cameron Shafer, *Punch* (January 18, 1911): 3.

Chapter 12

CREATING AND INSTRUMENTALIZING NATIONALISM

The Celebration of National Reunion in the Peace Jubilees of 1898

Fabian Hilfrich

> Those who witness or participate in the Chicago jubilee will be taking part in a unique historic function. Years afterwards they can tell a younger generation of the dramatic scenes and events witnessed in Chicago at the great peace jubilee of the Spanish war. Its memories will be worth cherishing, for it is an organic part in American history.[1]

THE *CHICAGO TRIBUNE'S* enthusiastic prediction proved to be wrong. Neither this nor any other of the four large jubilees following the Spanish-American War of 1898 remained long in contemporary memory, nor have they received serious scholarly attention. Nevertheless, these celebrations deserve a closer look because they are almost ideal manifestations of the increasing nationalistic spirit that scholars have detected in the United States of late nineteenth century. Stephen Skowronek, for example, has concentrated on commercial legislation, the civil service, and the professionalization of the army to show how local answers to national crises no longer proved adequate and thus had to be replaced by centralized responses. Analyzing the country's reaction to the crisis with Spain, on the other hand, Gerald Linderman has demonstrated

---

Notes for this section begin on page 251.

how for the first time localized public opinion gave way to a truly national response, which partially forced the hand of the administration in the crisis.[2]

As recent historical writing on the subject of the nation and nationalism has shown, however, symbols are at least as important as structural changes in promoting the idea of common nationality. For nations do not simply "exist," but are symbolically and discursively created either by a state or by interested groups within a given territory. If, in other words, the nation is an "imagined community," as Benedict Anderson has asserted, the peace jubilees of 1898 and 1899 did much to fire the American patriotic imagination at the time.[3] In their organization and content, they offer an excellent microscopic insight into a country on the threshold of a more national conception of itself, trying, but only partially succeeding, to supersede sectional, ethnic, and local allegiances with a larger national narrative, at the center of which stood the final reconciliation between North and South more than thirty years after the end of Civil War. This "new nationalism" was then instrumentalized to further the cause of an overseas empire, most notably in the Philippines. The new-found unity between the regions, however, was only to be had at the price of nationally sanctioning the inferior place of African Americans in the social and political hierarchy, a reinterpretation that aptly coincided with the racially based rationale for overseas colonial rule. This racism and the purposes for which national reunion was employed did not go unchallenged at the turn of the century, however. African Americans and the so-called anti-imperialists struggled against the dominant narrative of a white and expansive nationalism, and, although their voices were not much in evidence at the peace jubilees, they are crucial for a more complex evaluation of the "new nationalism."

Contrary to European traditions, there was no single national event celebrating the victory in the war with Spain. Although Robert Rydell has claimed that Omaha's Trans-Mississippi and International Exposition served as "the focal point for the national Peace jubilee," this was not mirrored in public opinion at the time. Originally designed to celebrate America's successful westward expansion and progress, the fair's role in celebrating the outcome of the "splendid little war" with Spain was extremely welcome, but rather accidental.[4] Following the war, peace jubilees sprang up spontaneously all over the country, frequently coinciding with the trips President William McKinley took to the West and the South in late 1898. Only the jubilees in Chicago, Philadelphia, Atlanta, and Washington, however, were so well orchestrated and large in design that they were recognized beyond regional borders. Hundreds of thousands, traveling from adjacent cities and states, visited these cities to witness the celebrations and to see the president. Being the first such major event, Chicago's celebration was sometimes touted as the "national peace jubilee," but like the others, it grew out of the efforts of a local committee, composed primarily of prominent businessmen and local boosters. Accordingly, the festivities were financed privately, by donations and subscriptions, or, if parades with floats were also featured, by the efforts of charitable organizations and local businesses.[5] These patriotic pageants, therefore, were not only designed to celebrate victory and the return of peace, but also to raise the cities' visibility and to provide the communities with financial profit. This purpose was most aptly illustrated by Washington's jubilee in March of 1899. The parade foreshadowed the twentieth-century habit of subsidizing national television through commercials, because it included a trades section which united advertising with patriotic spirit. This hybrid brought forth such eccentric contributions as a local butcher's "design of the American eagle, done entirely in 'links' of sausage, and another design of the United States shield, in the center of which was the head of a small pig."[6]

This mindset of local boosterism also manifested itself in the rivalry between the four cities, which tried to outdo each other by adding novelties to what quickly became the standard formula set in Chicago in mid-October 1898, two months before peace was formally concluded. All jubilee committees managed to secure the participation of President McKinley, his cabinet, and other national luminaries although, notably in the capital itself, the president only observed the parades, but did not give a major speech, as he had in the other three cities. The festivities lasted up to six days and included military and civic parades, banquets and balls, as well as a host of patriotic speeches. Chicago's jubilee was the most "orally" oriented, featuring speeches not only on one occasion, but on all six days, sometimes simultaneously in different locations. Philadelphia, trailing Chicago by just a week, could claim the largest military parade with 25,000 participants. In addition, the city presented an elaborate naval parade on the river, in which eight battleships from the recent war were greeted and surrounded by more than two hundred private boats. Finally, in its civic parade, Philadelphia added an elaborate historical pageant with numerous floats depicting crucial episodes in American history. Atlanta proudly hosted the first peace jubilee after the conclusion of the peace treaty with Spain in December, but in design, it was much more moderate than its precursors. Its only noted innovation was a floral parade, in which prominent local women drove carriages decorated with luscious flower arrangements. As we shall see, however, despite the moderate nature of its spectacles, Atlanta's jubilee was possibly the most significant in terms of its symbolic content. The organizers of the last jubilee in the nation's capital in May 1899 adopted all these features and added small-scale reenactments of the pivotal battles of the recent war. For the most popular one, the battle in Manila harbor, an artificial pond was built in front of Washington Monument so that a miniature American fleet could once again sink its Spanish counterpart amid extravagant fireworks and mock explosions.[7] Each successive city thus added novelties to its own jubilee, clearly wanting their celebration to stand out from the sweep of festivals around the country.

Local spirit and rivalries were also reflected in the newspaper coverage. Local papers devoted the majority of their space to minute descriptions of all events, whereas other papers only ran a brief summary. This tendency was particularly noticeable in the space the *St. Louis Post Dispatch* devoted to Chicago's celebration. While the paper described in detail President McKinley's visit to St. Louis itself, also labeling the surrounding events a "peace jubilee," it gave little space to the celebration by its neighboring rival for the title of "the gateway to the West."[8] Similar jealousies could be noted between Washington and New York. While the *Washington Post* and the city's organizing committee were so taken with the supposed success of their jubilee that they proposed the creation of an annual event that should rival New Orleans' Mardi Gras, the *New York Times* sarcastically commented that the expected boon to business was nowhere to be seen, that the supposedly grandiose fireworks had been poorly orchestrated, and that Washington's historical pageant, instead of exhibiting faithful representations of American history, had only been picturesque. The *Chicago Tribune*, moreover, conceded the success of Washington's jubilee, but referred to it as "strictly a local affair."[9]

With respect to symbolic and rhetorical content, on the other hand, the festivals were truly national, if not nationalistic. Although the celebrations were significantly dubbed as "peace" and not "victory" jubilees, reiterations of American military exploits and martial imagery clearly outweighed references to peace. Triumphal arches decorated with pictures of the crucial battles and the faces of victorious generals dominated the routes of the parades, while the national flag and colors decorated almost every building in the city centers. Taking advantage of the fact that peace had not yet been formally concluded at the time of Chicago's jubilee, the ardently nationalist and expansionist *Chicago Tribune* clarified that "this is not a jubilee of peace, but a jubilee of victory."[10] Oppositional voices criticized the abundance of military symbols and triumphalist speeches. Samuel Bowles, editor of the anti-imperialist *Springfield Republican*, for example, disgustedly commented on the "revelry of jingo sentiment which chiefly distinguished the so-called peace jubilee in Chicago." At the Illinois Federation of Women's Clubs meeting, which also took place in mid-October, Jane Addams criticized the abundance of martial symbols in the jubilee. Americans, she warned, were getting enamored with war as such, forgetting that the late struggle had had a decidedly idealistic purpose in liberating the Cubans from Spanish tyranny. Such criticism, however, was drowned out by the chorus of those celebrating the triumph in war. With thinly veiled satisfaction and sarcasm, the *Tribune* thus noted that few women listened to Addams's diatribe because they preferred to attend the jubilee festivities themselves.[11]

Superseding both the issues of peace and war, however, was the theme of national reunion, the reconciliation of North and South and, to a lesser extent, of East and West, rich and poor. After detailing the successes of American arms, George R. Peck, the chairman of Chicago's jubilee committee and a noted orator, concluded:

> But the greatest prize we have won in its consequences to us as a people, is the supreme victory which North and South have won over each other. Long ago all sensible and patriotic people in both sections knew that the hour had come. Today we hail it in the assured faith that, henceforth, we march together to the same music, under the same flag and to the same destiny. Verily, this is the year of jubilee.[12]

Speakers and commentators from the North and South agreed that this achievement almost eclipsed the "splendid little war" against Spain. As was indicated in Peck's speech, reconciliation between the regions had been a goal ever since the end of Reconstruction, but the war against Spain offered a unique possibility to cement these latent feelings.[13]

President McKinley never tired of emphasizing that, at the beginning of the war, "[t]here was no division in any part of the country. North and South and East and West alike cheerfully responded."[14] This outbreak of national enthusiasm had been genuine, but it was also consciously encouraged by the administration with gestures such as commissioning former Confederate officers Joseph Wheeler and Fitzhugh Lee as major generals. Selecting his high-profile "Rough Riders," Theodore Roosevelt paid similarly close attention to enlisting personnel from the North, South, East, and West.[15] The most evocative prewar effort at reconciliation, which entailed almost a rewriting of history, occurred when the Sixth Massachusetts was marched through Baltimore where, thirty-seven years before, the same regiment had been attacked by a secessionist mob. This time, the reception was markedly different, as Senator Henry Cabot Lodge described in a letter to his mother:

> First came the city people, bands and then the drums and fifes of the regiment playing '*Dixie*'—the drums and fifes of the 6th Massachusetts—and the crowd cheering wildly. Tears were in my eyes. I never felt so moved in my life. *The war of 1861 was over at last* and this great country for which so many died was one once again. It was a great, historic sight ...[16]

The postwar jubilees significantly embellished this symbolism. In each of the military parades, "Fighting" Joseph Wheeler, "whose fame has become world-wide because of heroism in two wars," was a guest of honor.[17] Civil War veteran detachments from both sides marched to broad acclaim, so much so, in fact, that the "heroes" of the Spanish-American War sometimes faded into the background. Thus, the *Washington Post* remarked that Civil War veterans from both regions, "after all, were the real heroes." In Chicago, these veterans formed the honor guard of the President's carriage, and, among the 3,000 veterans formed in various Grand Army of the Republic (GAR) posts, one small detachment of Confederate soldiers marched as well. The city's newspaper evaluated these scenes as "the significant proof of a reunited nation:"

> There are only a few of the Confederate veterans, but the crowd caught sight of their emblem, realized its significance, and cheered them lustily. A short time before they had been honored by having the thirteen of their number in the President's escort sent for by the President himself, who asked that he might meet each one of them.[18]

In the historical pageants held in Washington and Philadelphia, reunion was also accorded a prominent place. While battle scenes mounted on floats represented America's wars from 1776 to 1848, the Civil War float featured no martial scene but instead a scene that aptly reflected the titles of "The North and South United" or "Our Reunited Country." When the floats passed the president's reviewing stand, a Union and a Confederate officer shook hands while their troops jointly held the Stars and Stripes. The theme of reunion was thus designed to transcend the memories of war.[19] The most significant gesture, however, was extended by the president himself. After his trip to the West, during which he had attended the Omaha exposition and the Chicago jubilee, McKinley embarked on a tour of the South. Commenting on the prepared speeches the president was to deliver, his private secretary George B. Cortelyou noted in early December: "He is evidently going to make *unity*—a reunited country—the central thought."[20] The president not only bore out Cortelyou's predictions, but also sprang a dramatic surprise before the joint assembly of the Georgia legislature in Atlanta, where significantly he wore a Confederate badge:

> Every soldier's grave made during our unfortunate Civil War is a tribute to American valor ... And while, when those graves were made, we differed widely about the future of this government, those differences were long ago settled by the arbitrariment of arms; and the time has now come, in the evolution of sentiment and feeling under the providence of God, when in the spirit of fraternity we should share with you in the care of the graves of the Confederate soldiers. (Tremendous applause and long-continued cheering.)[21]

While in retrospect this may only seem to be a friendly gesture, contemporary audiences were thrilled at the promise that the national government would now treat Confederate and Union graves alike. All Civil War dead, in other words, would be treated as national heroes and no longer as loyal sons of the Union on one side and disloyal rebels on the other. The graves that had served as reminders of the bloody chasm and sectional separation were thus finally subsumed in a common American culture of remembrance. This symbolism was lost neither on the Southern audience nor on the Northern correspondents who witnessed the scene. One old Confederate soldier, so it

Political Cartoon Depicting President McKinley's Gesture at Atlanta.
Washington Post, December 17, 1898.

was reported, buried his head in his lap and "cried like a child," whereas the rest of the audience cheered so wildly that it was almost impossible for the president to finish his speech or for the ubiquitous Wheeler to add a few impromptu remarks. Equally as revealing was the president's thought process as related by the press. According to this—unprovable—narrative, McKinley had originally had this idea in 1886 when he visited the cemeteries at Fredericksburg, where he saw the stark contrast between well-kept Union and unkempt Confederate graves. From then on, he had supposedly waited for an opportunity to publicize his intentions.[22]

The rhetoric of most speakers at the jubilees revealed a consensus that the president had picked the ideal moment. Even before McKinley extended the central government's aegis to the graves of Confederate soldiers, Clark Howell, editor of the *Atlanta Constitution*, used the symbolism of death and sacrifice to visualize reunion. Opening his speech in Chicago with the inscriptions on two imaginary gravestones, one of a Confederate soldier, the other of a fictitious son of a Confederate veteran, Howell left no doubt that only war and bloodshed could have repaired the severed links:

> The iron sledge of war that rent asunder the links of loyalty and love has welded them together again. Ears that were deaf to loving appeals for the burial of sectional strife have listened and believed when the muster-guns have spoken. Hearts that were cold to calls for trust and sympathy have awakened to loving confidence in the baptism of their blood ... 'There is but one people of this Union, one flag for all.' The South will feel that her sons have been well given, that her blood has been well spilled, if that sentiment is to be, indeed, the true inspiration of our nation's future.[23]

Southerners in particular, but also Northerners, relished in pointing out that the first victim of the Spanish-American War had come from the South. Commenting on the death of Ensign Worth Bagley of North Carolina, the *Atlanta Constitution* wrote that "the blood of this martyr freely spilled upon his country's altar seals effectively the covenant of brotherhood between the north and south and completes the work of reconciliation which commenced at Appomatox."[24] Such emphases amounted to a highly dramatic and almost pagan narrative of human sacrifice that had been necessary to consecrate the reunion between the former enemies.

President McKinley preferred a slightly less pathetic version when he explained reunion in Atlanta: "Under hostile fire on a foreign soil, fighting in a common cause, the memory of old disagreements has *faded* into history."[25] Only through war, through the realization that a common enemy threatened both parts of the nation alike, McKinley argued, could Americans finally and truly realize that they were one people, irrespective of historical sectional animosities. The notion that the *national* soul could only be purified through war, sacrifice, and strife, moreover, fit neatly with the fin-de-siècle notion of a gendered nationality, most notably with Theodore Roosevelt's concept of the "strenuous life." According to this theory of national and international life, which was suffused with strong undercurrents of social Darwinism, *men* could only achieve their individual and social goals by courageously facing them and by being willing to sacrifice. Almost twenty years before Woodrow Wilson proclaimed the "war to end all wars," many of his compatriots had discovered the essence of this paradox, namely that "it is only through strife, through hard and dangerous endeavor, that we shall ultimately win the goal of true national greatness."[26]

For Civil War memory and the theme of reunion, the discourse on manliness and valor had particularly pertinent consequences. Viewed in the context of courage and bravery, the specific issues that had been at stake in the war faded into the background. In this context, the Southerner Wheeler celebrated the Civil War as proof of "the wonderful endurance and bravery of the *American* soldier—when every foe met 'foeman worthy of his steel.'"[27] Sectional memories were thus transformed into a national narrative of heroism, gallantry, and valor, sanitizing the Civil War into another glorious episode of American history, a model on par with the recent struggle against Spain. Suggestively connecting past and present in the names of officers from the recent war, Secretary of Agriculture James Wilson, speaking for Northern Republicans, thus proclaimed the end of sectional histories and the dawn of national history: "Lee and Wheeler commanded the men from the wheat fields of the North; Miles and Grant gave orders to the men from the cotton fields of the South. The valor of those who struggled for ideas as they understood them from 1860 to 1865 has become the heritage of a happy, prosperous, and united people." The *dedication* of both sides to their respective causes thus superseded the causes themselves.[28]

If jubilee speakers addressed the actual issues of the Civil War at all, they focused on a reading of history that facilitated reunion. "[A]t Gettysburg the Union was the issue," President McKinley insisted during the longest of his speeches at the Atlanta jubilee. The former Confederate officer and ex-Secretary of the Navy Hilary A. Herbert not only agreed with this limited understanding of the great confrontation, but fashioned it into a sweeping interpretation of American history:

> There have been three great eras in the history of our Republic—the first, the era which marked its beginnings—the settling of the colonies; second, the era in which the Constitution was framed and the new government launched on an uncertain sea, the era of an imperfect union when no man could tell how long that Union would last, and the third, the era of the perfected Union, the era that began with Fort Sumter, continued while the Union was being tried with fire and

sword, continued through the days of reconstruction and subsequent rehabilitation and reconciliation, and closes with this great jubilee.²⁹

The entire American past, Herbert asserted, had been overshadowed by the single question of a more perfect union. By subordinating the Civil War to the last of his three stages, Herbert furthermore robbed it of its seminal character and turned it into a mere segment of a teleological development toward a perfect union. With respect to the question of national over states' rights, then, Herbert and other Southerners accepted the verdict of the Civil War and thus gained readmittance to the American union, the region's worthiness to rejoin the union having been proven by their sons' loyal service in the war with Spain. When, in the same speech, Herbert openly blamed "anti-slavery agitation" for the actual outbreak of the Civil War, he indicated that most Northerners no longer demanded the South's consent to emancipation and Reconstruction as a precondition to that region's "re-entry" into the union.

This "single-issue" interpretation of the Civil War and the emphasis on individual valor instead of regional righteousness also guaranteed that the South could cling to the, albeit defused romanticism of the "Lost Cause" at the same time that it was being reintegrated into the nation. Michael Kammen and Cecilia Elizabeth O'Leary have emphasized the persistence of this "autonomous regional culture," evidence of which can also be found in the peace jubilees, most notably in Atlanta.³⁰ As we have seen, the president himself paid homage to this identity by donning a Confederate badge during the ceremonies. More importantly, however, General Wheeler wore his old Confederate uniform in the military parade and rode at the head of his former Confederate cavalry regiment. Obviously, his Confederate identity and his worth as a symbol of reunion were more important than his recent military contributions in the war with Spain. Northern newspapers observed this symbolism without any sign of disapproval, nor did they consider it inappropriate that, while Southern crowds cheered the national anthem, they only went truly wild when "Dixie" was played.³¹

With reunion achieved along these lines, it comes as no surprise that it was African Americans who had to pay the price for the reconciliation between the regions. Although many Northern politicians had long relinquished any plans to force the South to integrate the former slaves, the Spanish-American War threw the issue into stark relief once again. After all, black regiments had also participated in the war, and the community expected tangible rewards for this service to their country.³² Instead, African Americans were not given their symbolic place in the pantheon of American heroism, which their Southern oppressors now occupied instead. Focusing on

Theodore Roosevelt's account of the battle of San Juan Hill, Amy Kaplan has described how African Americans were robbed of their "manhood" and valor. Unable to tolerate the fact that his "Rough Riders" had been saved by a black regiment, Roosevelt propagated the myth that African Americans could not fight without the guidance of white officers and that it was he who drove them on to victory at San Juan Hill.[33] Similar exclusions could be observed in the peace jubilees. In Atlanta, at least, it is not astonishing that no black regiments marched in the military parade, but even black laborers were prohibited from participating in the civic parade, a move that, surprisingly, led their white colleagues to abstain from the festivities as well.[34] In the other three jubilees, black troop detachments did march, and they were duly noted by the press, albeit not with the special emphasis given to Southern troops and officers or to Confederate veterans. In Washington, African-American participation created a minor scandal as the white Norfolk Blues regiment from Virginia refused to take its allotted place behind the black troops. The *Washington Post* cited the white soldiers' reasons with an apparent, if involuntarily humorous, effort to downplay the incident: "They declared that they had never humiliated themselves to walk with negroes, and did not propose to begin at this stage in their military career. *There was no ill-feeling*, but the boys were determined in their refusal."[35] Voluntary black organizations also took part in these three jubilees but, compared to floats or groups that emphasized the theme of reunion, they elicited few special comments. The reason for this can be deduced from an African-American GAR post detachment in Chicago's parade who carried the likeness of the abolitionist John Brown on a banner. While the local paper did not comment on the imagery, we can safely assume that such contentious symbols did not endear them to Southerners nor did they further the previously mentioned process of reunion.[36] This little detail indicated that by 1898 African Americans had another "dissident" narrative of the Civil War, which could not coexist with the rhetoric of reunion and reconciliation between the two sides.

By the same token, while the individual names of Southern heroes in the late war with Spain were reiterated time and again in the addresses of white jubilee speakers, the role of African Americans elicited little response. The Reverend Dr. Thomas P. Hodnett was virtually the only one to acknowledge that "the newly enfranchised colored regulars bore no inconspicuous part" in the battle of San Juan Hill, during whose course they "were among the first to plant the flag which made them free." When Hodnett went on to list the immigrant groups that had made America a great country, however, African Americans were curiously absent.[37] Although many jubilee speakers agreed that the "melting pot" had been extremely beneficial in shaping the

American national character, they certainly did not include all of the groups that the black Reverend R. C. Ransom did:

> America is the most cosmopolitan nation on the globe; the children of African descent are here ten million strong; the Jew, the Indian, the Irishman, the German, the Italian, French and Anglo-Saxon are all here; but they have but one flag, and bear but a single name. They are all Americans. These demonstrate the virility, patriotism and courage of American manhood. The north and south, rich and poor, white and black were united in the contest. General Wheeler and Lee were side by side with Miles and Shafter.[38]

While Ransom was thus willing to acknowledge the Southerners' courage and patriotism, the latter, as well as the nation at large, were unwilling to respond in kind. Even in the president's behavior, the omissions were telling. Although black and white newspapers alike noted specifically that President McKinley repeatedly bowed in response to a speech by Booker T. Washington, these bows did not translate into tangible benefits or more specific mentions of the patriotic and heroic role of African Americans in the war with Spain. During his tour of the South, moreover, the president mentioned the recent war, Southern heroism, and reunion at almost every stop, but when he visited Washington's Tuskegee school, he spoke only about that institution's success in the advancement of the "colored race."[39] On the whole, then, blacks were largely omitted from the peace jubilees precisely because emphasizing their role would have detracted from the main narrative of reunion between the regions. While Southerners were "readmitted" on account of their recent military service, the same "proof" of loyalty by African Americans failed to reap the desired recognition and concrete rewards. Even their minimum demand, that black units be commandeered by black officers, was only hesitantly and incompletely fulfilled in the ensuing Philippine-American War. The reunion between the two sides was obviously only to be had on the basis of a nationwide acceptance of Southern views on race and segregation.[40]

Predictably, the African-American community reacted with mixed feelings toward the peace jubilees and the spirit of reunion. As patriotic Americans, black spokespeople wanted to partake in the jubilant mood sweeping the country, but as representatives of an oppressed minority, they pointed to the peacetime benefits they expected for their wartime military service.[41] In the black press, the jubilees found little mention, except when the stories had a specific relation to the concerns of the African-American community. With respect to the celebration in the capital, for example, the *Washington Bee* complained about the absence of blacks on the enormously large organizing committees for the event and demanded that at least black nurses of the recent war should be represented.[42] Extensive coverage, however, was given to the only speech by an African American in the official program of the peace jubilees, that of Booker T. Washington in Chicago. His speech was actually symptomatic of the predicament blacks faced at the end of the Spanish-American War. Throughout most of the address, Washington recounted how African Americans had always chosen "the better part," patriotic service, when the country had faced military threats from the outside. In the context of the Civil War, he emphasized, blacks had not only served on the side of the Union, but those in the South had even resisted "the temptation ... to burn the home and massacre wife and children during the absence of the master in battle" and had instead taken to "protecting and supporting the helpless, defenseless ones intrusted [sic] to his care." In their emphasis on continued devotion even to the oppressors, Washington's words constituted an almost desperate plea to the white majority to recognize those who had been in shackles for so long and who were once again being excluded from citizenship rights in the South. The only dissonant chord in his statement followed his praise for African Americans' role in the late war with Spain:

> But there remains one other victory for Americans to win ... We have succeeded in every conflict except in the effort to conquer ourselves in the blotting out of racial prejudices. We can celebrate the era of peace in no more effectual way than by a firm resolve on the part of Northern men and Southern men, black men and white men, that the trenches which we together dug around Santiago shall be the eternal burial-place of all that which separates us in our business and civil relations ... Until we thus conquer ourselves, I make no empty statement when I say that *we shall have a cancer gnawing at the heart of this Republic* that shall one day prove as dangerous as an attack from an army from without or within.

Washington thus sought to take advantage of the prevailing nationalist mood to effect a reconciliation between the races alongside that between North and South. Otherwise, he warned, the unreconciled strivings of African Americans could one day threaten the entire national fabric. Immediately thereafter, however, Washington almost defused this sentiment by heaping profuse praise on the chief executive and by offering him "the deep gratitude of nearly ten millions of my people ..." True to his gradualist approach, moreover, Washington indicated in another speech during the jubilee events that blacks would only demand full participation in political affairs "[w]hen we have ... prepared ourselves as a race" ... "for the highest duties of citizenship."[43] His speeches thus carefully straddled the gulf between expressions of nationalist fervor, gratitude, and the legitimate demands of his community.

Apprehension about reunion was pervasive in the black community in general, but its spokespeople knew that they could not withstand the white nationalist tide. This may be why the Republican editor Edward Cooper passed a generally positive judgment on McKinley's trip to the South, although he conceded that African Americans had valid reasons to be suspicious of reunion. "The Negro does not forget," Cooper concluded, "that he needs friends in the North; he needs them more in the South."[44] Republican Calvin Chase, on the other hand, warned McKinley to "beware of the wolves in sheep's clothing," because Southerners had thus far shown no "signs of repentence [sic]." Commenting on Southern suggestions to extend federal pensions to former Confederate soldiers, Chase furthermore lamented that these "rebels" now falsely viewed themselves as "patriots," and that this move amounted to "the open declaration on the part of the rebels that what they lost in war they will gain in peace."[45]

In its realization that Southerners were trying to be recognized as "patriots," Chase's analysis was particularly poignant, but it overlooked the crucial fact that the president, or the North, for that matter, had not been inadvertently deceived. On the contrary, few demanded the South's "repentance" as a prerequisite for its readmission to the union, because, in its response to the Spanish-American War, the South had exhibited all the patriotic loyalty the North had expected. Finally, Chase also pointed out that McKinley's gestures toward the South had failed to provide Republican gains in that region in the midterm elections, thus implying that the president may have had a short-term political objective in his efforts at reunion. Unspoken, but by no means absent in this observation was a reminder of the contrast between Southern loyalty to the Democratic party and that of African Americans to the party of Lincoln. Even if Chase intended his remarks as a veiled threat that his community might one day withdraw its support from the Republicans, its voting behavior only underlined the political powerlessness of African Americans at the turn of the century. Although they could theoretically threaten Republicans with a withdrawal of their support should that party abandon its commitment to further integration, African Americans simply had no realistic alternative in a Democratic party whose Southern wing vigorously discriminated against them. In other words, even if reunion did not turn Southern Democrats into Republicans, neither would it drive African Americans into the Democratic camp. Merely viewed from a political point of view, national reunion at the expense of African Americans was thus a "safe" strategy for a Republican administration.

What then were the purposes of national reunion? Obviously, the reconciliation between North and South after a murderous Civil War and a tumultuous period of reconstruction and sectionally-based politics was seen as a benefit in itself. After all, President McKinley was the last Civil War veteran in the White House and, according to his biographers, had been deeply traumatized himself by the seminal conflict.[46] Undoubtedly, despite the lack of success in the South, the 1898 congressional election was another factor on the president's mind when he emphasized not only unity, but also nonpartisanship for the time ahead. Political divisions had been particularly deep ever since the divisive presidential election of 1896, in which McKinley had been squarely identified with the interests of capital. This would explain why the president also emphasized national prosperity and a reconciliation between the "classes" on his westward trip. On the last day of Chicago's jubilee, for example, he became the first American president to visit a labor union, thus implicitly legitimizing organizations that had long been branded as criminal conspiracies in American political discourse.[47]

When the president visited Atlanta, however, the midterm elections had already passed and the South had voted Democratic as expected. McKinley's speeches there and earlier in Chicago, however, provide the clue to the other chief political purpose for which national reunion was instrumentalized, namely to elicit support for the new expansionist policies. At the time of Chicago's jubilee, the administration had not yet officially formulated its demands from Spain in the peace talks. However, the debate between the so-called imperialists and anti-imperialists, i.e. those who rejected the annexation of any territory or at least that of the Philippines, was in full force. In this climate, the president embarked on his trip to the West, which "is usually depicted as the time when a pliable chief executive heard the voice of the people on the subject of expansion and returned to Washington with his doubts removed and his commitment to the acquisition of the Asian islands crystallized." As Lewis Gould rightfully remarks, however, "[t]he opposite was true."[48] Just as McKinley had carefully influenced the impetus toward reunion by his overtures to the South, he was also actively, albeit carefully, promoting the new annexationist policies. In Chicago, he indicated what was in store when he spoke of the "grave responsibilities" and "the obligations of victory." After recounting how the war had been initiated for humanitarian reasons and how these broader considerations had to guide Americans in their future foreign policy, McKinley uttered his famous alliteration: "Duty determines destiny." This rather empty phrase was to become one of the most frequently used slogans of imperialists, who argued that, having freed the Philippines and other territories from Spanish tyranny, Americans could not now turn away and leave the islands to their own devices. Since the Filipinos and other "inferior races" were deemed incapable of self-government, imperialists argued that Americans were obligated to provide "good government" for them. As President McKinley implied in Chicago, this was a duty not only to the Filipinos themselves, but to "mankind."[49]

Within the context of the imperialism debate, the emphasis on national reunion and Civil War memory was extremely useful in a number of ways. First of all, as the president pointed out in Chicago, the inner logic of wars sometimes transcended their original objectives. Consistent with the above-mentioned reading of the Civil War, McKinley insisted that "Abraham Lincoln did not start out to free the slaves, but to save the Union." A similar change in consequences, which "may not be to our liking," the president continued, could transform the original promises made before the war with Spain. Then, the president and Congress had denied any intention of acquiring territories from Spain.[50] Secondly, the theme of national unity was instrumentalized as *ultima ratio*, as a self-explanatory proposition. In this context, McKinley warned the audiences during his trips throughout the West and South that unity had to be preserved "until we have settled our differences abroad ..."[51] These appeals thus demanded loyalty to the administration irrespective of the way in which it proposed to solve the difficult foreign policy questions. Occasionally, the pride of reunion was invoked to instill pure triumphalist and nationalist fervor. The president used this version of a "gut" appeal at the first jubilee after the conclusion of the treaty, in Atlanta, and thus in a region that was not sympathetic to the idea of expansion because racist Southerners feared "the injection into the body politic of the United States of that vitiated blood, that debased and ignorant people ...[i.e. the Filipinos]."[52] In Atlanta, however, the president roused the potentially hostile audience with some impassioned impromptu remarks:

> [Our] flag has been planted in two hemispheres, and there it remains the symbol of liberty and law, of peace and progress. (Great applause.) Who will withdraw from the people over whom it floats its protecting folds? Who will haul it down? Answer me, ye men of the South, who is there in Dixie who will haul it down? (Tremendous applause.)[53]

Elizabeth Marshall has described the effect of these sentences as "an electric shock," which prompted a "thunderous roar of 'No's" from the audience.[54] In fact, the president, in these few sentences, eloquently combined humanitarian pleas for a democratic mission to the "lesser peoples" with an instinctively patriotic appeal never to withdraw the flag, the emblem of national pride, once it had been planted by American soldiers. While political pressures and the Democratic leader William Jennings Bryan's decision to support the treaty certainly did more to procure the necessary votes to ratify the treaty in the Senate, McKinley powerfully demonstrated how nationalist pride could be instrumentalized to sweep potentially anti-imperialist audiences off their feet.

More than anything, however, the theme of national reunion created a consistent narrative of the past on which appeals for an expansionist future could be based. While McKinley merely implied expansion in Chicago, the city's vigorously imperialist newspaper concluded that the jubilee "told of sectional animosities now forever buried, and of a larger destiny for the reunited nation—a destiny reaching out to the islands of the seas. It was a national expansion parade in spirit and in fact."[55] National union, so the argument went, had been a potentiality, but never a reality, since American independence. The Civil War had been necessary to settle the outstanding issues between the regions, and the Spanish-American War to then close the old wounds with new blood. With national union thus finally realized, America could concentrate on the task of spreading civilization and democracy around the globe. No one captured this spirit better than the Chicago toastmaster Franklin MacVeagh:

> Democracy, in short, has seriously begun to rule humanity; and the illuminating truth is that democracy's ideals are not the ideals of isolation. Its concern is mankind. We are the greatest exponent of democracy, and we are appointed to live up to its ideals. And we must realize that a new democratic development is advancing which is characterized by broader demands of the democratic spirit—not demands for mere political institutions, important as they are, but for democratic civilization that shall reach all mankind, and for democratic human progress that shall include every corner of our earth.[56]

With its internal affairs rectified, America had to break out of the self-imposed confines of isolation, the imperialists argued, because its participation in world affairs was required to achieve the progress of mankind. More than that, nationalism itself was defined as progress, and the nation was biologically personified as a body that needed continued growth after domestic consolidation. In the context of his appeals to following the demands of "duty," the president warned his audience in Chicago: "The progress of a nation can alone prevent degeneration. There must be new life and purpose or there will be weakness and decay."[57] The Philippines and other overseas territories, he implied, would give America this "new life and purpose."

This rhetoric of America's new duties was mirrored in the peace jubilees' floats and decorations. Even the Omaha exposition, originally planned to depict America's westward movement across the continent, was quickly adapted to the new conditions. Instead of basing the "Indian exhibit" on models of previous American fairs, Edward Rosewater, primarily responsible for advertising, explicitly modeled it "after colonial exhibits at recent European fairs," thus suggesting that historical "Indian policy" ideally outfitted Americans for the tasks abroad. Sixteen Filipinos were quickly "imported" to form the nucleus of a Philippine village that served as an object lesson of that archipelago's primitiveness and incapability of self-government.[58] Washington's court of honor, a decorative staple of the jubilees, consisted not only of thirty-two columns representing each state of the union, but also of one column each for the Philippines and Hawaii. The organizers had apparently accepted the "white man's burden" quite quickly. The most stunning depiction, however, was in floats that appeared in Philadelphia and Washington, entitled "A Trifle Embarrassed:"

> In the center were two high columns, between which stood Uncle Sam and Miss Columbia. The happy couple, at this moment somewhat unhappy, were looking down upon a basket of *colored children*, tagged as follows: Hawaii, Porto [sic] Rico, Cuba, Philippines. All of the babies were bawling disconsolately, and evidently giving their uncle considerable trouble. These babies, however, like the basket in which they sat, were made of paper mache, while four beautiful children, two boys and two girls, standing at the other end of the float, represented the four possessions as living characters. The children were all smiling and happy. They were prettily costumed in white, with shades of red and blue.[59]

Such imagery combined the prevalent views of "inferior races" with expectations for America's civilizing mission. The "babies" in the basket represented "orphans" who had been left on the doorstep of the United States, through no fault of "Uncle Sam" himself. Their crying symbolized the desire to be assisted, to be "educated," by the United States. On the other side of the float, the four "live" children symbolized the progress that was sure to come as a result of American tutelage, a happy and clean future in America's national colors. The hierarchization of the races, implicit in this imperialist narrative, underscored the aforementioned reevaluation of African Americans' role in society, for if American blacks could not be entrusted to the care of their own officers or invested with the franchise in the South, how could other "inferior races" be expected to govern themselves? Relinquishing all pretense of equal rights and integration was thus not only the price of reconciliation with the South, but also the logical prerequisite of the imperial mission abroad. Thus, on the question of race as well, the themes of reunion and imperialism mutually reinforced one another. Imperialism facilitated what reunion required, namely that "inferior races", including African Americans, were defined as being outside the white re-United States. These races were supposedly mired in the "childhood stage" of development, still far removed from American "manhood," and whether they happened to reside within or outside of the United States, they required the guiding hand of their white American tutors.[60]

After war broke out in the Philippines in February 1899, imperialists instrumentalized Civil War memory in a final, more sectional way. Because of the timing, this theme was obviously not prevalent in the early peace jubilees, and in the Washington jubilee, the only one held after the outbreak of war, speakers refrained from sectional arguments, favoring the metaphors of reunion and unity. Nevertheless, this argument ought to be included because it added a slightly dissonant chord to an otherwise harmonious narrative of North and South. In this reading, imperialists argued that the Filipinos were rebelling against lawful American sovereignty, established through the peace treaty with Spain, just as the South had rebelled against the union. Attorney General Griggs was adamant in his conviction that the Civil War taught the appropriate lesson about how to respond to such provocations: "[T]he answer that is to be made to those who ask what we are to do about it, is the plain and simple answer that was given in 1861—'If any man attempts to haul down the American flag, shoot him on the spot.'"[61] The African-American *Indianapolis Freeman* similarly asserted:

> The independence of the Philippines is no part of the American program. We have nothing more to urge against the heroism of Aguinaldo than we have against the heroism of Gen. Lee or "Stonewall" Jackson. These had to submit and in this submission lost quite as much as Aguinaldo will loose ... The tears shed over the lost liberties of the Filipinos in the face of the past events are certainly insincere or the position of the North in 1862 was incorrect. If at that time it was right to coerce a people into a government without their consent it is still right. The fact of rebellion does not modify the condition at all for the principle of governing by consent is one and the same in either case.[62]

The president was slightly more cautious in his comparison of Filipinos and Confederates. After having once again described the Civil War as a conflict about the union, he asserted to great acclaim on the question of the Philippines: "We intend to put down that rebellion, just as we would put down any rebellion anywhere against the sovereignty of the United States."[63] Although such a comparison was consistent with the aforementioned basis of reunion between the sections, direct linkages between 1861 and 1899 were not designed to "sell" the imperialist message to Southern audiences. This associative argument thus remained more sectional than national since it reinvoked the Southern disloyalty that jubilee speakers had preferred to gloss over. Not surprisingly, the comparison was primarily made for Northern audiences.

This dissonant chord suggests, however, that reunion, as celebrated in the peace jubilees, was far from complete, especially when instrumentalized for such a specific purpose as imperial expansion. On the latter question, this impression was confirmed by the few dissident voices in Chicago's peace jubilee. While most speakers already dreamed of American world power and empire, Rabbi E. G. Hirsch admonished his audience that "[t]here is danger in a boastful national pride. Let us beware of colonial expansion."[64] During the second day of the jubilee, Samuel Gompers, the president of the American Federation of Labor, also spoke against colonial expansion and was, as the *Chicago Tribune* painstakingly noticed, jeered and hissed at by the audience. Warnings by a "melancholy idiot" were obviously not allowed to mar the triumphalism and expansionist fervor in evidence at the jubilee.[65] Although anti-imperialists were thus certainly underrepresented and not much appreciated at the peace jubilees themselves, their opinion about the way in which reunion was accomplished and instrumentalized is crucial in evaluating whether or not the jubilees had any lasting impact on contemporary thinking. While anti-imperialists were not opposed to the idea of reunion per se, they had their own version of Civil War memory, which they employed to fight the imperialist plans. Whereas, for President McKinley, the Union had been "the issue" at Gettysburg, the same battlefield symbolized the struggle for the doctrine of "the consent of the governed" to Senator George F. Hoar, the most prominent Republican anti-imperialist.[66] In this reading, the undemocratic institution of slavery had been the root cause of the fratricidal conflict. The annexation of the Philippines, anti-imperialists argued, erased the achievement of emancipation and nationwide democracy in one fell swoop because it subjected an entire country to government without consent. Alluding to the Emancipation Proclamation, William Lloyd Garrison, Jr., son of the famous abolitionist, thus lamented in a poem:

> When the great charter signed by Lincoln's pen
> From out the land of bondage brought a race,
> How little did ye dream that later men
> Would dare this seal of promise to efface!
> Has virtue vigor to uprise again,
> Or sinks one more republic in disgrace?[67]

Colonial rule in Asia, the anti-imperialists reasoned, was violating if not abrogating the mandate of those who had died for universal liberty. The Civil War thereby served them as a shibboleth of the cataclysm that could envelop American society should the consent of the governed be disregarded yet again. By the same token, many anti-imperialists thus felt called upon to don the abolitionist mantle one more time.

Having already sensed their exclusion in reunion, African Americans were similarly apprehensive about overseas expansion because it cemented white fantasies of racial hierarchy. Booker T. Washington, who was otherwise silent on the question of imperialism, warned in his second speech at Chicago that domestic racism still posed a powerful challenge to democracy, which could also endanger the entire imperialist enterprise:

> The further we go as a nation in the direction of engrafting into our system of government the *ignorant and irresponsible inhabitants of foreign islands*, the more will we be tempted to depart from those principles which have made us great as a nation ... It seems to me that the highest duty which this nation owes to itself and its traditions is to put the negro in the South on that plane of intelligence and civilization where no man will be tempted to degrade himself by interpreting the Constitution as meaning one thing when applied to a black man, and another thing when applied to a white man. If we permit the ignorance and poverty of the negro in the South to warp and corrupt our laws and degrade the public conscience the result will soon be felt in all parts of the North, *and the same hurtful influence will extend to our newly acquired territory*.[68]

While Washington denigrated the Filipinos, other black spokespeople confessed to sympathy with their plight and sometimes even to feelings of racial kinship. In general, it is fair to conclude with Willard B. Gatewood that the Philippine-American war represented "a dilemma that Negro Americans never completely resolved ..., a dilemma born of the conflict between their obligations as American citizens and their ideological and racial identity with the insurrectionists."[69] On the one hand, they wanted to appear as patriotic Americans, prepared to do their military duty in the Philippines. On the other hand, however, they were appalled at the spectacle of colonial oppression in the islands and, perhaps more importantly, feared the ominous consequences for their own position in the United States.

Their fears were borne out by the reaction of Southern anti-imperialists, who based their criticism of expansion primarily on racial fears of "amalgamation" and "miscegenation." During the debate on imperialism, they triumphantly and sarcastically pointed out that the imperialist rationale for subjecting "inferior races" ultimately "vindicated the South" and proved that Emancipation and Reconstruction had been wrongly conceived from the outset.[70] Like their Northern counterparts, they distilled a narrative of disfranchisement and disregard for the consent of the governed from the Civil War and warned that imperialism would repeat grievous mistakes from the past. Whereas Northern anti-imperialists spoke about the evil of slavery, Southern anti-imperialists insisted that it was the North who had disregarded states' rights and violated the consent of the (white) governed in the South.[71] Southern anti-imperialists thus resurrected the rhetoric of the "Lost Cause" in a highly contentious way that had not been envisioned by President McKinley when he honored the region by wearing the Confederate badge. It was not regional pride, but resentment over their recent "victimization" to which these anti-imperialists pointed.

Despite such challenges, the peace jubilees themselves undoubtedly reflected the mood of a country with a more national or even nationalist conception of itself. At first glance, this celebration of nationalism does not seem surprising following, as it did, the first successful foreign war the United States had waged in fifty years. On this level, the nationalist fervor sweeping the country seems somewhat comparable to that in Germany after the Franco-Prussian War of 1871, as an expression of a rather chauvinist and belligerent nationalism that gripped much of the Western world at the end of the century. A closer look at the messages transported in the peace jubilees, however, reveals how closely the "new nationalism" was shaped according to the particular historical circumstances of the late nineteenth-century United States. More than celebrating the "splendid little war" against Spain, speakers and images emphasized the victory Americans had won internally, over themselves and their recent divisive history. Memories of the Civil War quickly took center stage in the rhetoric and the representations during the peace jubilees. Common military service in the face of an external enemy, so the reasoning went, had finally demonstrated to the country that the chasm that separated North and South was now finally closed and sealed with fresh blood.

This newfound unity was quickly challenged, however, by groups that either disagreed with the particular terms of regional reconciliation or with the purposes for which reunion and Civil War memory were subsequently instrumentalized. African Americans realized that this reunion celebrated in the jubilees epitomized the process of their disfranchisement. Although black citizens, just like Southerners, had volunteered in the war against Spain, and although they had initially garnered considerable praise for their bravery and sacrifice, their role was belittled after the war and in the peace jubilees. While Southerners thus achieved symbolic reentry into the union by their military service in the recent war, African Americans were only further marginalized in response to their no less patriotic service. Such a more or less open redefinition of their place in society was the price their white compatriots were only too willing to pay for the South's acceptance of the verdict of the Civil War, a verdict that extended only to the notion that national rights superseded states' rights, but not to the emancipation of the slaves.

Overseas expansion, one of the purposes for which the newfound national unity was instrumentalized, only served to buttress the subordinate position of other races inside and outside of the United States. In the logic of the nationalist narrative in evidence at the celebrations, the Spanish-American War not only helped to resolve a divisive past, but also connected past and present with the important foreign policy questions of the future. The historical pageants and the jubilee speakers created a teleological interpretation of national history, stressing that the struggle for national unity and the conquest of the continent had been the dominant features of the first century of the United States' existence. The war with Spain closed this historical epoch and opened the way for a more active international role, through which America could realize its historical mission of spreading its democratic ideals around the globe. Such a millennial history strongly appealed to the exceptionalist beliefs with which America had always been invested.

The debate on expansion, as well as other divisive political questions of the age, also marked the boundaries of unity. Although not much in evidence during the celebrations themselves, anti-imperialists were quick to question this reading of history and they significantly appealed to Civil War memory themselves to legitimize their dissent. While unity and triumphant nationalism were the messages imperialists distilled from the seminal conflict, Northern anti-imperialists preferred the narrative of emancipation and democracy. Colonial rule, they argued, would only reintroduce slavery under another name and thus bring the country to the brink of destruction once again. More importantly, Southern anti-imperialists introduced decidedly sectional arguments, which directly undermined the *national* conception of America that jubilee speakers had so ardently tried to construct.

Accompanied by continued labor struggles and the question of a bimetallic currency, the imperialism debate was just one of the challenges that the narrative of national unity faced after the end of the war with Spain and the well-attended peace jubilees. Undoubtedly, the peace jubilees assisted in the construction of a more nationalist self-image, that coincided with structural changes at the turn of the century. Sectional, racial, class, and even local narratives—if one recalls the competitive boosterism in the various peace jubilees—persisted side by side, however, and could erupt under the strain of political controversies. The peace jubilees thus represent only a brief harmonious moment in historical time, which might be the very reason why they were so completely forgotten.

Notes

1. Editorial, "The Week of the Jubilee," *Chicago Tribune*, October 16, 1898.
2. The only article on one of the peace jubilees is largely descriptive and by no means analytical in design; Elizabeth Marshall, "Atlanta Peace Jubilee," *Georgia Historical Quarterly* 50 (Fall 1966): 276-82. Stephen Skowronek, *Building a New American State: The Expansion of National Administrative Capabilities, 1877-1920* (Cambridge, MA: Cambridge University Press, 1982). Gerald F. Linderman, *The Mirror of War: American Society and the Spanish-American War* (Ann Arbor, MI: University of Michigan Press, 1974), chapter 6. The author locates one cause for the more national response to war in the growing importance of a nationalized "yellow" press.
3. Benedict Anderson, *Imagined Communities: Reflections on the Origins and Spread of Nationalism* (London: Verso, 1991).
4. Robert W. Rydell, *All the World's a Fair: Visions of Empire at American International Expositions, 1876-1916* (Chicago: University of Chicago Press, 1984), 108. Since the fair had a different original purpose and since Rydell has covered it extensively, the event has been omitted from the analysis of this study. Rydell also writes, however, that the exposition was based on the efforts of local boosters and politicians. For the nineteenth-century absence of the national governments in the organization of nationalist celebrations and the comparison with Europe and Japan see Michael Kammen, *Mystic Chords of Memory: The Transformation of Tradition in American Culture* (New York: Alfred A. Knopf, 1991), 293-94. Cecilia O'Leary has also emphasized the role of private organizations and individuals, "'Blood Brotherhood:' The Racialization of Patriotism, 1865-1918," in John Bodnar, ed., *Bonds of Affection: Americans Define Their Patriotism* (Princeton, NJ: Princeton University Press, 1996), 60.
5. The label "national" peace jubilee was, for example, given by the *New York Times*, October 17, 1898. Chicago's organizing committee also included a number of the city's university professors, who then bestowed an honorary law degree on President McKinley; *Washington Post* and *Chicago Tribune*, October 18, 1898. In all cities, such organizing committees were very large. A detailed description of the capital's committee in the *Washington Post*, May 23, 1899, provides an idea of the size of the effort and of the occupations and connections of the committee members. The newspaper also noted that the committee had $24,000 at its disposal, which had been raised primarily through subscriptions from committee members. This information on financing, in turn, provides a clue as to why committee positions were so numerous.
6. *Washington Post*, May 25, 1899.
7. For elaborate descriptions of the various jubilees see: Chicago in *Chicago Tribune*, October 16-21, 1898; Philadelphia in *New York Times*, October 26-29, 1898; Atlanta in *Washington Post*, December 14-16, 1898; Washington in *Washington Post*, May 23-26, 1899. If one compares the newspapers' coverage of the historical pageants in Philadelphia and Washington, it is conceivable that the capital "recycled" Philadelphia's floats or at least used the same themes in its own civic parade. The *Washington Post*, May 26, 1899, also noted that the builder of the floats came from Philadelphia.
8. *St. Louis Post Dispatch*, October 14-18, 1898. The storm that ravaged Chicago during the jubilee and that destroyed a number of the triumphal arches received some of the most extensive coverage.
9. *Washington Post*, May 26, May 28, 1899. *New York Times*, May 28, 1899. *Chicago Tribune*, May 24, 1899.
10. Editorial, "The Jubilee Week," October 17, 1898.

11. Editorial, "Labor's Concern in the Matter," *Springfield Republican*, October 22, 1898; *Chicago Tribune*, October 20, 1898.
12. Peck, "The Year of the Jubilee," Address at the Peace Jubilee, Chicago, October 19, 1898, in Robert I. Fulton, Thomas C. Trueblood, eds., *Patriotic Eloquence Relating to the Spanish-American War and its Issues* (New York: Charles Scribner's Sons, 1900), 244. The same feeling pervaded an exchange of letters between the editor of the *Charleston News and Courier* who had to decline an invitation to Chicago, and Colonel Turner of the First Illinois Regiment. Turner wrote: "Chicago's great jubilee celebrates not so much the victory of the American army in the war with Spain as the reunion of our own country." *Chicago Tribune*, December 16, 1898.
13. On the political level, the rapprochement between the regions was initiated by the end of Reconstruction, which did not keep politicians from "waving the bloody shirt", however, whenever it suited their short-term goals, John A. Garraty, *The New Commonwealth, 1877-1890*, The New American Nation Series (New York: Harper Torchbooks, 1968), 240-44.
14. McKinley, "Speech at Decatur, Illinois, October 15, 1898," in idem, *Speeches and Addresses of William McKinley, from March 1, 1897 to May 30, 1900* (New York: Doubleday & McClure Co., 1900), 125-26.
15. For the veterans organizations' efforts at reconciliation before the Spanish-American War and Roosevelt's selection of the Rough Riders, see O'Leary, "'Blood Brotherhood,'" 60-70, 73. For the gestures toward the South at the beginning of the war and the nationalist response in that region, see Richard E. Wood, "The South and Reunion, 1898," *The Historian* 31 (May 1969): 415-30. On the careful and time-consuming process of selecting personnel for the war, compare Lewis L. Gould, *The Spanish-American War and President McKinley* (Lawrence, KS: University of Kansas Press, 1988), 70.
16. Lodge to Anna Cabot Lodge, May 22, 1898, Family Correspondence, Box 103, Henry Cabot Lodge Papers, Massachusetts Historical Society, Boston [emphasis mine]; compare also Wood, "South and Reunion," 425.
17. Quote from *Washington Post*, May 24, 1899.
18. For the quote, see *Washington Post*, May 24, 1899; for the description of the Chicago parade, see *Chicago Tribune*, October 20, 1898.
19. *New York Times*, October 29, 1898; *Washington Post*, May 26, 1899.
20. Cortelyou, Diary Entry, December 8, 1898, Box 52, Diaries, George B. Cortelyou Papers, Library of Congress, Washington, D.C. [emphasis in the original].
21. McKinley, "Speech before the Legislature in Joint Assembly at the State Capitol, Atlanta, Georgia, December 14, 1898," in idem, *Speeches and Addresses*, 159. On the significance of this Southern trip, see also Gould, *The Spanish-American War*, 111.
22. The reactions were detailed in *Chicago Tribune, New York Times, Washington Post*, December 15, 1898. The latter paper also related the story of McKinley's long-standing "secret" plan.
23. Howell, "Our Reunited Country," Extracts from Speech at Chicago Peace Jubilee, November [sic] 19, 1898, in Fulton, Trueblood, *Patriotic Eloquence*, 158-59.
24. *Atlanta Constitution*, May 13, 1898; quoted after Wood, "South and Reunion," 427.
25. McKinley, "Speech at the Auditorium, Atlanta, Georgia, December 15, 1898," in idem, *Speeches and Addresses*, 160 [emphasis mine].
26. Roosevelt, "The Strenuous Life," speech before the Hamilton Club, Chicago, April 10, 1899, in State of New York, ed., *Public Papers of Theodore Roosevelt, Governor, 1899* (Albany, NY: Brandow Printing Company, 1899), 293-307. On the cult of masculinity and strife see also Gail Bederman, *Manliness & Civilization: A Cultural History of Gender and Race in the United States, 1880-1917* (Chicago: Chicago University Press, 1995); John

Higham, "The Reorientation of American Culture in the 1890s," in idem, ed., *Writing American History: Essays on Modern Scholarship* (Bloomington, IN: Indiana University Press, 1970), 77-88; Kristin L. Hoganson, *Fighting for American Manhood: How Gender Politics Provoked the Spanish-American and Philippine-American Wars* (New Haven, CT: Yale University Press, 1998).

27. Wheeler's was the first address ever of a former Confederate general to a New England Grand Army post, cited in *Springfield Republican*, May 30, 1899 [emphasis mine].
28. Wilson, speech at the First Regiment Armory, *Chicago Tribune*, October 19, 1898. Similarly, Albert J. Beveridge also praised Southerners as "sons and daughters of a heroic race," Beveridge, "To the People of the South," speech manuscript for the Republican Mass Meeting, Louisville, KY, October 20, 1900, Box 297, Albert Jeremiah Beveridge Papers, Library of Congress, Washington, D.C. On this crucial reinterpretation see also O'Leary, "'Blood Brotherhood,'" 75.
29. Herbert, speech at the Washington Peace Jubilee, *Washington Post*, May 26, 1899.
30. O'Leary, "'Blood Brotherhood,'" 70-72; Kammen, *Mystic Chords of Memory*, 109-15; also David Blight, "'For Something Beyond the Battlefield': Frederick Douglass and the Struggle for the Memory of the Civil War," *Journal of American History* 75 (March 1898): 1165-67.
31. On the importance of Wheeler's appearance in the Atlanta Jubilee, see also Marshall, "Atlanta Peace Jubilee," 278. For the descriptions of reactions to "Dixie" and of Wheeler's appearance in the military parade, see *New York Times, Washington Post*, December 16, 1898.
32. On the predicament of the African-American community in the war and the ensuing imperialist period, see Willard B. Gatewood, Jr., *Black Americans and the White Man's Burden, 1898-1903* (Urbana, IL: University of Illinois Press, 1975); idem, ed., *"Smoked Yankees" and the Struggle for Empire: Letters from Negro Soldiers, 1898-1902* (Fayetteville, AK: University of Arkansas Press, 1987).
33. Kaplan, "Black and Blue on San Juan Hill," in Amy Kaplan, Donald E. Pease, eds., *Cultures of United States Imperialism* (Durham, NC: Duke University Press, 1993), 219-36.
34. *Washington Post*, December 15, 1898. The other papers surveyed for this study did not take note of this incident.
35. *Washington Post*, May 24, 1899 [emphasis mine]. The following day, the paper ran a small article denying the reasons given the previous day. Instead, regimental members claimed that their ranks had been too small for the inclusion in the parade, an explanation that seems highly unlikely, given the contemporary patriotic fervor and the chance to march in a well-attended military parade.
36. *Chicago Tribune*, October 20, 1898.
37. Hodnett, Address at Chicago peace jubilee, *Chicago Tribune*, October 17, 1898; for another description of the composite American nationality without blacks see Herbert, speech at Washington peace jubilee, *Washington Post*, May 26, 1899.
38. Ransom, "Past and Present," address at Chicago peace jubilee, *Indianapolis Freeman*, November 12, 1898. This speech could not be found among all the other reproduced speeches for the occasion in "white" newspapers. Most probably, it was not one of the speeches in the official program.
39. For the specific mention of McKinley's "curious gesture", see the African-American *Baltimore Ledger*, October 22, 1898; *New York Times*, October 17, 1898. McKinley, "Speech at Tuskegee Normal and Industrial Institute, Tuskegee, AL, December 16, 1898," in idem, *Speeches and Addresses*, 166-70. The *Washington Post*, December 15, 1898, labeled McKinley's visit to the institute a "surprise," but described his planned speech as one that would emphasize individual advancement and discourage a preoccupation with politics.

40. For background on black troops in the Philippines, see Gatewood, *Black Americans,* 207. For the notion of reunion on racial grounds see Rubin Francis Weston, *Racism in U.S. Imperialism: The Influence of Racial Assumptions on American Foreign Policy, 1893-1946* (Columbia, SC: University of South Carolina Press, 1972), 7-10.
41. The concept of the black citizen soldier reaping rewards for his community has been ably developed by Manfred Berg, "Soldiers and Citizens: War and Voting Rights in American History," in: David K. Adams, Cornelis A. van Minnen, eds., *Reflections on American Exceptionalism* (Staffordshire: Ryburn Publishing, 1994), 188-225.
42. "The Peace Jubilee," *Washington Bee,* April 15, 1898.
43. Washington, "The Better Part," address at peace jubilee, Chicago, October 16, 1898; "The Negro in the Late War," address, October 18, 1898, in Fulton, Trueblood, *Patriotic Eloquence,* 330-33, 333-36 [emphasis mine].
44. Editorial, "President McKinley in the South," *Colored American,* December 24, 1898.
45. Editorials, "The President South," "There are no Rebels Now," *Washington Bee,* December 17, 1898; February 4, 1899.
46. On McKinley's emotional views of the Civil War and on his deeply held conviction that national unity was essential for the progress of the country, see Linderman, *Mirror of War,* 9-11.
47. McKinley, "Speech at First Regiment Armory, Chicago, before the Allied Organizations of Railroad Employees, October 20, 1898," in idem, *Speeches and Addresses,* 136-38. The *Chicago Tribune,* October 21, 1898, noted the significance of the event. At the same occasion, moreover, Colonel Turner reinvoked the theme of reunion this time but tied it to the reconciliation between labor and capital. For the divisiveness of the 1896 elections see Nell Irvin Painter, *Standing at Armageddon: The United States, 1877-1919* (New York: W.W. Norton & Co., 1987), 135-39. That the political divisions were difficult to overcome was foreshadowed in the act of a Democratic prankster during Chicago's civic parade. As the city's Republican clubs passed the window in which he was positioned, he showered them with silver snippets, thus alluding to the highly divisive monetary issues separating Republicans, who favored the gold standard, from Democrats, who desired a more inflationary bimetallic standard; *Chicago Tribune,* October 20, 1898.
48. Gould, *The Spanish-American War,* 104. For the traditional view of McKinley as a rather weak chief executive who followed instead of listened to the people on the question of expansion see, for example, Julius W. Pratt, *Expansionists of 1898: The Acquisition of Hawaii and the Spanish Islands* (1936; Chicago: Quadrangle Books, 1964), 337.
49. McKinley, "Speech at the Citizens' Banquet in the Auditorium, Chicago, October 19, 1898," in idem, *Speeches and Addresses,* 133-36. Providing the twin themes of duty and destiny with religious content, the president recalled later in front of a church delegation how he had had a kind of revelation late at night, which finally prompted him to demand the cession of the entire Philippine archipelago, report by General James F. Rusling, *The Christian Advocate,* January 22, 1903, reported in Charles S. Olcott, *The Life of William McKinley,* 2 vols. (Boston and New York: Houghton Mifflin Company, 1916) 2: 109-111. Still unsurpassed on the themes of duty and destiny is Albert K. Weinberg, *Manifest Destiny: A Study of Nationalist Expansionism in American History* (1935; Chicago: Quadrangle Paperbacks, 1963), chapter 9.
50. See the Teller-Amendment to the congressional resolution that authorized the president to take any means necessary to secure a resolution of the Cuban question in *Congressional Record,* 55th Cong., 2nd sess., 1898: 4040-41. For the president's previous denial of any annexationist designs, see McKinley, "First Annual Message," December 6, 1897, in *A Compilation of the Messages and Papers of the Presidents, 1789-1897,* ed. James D. Richardson, (Washington: GPO, 1899) 10: 131.

51. McKinley, "Speech at Clinton, Iowa, October 11, 1898;" for a similar example on his Southern tour, see idem, "Speech at Augusta, Georgia, December 19, 1898," in idem, *Speeches and Addresses*, 85, 182.
52. Senator Benjamin Tillman in *Congressional Record*, 55th Cong., 3rd sess., 1899: 837.
53. McKinley, "Speech at the Auditorium, Atlanta, Georgia, December 15, 1898," in idem, *Speeches and Addresses*, 161. The *Washington Post*, December 15, 1898, remarked that the president himself had added the rhetorical questions to his prepared remarks.
54. Marshall, "Atlanta Peace Jubilee," 280.
55. Editorial, "The Jubilee Parade," *Chicago Tribune*, October 20, 1898.
56. MacVeagh, Address at the Jubilee Banquet, *Chicago Tribune*, October 20, 1899 [emphasis mine]. In an editorial of the following day, the imperialist *Chicago Tribune* was quick to seize on the speech's significance, namely that it realized the logically global concern of democratic theory and practice, "Mr. MacVeagh's Speech," *Chicago Tribune*, October 21, 1899. For another invocation of the "new era", see Bishop John Ireland, "Extracts from Speech at the Peace Jubilee, Chicago, October 18, 1898," in Fulton and Trueblood, *Patriotic Eloquence*, 167-73.
57. McKinley, "Speech at Citizens' Banquet in the Auditorium, Chicago, October 19, 1898," in idem, *Speeches and Addresses*, 135. At the Washington peace jubilee, Senator Shelby Cullom similarly stressed that the nation was governed "by the law of growth," *Washington Post*, May 26, 1899. On the contemporary conviction that nationalism and patriotism themselves were marks of progress, see Rydell, *All the World's a Fair*, 59.
58. Rydell, *All the World's a Fair*, 112, 120. "Indian policies" were indeed the model on which American colonial administration was to be based, Walter L. Williams, "United States Indian Policy and the Debate over Philippine Annexation: Implications for the Origins of American Imperialism," *Journal of American History* 66 (March 1980): 810-31.
59. *Washington Post*, May 26, 1899 [emphasis mine]; for the same float in Philadelphia see *New York Times*, October 29, 1898.
60. Although Amy Kaplan does not address the question of reunion, she eloquently describes the re-definition of American manhood at the close of the Spanish-American War. Roosevelt's account of the battle of San Juan Hill, she argues, defined African Americans as incomplete males. External empire and internal racism, she concludes, mutually conditioned one another, "Black and Blue on San Juan Hill," 219-36.
61. Speech of Attorney General Griggs at Quincy, IL, October 6, 1899, Reel 83, Series 4, William J. McKinley Papers, Library of Congress, Washington, D.C. By the turn of the century, the flag as a symbol had also undergone a dramatic reinterpretation as it was freed from local or regional connotations and invested with truly national meaning, Stuart McConnell, "Reading the Flag: A Reconsideration of the Patriotic Cults of the 1890s," in Bodnar, *Bonds of Affection*, 102-19.
62. *Indianapolis Freeman*, April 22, 1898.
63. McKinley, "Speech at Sioux Falls, SD, October 14, 1899," in idem, *Speeches and Addresses*, 294-97.
64. Hirsch, Sermon at Sinai Temple, Chicago, October 16, 1899; in the central Thanksgiving sermon preceding the jubilee exercises, Hirsch was more equivocal on the subject but nevertheless also warned of colonial expansion, *Chicago Tribune*, October 17, 1898.
65. The quotation on Gompers is from an editorial, "Gomper's Crazy Predictions," *Chicago Tribune*, October 20, 1898.
66. Hoar, Address at Gettysburg, *Worcester Spy*, September 17, 1900, Box 24, Scrapbooks, George F. Hoar Papers, Massachusetts Historical Society, Boston.
67. Garrison, "Invocation," April 30, 1899, in idem, *The Nation's Shame: Sonnets* (n.d., n.p.).

68. Washington, "Address at Peace Jubilee, Chicago, October 18, 1898," in Fulton and Trueblood, *Patriotic Eloquence*, 335 [emphasis mine].
69. Gatewood, *Black Americans*, 187-88. Chapter 8 of this book details the complicated responses of black Americans gave to the question of imperialism.
70. Senator McLaurin in *Congressional Record*, 55th Cong., 3rd sess., 1899: 639; see also Representative Williams, *ibid.*: 339. For this charge by Southern Democrats see also Weston, *Racism in U.S. Imperialism*, 12. Weston also concludes (p. 15) that the new imperialism spelled the victory of Southern ideas on race.
71. For this view compare Representative John Lamb in *Congressional Record*, 55th Cong., 3rd sess., 1899, Appendix: 97-98.

Chapter 13

HISTORICAL BONDING WITH AN EXPIRING HERITAGE

Revisiting the Plymouth Tercentenary Festivities of 1920/21[1]

Udo J. Hebel

The Plymouth Tercentenary and the Retreat of Forefathers' Day from the National Stage of Commemoration after the Civil War

WHEN CHARLES C. EVERETT ascended the Forefathers' Day rostrum in Bangor, Maine on December 17, 1865, he imagined himself to be still in command of the cultural force and national clout which the anniversary of the so-called landing of the Pilgrim Fathers on Plymouth Rock in 1620 had exerted all across the North American continent throughout the first half of the nineteenth century.[2] "This week," he claimed with a rhetorical gesture reminiscent of such antebellum orators as John Quincy Adams, Horace Bushnell, Lewis Cass, Rufus Choate, Edward Everett, Oliver Wendell Holmes, Truman Post, Richard Storrs, Charles Sumner, Charles Wentworth Upham, and Daniel Webster, "will occur the grandest and the most sacred anniversary which marks the national year."[3] In keeping with the repertoire of his more famous predecessors on the privileged platform of New England ancestor worship, the commissioned speaker of the day once again advanced

---

Notes for this section begin on page 289.

a Plymouth Rock-based construction of the United States and pronounced a New England-centered formulation of national history as the exclusive key to a glorious future for the recently reunited nation:

> The great West is mainly an outgrowth of New England. And now the South is becoming New Englandised. The very year, that the Mayflower reached Plymouth, with its freight of Liberty, came, like its dark shadow, the first slave ship to Jamestown. From these two germs sprang two powers, one of light and one of darkness, one of order and one of chaos. The continent was not large enough for both. At last they met, they touched; and for them to meet and to touch, was a life and death struggle.—Now at last we can hail Fore Fathers day, with the welcome greeting of final triumph. The Puritan has conquered the Cavalier. The South itself is overrun by Northern emigrants and Northern ideas, as it has been overrun by Northern armies. Ideas of the dignity of labor and of the rights of man are taking the place of the Feudal notions of the right of oppression and of the dignity of idleness. Plymouth Rock is becoming the center, Forefathers day the anniversary, of the whole nation. The Puritan is supreme. And it is the Puritan principles that are to be the cement and the guarantee of our new Union.[4]

Everett's vision of the absolute power of New England's heritage and his trust in the uncontested centrality of Forefathers' Day in the collective cultural memory[5] of the United States did not materialize in the expected manner. The Civil War had dealt a fatal blow to New England's claim to rule supreme on the increasingly competitive field of commemorative production.[6] The mass immigration of the Gilded Age and the Progressive Era prompted demographic, cultural, and social changes that eroded the influence of the New England societies outside New England proper[7] and supported the ethnic pluralization of American festive culture, in whose future calendar "the grandest and most sacred anniversary" was to occupy considerably less space than in the time period between the American Revolution and the Civil War.[8]

Sure enough, the veneration of the Pilgrim Fathers as cultural icons of mythic stature and national implication was continued with continued fervor in and around Plymouth, and the enshrinement of Plymouth Rock and December 21, 1620[9] as the only true origin of the United States reached new dimensions on the occasions of the 250th anniversary in 1870, the dedication of the National Pilgrim Monument in 1889, and the return from England of the manuscript of William Bradford's history of Plymouth's beginnings in 1897.[10] Performances by Mark Twain and Ulysses S. Grant at the annual dinners of the unrelenting New England Society in the City of New York in the late 1870s and early 1880s stirred up considerable media attention[11] although Mark Twain's irreverent approach to the honorable forefathers introduced a new tone into the discourse of the filiopietistic rite.[12] In contrast, and probably symptomatic of the ongoing transformation of American commemorative and festive cultures, functions in Charleston, Philadelphia, St. Louis, and Chicago[13] pursued the tradition of Forefathers' Day banquets with more modesty and less continuity in the decades after the Civil War and were hardly able to match the grandeur of their antebellum models. The New England Society of Charleston, South Carolina, seems to have been rather isolated in its muted support for the "New Englandisation" of the South.[14] Scattered references to newly installed but soon-to-be-discontinued observances of Forefathers' Day in Wisconsin after the Civil War and in Minnesota around the turn of the twentieth century may be taken as gauges of a different kind to the loosening hold of New England anniversary celebrants on the reins of national memory.[15] Never again after the Civil War did the commemorative energy stirred by the arrival of William Bradford and the Pilgrims on the shores of the Old Colony reach the magnitude of the 1820s, 1830s, 1840s, and 1850s, when the desire to observe December 21, 1620 as an historic event of exceptional significance for the nation was gratified by large-scale festivities held simultaneously with the celebration at Plymouth in major cities from Boston, Philadelphia, and New York to Charleston, New Orleans, Louisville, Cincinnati, Detroit, Chicago, St. Louis, Sacramento, and San Francisco.

By the time the first initiatives for the observance of Plymouth's tercentenary were launched during the years of the First World War, Forefathers' Day had become a site of memory[16] whose visibility as an extralocal cultural practice needed resuscitation. Reports of unexpected financial problems[17] were a trustworthy indicator that the civic rite, which the *Massachusetts Mercury* had long ago on December 25, 1798 called "the celebration of the most important day in our History", and which Charles C. Everett was still sure to carry to unprecedented heights as the foundational anniversary "of the whole nation," had exhausted its funds. When preparations for the tercentenary festivities were getting underway, the Anglocentric definitions of American history and culture that had fueled Forefathers' Day celebrations since the late eighteenth century had been rendered problematic, if not obsolete, by the political and social realities of the early twentieth-century United States. Monolithic conceptualizations of an Anglo-Saxon America were seriously challenged by the emergence of new notions of cultural pluralism.[18] In an uncommonly radical way, Randolph Bourne's projection of a "trans-national America" exposed the "failure of the melting-pot," attacked the assimilationist programs of Americanization flourishing in the 1910s,[19] and rejected the "narrow 'Americanism'" and "forced chauvinism" of "native 'American' culture."[20] While tercentenary organizers imagined a technologically modernized repetition of the glorious Plymouth Bicentennial of 1820 and the triumphant revalidation of the retrospective politics of Forefathers' Day on the stage of national festive culture, H.L. Mencken braced himself for a first, trend-setting round of Puritan-bashing,[21] and Carter G. Woodson advocated his specific revision of white interpretations of (African) American history from the pages of the newly founded *Journal of Negro History*.[22] Together with the shift in immigration politics towards restrictive legislation, the resurfacing of deep-rooted xenophobic sentiments in the wake of the Red Scare, the expulsion of anarchist dissidents, the impending Sacco and Vanzetti trial, and the controversy over the role of the United States in the post-war world, such oppositional voices revealed undeniable cracks in the glossy surface of traditional constructions of America.[23] Tercentenary exercises in Connecticut, Charleston, St. Louis, Indianapolis,[24] and, most importantly, in Plymouth itself continued to raise the rhetorical question "[w]hat meaning have the Pilgrims to us?"[25] That the tercentenary orator, Henry Cabot Lodge, defined the festive community as including all those "who have one and all been bred up in the nineteenth-century spirit" is more than a negligible detail in the texture of the official tercentenary oration. Lodge's collective self-conceptualization contains the involuntary admission of the retrospective character of the event as well as the impending expiration date of the heritage it staged. If the blueprint for the festivities of 1920/21, the Plymouth Bicentennial of 1820, had indeed managed to ultimately install Plymouth Rock and the Pilgrim myth as a crystallizing focus of nineteenth-century national(ist) sentiment, the Plymouth Tercentenary may be taken as the coda to the national demise of New England anniversary celebrations after the Civil War and as the final seal to "the passing away of a New England that would not return."[26]

The following retraces the Plymouth Tercentenary jubilee in its entirety from the early summer of 1920 to the late summer of 1921. Instead of providing for specific interpretations of the central texts, including Henry Cabot Lodge's "The Pilgrims of Plymouth: An Address at Plymouth, Massachusetts on the Three Hundredth Anniversary of Their Landing December 21, 1920," Le Baron Russell Briggs's "1620-1920: A Poem," and George P. Baker's pageant *The Pilgrim Spirit*,[27] the present study will explore the choreography of the festivities at large and the symbolic implications of individual parts of the cultural performance. Drawing on the press coverage that the tercentenary received in local, regional, and national papers throughout the festive year[28] as well as on major contemporary documents,[29] this return to the sites of the tercentenary will assess the unifying political rationale governing the commemoration throughout the course of public action. The analysis of contemporary newspaper representation will trace the circulation of the desired ideological impact to a wider—national—

audience. Despite the magnitude of the endeavor and initial doubts about the "confused congeries of uncertain projects ... clouding the plans" (*Old Colony Memorial*, January 23, 1920), the tercentenary became a celebration "in which, through a multiplicity of forms and a series of coordinated events, participate directly or indirectly and to various degrees, all members of a whole community united by ethnic, linguistic, religious, historical bonds, and sharing a world view."[30] Like Forefathers' Day celebrations of earlier days, the Plymouth Tercentenary featured a "sequence of practices,"[31] and, even over the course of more than a year, accomplished the "high degree of functional interdependence among its components"[32] which had determined these earlier events and which interpreters of public events have recognized as an important requirement for the emotional appeal and political success of collective celebrations as symbolic formations. The Plymouth Tercentenary took to perfection preexisting scripts of New England filiopietism and employed with unrivaled mastery the festive "building blocks"[33] which regular attendants of previous functions and newcomers to the order of anniversary exercises expected to be (re)enacted in due fashion. Yet, if acts of cultural commemoration are "re-constructive semiotic operation[s]" and, under certain circumstances, indeed related to experiences and sentiments of collective crisis, "constituting an aggressive-defensive, essentially *political* reflex to some threat of collective marginalization or defeat,"[34] the pompous grandeur of the Plymouth Tercentenary bears involuntary witness to the pressures under which the supporters of a New England-centered formulation of American history and culture operated by 1920-21—and unknowingly (?) bid farewell to the exclusive position of the heritage rehearsed.

The Plymouth Tercentenary: A Consolidated Effort of National Revalidation and Continuing (Anglo-)Americanization

The scope of the Plymouth Tercentenary as a consolidated effort from within the camps of the older, New England-oriented elite to recertify the historical and political validity of the Pilgrim heritage against the ongoing cultural transformation of the United States is manifested by the roster of local, regional, and national organizations involved at one point or another, and to different degrees, in the planning of the festivities. The continuous coverage of preparatory measures and meetings in Plymouth's *Old Colony Memorial*—usually under headings such as "Tercentenary Matters," "Tercentenary Developments," or "Tercentenary Plans"—includes references to the following agencies, with exact titles changing at times: the Town Tercentenary Committee (with its Executive Committee), the (Massachusetts) State (Pilgrim) Tercentenary Commission, the (Federal) Pilgrim Tercentenary Commission (with its National Executive Committee), the National Finance Committee of the Pilgrim-Plymouth Tercentenary Committee (first trying to raise a minimum of $300,000, then raising the stakes to $500,000), the Society of Mayflower Descendants (with its California chapter being among the most active contributors), the New England Society in the City of New York, the Daughters of the American Revolution, the Colonial Daughters of the Seventeenth Century, the Improved Order of the Red Men, the National Society of New England Women, the Society of Colonial Dames, the National Society of the Sons and Daughters of the Pilgrims, and, of course, the Pilgrim Society[35] that had sponsored Plymouth Forefathers' Day celebrations since the grand old days of the 1820 bicentennial. Innumerable subcommittees concerned themselves with the coordination of various responsibilities, e.g., "Railroad and Steamboat Transportation," "Housing and Feeding," "Reception and Entertainment," Traffic and Highway," "Law and Order," "Publicity," and "Tablet and Markers."[36] The organizing and supporting agencies provided the platform for a seemingly heterogeneous, but inherently monolithic, gathering of dignitaries, enthusiasts, administrators, educators, historians, and, above all, politicians. The organizational apparatus fueling the festive operation went beyond anything traceable in the 151-year-old history of Forefathers' Day celebrations in Plymouth. By 1920, Forefathers' Day had come a long way since its inception as a rite of politically interested ancestor worship in 1769 and the earliest days of the Old Colony Club in pre-revolutionary Plymouth.[37]

Repeatedly, the high degree of administrative institutionalization of the singular event stirred warnings that the "memorial work" might end in "memorial confusion" and that the "realization of the significance of the Pilgrim emigration" might be seriously endangered by festive competition (*Old Colony Memorial,* January 23, 1920). The local paper took care to ensure that the imagined community of readers and celebrants kept their faith in the successful completion of the collective venture and thereby in the unbroken power of the history to be invoked for (re)sanctification. The *Old Colony Memorial* of July 23, 1920, e.g., put special emphasis on the fact that Louis K. Liggett, chairman of the State Pilgrim Tercentenary Commission, had been elected as a member of the National Executive and National Finance Committees so that "there will be the fullest co-operation between the State Commission, the Federal Commission, and the Plymouth National Committee, and a complete co-ordination between them of all plans and purposes." A few weeks later, the same paper dispersed doubts about the progress and accomplishment of the project:

There being some confusion on the part of many as to what the various committees on the Tercentenary celebration are to do, it can be stated that there are the Federal Committee, the State Committee and the Plymouth Committee, while there is also the National Committee which is merged with the Plymouth Committee, or in other words, the local organization is now nationalized, with some of the best known and prominent men and women of the nation as members. All of these committees are co-operating for the same end, the great success of the coming observance, and all are in complete agreement.[38]

It seems that destabilizing thoughts about the feasibility of the enterprise were to be overruled by three impulses: the desire to invest the Plymouth Tercentenary with the cultural clout which the various old-stock societies participating in the preparations had commanded until then; secondly, the urge to confirm in advance the national significance of the jubilee and its political agenda by means of references to the unanimous consent among all agencies involved; thirdly, the trust that the embattled Anglo-American heritage could be reinforced by an effective demonstration of cultural and political energy and the systematic circulation of this demonstration to the wider American populace. The emphasis on the 'merging' (again) of the 'local' practice with 'national' interests—with the help of "some of the best known and prominent men and women of the nation"—is a noteworthy expression of the underlying purpose of the Plymouth Tercentenary, i.e., the political empowerment of a receding heritage and the (re)affirmation of Plymouth Rock as the cornerstone of the American civil religion.[39]

The seriousness of the joint effort to (re)claim Plymouth's foundation as the only acceptable origin of the United States and its ideological self-construction as "American" is mirrored in the magnitude of the festivities. From their earliest beginnings, observances of New England's anniversary in Plymouth had been multidimensional cultural performances, featuring commissioned orations, festive poems, dinners, balls, decorations of the entire town, parades, and occasional historical plays. Plymouth had always honored Forefathers' Day as a holiday of national significance, with more participation on the side of the local population than anywhere else across the nation, and out-of-town visitors, guests of honor, and performers gladly journeying to the supposed starting point of the nation for obvious reasons of political expediency and popular legitimization. But even such special occasions as, e.g., the bicentennial of 1820 or the Pilgrim memorial fundraiser of 1853[40] had been limited to one day, either Forefathers' Day proper or August 1, frequently referred to in the sources as Plymouth Day. The tercentenary, however, was celebrated with a "large program of public exercises that [was to] be national in scope" (*Old Colony Memorial* June 11, 1920). It might be assumed that the course of action from the summer of

1920 to the late summer of 1921, was to make celebrants and sympathizers reimagine the immigrants' experience from their departure from Europe in the summer of 1620 to the moment of their first harvest in the early fall of 1621. The festive program of 1920-21 might be read as an evocative trajectory symbolically spanning the earliest period of Plymouth history glorified by New England historians since William Bradford, Nathaniel Morton, and Cotton Mather. At a moment of cultural reorientation, if not historical rupture, the Plymouth Tercentenary performed a grand gesture of connectedness, an emotionally appellative act of collective historical bonding. The tercentenary staged a historical and cultural (re)linkage with William Bradford and the Pilgrims whose singular role in the maintenance of national American ideologies had become seriously contested after Bourne and others had announced an end to "the search for our native 'American' culture."[41]

To such subversion, however, the supporters of the Plymouth Tercentenary responded with J.F. McGrath, the leading organizer of the national celebration at Plymouth, who had formulated and circulated to the public in advance the jubilee's self-conception:

> ... the celebration is to be a national one and therefore will be non-secterian and non-political in any of its aspects, the idea being to draw salutary lessons of Americanism from the ideals and accomplishments of the Pilgrim Fathers. ... This is an American celebration and in no way connected with private organizations seeking to inject foreign propaganda, religious propaganda, or political propaganda into the Tercentenary of the Landing of the Pilgrim Fathers. ... The celebration is to be 100 per cent American, despite the statements of the ignorant, misinformed or manevolent [sic], seeking to give the public a contrary view.[42]

McGrath drapes the political interest of the event with a coat of festive bipartisanship, obviously downplaying the exclusive nature of the very concept of (Anglo-)Americanization. In view of the almost too ready-made contradiction between Bourne's call for a "trans-national America" and McGrath's determination to convey "salutary lessons of Americanism," the Plymouth Tercentenary festivities appear like an outwardly climactic but inwardly erosive, retrospective summons to rededicate a heritage whose expansive, nationally cohesive power had exhausted itself.[43]

Stepping Stones on the Path to Forefathers' Day: Historical Bonding and Political Symbolism

The ideological rationale and symbolic force of the tercentenary already surfaced in the wide range of preparatory activities staged in the second half of 1920 and regularly registered in the *Old Colony Memorial* and, though more occasionally, in regional and national newspapers. Under the title "Hands Across the Sea," the *Old Colony Memorial* of June 25, 1920, reported the visit to Plymouth of a delegation from "Old Plymouth, England" and, in a manner characteristic of numerous following accounts, highlighted the implications of the visit of Mr. A. N. Hollely, the "representative of the town the Mayflower left in September, 1620." Although Hollely had "arrived from Boston by automobile during the forenoon," the local hosts, including the president of the Pilgrim Society, the Hon. Arthur Lord, first took the visitor to Plymouth Rock so that he "had been properly 'landed' on the famous boulder" and photographs of this "official joining of the old and new Plymouth" had been secured before the exchange of messages and speeches got underway. This ceremony, which was then followed by a similarly symbolic embrace on Town Square (also documented in a photograph of "the representatives of the two Plymouths with clasped hands"), was to underscore the original bond between England and the United States, whose future confirmation determined the afternoon function in the Old Colony Theatre. There, against the backdrop of a finely dressed podium with "a large painting of the Mayflower sailing from Plymouth, England, this being draped with the American and British flags," the envoy from the Old World gratified the expectations of his hosts when he delivered his message:

> Perhaps there is no more historic spot in the terrestrial territories of the Anglo-Saxon race than that on which I now stand, for, as the centuries roll on, this town of Plymouth will remain the hallowed cradle out of which sprang the most astonishing development of human progress and endeavor known to modern life and I am sure it has been, and will continue to be, as long as history continues to record the actions and guiding principles of the human race, to every generation of Plymoutheans a source of pride and satisfaction that those hundred souls who landed on your shores—the precursors of this great nation of the United States of America—were in character, in endurance and in their perfect faith in Almighty God, representative of the noblest examples of human virtue.

Hollely affirmed the status of the Mayflower Compact as "the first American Constitution" and praised the Pilgrim Fathers as the ancestors who had sown "the seed of true democracy" before he returned to the main theme of his address:

> In this process of seeking for the greatest happiness of mankind it is inevitable that, by the way, disappointment and discouragements should be encountered but in the majestic onward march of the Anglo-Saxon race such disappointment and discouragements are but the fleeting difficulties which serve to stimulate a jaded spirit and throw into the brightest relief of the ultimate goal toward which we strive.

The spokesperson from "Old Plymouth" concluded with a welcome interpretation of the most recent reversal of the great transatlantic migration and the British-American wartime alliance "for the preservation of the freedom of the world" as proof that the special "bond of union" went back to 1620. After the formal presentation of a "Greeting Scroll,"[44] the ceremony was rounded out by the president of the Pilgrim Society, "whose address of a historical character occupied about an hour and was interesting throughout to a student of history and the spread of the Anglo-Saxon race through this part of the world." Half a year before the actual Tercentenary, Plymouth celebrants thus performed a model act of political and historical bonding which reiterated their vision of an exceptionalist New England history at the core of America's manifest destiny.

The Anglo-American bonding of June 24, 1920,[45] may be taken as the overture to a long series of preparatory meditations on the larger significance of the event to be observed later in the year. The official authority, national scope, didactic impetus, and political support hoped for by organizers, sponsors, and prospective celebrants were bestowed onto the civic rite when

> President Wilson issued a proclamation suggesting and requesting that December 21 next, the date of the landing of the exploring party of the Pilgrims in this town in 1620 be given a proper observance throughout the country, with special patriotic exercises ... with the end in view that lessons may be learned from the bravery and energy and ideals of the Mayflower Pilgrims, who established on this country the first self-determined government.[46]

On August 13, 1920, the *Old Colony Memorial* noted that

> the tercentenary of the sailing of the Mayflower from Southhampton, Eng., was observed in that port on July 24, the event including a luncheon, which was attended by visitors of note and public men, a pageant play and aquatic sports. ... The place where the pageant ["John Alden's Choice"] was produced was the identical one whence the Pilgrims embarked in the Mayflower and the Speedwell for their voyage across the Atlantic to Cape Cod.

In order to strengthen the genealogy to be remembered, the article stressed that "[o]ne of the speakers at the observance pointed out that there was a greater English strain running through the blood of the presidents of this country than was realized, for out of the 28 of them, 15 were of pure English parentage; 6 Scottish and Irish; 3 Scottish and 1 Welsh."[47] Occasionally throughout the following weeks, the historic course of the Mayflower served as a point of reference to make future celebrants and sympathizers approach in due spirit the portentous moment of the first encounter between the old world emigrants and their new world. Eventually, the *New York Times* of November 21, 1920, reminded its readers of the first landfall on Cape Cod and commemorated the day with a summary of the historic events of the 1620s, presenting Plymouth's early economic development as a case study in the pitfalls of the "outrageous communist scheme" over against the virtues and advantages of "individual self-interest" and "private property." On a minor scale, the issuing of stamps and coins was heralded as a suitable means to give "the event a wonderful amount of publicity" (*Old Colony Memorial*, August 13 and 17, 1920). In September, the first (semi-private) performances of the three-act piece "Mayflower"—"a new operatic epic of the Landing of the Pilgrims" by H. Gratton Donnelly of Plymouth and Helen Merrill Shoate of Boston—received front-page attention in the local paper, with details about stage settings, quotations from the opening chorus and the speeches of Elder Brewster, and laudatory remarks about the "historically accurate" rendition of the course of action from the beginnings in Scrooby to the time of the transatlantic passage and the arrival in New England (*Old Colony Memorial*, September 24, 1920). What had been announced in June "as a contribution toward the Tercentenary celebration" by the Massachusetts Society of the Sons of the American Revolution—"a reproduction of the old powder house [of] early colonial days" (*Old Colony Memorial*, June 18, 1920)—became, as the headlines have it, the "first tercentenary memorial" four months later. Both the completion and dedication received extended appreciation in the *Old Colony Memorial* of October 8 and 15, 1920, with special emphasis given to the link between 1620 and "the successful prosecution of the War of the Revolution which gained the freedom of this country." In continuation of nineteenth-century national historiography in the vein of George Bancroft, "[t]he landing of the Pilgrims in 1620 and the American Revolution in 1776 are but successive steps in one great plan" to the journalistic interpreter of the event and its impact. In the eyes of interested celebrants, such a teleological fusion of historically distant events added welcome weight to the lineage which the tercentenary endorsed so fervently. That the dedication was held on "the 438th [*sic*] anniversary of the Landing of Columbus" shows even more dramatically the will to festive empowerment on the side of all those involved in the maintenance of New England anniversary rites at a moment of cultural reorientation.

One important stepping-stone on the way to filiopietistic fulfillment was reached four weeks before Forefathers' Day proper, when the National Society of the Sons and Daughters of the Pilgrims, together with the Plymouth town authorities, the public schools, the American Legion, and the Compact Committee of the Plymouth Women's Club, staged "Compact Day" on Sunday, November 20, 1920.[48] With their society's purpose clearly in mind— "to perpetuate the memory and to foster and promote the principles and virtues of the Pilgrims" (*Old Colony Memorial*, November 5, 1920)—the

Sons and Daughters of the Pilgrims honored the signing of the Mayflower Compact in a ceremony which turned into a tercentenary of its own and gave a foretaste of what was to be accomplished one month later.[49] The impetus of the ceremony lies condensed in the title of L. Bradford Prince's commissioned address, "The Pilgrims: Their Contribution to the Nation and the World"; it was publicly enacted in the recital of filiopietistic hymns and the reading out of the Mayflower Compact as a scripture in its own right. The *Old Colony Memorial* of November 19 and 26, 1920,[50] took the opportunity to recount the events immediately preceding the Pilgrims' arrival on the shore of Plymouth, reprinted the full text of the compact for those who might have been in need of it, and rendered the details of the festivity which started with an overtly symbolic approach to of the granite presence of the monolithic heritage to be invoked:

> The gathering place was at Plymouth Rock where Thomas W. Bicknell, L.L.D., of Providence, the founder of the Society, and its secretary general opened the exercises by getting all of the party to assemble close to the boulder on which their ancestors had landed, to sing, "Praise God, from whom all blessings flow."

At least for those embracing the boulder, all that was good and praiseworthy in American history and politics had sprung from Plymouth Rock just as "all blessings flow" from God. In the further course of the proceedings, the full repertoire of anniversary rites was employed to give credit to the supposed origin of the United States government, including prayers, Thomas W. Bicknell's poem "The Mayflower," Sherman L. Whipple's oration "The Compact," greetings by local dignitaries, politicians, and a leading representative of the Daughters of the American Revolution, and, eventually, the communal singing of Felicia Hemans's notorious Pilgrim anthem, "The First Landing of the Pilgrim Fathers" (1824).[51] This hymn had been used as the poetic centerpiece of most nineteenth-century Forefathers' Day celebrations and was now to invest this preparatory exercise with the reputation of all the ceremonies of which it had been part. Because of prohibition, the only traditional "building block" missing from this day of commemoration, as from all others in 1920-21, was the toasting which had been so prolific since the late eighteenth century.[52] Throughout its coverage of "the eventful day for the colony, for America and the world," the *Old Colony Memorial* emphasized the spirit of historical bonding which governed the rite instead: "From Plymouth Rock the party proceeded in groups up Leyden Street, the first laid out in New England and plotted by the Pilgrims themselves in 1621, to the First Church where more formal exercises took place." The national(ist) politics of the performances inspired the decoration of the stage in the Old Colony Theatre, "which was exclusively of American flags," and the collective singing of "America" towards the end of the exercises. When the singing of "America" by—as the paper put it—"the congregation" merged with the benediction of the minister, American civil religion had been 'New Englandized' one more time at Plymouth. The *New York Times* of November 22, 1920 reported about several similar observances in New York City, including one sponsored by the Society of Mayflower Descendants held at the Cathedral of St. John the Divine and attended by "representatives of other patriotic organizations, representatives of Great Britain, and the Netherlands," which highlights a growing national interest as the actual tercentenary came closer on the calendar. At the same time, however, Bishop Chauncey B. Brewster's call for "freedom in religious thought," his stress on the present time as a "period of transition and readjustment," and his subtle admonition "to look backward and see what should be kept of this compact and what should give way to the new order just dawning," questioned neither "[the Pilgrim Fathers'] conviction of the superiority of the individual over the State" nor the status of the Mayflower Compact as "the foundation of the nation," but added a thoughtful undertone to the event which the final singing of "The Star-Spangled Banner" still muted, at least for the time being and for those invited to the service.

The commemorative energy of associated clubs and local chapters of national New England societies knew few limits. The California Society of Mayflower Descendants decided

> that its contribution to the Pilgrim Tercentenary is to be something more enduring than a memory of a series of pageants and the reports of many speeches, and it has accordingly fixed on the plan to contribute a bronze chest which is to contain the official documents of the society; tangible material relative to the career of Mayflower descendants of public distinction ... . Among the contents of the chest will also be copies of maps of the United States, Plymouth County and the town of Plymouth ... .[53]

In a kind of re-produced foundational ceremony, the California Society of Mayflower Descendants seems to have aimed at the preservation of the historical accomplishments of the Plymouth immigrants and their kin as well as at the documentation of the national expansion initiated by their arrival. The New York Historical Society staged an exhibition of books and manuscripts related to early New England history "in commemoration of the tercentenary of the landing of the Pilgrims at Plymouth, Mass, on December 21, 1620, and the beginning of free institutions in America" (*New York Times,* November 14, 1920). The collection included rare originals of the works of John Brereton, James Rosier, John Smith, Christopher Levett,

William Alexander, and John Underhill and was focused on early travel literature and ethnographic representations rather than on those texts of seventeenth-century Puritan New England that might have blurred the commemoration of "the beginning of free institutions in America."

On November 24, 1920, President Woodrow Wilson reviewed a Washington parade "in commemoration of the landing of the Pilgrim Fathers at Plymouth" which featured military units as well as "patriotic organizations, with a dozen bands and floats" (*New York Times*, November 25, 1920). Yet Irish protesters, with scrolls asking "What Did England Do for the Pilgrims When They Were Starving?" questioned the historical harmony of Anglo-American relations celebrated by the parade, drew popular attention to the contemporary Irish crisis, and reminded the cheerful crowd of larger problems looming not only in the transatlantic background. After similar disruptions of the festive mood by Irish protest against the British flag, anniversary celebrations in New York were protected by the police and unwelcome opponents excluded from further functions:

> Irish and Irish sympathizers, who attacked the Union Club on Sunday for displaying the British flag, were not represented at the Tercentenary Celebration in honor of the Landing of the Pilgrims at Carnegie Hall last night, where the British flag was displayed with others, tributes paid to England and other countries of the Allies, and a message read from King George. The hall was surrounded by policemen. The celebration, however, was attended with perfect peace inside and outside of the hall.[54]

The Carnegie Hall gathering served as the platform for General Robert Georges Nivelle, "the hero of France, who was at the celebration as a descendant of the Huguenots, the French spiritual kin of the Pilgrim Fathers." Nivelle honored the American soldiers fighting in World War I and evoked the image of the Mayflower as a warship that "sailed in 1917 side by side with [other American ships] and that brought also to France her share of the American troops." The message from King George must have been especially welcome as he heralded the "men and women of the Mayflower whose memory is one of the abiding inspirations of America" (*New York Times*, November 27, 1920) and thus expressed the trust in the lasting potential of the heritage which the celebrants cherished so ardently. The fact that General Nivelle's official itinerary did not take him to Plymouth but rather had him attend tercentenary commemorations in Boston—much to the surprise of the *Old Colony Memorial* (December 10, 1920)—makes for a curious detail in the records of the Plymouth Tercentenary.

Forefathers' Day 1920: Climactic Summation of a Retrospective Cultural Practice

When the anniversary of the Pilgrim arrival in America approached and passed, regional and national newspaper coverage became more intense and diverse. The reports about an exhibition of commemorative medals in the *Hartford Daily Courant* of December 21, 1920, and the presentation of a set of chimes to the First Church in Plymouth by the Brooklyn New England Society in the *New York Times* of December 29, 1920 illustrate the scope and substance of journalistic miscellanies of this sort. At the same time, the complete reprint of Daniel Webster's bicentennial oration in the *New York Times* of December 19, 1920[55] marked a quantitative climax in the media coverage of preparatory events and voiced the high expectations for a successful, nationwide repetition of such themes on the part of tercentenary sympathizers.[56] The political agenda of this repetition was formulated in a long editorial on "The Pilgrims" also published in the *New York Times* of December 19, 1920. The article characterizes the New England ancestors as "these pioneers, these establishers of ordered freedom and self-government" and hails them as advocates of "individualism, independence, and public spirit" over and against the alleged, but ultimately deceptive, advantages of "the communist system." Throughout the month of December, the *Old Colony Memorial* abounded with announcements of collateral activities such as a high school "pilgrim pageant symbolizing the development of the country in three hundred years" and a "Pilgrim Christmas" held at the junior high school.[57] On "the night before Forefathers' Day" (*Old Colony Memorial*, December 17, 1920), as the local paper put it in reverberation of the joyous, childlike anticipation of stories of "The Night Before Christmas," the Plymouth Antiquarian Society enacted a series of tableaux in Kendall Hall, which featured the usual historical scenes (departure from Holland, signing of the Compact, landing, encounter with the Indians, first winter, sailing of the Mayflower, first harvest) but gave uncommon prominence to the recital of the time-honored anniversary poems and hymns of Samuel Davis, Felicia Hemans, William Cullen Bryant, John Pierpont, and others.[58] In its preview, the *Old Colony Memorial* emphasized that "[i]n arranging the program the Committee has tried to include as many as possible of the hymns which have been sung for so many years on Forefathers' Day" (December 17, 1920), thus underscoring the summary nature of the preparatory, mood-setting function. That this overture was indeed recognized as part of the overall dramaturgy of the tercentenary becomes evident in its description as a "curtain-raiser" in the *Providence Journal* of December 21, 1920.[59] The staff correspondent of the *Boston Post* drew special attention to the participation of "many prominent Plymouth people" (December 21, 1920) in the tableaux and therewith to the communal effort traceable also at this point in the festive cycle. Reading scripture and concluding by singing "America" testify to the intention of the Plymouth Antiquarian Society to perform a representation of American civil religion as primarily anchored in the traditions of New England. The expectancy, excitement, and suspense that seem to have ruled Plymouth during those days are best contained in a headline in the commercial section of the *Old Colony Memorial* of December 17: "Forefathers' Day—Christmas—New Year." The foundational anniversary is placed within a sequence of religious and secular rites of rebirth and renewal and thus embedded in a symbolic context much larger than its own history.

Forefathers' Day itself was orchestrated on December 21, 1920, as the first climax in the year-long trajectory of Plymouth tercentenary festivities. Plymouth's observance of its own and the nation's anniversary was given extensive extralocal media recognition.[60] Because of the limited space in the Old Colony Theatre, which seated some 900 people, the various organizing committees had agreed to stage a two-part celebration, with the morning reserved for the official state function of the Massachusetts Tercentenary Commission and the afternoon left for what came to be known in contemporary media accounts and documentations as "Plymouth's Own Celebration."[61] In an article published on December 10, 1920, the *Old Colony Memorial* explained the specific character of both installments and especially the diverging admission policies. Upon closer inspection, the report reveals traces of the delicate balance between exclusiveness and populism, between participatory enthusiasm and political expediency, which must have determined the proceedings to a considerable extent. Unlike in the early days of the civic rite, the number of celebrants actually present was no longer symbolically restricted, e.g. to the alleged number of Mayflower passengers, but rather according to reasons of public relations and social clout:

> The [Pilgrim Tercentenary] Commission regrets that there is not available in Plymouth a hall large enough to accommodate all who might like to attend these exercises. It has selected what seemed to be the best and most commodious place of meeting, but this necessarily limits the number who may be provided for. Invitations are being sent out by the commission to representatives of the nation and state, of patriotic and historical societies, and certain foreign representatives of England and Holland, also to many local societies and officials. Those receiving invitations become official guests of the commission … . The balcony of the theatre, which accommodates 437 people, or about the same number as the floor, will be thrown open to the public and the doors will be opened at 10:30 o'clock, or thereabouts, to admit those who desire balcony seats, to be accommodated in the order in which they reach the theatre, as far

as possible. There is no admission charge of any kind in connection with the exercises. ... On Wednesday evening the town's Tercentenary Committee approved and adopted plans suggested by the local committee for the citizens' celebration of the Pilgrim Tercentenary, on the afternoon of December 21, in the Old Colony Theatre. Mills and factories in town will be closed and the day will be made a general holiday. In the theatre there is to be good music, good speaking, and Dean Le Baron Briggs is to read his original poem written for the State Commissions' [sic] observance, during the afternoon observance, while the presence of important state officials is expected. This gathering is in no way a duplication of the morning exercises and is to have no references to them, except as a commemoration of the same event. No tickets will be required, everything being free and all who desire to attend may consider themselves invited to come to the Plymouth town celebration of the Tercentenary.

Civic pride, community spirit, and localist independence, on the one hand, and the desire for national visibility, societal bonding, and public relations, on the other, seem to have stirred an unpronounced rivalry which can only be traced in and between the lines of Plymouth's own newspaper. The *Old Colony Memorial* also stands alone with its reproduction of the full program and details of the afternoon exercises that indeed featured the intended mixture of "good music" and "good speaking"[62] but hardly reached the political weight given to the morning exercises by the presence and performance of Henry Cabot Lodge.

The larger part of all newspaper accounts focused on the official morning exercises—"the leading event of the day from a public standpoint," as the *Old Colony Memorial* (December 24, 1920) phrased it with a subtle qualification. These contemporary documentations and interpretations of the festive activities show that their general choreography followed the scripts introduced before the American Revolution and developed to ever-expanding dimensions throughout the nineteenth century, from the opening parade, music, and prayer to the climactic oratorical performance, and on to the concluding singing of religious, anniversary, and national hymns and the final procession to Plymouth Rock. Besides reproducing the addresses by Governor Coolidge and Senator Lodge and the traditional or newly commissioned poems by Felicia Hemans, John Pierpont, and Le Baron Russell Briggs, newspaper coverage followed the course of action, evoked the festive mood, and paid tribute to the prominent participants. The following excerpt from the front-page report in the *Boston Evening Transcript* of December 21, 1920 serves to illustrate the mode of journalistic rendition generally produced in the coverage of Plymouth Forefathers' Day 1920:

> Only four spans of life, and a little more—a brief period as the histories of people are measured—since the foundation was laid in this spot of a nation of today more than a hundred million souls, the most progressive, most powerful

and richest nation on the face of the earth, the leader in trade, in finance, in the arts and industries. Today a handful of the latest beneficiaries of the great structure that the Pilgrims made a beginning of at Plymouth, assembled to do them honor. ... For the occasion Plymouth was en fete. From the country roundabout a large number of people had assembled and the streets were decorated for the parade which preceded the exercises in the theatre. The distinguished guests of the Pilgrim Tercentenary Commission of Massachusetts included Governor Coolidge, Senator Henry Cabot Lodge, the orator; Dean Le Baron Russell Briggs of Harvard, the poet, the Belgian ambassador and others, most of them arriving by special train. ... Unfortunately, the little theatre, with its tawdry decorations was ill-suited to the solemnity and dignity of such an occasion, and the draughty stage was very evidently uncomfortable for those who had to sit there. Indeed, Senator Lodge crouched in his overcoat until he had to speak and wore his muffler throughout his oration, while Dean Briggs used his coat for a lap robe. Notwithstanding the incongruity of such a setting, it was the best Plymouth had to offer, and the eminence of the speakers and the distinguished guests drew attention from the surroundings. A pleasing touch was the women ushers in Pilgrim garb.

Most press coverage was similarly appreciative of the national growth, singular achievement, and universal progress initiated by the Pilgrims and equally reverent towards the assembly of representatives of the established cultural and political powers.[63] Articles varied in their reproduction of details of the festive proceedings, as, e.g., the emphasis on the collective "pilgrimage to the Rock" after the exercises in the *New York Times* (December 22, 1920) or the regret in the *Old Colony Memorial* about the circumstance that "the dressing [of the business buildings in the center of the town] was not on a scale of that of the dedication of the National Monument to the Forefathers in August 1889" (December 24, 1920) shows. No other paper, however, conveyed a picture of more symbolic potential than the *Boston Evening Transcript*, whose rendition of the freezing, bundled-up dignitaries may entice the interpreter to read the scene as an involuntarily comic portrayal of the old guard publicly entrenched on stage against the frosty winds of change. The fact that even the smallest contribution to the festive arrangement contained the political rationale underlying the tercentenary festivities at large—and that these implications radiated from the pages of the newspapers covering the activities—becomes manifest in the introductory blessing offered by Rev. Arthur B. Whitney, minister of the First Church. Reeenacting the old practice of opening Forefathers' Day celebrations with a prayer, Whitney did not hesitate to include an obviously political plea which reveals both the retrospective politics of Forefathers' Day and the deeper anxieties on the side of its celebrants and supporters: "O strong and loving Father of mankind, to our dear country bring in again the good and godly order, as of old, that the days of this free people may be long in the land the Lord their God gave to our fathers" (*Old Colony Memorial*, December 24, 1920). To furthermore stress the backwards orientation of the gathering, Whitney's prayer was followed by the singing of John Pierpont's hymn of 1824, "The pilgrim fathers—where are they?" by Plymouth's men's chorus.

In continuation of the practice of their nineteenth-century predecessors, the organizing committees had pushed for a most effective realization of two seminal "building blocks": the festive oration and the commissioned poem. Together with a programmatic introduction by Governor Calvin Coolidge, Henry Cabot Lodge's "The Pilgrims of Plymouth: An Address at Plymouth, Massachusetts on the Three Hundredth Anniversary of Their Landing December 21, 1920" and Le Baron Russell Briggs's "1620-1920: A Poem" made for the choreographic and ideological backbone of the morning exercises in the Old Colony Theatre. These texts were reproduced in their entirety, or at least in substantial excerpts, in most newspapers, published in book form by the Pilgrim Tercentenary Commission, incorporated in Bittinger's *The Story of the Pilgrim Tercentenary Celebration At Plymouth*—and thus circulated to an audience much larger than the one actually present. These statements voice the essence of New England filiopietism and advance the traditionalist agenda of continuing Anglo-Americanization which J.F. McGrath had proclaimed as the overarching purpose of the tercentenary enterprise.

Speaking from the position of Massachusetts governor and vice president-elect of the United States, and still radiant with the reputation gained by his fervent opposition to the Boston police strike of 1919, Coolidge rehearsed the rhetoric of numerous nineteenth-century Plymouth orators when he invoked the conventional image of the Pilgrims as persecuted, virtuous, idealistic founders of a democratic American empire. No other point of reference in all of world history offered a more suitable model for future generations of Americans than 1620, especially in the post-World War I period of crisis and reorientation. The excerpt chosen by the *New York Times* of December 22, 1920 illustrates what sympathetic observers deemed worthy to emphasize and circulate further as the gist of Coolidge's speech:

> They came not merely from the shores of the Old World. It will be in vain to search among records, maps and history for their origin. They sailed up out of the infinite. There was among them small trace of the vanities of life. They came undecked with orders of nobility. They were not children of fortune but of tribulation. Persecution, not preference, brought them hither, but it was a persecution in which they found a stern satisfaction. They cared little for titles, still less for the goods of this earth, but for an idea they would die. Measured by the standard of men of their time they were the humble of the earth. Measured by later accomplishments they were the mighty.

For the *Old Colony Memorial*, it seemed appropriate to quote Coolidge more extensively, giving particular attention to his quasi-religious stress on the lasting and universal significance of the spiritual heritage springing from Plymouth Rock: "No like body ever cast so great an influence on human history. Civilization has made of their landing place a shrine. ... Plymouth Rock does not mark a beginning or an end. It marks a revelation of that which is without beginning and without end, a purpose, shining through eternity" (December 24, 1920). When the *Providence Journal* of December 22, 1920 titled the report of the correspondent of the Associated Press "Lodge and Coolidge Call for Faith to Stem Tide of National Doubt," the paper highlighted the unifying theme of the exercises as it first emerged from Coolidge's opening remarks. That 'national' revitalization and 'purposeful' inspiration may no longer arise solely from the Anglo-Saxon heritage did not occur to a speaker so deeply attached to older formulations of America as Calvin Coolidge.

Before Lodge gave his longer oration, the audience was presented with the recital of Le Baron Russell Briggs's anniversary poem "1620-1920: A Poem" by the author himself. Two months before, the *Old Colony Memorial* of October 22, 1920 had published a brief laudatory biography of the Harvard Boylston Professor of Rhetoric and Oratory and dean of the Faculty of Arts and Sciences and announced that Briggs's poem had been selected "after careful consideration" and in full trust that it will help to "maintain the high character of the notable anniversary." Endowed with the cultural force of the institution he represented, Briggs pronounced "something of a jeremiad, aimed at that traditional target, the rising generation."[64] In the same year that F. Scott Fitzgerald in *This Side of Paradise*, ended his portrait of "the new generation" on a note of collective disillusion with "the spirit of the past" and "the old creeds,"[65] Briggs made a conscious effort to "span the years from 1620 to 1920 in verse" (*Providence Journal*, December 21, 1920). Criticizing contemporary hedonism and materialism as "a carnival of death" and calling the "slaves of sloth and the senses / clippers of Freedom's wings" to repent and "come back to the Pilgrim's army," he tried to energize present and future generations with the old Pilgrim spirit:

> And when we sail as Pilgrims' sons and daughters
> The spirit's Mayflower into seas unknown,
> Driving across the waste of wintry waters
> The voyage every soul shall make alone,
>
> The Pilgrim's faith, the Pilgrim's courage grant us;
> Still shines the truth that for the Pilgrim shone.
> We are his seed; nor life nor death shall daunt us.
> The port is Freedom! Pilgrim heart, sail on!

After this invocation of the traditional Pilgrim muses and Briggs's poetic declaration of war on the dawning Jazz Age, the audience was ready for Henry Cabot Lodge, seventy years of age at the time, long-time professional politician of national, if not international stature, Boston Brahmin by birth and self-conception, and certainly one of the most prominent figureheads of old-stock Republican conservatism. Lodge did not disappoint his audience and delivered an oration which John Seelye in his conclusive interpretation characterized as a speech "containing personal resonances reflected in his obsequies for Webster and the nineteenth century, being something by way of a eulogy for his generation and an elegy for himself."[66] Ascending the podium as the herald of times past, Lodge's "peculiar appropriateness [...] as the celebrant of the Pilgrim tercentenary at Plymouth"[67] arose from his very personal anchorage in traditional, nineteenth-century paradigms, which he had so aptly articulated during his performances at New England anniversaries in the 1880s.[68] Echoing the stock elements of epideictic Forefathers' Day oratory since John Quincy Adams and Daniel Webster—and indeed drawing heavily on Webster's bicentennial address and its prophecy of national progress—Lodge praised the Pilgrims as those ancestors laying "the cornerstones of the foundations upon which the great fabric of the United States has been built up."[69] Lodge reaffirmed the myth of the New England origin of the United States and the grand saga of the historic march from Plymouth Rock towards national progress, global empire, and universal salvation. With his elaborations on the "lessons they teach which will help us in the present and aid us to meet the imperious future ever knocking at the door,"[70] Lodge clung to the assumed adaptability to ever-changing historical contexts of the Pilgrims who had "meant to be Americans," who had "decided that the right of man to private property honestly obtained was essential to social stability and to civilization," and who still functioned as models of "unfailing courage" and a "strong and active sense of public duty."[71] Consequently, and fully in line with the spirit of the jubilee, the *New York Times* of December 22, 1920 saw Lodge speaking up against the "present pessimism growing out of the war" and titled its coverage: "Senator Sees Pessimism—Declares It Is a War Legacy and Urges Spirit of the Founders as Corrective."

The theatrical climax of the filiopietistic rites in the Old Colony Theatre on the morning of December 21, 1920 was reached when all of a sudden—at least for the audience—a telephone rang on stage and interrupted Lodge's oration at the very point when he was evoking Daniel Webster's much quoted vision of transcontinental expansion. Representations of this incident were included prominently in all newspaper accounts and generally read as follows:

> In the midst of his address, just after he had spoken of the significance of Webster's speech in 1820, a telephone bell rang. The Senator went on to recite Webster's prophecy that "from those who shall stand here a hundred years hence the voice of acclamation and gratitude commencing on the Rock of Plymouth shall be transmitted through millions of sons of the Pilgrims till it lose itself in the murmurs of the Pacific seas." The bell rang again and the receiver was lifted. Across the continent came a voice from California. A moment later Governor Coolidge, speaking from the chair of a Governor of the Plymouth Colony, delivered a greeting to Governor Stephens and the Golden Gate from the Governor of Massachusetts and from Plymouth Rock.[72]

As usual, the *Old Colony Memorial* of December 24, 1920 added further details and major elements to the public interpretation of the dramatic episode:

> The instrument was passed to his Excellency and the latter took up the conversation which was fulfilling the prophetic utterances of Webster a century previous, saying, "Governor Stephens? Yes. This is Governor Coolidge of Massachusetts. Yes. I am seated in the chair of Governor Bradford at Plymouth. I wish to say that Massachusetts and Plymouth Rock greet California and the Golden Gate and send the voice which is to be lost in the waves and roar of the Pacific. I'll do so. Goodbye." As Senator Lodge resumed his discourse he remarked: "It was the merest accident that I read that sentence."

Although the telephone call and its timing had been carefully planned in advance and was anything but a providential interference to enhance the message of the gathering (and Governor Stephens had rather gone hunting than play the Western caller for a far-removed New England audience), this interruption of the proceedings dramatized most effectively the national embrace and historical bonding aimed at by the tercentenary's organizers. The telephone communication from the very chair that Governor Bradford had supposedly used and that had been a central relic on display at Forefathers' Day celebrations since 1769 established an emotionally appealing link across both spatial and temporal trajectories, from the Atlantic to the Pacific, from 1620 to 1820 and 1920. The greetings sent from Plymouth Rock to the Golden Gate tried to recertify the unbroken extension of the Pilgrim heritage into modern times and far beyond New England. Whether it stretches the limits of thick description to read the absence of the Governor of California from the other end of the telephone conversation as a reliable gauge of Western disinterest in the New England heritage invoked thousands of miles away—and thus as a symptom of the illusionary nature of the tercentenary endeavor—is open to interpretation.

On to Plymouth Day 1921: From Traditional Anniversary Rites to Living History Performances and Filiopietistic Public Recreation

No matter how far one is willing to go in analyzing the telephone episode, it certainly marked a theatrical fulfillment, if not the climactic endpoint, in the history of Plymouth anniversary festivities and their unrelenting attempts to (re)affirm the validity and adaptability of the Pilgrim spirit over time and space. If, as Peter Gomes phrased it in his survey of "the so-called Pilgrim Century, from 1820 to 1920," "the high-water mark of [the Pilgrims'] appeal had already passed"[73] by the end of the nineteenth century, the recourse to technological tricks in the early twentieth century almost appears like a short-lived attempt to compensate for the diminishing force of the ideological positions once again submitted for collective approval. By the time of the Plymouth Tercentenary and the almost simultaneous arrival of modern mass media and popular culture, the celebratory rehearsal of Forefathers' Day proper was not enough anymore to assure lasting visibility on the stage of national commemoration and to gratify the desire for ever more grandiose spectacles on the side of both local celebrants and the larger American public. The further extension of the festivities throughout the year 1921 relativized the ancient singularity of Forefathers' Day, bearing witness to the urge of their organizers to present more than the conventional anniversary rites of December 21. A comprehensive documentation of the various festive functions leading up to Plymouth Day and a thorough exploration of the multifarious, multimedia events of August 1, 1921 itself, with its large-scale civic parade of floats, groups, and musical bands, its numerous addresses by local and national dignitaries, and, above all, its outdoor performance of George P. Baker's mass pageant, *The Pilgrim Spirit*, goes far beyond the scope of one article. The illustrations and texts collected in Harry Bloomingdale's 1921 documentation, *Plymouth Tercentenary, Illustrated with a Brief History of the Life and Struggles of the Pilgrim Fathers. Including the Original Program of the "Pilgrim Spirit" by Professor George P. Baker, President Harding's Visit, All Scenes, Episodes, and Official Photographs*, Frederick W. Bittinger's 1923 *Story of the Pilgrim Tercentenary Celebration at Plymouth*, and the extensive coverage of the activities on Plymouth Day 1921 in the *Old Colony Memorial* (July 22 and August 5, 1921), *Boston Evening Transcript* (August 1, 1921), *Boston Post* (August 1 and 2, 1921), *Providence Journal* (August 1, 1921), *Manchester Union* (August 1, 1921), *New York Times* (August 1, 2, and 7, 1921), *Chicago Daily Tribune* (August 1 and 2, 1921), and *Washington Post* (August 1 and 2, 1921) all lend themselves well to detailed studies of the intricate festive webwork of the tercentenary and the politics of its representation. The last section of the present article will therefore concentrate on major aspects of the 1921 tercentenary festivities and submit still tentative assessments of some transformations traceable in the public Pilgrim commemorations in 1921, hoping that this all but conclusive sketch will induce further readings of the events and their media coverage.

The months of January through August saw a sequence of commemorative activities comparable to those preceding Forefathers' Day 1920. In its issue of January 28, 1921, Plymouth's local paper published the plans for the ongoing celebration of the tercentenary in that year and quoted the desire of the town's tercentenary committee "that there be fitting observances of important Pilgrim anniversaries. The first of these will be April 15th, the date of the return of the Mayflower, for which an appropriate program will be arranged in due time."[74] Between Forefathers' Day and Plymouth Day, the anniversary of "The Return of the Mayflower" became the most publicized intermediate event—in the words of William S. Kyle, chairman of the local tercentenary committee, "a sincere tribute to the sublime faith and fortitude of the heroic men and women of the Mayflower company" (*Old Colony Memorial*, April 22, 1921). The festive evening in the Old Colony Theatre offered music, poems, tableaux, and addresses by Governor Cox and Rev. Paul Revere Frothingham on "the beginning of a new civilization" in 1620, the "living consciousness of ties that bound [the Pilgrims] to the country of their birth," and the Pilgrims' political advice to those present: "'If the Pilgrim Fathers could speak to the children here tonight, who would doubt what they would say? They would counsel the English speaking nations of the world to stand together. They would bid them live and work together in the days of peace as they worked and fought together in the days of war." That Rev. Frothingham was a descendant of Elder Brewster, and expressly spoke as such, gives the performance and the advice the authority of direct Pilgrim lineage. Other such "fitting observances" in the course of the spring and summer of 1921 included the celebration of the "approach to the home of the Pilgrims" (*Old Colony Memorial*, July 8, 1921) of the Mayflower replica prepared for participation in Barker's tercentenary pageant and peopled with "impersonators" of historic figures for "the movie men and newspaper men" awaiting their symbolic landing, or the ceremonial unveiling of the Howland Memorial in the presence of descendants of John Howland from fifteen different states as far away as Nebraska and Tennessee (*Old Colony Memorial*, August 19, 1921).

Whereas the Mayflower and Howland memorial functions were traditional in choreographic arrangement, the "Pilgrim Progress" of the summer of 1921, despite its retrospective allusion to John Bunyan's seventeenth-century religious allegory, introduced a new dimension into Plymouth filiopietism. It may be regarded as an early, modest enactment of more recent conceptions of living history.[75] The design and purpose of this addition to the repertoire of Plymouth ancestor worship was related to the public in advance by the *Old Colony Memorial* of May 13, 1921:

> One feature of the Pilgrim Tercentenary celebration to be held next summer will be a Pilgrim Progress under the auspices of the Pilgrim Tercentenary Committee, in which all who reverence the Pilgrims are cordially invited to take part. The participants will assemble daily, in Pilgrim costume at Plymouth Rock and proceed, according to the Pilgrim custom, through the first street to the Burial Hill, where there will probably be a short service, including the singing of Pilgrim hymns, on the site of the Old Fort, once the Pilgrim meeting house. ... A knowledge of the approximate age of the participants, and the Pilgrim families to which they belong, if they are of Mayflower descent, will help the committee very much in assigning the various parts. ... As the Pilgrim Progress is commemorative rather than theatrical in character, a sincere feeling for the spirit of the occasion is of more importance to the participants than ability to act. The committee is sending notices of the Progress to patriotic and historical societies all over the country, for it feels that many of those who are planning to come to Plymouth next summer will be glad of the opportunity to take part, especially those descendents of the Pilgrims who are coming here, eager to re-live the great adventure of their ancestors. The main stay of the Progress, however, must be the Plymouth people themselves; it cannot be successful without them. ... The Pilgrim Progress will serve as a link uniting the various celebrations of next summer, as a constant event of interest and inspiration to our visitors, and as a daily reminder to ourselves of the heroic experiment in faith and in democracy which we are celebrating.

The "Pilgrim Progress" comes across here as a ritualistic community effort to perform on site and in original attire scenes of seventeenth-century Plymouth life. The historical bonding, recognized as a primary purpose of the 1920/21 festivities in the present study, now took the form of 're-living' in person the ancestral times and legacy. The participation of outside visitors and representatives of interested societies from "all over the country" nationalized the reenactment and showed traces of filiopietistic tourism. The symbolic performance of the procession from Plymouth Rock to the site of the seventeenth-century meetinghouse, "according to the Pilgrim custom," was no longer restricted to special occasions but was to become "a constant event of interest and inspiration." The anniversary and its mood was to be transformed into a heritage alive within the daily course of modern life. Despite the paper's stress on its commemorative character, the "Pilgrim Progress" turned into a theatrical "spectacle" which might be considered a small-scale living history production. The account of the first enactments in the *Old Colony Memorial* of June 24, 1921, with its emphasis on the 'realism' and 'originality' of the performance, supports such a reading:

It has attracted much attention already, and is drawing larger crowds of spectators on each appearance. Real Pilgrim descendants assemble at the beat of the assembly on Leyden street, the original first Pilgrim street. The groups come from the sites of the old Pilgrim dwellings and joining the others march slowly headed by the officials of the colony up the street, the men bearing their long barrelled guns, and the women and children in the centre. ... The impersonators are dressed in Pilgrim costume, and the whole spectacle gives one a strong impression of realism in its portrayal of the old time custom.

Living history of a different kind was staged at the so-called "Indian Village," which was a far cry from today's presence—and contested exhibition—of Native Americans and Native American history in and near Plimoth Plantation:

One of the most picturesque attractions of the town in connection with the tercentenary is the camp of the Passamaquoddy Indians at Little Pond in Morton Park, and beginning tomorrow, Saturday afternoon at 3 o'clock, there will be water sports on the pond followed by war dances in full native costumes. The public is invited without charge. ... One of the large motor busses is making frequent trips from the town centre to the camp at the reasonable charge of thirty-five cents for the round trip.

This announcement in the *Old Colony Memorial* of July 15, 1921, reads like a commercial for an early variant of a (post)modern theme park, with Native Americans as true-to-life actors and fashionable leisure-time entertainment for the sight-seeing tercentenary celebrants. Coming to Plymouth "under a contract with the Tercentenary Committee," the members of the Passamaquoddy tribe and their display of Native American culture turned out to be "one of the most popular attractions of the Tercentenary Celebration," and the "success of the village" was cited to justify the contract price (*Old Colony Memorial* September 9, 1921). The ethnocentric paternalism of this appropriation of Native American culture shows in the "picturesque" quality of the display and in the stereotypification in the *Old Colony Memorial* (September 9, 1921) on the occasion of the closing of the site: "The Indians were a fine lot of people. Plymouth people who came in contact with them found them honest and upright. They are a kindly and intelligent lot of folks."

Entertainment culture and historical tourism also contributed to the choreography of Plymouth Day 1921, which, in hindsight and on the basis of the contemporary documentation available, appears like an intricate merger of conventional anniversary scripts and modern fair culture. If we can trust previews such as the one published in the *Boston Post* on August 1, 1920, under the heading "Biggest of Days for Plymouth," the sentiment of festive anticipation ruling Plymouth prior to and on August 1 even exceeded that of December 1920. The organizers produced a day-long civic rite whose desired emotional impact and actual scope transcended all previous anniversaries, including Plymouth Day 1853 and the dedication of the National Pilgrim Monument in 1889. Throughout the day, large numbers of spectators crowded Plymouth[76] and watched the various parts of the proceedings, which extended over the entire town and its shoreline surroundings. The space of historical bonding had been lavishly adorned with greens and decorated programmatically with arrangements of colonial, early national, and contemporary American as well as ancient and present-day British flags in order to underscore not only historical continuity and the claim to nationwide significance but also a specific cultural and political affinity (cf. esp. *Boston Evening Transcript,* August 1, 1921). In an overture to the festive exercises, the presidential yacht (with the fitting name *Mayflower*) sailed out of the morning haze and into Plymouth harbor, evoking the historic approach of the Pilgrim Fathers aboard the Mayflower in 1620. In an equally symbolic act, which the *Chicago Daily Tribune* (August 1, 1921) described as "retrac[ing] old steps," the chief executive of the United States landed close to "the historic boulder that served as a foundation for the greatest nation in the world" (*Boston Post* August 1, 1921). Before President Harding gave the keynote address of the holiday, a long sequence of welcomes and greetings was extended by the local, regional, and national dignitaries who were by then well-known to regular attendants of tercentenary activities and especially to those present at Forefathers' Day 1920.[77]

The most noteworthy feature of the arrival ceremony, which was recognized for its symbolic weight in most accounts, was President Harding's awarding of medals of achievement to selected school children:

> Following this brief [welcome] ceremony occurred an incident that was especially significant of the Pilgrim spirit. Twenty-seven school children from New Bedford, Poles, French, Italians and Portuguese boys and girls were marshaled in front of Mr. Harding and to each he handed a medal awarded in the contest of the New England standard for excellence in the reading of English offered to children of non-English speaking parents.[78]

The ideological implications of the award ceremony becomes even more evident in the *Old Colony Memorial's* emphasis on the winners' "proficiency in the studies of the English language and American ideas" (August 5, 1921). The immigrant children were commended for their successful Americanization that, in turn, was associated with the original "Pilgrim spirit" and its unquestioned continuation into the present time of demographic changes. Senator Lodge's ensuing remarks about "the early Americanism of the Pilgrims"—when "pointing out that once they had set foot in the new country they had cut loose from virtually all ties in the old and had begun to love America" (*Washington Post* August 2, 1921)—provide for an unmistaken explanation of the equation of "Pilgrim spirit" and "Americanism" and demonstrate how closely interrelated symbolic acts and festive addresses were during the proceedings of August 1, 1921.[79] The densely woven choreographic fabric of Plymouth Day is borne out in another way by a carefully staged handshake between President Harding and "Mrs. Charlotte Mitchell, a direct descendant of Chief Massasoit, the Pilgrims' staunchest Indian friend" (*New York Times*, August 2, 1921) after a convivial luncheon at the Samoset Hotel.

In the central address of the day, which was excerpted at length in all the regional and national papers cited above and later reprinted in Bittinger's semi-official documentary,[80] President Harding gave what the *Chicago Daily Tribune* of August 2, 1921 called "a eulogy to the achievements of the English-speaking race everywhere."[81] During his speech, Harding reportedly stood facing Cole's Hill, with the audience seated on its slopes—an arrangement which had the presidential orator address both the honored dead and their living heirs in a posture reminiscent of Edmund Burke's call for "always acting as if in the presence of canonized forefathers"[82] as the basis of public virtue and communal stability. Like Lodge, Harding expressed a nineteenth-century mix of historical didacticism, demonstrative adaptation of proven (New England) values to ever-changing cultural moments, and collective admiration for all that Plymouth Rock had given rise to, hardly missing the chance to invest his own agenda of 'back to normalcy' and his new administration with the moral integrity radiating from the Pilgrim Fathers—to little avail as the future course of his presidency would show. In August 1921, newspapers still deemed it important to focus their readers on Harding's rededication of Plymouth Rock as "a landmark of American freedom" (*Boston Post,* August 2, 1921), on his praise for the New England settlers as those ancestors planting "the seeds of representative democracy, the new ideals of nationality through association and representation" (*Washington Post,* August 2, 1921), and on his warnings against undue centralization as "the one outstanding danger of today" (*New York Times,* August 2, 1921). The national implications of Harding's speech were underscored by the singing of "America" towards the conclusion of morning exercises which conveyed the impression of an enlarged, dramatically enhanced outdoor version of traditional Forefathers' Day rites.

The grand parade through the streets of Plymouth and the evening performance of *The Pilgrim Spirit* turned the tercentenary celebration into an anniversary show. Civic processions[83] had been part of Plymouth observances since 1769 but the 1921 parade reached unprecedented dimensions in magnitude, historical extension, and national ambition. The official announcement of the "Parade Order" in the *Old Colony Memorial* of July 29, 1921, allows for insight into the planning of the route and the timing; the formation of the various divisions; and the locations of reviewing stands for guests of honor and judges, points of dismissal, first aid stations, and even "drinking water and latrines." Press accounts paid special attention to the participation of military units as the following excerpt from a much longer passage on the parade in the *Boston Evening Transcript* of August 1, 1921 shows:

> In the first division were Massachusetts national guardsmen with the First Coast Defense Command and Battery, with the First Regiment Field Artillery in the van. Directly ahead of President Harding was the troop of United States cavalry from Fort Allen. In this division also were the sailors from the United States battleships in the harbor and from the British cruiser. Near the head of the second division were the Grand Army men of the Old Colony posted in automobiles and they received a good part of applause. The Spanish War veterans were followed by the American Legion and they made a feature of the trooped flags of the numerous posts in the Old Plymouth Colony territory. At the start of the procession the World War veterans began to call the attention to [the flags].

The military divisions of the parade presented the spectators with veterans of the major wars of the last sixty years and thus reviewed United States military history rather than the Pilgrim heritage. The military units were followed by several further divisions with more than forty floats, most of them from towns in the counties of Plymouth and Barnstable. The floats showed a kaleidoscope of American history as New England history, including the inevitable landing scene, renditions of early intercultural encounters, and tableaux related to the Revolutionary and the Civil War.[84] The first prize went to the float from Marshfield, Massachusetts, which presented an arrangement of descendants of Governor Winslow in front of a miniature version of the home of Daniel Webster and the stage coach Webster had used in the 1840s. The design of the float connected the Pilgrim heritage and one of its leading advocates by means of a central symbol of nineteenth-century expansion and progress. Newspapers again did not hesitate to formulate interpretations of the political implications of the parade and individual floats:

> The Plymouth Portuguese National Club presented probably the oldest feature by its float, depicting Vasco da Gama, the great navigator, and his crew in the ship St. Gabriel. The crowds were quick to catch the spirit of the float, which pictured Abraham Lincoln, Washington, an Indian, a Pilgrim, World War veterans and an all surrounding "Liberty." It was America and Americanism.[85]

For more than two hours, the procession of such specimens of "Americanism" was the stage for the very fusion of "genuine entertainment" and "wonderful object lessons in history" (*Boston Evening Transcript* August 1, 1921) that can be traced back to the earliest beginnings of Forefathers' Day celebrations in Plymouth and Boston in the late eighteenth century. The history lesson in the guise of a street carnival was commanded by Chief Marshal Sherman Whipple with a baton "made of historic relics":

> Three pieces of wood composed [the baton], one end being of wood from the Howland House, Sandwich street, erected in 1667; the centre piece of elm from the Town Tree, set out in 1783 in Town square and long used for a bulletin board, until it was blown down in a storm, Dec. 26, 1885; while the other end was a piece of oak taken from one of the timbers of the old fort which stood on Fort (now Burial) Hill, an extension of the original fort of 1621-22. A piece of Plymouth Rock was set in one end and in the other a bit of stone from the National Monument to the Forefathers.[86]

It seems that the tercentenary's rationale, i.e., to enact a collective act of historical bonding and reaffirm the rule of Plymouth Rock over American history and its future course, lies condensed in the composition of this parade baton and its symbolic presentation to Sherman Whipple before the commencement of the parade.

The exercises of the day were concluded with a special performance of George P. Baker's *The Pilgrim Spirit*. In the wider context of the development of American pageantry into "a form of public holiday celebration" and "public recreation"[87] in the early years of the twentieth century, the Plymouth pageant had become a regional attraction since its opening on July 20, and would remain so through its last performance on August 13. Certainly one of the most elaborate and prestigious attempts to stage American history and use historical pageantry as a "public ritual of communal self-discovery,"[88] Baker's theatrical version of early Plymouth history was projected by the organizers of the tercentenary as a platform "to visualize the Pilgrim story and form the dominant note in the tercentenary exercises during the months of July and August, 1921" (*Old Colony Memorial*, February 20, 1920). Preparations for the pageant, which were not at all free of worries over the financial burden and the danger of failure because of a "lack of help by local people," were regularly recorded in the local paper and later supplemented by synopses and similar information material in order to maintain the support from within the Plymouth community and attract outside visitors.[89] Yet, the cast of more than 1,300 and audiences of more than 5,000 "from all parts of the country, and many places overseas" (*Old Colony Memorial*, July 22, 1921) turned the opening performance and all those to follow into more than a Plymouth community affair, and the jubilee enactment in the presence of President Harding on August 1, 1921, achieved national attention and critical approval.[90] The ideological didacticism of the pageant and its performances is maybe best preserved in a commercial announcement published in the *Old Colony Memorial* of July 29, 1921, under the heading "Make It Your Duty to See the Pageant." The summary description of the production for the sake of advertisement culminates in the statement: "That pageant with its inspiration to patriotism, ought to make a better American of every person who lets its lessons sink into his mind and heart." Consequently, the unifying voice of the monumental on-site recreation of Plymouth history, Plymouth Rock itself, opens the prologue to the play with the words "I, the rock of Plymouth, speak to you, Americans,"[91] and exhorts audiences accordingly throughout the play: "This is your heritage, All you Americans."[92] Interpretations of *The Pilgrim Spirit* as a contribution to contemporary agendas of Americanization and a New England-centered American civil religion[93] expose the political core of the pageant and (re)situate it in its larger cultural contexts. The conservative, if not nativist, stance of Baker's version of early colonial history furthermore manifests itself in the lengthy inclusion of the 1624 trial of John Oldham and John Lyford for "plott[ing] to disestablish our church and overthrow our government."[94] As a conclusion to this trial, Governor Bradford issues a solemn warning to future opponents to the Pilgrim spirit and the political and social order it was to support over the centuries: "Let this be a warning that what we established here for personal liberty and self-government, that will we hold as a heritage for our children and our children's children."[95] The interpreter is tempted to take the voice of the most prominent Pilgrim Father of them all as the voice of the Anglo-American elite of 1920 who employed the platforms of the Plymouth Tercentenary to defend and recertify this very heritage.

A Brief Coda to a Long Story

When a series of articles in the *Old Colony Memorial* (esp. September 9 and 16, 1921) recorded the final activities and closing reports of the various tercentenary committees, the organizers, supporters, and celebrants of the Plymouth Tercentenary rested assured of the grandeur and success of their year-long effort. They did not yet know that the festivities of 1920-21 would not inaugurate a new "Pilgrim century" and that, unlike the bicentennial, the tercentennial would mark an endpoint rather than a beginning. Maybe the members of the committee who selected festive poems had already sensed the approach of the expiration date of the heritage to be invoked for revitalization when they rejected Edward F. Sutton's playfully ironic "Ye Pilgrim Father" and thus revealed their deeper anxieties and sensibilities even towards mild poetic subversions of Plymouth Rock.[96] Ultimately, the theatrical 'normalcy' of the Plymouth festivities turned out to be deceptive because the national attractiveness of the Pilgrim myth had passed its zenith and the ideological power of what McGrath had proclaimed as "salutary lessons of Americanism" became increasingly contested. Suspended in the middle between Randolph Bourne's claim to a "trans-national America" of 1916 and Alain Locke's call for "a new democracy in American culture" and "a new American attitude"[97] of 1925, the Plymouth Tercentenary appears like a retrospective and exhausted rather than a prospective and energizing enterprise. Harvard President Eliot betrayed a partisan, old-stock conception of "America" when he welcomed the tercentenary preparations with the statement that "America needs just this program at just this time" (*Old Colony Memorial*, June 11, 1920). The Puritan might have conquered the Cavalier on the battlefields of the Civil War, as Charles Everett had put it in 1865, but on the stages and platforms of national commemoration, rebels, cowboys, and an ever more diverse gathering of ethnic, non-English speaking ancestors had reduced, and would further reduce, the radius of the Pilgrim Fathers. The much publicized second cracking of Plymouth Rock in the course of its transportation and re-enshrinement on the eve of Forefathers' Day 1920[98] could hardly be read as a positive omen—as it had been after its first breaking shortly before the American Revolution when the rupture was taken as a justification of the separation from Great Britain—and observers were quick to affirm that "[t]he rock will present a united face again when it is cemented and restored to its original base at the waterline" (*Providence Journal*, December 21, 1921). In the years to come, the Boston Tercentenary stirred noteworthy, but in no way comparable, festivities,[99] and Plymouth anniversary observances outside of Plymouth hit the national press only on special occasions such as the 320th jubilee in 1940.[100] Although Forefathers' Day continued to be observed in Middlebury, Vermont until 1974,[101] post-World War II records of festivities are limited. While Plymouth has developed into "one of the sacred spaces of American tourism"[102] and draws massive crowds of summer travelers, Forefathers' Day celebrations have succumbed to the attractions of the December shopping season even in traditional centers of New England ancestor worship. Plymouth remains as the lone(ly) celebrant of its own (national) heritage three days before Christmas. The Old Colony Club of Plymouth still honors the event and even circulates its observances out into the global village from the virtual platform of "http://www.plimoth.org/occ.htm", despite—or because of (?)—"the Rock's present state of national neglect."[103]

Notes

1. I wish to express my special gratitude to Lee Regan and the staff volunteers of the Plymouth Public Library in Plymouth, MA, and to Peggy M. Baker of the Pilgrim Society at Pilgrim Hall, Plymouth, MA. Their generous help provided access to documentary materials and newspaper accounts I would not have been able to include otherwise.
2. For accounts of the history of Forefathers' Day since the inception of this civic rite in 1769, cf. John Seelye, *Memory's Nation: The Place of Plymouth Rock* (Chapel Hill: University of North Carolina Press, 1998); Udo J. Hebel, "'A Proper Recollection of These Things': New England Forefathers' Day Orations 1769-1820 and the National Consecration of a Colonial Past," *Remembering the Individual / Regional / National Past*, ed. Waldemar Zacharasiewicz (Tübingen: Stauffenberg, 1999), 31-58; idem, "The Forefathers' Day Celebrations of 1802 and the Enactment of Federalist Constructions of the American Republic," *The Construction and Contestation of American Cultures and Identities in the Early National Period*, ed. Udo J. Hebel (Heidelberg: Winter, 1999), 303-30; idem, "New England Forefathers' Day Celebrations Between the American Revolution and the Civil War," in *Ceremonies and Spectacles: Performing American Culture*, eds. Teresa Alves et al. (Amsterdam: VU University Press, 2000), 111-43; earlier Robert J. Myers, *Celebrations: The Complete Book of American Holidays* (Garden City, NJ: Doubleday, 1972), 295-301; Albert Matthews, "The Term Pilgrim Fathers and Early Celebrations of Forefathers' Day," *Publications of the Colonial Society of Massachusetts* 17 (1914): 293-391; William T. Davis, *Plymouth Memories of an Octogenarian* (Plymouth, MA: Memorial Press, 1906). In a wider context, including the so-called Pilgrim myth, George F. Willison, *Saints and Strangers* (New York: Time, 1945); Wesley F. Craven, *The Legend of the Founding Fathers* (1956; Westport, CT: Greenwood, 1983); Francis Russell, "The Pilgrims and the Rock," *American Heritage* 13.6 (1962): 48-55; Rose T. Briggs, *Plymouth Rock: History and Significance* (Plymouth, MA: Pilgrim Society, 1968); Peter Gomes, *The Pilgrim Society 1820-1920: An Informal Commemorative Essay* (Plymouth, MA: Pilgrim Society, 1971); idem, "Pilgrims and Puritans: 'Heroes' and 'Villains' in the Creation of the American Past," *Proceedings of the Massachusetts Historical Society* 95 (1983): 1-16; Robert D. Arner, "Plymouth Rock Revisited: The Landing of the Pilgrim Fathers," *Journal of American Culture* 6 (1983): 25-35; Lawrence Buell, *New England Literary Culture: From Revolution through Renaissance* (Cambridge, MA: Cambridge University Press, 1986); Michael Kammen, *Mystic Chords of Memory: The Transformation of Tradition in American Culture* (New York: Knopf, 1991), 63-64, 208-11; Deborah Gussman, "Remembering Plymouth Rock: The Making of Citizenship in Nineteenth-Century Narratives of Colonial New England," Ph.D. diss., Rutgers University, 1993 [DAI 54.11 (1994): 4092-93A]. Ann U. Abrams, *The Pilgrims and Pocahontas: Rival Myths of American Origin* (Boulder, CO: Westview, 1999) became available after the completion of this study.
3. Charles C. Everett, *A Sermon Preached December 17th, 1865, The Sunday Preceding The Anniversary of the Landing of the Pilgrims* (Bangor, ME: Burr, 1865), 3.
4. Ibid., 10.
5. For a concise discussion of the recent theoretical debate on collective cultural memory and further bibliographical references, cf. Hannah Möckel-Rieke, "Introduction: Media and Cultural Memory," *Amerikastudien/American Studies* 43 (1998): 5-17.
6. For accounts of post-Civil War cultures of memory, cf. Jim Cullen, *The Civil War in Popular Culture: A Reusable Past* (Washington, DC: Smithsonian Press,1995) and Kirk Savage, *Standing Soldiers, Kneeling Slaves: Race, War, and Monument in Nineteenth-Century America* (Princeton, NJ: Princeton University Press, 1997).

7. Pershing Vartanian, "The Puritan as a Symbol in American Thought: A Study of the New England Societies, 1820-1920," Ph.D. diss., University of Michigan, 1971 [DAI 32.7 (1972): 3939A] on the rise and demise of New England societies throughout the nineteenth century.
8. On the development of ethnic—and especially immigrant—festive culture in the United States, cf., Kenneth Moss, "St. Patrick's Day Celebrations and the Formation of Irish-American Identity, 1845-1875," *Journal of Social History* 29 (1995): 123-48; April Schultz, "'The Pride of the Race Had Been Touched': The 1925 Norse-American Immigration Centennial and Ethnic Identity," *Journal of American History* 77 (1991): 1265-95 [repr. *Norwegian-American Studies* 33 (1992):267-307]; April Schultz, *Ethnicity on Parade: Inventing the Norwegian American Through Celebration* (Amherst: University of Massachusetts Press, 1994); David Glassberg, *American Historical Pageantry: The Uses of Tradition in the Early Twentieth Century* (Chapel Hill: University of North Carolina Press, 1990); Dag Blanck, "History at Work: The 1988 New Sweden Jubilee," *Swedish-American Historical Quarterly* 39 (1988): 5-20; Robert Orsi, "Parades, Holidays, and Public Rituals," *Encyclopedia of American Social History*, eds. Mary K. Cayton et al. (New York: Scribner, 1993), 1916-17. For case studies in local commemorative civic traditions, cf. John Bodnar, "Commemorative Activity in Twentieth-Century Indianapolis: The Invention of Civic Traditions," *Indiana Magazine of History* 87 (1991): 1-23 and David Glassberg, "Public Ritual and Cultural Hierarchy: Philadelphia's Civic Celebrations at the Turn of the Twentieth Century," *Pennsylvania Magazine* 107 (1983): 421-48. For a summary account of American public commemoration, cf. John Bodnar, *Remaking America: Public Memory, Commemoration, and Patriotism in the Twentieth Century* (Princeton, NJ: Princeton University Press, 1992).
9. The controversy over the exact anniversary, i.e. December 21 or December 22, was resolved in 1850; cf. *Report of the Pilgrim Society on the Expediency of Celebrating the Landing of the Pilgrims December 21 Instead December 22* (Boston: n.p., 1850). The anniversary observes the arrival at Plymouth (according to New Style), not the first landfall of the *Mayflower* on Cape Cod in November 1620.
10. *Proceedings of the Pilgrim Society at Plymouth, 1870* (Cambridge, MA: Pilgrim Society, 1871); *Proceedings at the Celebration of the Pilgrim Society, 1889* (Plymouth, MA: Pilgrim Society, 1889); *Proceedings at the Celebration of the Pilgrim Society, 1895* (Plymouth, MA: Pilgrim Society, 1896); furthermore Davis, *Plymouth Memories*, 380-88 and James F. O'Gorman, "The Colossus of Plymouth: Hammatt Billings's National Monument to the Forefathers," *Journal of the Society of Architectural Historians* 54 (1995): 278-301 as well as *Bradford's History "Of Plimoth Plantation" From the Original Manuscript. With a Report of the Proceedings Incident to the Return of the Manuscript to Massachusetts* (Boston: Wright, 1898).
11. E.g. *New York Times*, December 23, 1876; ibid., December 23, 1882; *New York Herald*, December 23, 1882; *New York Evening Post*, December 23, 1882. Cephas Brainerd and Eveline W. Brainerd, eds., *The New England Society Orations: Addresses, Sermons and Poems Delivered Before the New England Society in the City of New York 1820-1885*, 2 vols. (New York: Century, 1901), gathers orations delivered in New York throughout the nineteenth century. On the New England Society in the City of New York, cf., Horace Hatch, *The New England Society in the City of New York, 1805-1957* (New York: New England Society, 1958).
12. For texts of Twain's addresses, "The Oldest Inhabitant—The Weather of New England" (1876), "Plymouth Rock and the Pilgrims" (1881), and "Woman—God Bless Her" (1882), cf. Paul Fatout, ed., *Mark Twain Speaking* (Iowa City: University of Iowa Press, 1976), 100-03, 162-66, 173-75. Artemus Ward's passing remarks on "the growth of

Ameriky frum the time when the Mayflowers cum over in the Pilgrim and brawt Plymmuth Rock with him" in his "Fourth of July Oration, Delivered July 4th, at Weathersfield, Conn., 1859" make for an earlier, but even more isolated, example of satirical representation of the Pilgrim Fathers; Artemus Ward, *Selected Works*, ed. Albert J. Nock (New York: Boni, 1924), 52-57, quote on page 53.

13. Cf. by means of an exemplary selection, William Way, *History of the New England Society of Charleston, South Carolina For One Hundred Years, 1819-1919* (Charleston, SC: New England Society, 1920), 65-70, 184-87, 275-92; *Philadelphia Press*, December 23, 1881; *Proceedings of the New England Society of St. Louis* (1885; St. Louis, 1900), *Annual Dinner of the New England Society of Chicago* (Chicago, 1907).

14. Cf. the chapters on the post-Civil War activities of the New England Society of Charleston, SC, in Way, *History of the New England Society of Charleston, South Carolina*.

15. Cf. a respective note in *The Milwaukee Sentinel*, December 25, 1865, and Dan Freeman Bradley, *The Development of Fellowship in the Congregational Churches: An Address Delivered before the Minnesota Congregational Club at Its Forefathers's Day Meeting, 1902* (Minneapolis, MN: Hall, 1902).

16. For relevant discussions and applications of the term 'site of memory,' cf., Aleida Assmann, *"Erinnerungsräume": Formen und Wandlungen des kulturellen Gedächtnisses* (München: Beck, 1999); Toni Morrison, "The Site of Memory," in *Inventing the Truth: The Art and Craft of Memoir*, ed. William Zinsser, rev. and exp. ed. (Boston: Houghton Mifflin, 1995), 83-102; Geneviève Fabre, "Lieux de fête et de commémoration," *Revue Francaise d'Etudes Américaines* 51 (1992): 7-17; and, of course, Pierre Nora, *Les Lieux de Mémoire*, 3 vols. (Paris: Gallimard, 1984-1992), now also in English as *Realms of Memory* (New York: Columbia University Press, 1996-1998); for an earlier English version of his theoretical approach, cf. Pierre Nora, "Between Memory and History: Les Lieux de Mémoire," *Representations* 26 (1989): 7-25; for a summary review of Nora's work, cf. Tony Judt, "A la recherche du temps perdu," *New York Review of Books*, December 3, 1998, 51-58.

17. E.g. the *Old Colony Memorial* of February 20, 1920: "The commission, handicapped as it has been by the war and restrained as it is even now by the fact that the Federal appropriation for the celebration has been delayed by conditions at Washington, has not felt justified in making public any considerable part of its plan [...]." Also reports in the same paper on April 2, 1920, April 9, 1920, and June 11, 1920, about funding needed improvements along the Plymouth waterfront.

18. For a contextualizing account of cultural pluralism in the second and third decade of the twentieth century, and especially on Horace Kallen, cf. Alfred Hornung, "The Birth of a Multicultural Nation: Horace M. Kallen's Cultural Pluralism," *Transatlantic Encounters: Studies in European-American Relations*, eds. Udo J. Hebel and Karl Ortseifen (Trier: WVT, 1995), 347-58.

19. For further contextualization and a thorough discussion of patterns of nativism and Americanization in the 1900s and 1910s, cf. chapters 7 through 11 in John Higham, *Strangers in the Land: Patterns of American Nativism 1860-1925* (1963; Westport, CT: Greenwood, 1981).

20. Randolph Bourne, "Trans-National America" (1916), in *History of a Literary Radical and Other Essays* (New York: Huebsch, 1920), 266-99, quotes on 287, 289, 292, 282.

21. H.L. Mencken, *Prejudices*, 6 vols. (New York: Knopf, 1919-1927).

22. The *Journal of Negro History* was founded in 1916 with Woodson as editor and major contributor. For a summary account of the influence of Woodson in those years, cf. Willis Richardson, ed., *Plays and Pageants from the Life of the Negro* (1930; Jackson, MS: University of Mississippi Press, 1993), vii-xii; on the emergence of early twentieth-century

African American drama and theater as a means to perform the work of collective memory, cf. Udo J. Hebel, "Early African American Women Playwrights (1916-1930) and the Remapping of Twentieth-Century American Drama," *Arbeiten aus Anglistik und Amerikanistik* 21 (1996): 267-86; furthermore William H. Wiggins, *O Freedom! Afro-American Emancipation Celebrations* (Knoxville: University of Tennessee Press, 1987).

23. For a synchronic exploration of the cultural moment 1920, cf. Udo J. Hebel, "'The Whole Evanescent Context'?: Möglichkeiten und Grenzen synchroner Kulturpoetik am Beispiel von Sinclair Lewis' *Main Street* (1920)," *Literaturwissenschaftliches Jahrbuch* 37 (1996): 261-82.

24. *Proceedings by the State of Connecticut in Commemoration of the Tercentennial Anniversary of the Landing of the Pilgrims* (Hartford, CT: n.p., 1920), Way, *History of the New England Society of Charleston, South Carolina, St. Louis Daily Post-Dispatch*, December 22, 1920, *St. Louis Globe*, December 22, 1920, *Indianapolis News*, December 22, 1920.

25. Henry Cabot Lodge, *The Pilgrims of Plymouth: An Address at Plymouth, Massachusetts on the Three Hundredth Anniversary of their Landing, December 21, 1920* (Boston: Pilgrim Tercentenary Commission, 1920), 33.

26. Seelye, *Memory's Nation*, 588. Although the Plymouth bicentennial certainly marks a decisive point in the nationalization of Forefathers' Day, there had already been widely recognized observances prior to 1820. For differing accounts of the significance of 1820 as the supposed starting point of the so-called "Pilgrim century" between 1820 and 1920, cf. Buell, *New England Literary Culture*, 197-98 and Gomes, "Pilgrims and Puritans," on the one hand, and Hebel, "'A Proper Recollection of These Things,'" on the other. Werner Sollors, "Konstruktionsversuche nationaler und ethnischer Identität in der amerikanischen Literatur," *Nationale und kulturelle Identität: Studien zur Entwicklung des kollektiven Bewußtseins in der Neuzeit*, ed. Bernhard Giesen (Frankfurt/Main: Suhrkamp, 1991), 551-52, traces the national popularity of the Pilgrims to the late nineteenth century.

27. Lodge, *The Pilgrims of Plymouth*; Le Baron Russell Briggs, "1620-1920: A Poem," in Henry Cabot Lodge, *The Pilgrims of Plymouth*, 41-46; George Pierce Baker, *The Pilgrim Spirit* (Boston: Jones, 1921).

28. I will especially draw on the coverage in the *New York Times, Washington Post, Chicago Daily Tribune, Boston Evening Transcript, Boston Post, Providence Journal, Hartford Daily Courant, Manchester Union*, and, most significantly, Plymouth's own *Old Colony Memorial*. References to these papers will be documented parenthetically. In his seminal study of early national American festive culture, Waldstreicher has emphasized "the printed discourse that surrounded these events and gave them extralocal meaning" and called for the exploration of public events beyond "a narrowly anthropological definition of ritual that does not do justice to the cultural complexity, much less the political significance, of modern American celebrations"; David Waldstreicher, *In the Midst of Perpetual Fetes: The Making of American Nationalism, 1776-1820* (Chapel Hill: University of North Carolina Press, 1997), 11. Benedict Anderson's views on print media as important factors in the ceremonious creation of shared (national) communities and identities furthermore support the prominent consideration of newspapers in the interpretation of public celebrations as sites of collective memory; cf. Benedict Anderson, *Imagined Communities: Reflections on the Origin and Spread of Nationalism*, rev. ed. (London: Verso, 1991).

29. Cf. esp., Frederick W. Bittinger, *The Story of the Pilgrim Tercentenary at Plymouth in the Year 1921* (Plymouth, MA: Memorial Press, 1923); Harry Bloomingdale, *Plymouth Tercentenary, Illustrated with a Brief History of the Life and Struggles of the Pilgrim Fathers. Including the Original Program of the "Pilgrim Spirit" by Professor George P. Baker, President Harding's Visit, All Scenes, Episodes, and Official Photographs* (New Bedford,

MA: n.p., 1921); *Pilgrim Tercentenary Observance of the Three Hundredth Anniversary of the Landing of the Pilgrims at Plymouth July—August—September 1921* (Plymouth, MA: Tercentenary Commission, 1921); *Exercises on the Three Hundreth Anniversary of the Landing of the Pilgrims, Held at Plymouth* (Boston: Tercentenary Commission, 1921).

30. Alessandro Falassi, ed., *Time out of Time: Essays on the Festival* (Albuquerque: University of New Mexico Press, 1987), 2. Following Roger D. Abrahams, "An American Vocabulary of Celebration," in *Time Out of Time*, ed. Falassi, 173-83, "celebration" may indeed be taken as an over-arching term to describe the (American) field under consideration. Theoretical points of reference for the exploration of public events as political rituals and cultural performances are furthermore provided by Don Handelman, *Models and Mirrors: Towards an Anthropology of Public Events* (Cambridge, MA: Cambridge University Press, 1990); John J. MacAloon, ed., *Rite, Drama, Festival, Spectacle: Rehearsals Towards a Theory of Cultural Performance* (Philadelphia: Institute for the Study of Human Issues, 1984); Sally F. Moore and Barbara G. Myerhoff, eds., *Secular Ritual* (Amsterdam: Van Gorcum, 1977); Steven Lukes, "Political Ritual and Social Integration," *Sociology* 19 (1975): 289-308; Milton Singer, ed., *Traditional India: Structure and Change* (Philadelphia: American Folklore Society, 1959). Also Henry Sayre, "Performance," in *Critical Terms for Literary Study*, eds. Frank Lentricchia and Thomas McLaughlin (Chicago: University of Chicago Press, 1990), 91-104; Mary Ryan, "The American Parade: Representations of the Nineteenth-Century Social Order," in *The New Cultural History*, ed. Lynn Hunt (Berkeley: University of California Press, 1989), 131-53; Roger D. Abrahams and Richard Bauman, "Ranges of Festive Behavior," in *The Reversible World: Symbolic Inversion in Art and Society*, ed. Barbara A. Babcock (Ithaca, NY: Cornell University Press, 1978): 193-208. The familiar approaches to (cultural) performance, social drama, symbolic action, and (collective) identity as advanced by Victor Turner, Erving Goffman, Kenneth Burke, Dell Hymes, Clifford Geertz, and Emile Durkheim inform most of these studies; for a concise assessment of these approaches in the present context, cf. MacAloon, ed., *Rite, Drama, Festival, Spectacle*, 1-15.
31. Handelman, *Models and Mirrors*, 12-13. Handelman lists "formality, replicability, intentionality, symbolic formation, and a connectivity that extends beyond itself" as basic features of such a festive "sequence of practices."
32. Ibid., 5.
33. Falassi, *Time out of Time*, 3. Falassi recommends the "fragmentation of the festive complex into events" (6) in order to account for the festivity in its entirety.
34. Klaus Poenicke, "Engendering Cultural Memory: 'The Legend of Sleepy Hollow' as Text and Intertext," *Amerikastudien/American Studies* 43 (1998): 19-32, quote on 21 (italics in the original).
35. "History of the Pilgrim Society," *New England Historical and Genealogical Register* 1 (1847): 114-25.
36. *Old Colony Memorial* June 11, 1920; also *Old Colony Memorial*, July 23, 1920, August 13, 1920, and August, 27, 1920, for further details, including extended lists of committee chairpersons and members, as well as specific projects at certain stages in the planning.
37. For a comparison, cf. "Records of the Old Colony Club," *Proceedings of the Massachusetts Historical Society* Vol. 3, Second Series (1886/1888): 381-444, and "First Celebration of the Landing of the Pilgrims at Plymouth, by the Old Colony Club," *New England Historical and Genealogical Register* 4 (1850): 367-68.
38. *Old Colony Memorial*, August 13, 1920.
39. Discussions of American civil religion still draw on Robert Bellah, "Civil Religion in America," *Daedalus* 96 (1967): 1-21 [repr. in Russell E. Richey and Donald G. Jones, eds., *American Civil Religion* (New York: Harper, 1974): 21-44].

40. A most comprehensive documentation of this frequently forgotten celebration is available in *An Account of the Pilgrim Celebration at Plymouth, August 1, 1853, Containing a List of the Decorations in the Town, and Correct Copies of the Speeches Made at the Dinner-Table* (Boston: Nichols, 1853).
41. Bourne, "Trans-National America," 282.
42. *Old Colony Memorial*, September 24, 1920.
43. Seelye stresses the "ideological conservatism virtually inherent in most publicly sponsored activities of this kind" and the "conservative, even reactionary impulse underlying the events"; *Memory's Nation*, 608.
44. For the full text of the scroll, cf., *Old Colony Memorial*, June 25, 1920.
45. For further reports about tercentenary visits from England and Canada, cf. *New York Times*, October 1, 1920, and *Old Colony Memorial* October 22, 1920.
46. *Old Colony Memorial*, August 6, 1920.
47. Reports about anniversary activities in England were repeatedly reprinted from English newspapers throughout the latter half of 1920. Cf. *Old Colony Memorial*, September 10 and October 1, 1920, on celebrations in Plymouth, England, as reprinted from the *Western Morning News*. Less frequent were reports about related festivities in other countries; cf. *New York Times*, November 29, 1920, on a function held by the French Protestant Historical Society in Paris and featuring O.W. Goodrich, pastor of the American Church in Paris, as the main speaker. In all instances, the reports establish some kind of link to wartime alliances.
48. On the Mayflower Compact in American cultural history, cf. Mark L. Sargent, "The Conservative Covenant: The Rise of the Mayflower Compact in American Myth," *New England Quarterly* 61 (1988): 233-51.
49. For reprints of the program, cf. *Old Colony Memorial*, November 12 and 19, 1920.
50. The *Old Colony Memorial* of November 19, 1920, also took the opportunity to refer extensively to John Quincy Adams's canonical interpretation of the Mayflower Compact as pronounced on Forefathers' Day 1802; cf. John Quincy Adams, *An Oration Delivered at Plymouth, December 22, 1802, at the Anniversary Commemoration of the First Landing of Our Ancestors* (Boston: Russell, 1802).
51. For the full text, cf. Felicia Hemans, *The Poetical Works* (London: Ward, 1912), 308.
52. For examples of New England anniversary toasting and its political implications, cf. Hebel, "The Forefathers' Day Celebrations of 1802."
53. *Old Colony Memorial*, November 26, 1920.
54. *New York Times*, November 27, 1920.
55. For a scholarly edition, cf. Daniel Webster, "The First Settlement of New England" (1820), *The Writings and Speeches*, 18 vols. (Boston: Little, 1903), 1: 179-230.
56. Almost simultaneously, the *Old Colony Memorial* of December 17, 1920 announced that "fitting quotations from Webster's oration" were now available on greeting cards depicting "famous events in Pilgrim history."
57. *Old Colony Memorial*, December 3, 1920. The high school pageant is a good example of the didactic nationalization of Plymouth Pilgrim history. Among the "characters" were the expected "men and women of the Mayflower" but also allegorical figures such as "America" and "The Spirit of Progress" as well as "historic characters like Washington, Penn, Franklin, and Lincoln."
58. For a detailed program and full titles of the tableaux, cf., *Old Colony Memorial*, December 17, 1920. Reliable texts of Plymouth anniversary poems are available in the following compilations: "Hymns, Odes, etc. Written for the Anniversary of the Landing of the Pilgrims," in James Thacher, *History of the Town of Plymouth, From Its First Settlement in 1620 to the Present Time*, enl. ed. (1835; Yarmouthport: Parnassus, 1972), 341-52;

"Appendix: Airs of the Pilgrims," in William Russell, *Guide to Plymouth and Recollections of the Pilgrims* (Boston: Coolidge, 1846); Z.H. Spooner, ed. *Poems of the Pilgrims*. Boston: Williams, 1881); Marvin D. Bisbee, ed., *Songs of the Pilgrims* (Boston: Congregational Publishing Society, 1887).
59. The *Providence Journal* reprinted the account offered by the Associated Press.
60. In the following, I will draw on representative coverage in *Old Colony Memorial*, December 24, 1920, *Boston Evening Transcript*, December 21, 1920, *Boston Post*, December 21 and 22, 1920, *Providence Journal*, December 21 and 22, 1920, *Hartford Daily Courant*, December 21 and 22, 1920, *New York Times*, December 22, 1920.
61. Cf. e.g., Bittinger, *The Story of the Pilgrim Tercentenary*, 17.
62. *Old Colony Memorial*, December 24, 1920. Musical recitals included the singing of Felicia Hemans's "The Breaking Waves Dashed High" as well as "Our Country" and "America"; Le Baron Russell Briggs repeated his poem "1620-1820: A Poem" and Ashley D. Leavett of Brookline, MA, spoke on "The Day We Commemorate: Its Privileges and Responsibilities—Our Heritage." Unfortunately, two shorter addresses, one by Vittorio Orlandini on "The Immigrant's Share in Our Heritage—What Part May He Fairly Expect?" and the other by Frank V. Thompson (Superintendent of Schools, Boston) on "For the Rights Accorded the Immigrant—What May America Justly Expect of Him?" have not been preserved. These evidently dialogic presentations might provide further insights into the ideological intricacies and tensions governing the tercentenary.
63. A good point of comparison may be provided by the article in the *New York Times*, December 22, 1920. Under the title "Honor Pilgrims on Tercentenary," the *New York Times* circulated to a nationwide audience a comprehensive representation of "the formal exercises before a distinguished audience in observance of the 300th anniversary of the landing of the Pilgrims." The most detailed account of the proceedings (complete with titles of all songs, hymns etc. and names of the persons giving individual presentations) was given by the *Old Colony Memorial*, December 24, 1920. Accounts representative of the coverage in New England papers are those in the *Boston Post* of December 22, 1920, and the *Providence Journal* of December 22, 1920.
64. Seelye, *Memory's Nation*, 573.
65. F. Scott Fitzgerald, *This Side of Paradise* (1920; New York: Scribner, 1970), 282.
66. Seelye, *Memory's Nation*, 587.
67. Ibid., 567.
68. For details of Lodge's previous participation in Forefathers' Day celebrations, cf. ibid., esp. 583.
69. Lodge, *The Pilgrims of Plymouth*, 7.
70. Ibid., 11.
71. Ibid., 12, 36, 34.
72. *New York Times*, December 22, 1920.
73. Gomes, "Pilgrims and Puritans," 2, 14.
74. *Old Colony Memorial*, February 18, March 4, April 8, and April 15, 1921.
75. For a detailed discussion of living history at Plymouth, cf. Stephen E. Snow, ed., *Performing the Pilgrims: A Study of Ethnohistorical Role-Playing at Plimoth Plantation* (Jackson: University of Mississippi Press, 1993).
76. Papers record a total of 100,000 spectators (*Old Colony Memorial* August 5, 1921) and up to 30,000 for individual parts of the day-long event (*New York Times* August 2, 1921). The large audiences are documented and highlighted in the photographs included in Bloomingdale, *Plymouth Tercentenary* and newspaper coverage such as the one in the "Picture Section" in the *New York Times*, August 7, 1921. Most render the movement of

the masses towards and into Plymouth in a way which evokes in enlarged proportion the advance of the Pilgrims towards Plymouth Rock.
77. The welcome committee was headed by Vice President Calvin Coolidge, Senator Lodge, Governor Cox, and Tercentenary Committee Chairman William S. Kyle.
78. *Boston Evening Transcript*, August 1, 1921.
79. Cf. also the greetings of Captain Bailey of the Royal Navy, representative of the British Ambassador; Bailey emphasized English traits as "the most outstanding in the complex of American traits."
80. Bittinger, *The Story of the Pilgrim Tercentenary*, 76-95.
81. The same paper also singled out Harding's stress on "the mission of the race" and "the leadership of the English speaking peoples in the present world crisis." Reports and summaries in other papers, e.g., *Boston Post*, August 2, 1921, record the same passages.
82. Edmund Burke, *Reflections on the Revolution in France* (London: Dodsley, 1790), 49.
83. For investigations of earlier American festive culture and parade culture, cf., Brooks McNamara, *Day of Jubilee: The Great Age of Public Celebrations in New York, 1788-1909* (New Brunswick, NJ: Rutgers University Press, 1997); Simon P. Newman, *Parades and the Politics of the Street: Festive Culture in the Early American Republic* (Philadelphia: University opf Pennsylvania Press, 1997); Mary Ryan, *Civic Wars: Democracy and Public Life in the American City during the Nineteenth Century* (Berkeley: University of California Press, 1997); Len Travers, *Celebrating the Fourth: Independence Day and the Rites of Nationalism in the Early Republic* (Amherst: University of Massachusetts Press, 1997); Waldstreicher, *In the Midst of Perpetual Fetes*; Jürgen Heideking, "The Federal Processions of 1788 and the Origins of American Civil Religion," *Soundings* 77 (1994): 367-87; Diana Appelbaum, *The Glorious Fourth: An American Holiday, an American History* (New York: Facts on File, 1989); Susan G. Davis, *Parades and Power: Street Theatre in Nineteenth-Century Philadelphia* (Philadelphia: Temple University Press, 1986).
84. For a complete list of the town floats, cf. *Old Colony Memorial*, July 29, 1921; for detailed descriptions of specific floats and reactions of the spectators, cf. esp. *Boston Evening Transcript*, August 1, 1921; for photographs showing selected floats, cf. Bloomingdale, *Pilgrim Tercentenary*.
85. *Boston Evening Transcript*, August 1, 1921.
86. This detail in the choreography was recorded by most papers; cf. for a similar description *Boston Evening Transcript*, August 1, 1921.
87. Glassberg, *American Historical Pageantry*, 281, 283.
88. Ibid., 283.
89. Esp. *Old Colony Memorial* January 28, February 11, June 3, and June 10, 1921. Also the well-timed publication of the pageant master's own account; George P. Baker, "The Pilgrim Spirit in Pageantry," *The New York Times Book Review and Magazine* (July 17, 1921): 6.
90. The scope of the theatrical apparatus and the immediate effect of the productions on observers and participants is captured in this long report of the *Old Colony Memorial* entitled "'The Pilgrim Spirit': First Performance of Beautiful, Spectacular, Historic Pageant Played by Old Colony People." Also *New York Times*, July 21, 1921, under the heading "See Pilgrims Land on Flash-Lit Rock." On Baker's *The Pilgrim Spirit*, its reception, and major lines of interpretation, cf., Seelye, *Memory's Nation*, 596-606; Winfried, Herget, "Amerikanisches Historienspiel als nationale und ethnische Identitätsbindung," in *Aspekte des Geschichtsdramas: Von Aischylos bis Volker Braun*, ed. Wolfgang Düsing (Tübingen: Francke, 1998), 181-93; Glassberg, *American Historical Pageantry*, 259, 265-66; Naima Prevots, *American Pageantry: A Movement for Art and Democracy* (Ann Arbor, MI: UMI, 1990), 113-14; Norreys J. O'Connor, "The Plymouth Pageant," *The*

Bookman 54.2 (October 1921): 166-68; Ludwig Lewisohn, "The Plymouth Pageant," *The Nation* 113 (August 24, 1921): 210-11.
91. Baker, *The Pilgrim Spirit*, 5.
92. Ibid., 79. Already reviews of the first performance emphasized the effectiveness of the "Voice of Plymouth Rock" as part of the dramatic design; cf. e.g., *New York Times*, July 21, 1921.
93. Herget, "Amerikanisches Historienspiel," 183-86.
94. Baker, *The Pilgrim Spirit*, 108-31, quote on 122. For historical details, cf. William Bradford, *Of Plymouth Plantation, 1620-1647*, ed. Samuel E. Morison (1952; New York: Knopf, 1987), 146-63. Whether Baker drew on Joseph Croswell's play, *A New World Planted; Or, The Adventures of the Forefathers of New England, Who Landed in Plymouth, December 22, 1620* (Boston: Larkin, 1802), must remain speculation, although the similarities in presenting the Oldham and Lyford affair and the parallels of historic contexts (Alien and Sedition Acts of 1798 and Red Scare of 1919-1920) are quite striking.
95. Baker, *The Pilgrim Spirit*, 131.
96. The poem is preserved in typescript and contained in a folder of notes and clippings on New England anniversary festivities held by the Houghton Library of Harvard University. For satiric poems on the Pilgrim Fathers and Plymouth Rock by ethnic writers, cf. Sollors, "Konstruktionsversuche nationaler und ethnischer Identität," 566-68.
97. Alain Locke, "The New Negro," *The New Negro*, ed. Alain Locke (1925; New York: Macmillan, 1992): 1-16, quotes at 10, 11.
98. Cf. esp. *Old Colony Memorial*, December 24, 1920; *New York Times*, December 21, 1920; *Chicago Tribune*, December 21, 1920; *Boston Post*, December 21, 1920; *Providence Journal*, December 21, 1921.
99. Cf. *Celebrating a Three Hundredth Anniversary: A Report of the Massachusetts Bay Tercentenary of 1930* (Boston: Tercentenary Commission, 1931) and *Materials Suggested for Use in the Schools in Observance of the Tercentenary of Massachusetts Bay Colony* (Boston: Commonwealth of Massachusetts, 1930).
100. E.g. the *New York Times*, December 21, 22, 23, 1940 and the indicative headline "Dictators Scored at Pilgrims' Fete." Cf. *Anniversary Celebration of the New England Society in the City of New York* (New York: Bryant, 1930) and *Annual Report of the New England Society in the City of New York* (New York: n.p., 1931) for accounts of activities in New York City around 1930.
101. For an account of pre-World War II celebrations, cf. W. Storrs Lee, "Forefathers Day," *The Middlebury College News Letter* 15.2 (1940): 10-11, 18. In 1974, the Middlebury Historical Society canceled the already scheduled event after Jessica Swift, then 103 years old and for decades the main supporter of festivities, had withdrawn her support. I am indebted to The Sheldon Museum at Middlebury, VT, for copies of the correspondence documenting the circumstances of the termination of celebrations there.
102. Mark L. Sargent, "The Encounter on Cole's Hill: Cyrus Dallin's 'Massasoit' and 'Bradford,'" *Journal of American Studies* 27 (1993): 399-408, quote at 399.
103. Seelye, *Memory's Nation*, 629.

List of Editors and Contributors

Tobias Brinkmann is currently working at the Center for Advanced Studies at the University of Leipzig. He recently completed his PhD-thesis titled "'We American-German Jews': Jewish Immigrants in Chicago 1840-1900," at the Technical University Berlin. Brinkmann has worked for several German museums and holds MA-degrees of Indiana University (Bloomington) and the Technical University Berlin. He has published several articles on Modern Jewish History.

Heike Bungert is assistant professor of history at the University of Cologne, Germany. She received her M.A. at the University of North Carolina in Chapel Hill in 1990 and her Ph.D. from the University of Tübingen, Germany, in 1995. Her dissertation was published in 1997 as *Das Nationalkomitee und der Westen: Das NKFD und die Freien Deutschen Bewegungen aus der Sicht der Westalliierten, 1943-1948* by the Steiner Verlag, Stuttgart. Currently, she is working on her "Habilitation" or second book, a project examining the festive culture of German Americans in the United States, 1848-1925. She has published articles in the areas of diplomatic history, intelligence history, Civil War history, and ethnic history.

Bénédicte Deschamps is assistant professor at the Institut Charles V, University of Paris 7, Denis Diderot. In 1996 she received her Ph.D. in American Studies at the University of Paris 7, Denis Diderot. Her dissertation was titled "From 'Colonial' Press to Italian American Press, the Evolution of Six Italian Periodicals in the U.S." She has published several articles on the history of Italian Americans and is co-editor of the book *L'immigration aux États-Unis de 1607 à nos jours*, Paris (Ellipses), 1998. She is also author of the forthcoming book *La presse italo-américaine (1910-1935)*.

Kai Dreisbach is research fellow at the Institute of Anglo-American History, University of Cologne. Currently he is completing a dissertation titled "The United States and Regional Cooperation in Southeast Asia. American Foreign Policy towards ASEAN since the Vietnam War." He holds a MA-degree of the University of Cologne. Forthcoming are articles on U.S. foreign policy towards the Third World in the 1960s and on the American role in the origin of regional cooperation in Southeast Asia.

Geneviève Fabre is professor at the University of Paris 7 where she is also director of the Center of African American Research. Author of books on James Agee, and Afro-American Theatre (Paris, CNRS and Harvard University Press), she has published many essays on American theater and literature, on Hispanic theater and fiction and has contributed to several collective volumes and encyclopedias. Co-author of books on Francis Scott Fitzgerald and American minorities, she has edited or co-edited several volumes: on European Perspectives on Hispanic literature in the United States, on Barrio culture in the United States, on ethnicity, and "Parcours identitaire", and on Toni Morrison. She has also edited two volumes on *Feasts and Celebrations among Ethnic Communities*, and a book on history and memory in African American Culture. She is now co-editing two books on J. Toomer and on the Harlem Renaissance. A Fellow at the Du Bois Institute, Harvard University, The National Humanities Center, and the American Antiquarian Society, she is currently working on a study of African American celebrative culture (1730-1880).

Annick Foucrier is associate professor at the University of Paris 13. She defended her Ph.D. in history, "La France, les Français et la Californie avant la ruée vers l'or, 1786-1848" at the École des Hautes Études en Sciences Sociales, Paris in 1991. She has published articles in French and in English on the history of California, on immigration, and on ethnic relations and citizenship in the United States. She is the author of *Le rêve californien. Les migrants français sur la côte Pacifique, 18e-20e siècles* (The California Dream. History of French Migrants on the California Coast from the 18th to the 20th Century), Paris: Belin, 1999.

Udo Hebel is Professor and Chair of American Studies at the University of Regensburg. He taught at the Universities of Mainz, Potsdam, and Freiburg, and was a Visiting Scholar to the University of Michigan, Ann Arbor, and Harvard University. He also was a Fellow at the American Antiquarian Society in Worcester, MA. He published *Romaninterpretationen als Textarchäologie* (1989), *Intertextuality, Allusion, and Quotation* (1989), and *'Those*

Images of Jealousie': Identitäten und Alteritäten im puritanischen Neuengland (1997); he edited *Transatlantic Encounters* (1995) and *The Construction and Contestation of American Cultures and Identities in the Early National Period* (1999). His articles include studies of twentieth-century American literature, African-American drama, early national festive culture, seventeenth- and eighteenth-century New England culture, German American imagology, intermediality, and theories of American Studies.

Jürgen Heideking (†) was director of the Institute of Anglo-American History at the University of Cologne. Since 1994 he has been a member of the advisory council of the German Historical Institute (GHI) in Washington, D.C. His latest publications include *U.S. Intelligence and German Resistance in World War II* (eds. J. Heideking and Christof Mauch, 1996), *Die amerikanischen Präsidenten. 41 historische Porträts von George Washington bis Bill Clinton* (ed., 1997) and *Geschichte der USA* (2nd ed., 1999). He has also published various articles on United States constitutional history, American national identity, and United States foreign policy in the twentieth century. His "Habilitation" (*Die Verfassung vor dem Richterstuhl: Vorgeschichte und Ratifizierung der amerikanischen Verfassung, 1787-1791*) will soon be published in an English edition.

Fabian Hilfrich was Bosch-Lecturer for German and American History at the Latvian Academy of Culture, Riga, 1999-2000. In 2000 he received his Ph.D. in Modern and American History at the Free University of Berlin. He holds a MA degree from Washington University in St. Louis. His publications include "Patriotismus zwischen Macht und Moral: Die Beschwörung des Nationalstolzes in der Auseinandersetzung über den Vietnamkrieg 1964-1968" (in Manfred Berg et al., eds., *Macht und Moral: Ideologie und Praxis der amerikanischen Außenpolitik im 20. Jahrhundert*, Münster 1999) and "Falling Back into History: Conflicting Visions of National Decline and Destruction in the American Imperialism Debate" (in Studies in North American History, Politics and Society 1, 1997).

Adrien Lherm teaches American Civilization and English Translation at the Department of English and North American Studies of the University of Strasbourg 2, Marc Bloch, after serving as teaching assistant at the Department of Modern History, University of Paris 1, Sorbonne. He received his Ph.D. from the Sorbonne with a dissertation about the history of Halloween in North America and Great Britain from the eighteenth to the twentieth century.

Bernard Mergen is Professor of American Studies at George Washington University in Washington, D.C. and senior editor of *American Studies International*. In 1996 he was Fulbright Professor of American Studies at the National University of Mongolia in Ulan Bator. He has published in the fields of labor history, the history of childhood, and environmental history. His most recent book is *Snow in America* (Smithsonian Institution Press, 1997). He is currently working on a book on American attitudes toward weather and climate in the twentieth century.

Marie-Jeanne Rossignol has studied at the École Normale Supérieure in Paris (Ulm-Sèvres). She teaches American Civilization at the Institute Charles University of Paris 7 Denis Diderot. Her book *Le ferment nationaliste: aux origines de la politique extérieure des Etats-Unis 1789-1809* received the Organization of American Historians' Prize for Best Foreign Book in 1996 and is to be translated into English by Ohio State University Press. She has edited a collection of papers on early American cultural history with Elise Marienstras, *Mémoire privée, mémoire collective*, and is currently preparing a special issue of the Institute's journal of the cultural dimension on United States foreign relations.

Dietmar Schloss teaches American literature and cultural studies at the University of Heidelberg. His publications include *Culture and Criticism in Henry James* (1993) and articles on eighteenth- and nineteenth-century British and American literature. He recently completed a book-length study on the interrelationship between political ideology and literature in the early American republic, which will be published in 2001. Presently he is investigating the changing conceptions of the intellectual in American society from the Revolution to the present.

Michael Wala has taught American, British, and Canadian History at the University of Cologne and the University of Erlangen-Nürnberg. Currently, he is Visiting Professor at St. Olaf College, Minnesota. In addition to a number of scholarly articles published in Europe and the United States, he is author of *The Council on Foreign Relations and American Foreign Policy in the Early Cold War*, and the editor of *The Marshall Plan*, by Allen W. Dulles, and *Gesellschaft und Diplomatie im transatlantischen Kontext*. He has just published a collection of papers on European perceptions of American technology and Culture (with Ursula Lehmkuhl). Forthcoming is a book on German-American relations during the period of the Weimar Republic.

CONTENTS

A

abolitionism 6, 13, 68, 93, 103
"Account of the Grand Federal Procession in Philadelphia" 47
Adams, John 5, 25, 257, 277
adaptation *see* assimilation
Adler, Liebman 168, 170
aesthetics 15, 47, 56, 58, 59
Africa 95, 96, 99, 100, 101, 142
African-American courts 9, 45
African-Americans 4, 6, 10, 12, 13, 16, 21, 68, 88, 92, 101, 104, 111, 112, 113, 200, 229, 237, 238, 239, 240, 241, 245, 246, 247, 249
allegory 15, 47, 52, 54, 58, 59, 280
Allen, Merton C. 150
Alsace-Lorraine 143, 148
"America" (hymn) 269, 272, 284, 288
American Constitution 265
"American Creed" 8
American Eagle 29, 52, 230
American Empire 33, 35
American Revolution 34, 35, 40, 68, 75, 77, 80, 176, 258, 267, 273, 288
Americanization 10, 14, 140, 165, 209, 259, 261, 264, 283, 287
Anderson, John 102
Anglo-Americans 177, 178, 179, 184, 263, 266, 270, 287
antebellum era 93, 104
anti-Federalists 29, 31, 32, 37, 38, 46, 52, 77
anti-imperialists 9, 21, 229, 231, 242, 243, 247, 248, 250

assimilation 3, 10, 18, 141, 149, 151, 155, 158, 168, 180
Atlanta 20, 229, 230, 233, 235, 236, 237, 238, 242, 243
August 15 143, 145, 155

B

B'nai B'rith 161, 163, 166
Babeuf 147
Baker, George P., "The Pilgrim Spirit" (pageant) 260, 279, 286
Baldwin, Roger S. 103
Baltimore 27, 33, 81, 83, 125, 232
Bancroft, George 267
Barsotti, Carlo 127
Bastille Day 81, 140, 147, 149, 150, 151, 152, 154, 155
Beard, Charles A. 9
Bellah, Robert N. 2
Bentley, William 95, 105
Bicentennial 1, 18, 178, 179, 259, 260, 262, 263, 271, 277, 287
Bicknell, Thomas W., "Mayflower" (poem) 268
Bildung 161, 164
Bill of Rights 33, 38
black coronation 50
Bonfire Night 198
Boston 3, 10, 26, 27, 32, 34, 44, 78, 80, 81, 82, 83, 84, 85, 86, 92, 95, 97, 101, 103, 125, 126, 132, 133, 169, 217, 224, 259, 265, 267, 270, 271, 273, 274, 275, 277, 279, 282, 283, 284, 285, 286, 288

Boston Trow Trow 101, 103
Bourne, Randolph 259, 264, 288
Bowles, Samuel 231
Bradford, William 258, 259, 264, 268, 278, 287
Brentano, Lorenz 167
Brewster, Chauncey B. 269
Brewster, Elder 267, 280
Brown, William Wells 103
Buffalo 9
Bushman, Claudia 125

C

Cabot, John 128
Caillois, Roger 124
Caledonian societies 205
Callithumpians 200
Canada 85, 128, 205, 221
carnival 20, 107, 205, 216, 218, 219, 220, 222, 223, 224, 225, 276, 286
Catholics 4, 6, 17, 128, 129, 130, 134, 135, 142, 146, 154, 155, 159, 178, 185, 199, 207
Charleston 3, 15, 27, 32, 63, 64, 69, 71, 80, 259, 260
Chase, Calvin 241
Chesapeake (U.S. navy vessel) 76
Chicago 11, 18, 20, 125, 129, 130, 131, 133, 153, 157, 158, 159, 160, 161, 162, 163, 166, 167, 168, 169, 170, 181, 208, 228, 229, 230, 231, 232, 233, 235, 238, 240, 242, 243, 244, 246, 247, 259, 279, 283, 284
Chicago jubilee 228, 233
Christmas 19, 85, 94, 107, 195, 198, 199, 200, 201, 202, 203, 204, 206, 217, 271, 272, 288
Church of Notre Dame 146, 154
civil religion 2, 3, 7, 19, 21, 38, 46, 194, 203, 206, 263, 269, 272, 287
Civil War 3, 6, 7, 8, 9, 16, 18, 20, 70, 145, 158, 160, 167, 168, 169, 177, 222, 229, 233, 234, 236, 237, 238, 240, 241, 243, 244, 245, 246, 247, 248, 249, 250, 257, 258, 259, 260, 285, 288
colonial rule 229
Columbian order 4, 125
Columbus Day 17, 124, 125, 128, 129, 130, 131, 132, 133, 134, 135, 136
Columbus, Christopher 125, 126, 127, 128, 129, 131, 133, 134, 135, 136
commemorative culture 17, 258

Confederates 167, 232, 233, 234, 235, 236, 237, 238, 241, 246, 248
Connecticut 26, 92, 96, 102, 260
Constitution 1, 3, 4, 7, 8, 9, 10, 11, 14, 25, 26, 27, 29, 30, 31, 32, 33, 34, 35, 37, 38, 39, 40, 44, 45, 47, 49, 50, 51, 52, 53, 54, 58, 59, 72, 77, 132, 142, 165, 235, 236, 248
Constitutional Convention 44, 49, 53
Convention Movement 104, 105
Conzen, Kathleen 159, 176, 185
Coolidge, Calvin 273, 274, 275, 276, 278
coquetry 219
Cotton Mather 264
Cuba 232, 245
Cuff 102
cultural memory 175, 184, 258
cultural pluralism 21, 259
culture of labor 46

D

Dame Shirley (Louise Clapp) 145
Daughters of the American Revolution 262, 268
Davis, Susan 200
Declaration of Independence 3, 5, 6, 7, 8, 40, 45, 47, 49, 52, 72, 75, 77, 78, 80, 82, 84, 85, 86, 142, 143
Democratic-Republican 67, 77
Democratic-Republican Party 77
Democrats 67, 82, 161, 241
Detroit 169, 259
Deutsche Gesellschaft (Chicago) 161
Dickens, Charles 202
Donnelly, Gratton and Helen Merrill Shoate, "Mayflower" (pageant) 267
Douglass, Frederick 13, 103
Du Bois, W.E.B. 10

E

Easter 94, 204
Election Day 4, 93, 94, 95, 96, 97, 98, 101, 105, 106, 107, 109
Embargo Act 79
ethnicity 20, 140, 161, 163, 176, 180, 184, 185, 216, 220
Everett, Charles C. 257, 258, 259, 288

F

February 24 143, 147
Federal Convention 26, 27

Federal Processions 8, 15, 25, 26, 27, 29, 31, 32, 33, 34, 36, 37, 38, 40, 45, 46, 54, 177
"Federal Ship" 26, 33
Federalist Party 16, 77, 86, 87
Federalists 4, 26, 31, 32, 33, 34, 36, 37, 38, 40, 45, 46, 52, 59, 67, 77, 78, 79, 80, 82, 83, 84, 86, 87
Felsenthal, Bernard 163, 164, 165, 166
festive culture 2, 3, 4, 5, 7, 8, 10, 11, 12, 13, 14, 15, 18, 19, 21, 22, 26, 176, 185, 258, 259, 260
filiopietism 261, 275
Filipinos 242, 243, 244, 246, 248
Fitzgerald, F. Scott 225, 276
flirtation 219
floats 10, 15, 26, 29, 33, 38, 44, 45, 47, 48, 49, 52, 53, 54, 130, 134, 148, 177, 179, 180, 208, 224, 230, 233, 238, 243, 244, 245, 270, 279, 285
Fort Worth 208
Fourth of July 4, 5, 6, 10, 11, 13, 15, 27, 36, 40, 45, 47, 52, 75, 77, 78, 80, 81, 84, 85, 86, 87, 142, 143, 150, 159, 201
France 1, 18, 36, 38, 63, 64, 65, 66, 67, 68, 75, 76, 78, 79, 140, 141, 142, 143, 145, 146, 147, 149, 150, 151, 153, 154, 155, 209, 217, 270
Franco-Prussian War 18, 143, 176, 249
Frankfurter, Felix 135
freethinkers 178, 179, 183
French consul 145
French Legion 152
French quarter 141
French Republic 65, 67, 142, 145, 147
French Revolution 1, 4, 15, 40, 63, 65, 66, 68, 75, 145, 148, 149
French Zouaves 143, 147, 152
frontier 6, 35

G

Gaelic Clubs 205
Gemüthlichkeit 175, 180
General Barnes 149
Genêt, Edmond-Charles 64, 65, 66, 67, 69, 70, 71
Genovese, Eugene D. 69
German Aid Society (Chicago) 159, 161
German-Americans 18, 19, 160, 161, 170, 175, 176, 177, 178, 179, 180, 181, 182, 183, 184, 185, 221
Germany 18, 19, 29, 39, 158, 159, 160, 161, 162, 163, 164, 165, 166, 167, 168, 169, 175, 176, 177, 178, 179, 180, 181, 182, 183, 184, 185, 209, 221, 224, 239, 249
Gettysburg 7, 236, 247
Gilded Age 7, 258
Gilje, Paul 200
Grand Army of the Republic (GAR) 222, 224, 225, 233, 238
"Grand Federal Edifice" 29, 52
Grand Federal Processions 3, 14, 29, 44, 45, 47, 50, 51, 58, 59
Grant, Ulysses S. 221, 236, 258
Great Britain 16, 21, 34, 67, 72, 75, 76, 77, 78, 79, 83, 84, 85, 269, 288
Great Western Railroad 223
Greenebaum, Henry 159, 160, 161, 166, 169
Guy Fawkes' Day 198
gymnastics *see* gymnasts
gymnasts 35, 177, 178, 179, 180, 181, 183, 184, 221

H

Haiti 63, 70
Hamilton (miniature fregate) 30
Hamilton, Alexander 29, 30, 40
Harding, Warren G. 279, 283, 284, 285, 286
Harrison, Benjamin 129
Hartford Convention 86
Hawaii 245
Hecker, Friedrich 167, 178
Heman, Felicia, "The First Landing of the Pilgrim Fathers" (anthem) 268
Henry, Prince of Prussia 18, 127, 159, 160, 166, 181, 182, 183, 217, 221, 232, 260, 273, 274, 275, 277
Herbert, Hilary A. 236
Hill, James J. 217
Hollely, A.N. 265
Hopkinson, Francis 45, 47, 49, 50, 51, 52, 53, 54, 57, 59
Hotel d'Europe 145
Howell, Clark 235
Howland Memorial 280

I

ice palaces 221, 222, 225
identity 1, 2, 3, 10, 13, 15, 16, 18, 19, 20, 34, 46, 67, 72, 75, 77, 79, 83, 84, 86, 87, 96, 99, 110, 130, 132, 136, 142,

Index 305

143, 150, 151, 154, 166, 169, 178, 179, 180, 184, 185, 198, 203, 207, 208, 209, 215, 216, 217, 219, 220, 222, 224, 237, 248
Il Progresso Italo-Americano 127
Il Proletario 133
imperialism 243, 245, 247, 248, 250
imperialists 242, 244, 245, 246, 247, 248, 250
inauguration 3, 5, 38, 39, 56, 168
Independence Day 13, 16, 25, 29, 75, 77, 79, 80, 81, 82, 83, 84, 86, 141, 142, 143, 150
"inferior races" 242, 245, 248
inversion 110, 196, 197, 198, 202, 205
Irish Guards 146
Irish National League 150
Irving, Washington 127, 201, 202, 203
Italian Bersaglieri 148
Italian Unification 132
Italian-Americans 17, 124, 125, 126, 127, 128, 130, 131, 132, 133, 134, 136

J

Jackson, Andrew 4, 5, 16, 82, 145
Jacobins 67, 68
Jefferson, Thomas 4, 5, 40, 64, 65, 67, 75, 76, 77, 78, 79
Jews 18, 37, 157, 158, 159, 160, 161, 162, 163, 164, 165, 166, 167, 168, 169, 170
Juarez Guards 148

K

Key, Francis Scott 4
King Borealis 222, 224
King Caesar of Dunham 101
Kiwani 207
Knights of Columbus 17, 128, 129, 130
Kupperman, Kaen Ordahl 216, 217

L

L'Enfant, Pierre 30
L'Italia 126, 127, 128, 130, 132, 133, 134
Lady of Mount Carmel 130
Lafayette Club 153
Lafayette Guards 147, 152
Lafayette Hook and Ladder Company 142, 146
Lane, F.K. 151
Lanson, William 100

Larson, Paul 218, 219, 224
Latin Quarter 148
Le Baron Russell Briggs, 1620-1920 A Poem 260, 273, 274, 275, 276
Leopard (Royal Navy vessel) 76
Lévy, Daniel 143
Lincoln, Abraham 6, 7, 147, 168, 241, 243, 247, 285
living history 282
Locke, Alain 288
Lodge, Henry Cabot 104, 127, 163, 232, 260, 273, 274, 275, 276, 277, 278, 283, 284
Lord Mayor's Shows (London) 54, 56
Luddists 197

M

Madison, James 10, 40, 79, 80, 81, 82, 83, 84
manifest destiny 199, 266
Manila 230
manliness 180, 220, 236
"march of civilization" 35
Marque, Emile 146
Marseillaise 140, 142, 145, 148
Massachusetts 9, 21, 25, 26, 32, 44, 80, 81, 85, 95, 129, 232, 259, 260, 262, 267, 272, 274, 275, 278, 285
masters 27, 54, 69, 70, 93, 94, 95, 98, 99, 102, 103, 104, 106, 107, 109, 113, 196
Mayflower 21, 258, 262, 265, 266, 267, 268, 269, 270, 271, 272, 276, 280, 281, 283
Mayflower Compact 21, 265, 268, 269
Mayor Phelan (of San Francisco) 150
McAndrew, William 208
McGrath, J.F. 264, 275, 288
McKinley, William 20, 229, 230, 231, 232, 233, 235, 236, 239, 241, 242, 243, 244, 247, 248
Michelet, Jules 15, 65, 66, 68, 70
Milwaukee 10, 18, 19, 162, 175, 176, 177, 178, 179, 180, 181, 182, 183
Minnesota 19, 215, 216, 218, 220, 222, 259
Monroe, James 16, 76, 84, 85
Montreal Winter Canival, 1883 218
Moore, Clement 201, 202
Mount Vernon 27, 39
mutual benefit associations (mutual benefit society) 177, 179

N

Napoleon I 141, 145, 151
Napoleon III 141
National Pilgrim Monument 258, 283
national reunion 3, 20, 229, 232, 233, 235, 236, 237, 238, 239, 240, 241, 242, 243, 244, 245, 246, 247, 249
nationalism 1, 4, 12, 37, 46, 86, 150, 184, 229, 244, 248, 249, 250
Native Americans 6, 35, 50, 85, 208, 221, 224, 271, 282
Negro election 4, 6, 35, 94, 95, 96, 97, 99, 100, 102, 104, 105, 109, 111, 163, 242
Negro Election Day 16, 88, 112, 113
Negro governors 86, 88, 94, 95, 96, 97, 98, 99, 100, 101, 102, 103, 104, 106, 108, 112, 151, 183, 221, 223, 275
Negro kings 84, 88, 99, 100, 101, 104, 112, 177, 184
neoclassical 47, 58
New England 16, 21, 49, 78, 79, 80, 81, 82, 84, 86, 88, 92, 94, 95, 100, 104, 106, 108, 109, 112, 141, 145, 217, 257, 258, 259, 260, 261, 262, 263, 264, 266, 267, 268, 269, 270, 271, 272, 275, 277, 278, 283, 284, 285, 287, 288
New England Society 258, 259, 262, 271
"new nationalism" 229, 249
New Year's Day 201
New York 4, 5, 7, 8, 10, 26, 29, 30, 32, 33, 39, 78, 82, 83, 84, 86, 125, 126, 127, 129, 130, 135, 136, 141, 167, 169, 200, 201, 202, 204, 205, 219, 222, 231, 258, 259, 262, 266, 269, 270, 271, 274, 275, 277, 279, 284
New York Herald 129
New York Historical Society 201, 269
New York Times 129, 204, 205, 231, 266, 269, 270, 271, 274, 275, 277, 279, 284
Nissenbaum, Stephen 202
Nivelle, Robert Georges 270
Non-Intercourse Act 79
North American Gymnasts Union 18
Northern Pacific Railway 221

O

October 12 125, 132, 133
Old Colony Memorial 261, 262, 263, 264, 265, 266, 267, 268, 270, 271, 272, 273, 274, 275, 276, 278, 279, 280, 281, 282, 283, 285, 286, 287, 288

Oldham/Lyford trial 287
Omaha 229, 233, 244
orations 21, 75, 80, 95, 103, 105, 150, 152, 154, 166, 263
Orsi, Robert Anthony 130
overseas empire 229
overseas expansion 247
Ozouf, Mona 2, 15, 65, 66, 68, 70

P

pageants 8, 9, 10, 12, 20, 47, 48, 50, 54, 56, 57, 58, 135, 208, 230, 231, 233, 249, 260, 266, 269, 271, 279, 280, 286, 287
parades 3, 4, 5, 6, 8, 9, 10, 12, 14, 15, 18, 19, 20, 21, 25, 26, 27, 29, 30, 31, 32, 33, 34, 35, 36, 37, 38, 39, 40, 44, 45, 46, 47, 48, 49, 50, 51, 52, 53, 54, 56, 57, 59, 75, 77, 80, 84, 85, 86, 94, 95, 97, 98, 99, 104, 125, 126, 129, 130, 131, 134, 141, 142, 143, 145, 148, 152, 158, 159, 160, 161, 166, 169, 170, 171, 177, 178, 179, 180, 181, 184, 194, 195, 198, 199, 200, 201, 205, 208, 216, 219, 221, 222, 223, 224, 225, 230, 231, 233, 237, 238, 244, 263, 270, 273, 274, 279, 281, 284, 285, 286
parent-teacher associations 207
Passamaquoddy tribe 21, 282
peace jubilees 18, 20, 177, 178, 228, 229, 230, 231, 237, 238, 239, 240, 244, 246, 247, 248, 249, 250
Peale, Charles Wilson 29, 39, 45, 50, 52
Peck, George R. 232
Penn, William 208
Philadelphia 6, 7, 8, 9, 14, 15, 20, 25, 26, 27, 29, 34, 36, 39, 44, 45, 47, 48, 49, 51, 57, 58, 63, 64, 70, 71, 77, 78, 79, 80, 83, 126, 178, 200, 229, 230, 233, 245, 259
Philippine-American War 239
Philippines 21, 229, 242, 244, 245, 246, 247, 248
picnics 9, 152, 177, 184
Pilgrim Fathers 257, 258, 264, 265, 268, 269, 270, 279, 280, 283, 284, 288
Pinkster 4, 16
Pintard, John 201, 202
Plymouth Day 263, 279, 280, 282, 283, 284

Plymouth Rock 257, 258, 260, 263, 265, 268, 273, 276, 277, 278, 281, 284, 286, 287, 288
Plymouth Tercentenary 21, 257, 260, 261, 263, 264, 270, 279, 287, 288
popular sovereignty 3, 35, 36, 38, 59
President's Birthday 43
processions *see* parades
Progressive Era 9, 10, 14, 20, 258
Protestants 4, 17, 129, 185, 194, 195, 199, 206, 207, 209
public celebrations 2, 3, 5, 7, 14, 16, 18, 19, 20, 22, 26, 37, 40, 46, 50, 66, 72
public sphere 1, 12, 22, 98, 99, 103, 110, 141, 206
Pulaski, Kazimierz 136
Puritans 49, 177, 183, 199, 258, 270, 288

Q

Quakers 208
Quosh Freeman 100, 103

R

Ransom, R.C. 239
Rapp, Wilhelm 167
realist 47, 60
reconciliation 9, 16, 20, 21, 70, 78, 84, 222, 229, 232, 235, 237, 238, 240, 241, 242, 245, 249
Reconstruction 7, 8, 232, 237, 248
red-letter days 197, 198, 199, 204
Reform Judaism 161, 162, 164, 165
regeneration 7, 175, 176, 181
republicanism 3, 5, 6, 15, 34, 38, 39
Republicans 4, 17, 40, 65, 77, 78, 79, 81, 83, 84, 85, 86, 141, 161, 236, 241
Rochefort 147
Roosevelt, Theodore 135, 232, 236, 238
Rosenthal, Julius 160, 161
Roswell Quosh 100
"Rough Riders" 232, 238
Rush, Benjamin 34, 36, 37, 45, 51, 141
Ryan, Mary 159, 160, 170

S

Salomon, Edward 158, 159, 169
San Domingo 63, 64, 69, 70, 71
San Francisco Chronicle 141, 149
San Juan Hill 238
Santa Claus 201, 202, 203

Schiavo, Giovanni 125
Schiller, Friedrich 164
Scots 49, 207, 219, 266
Second War of Independence 72, 87
self-confidence 19, 33, 179, 180, 181
Sinai Congregation (Chicago) 165
singers 70, 140, 142, 176, 177, 179, 184, 268, 269, 272, 273, 275, 281, 284
site of memory 259
Sketchbook of Geoffrey Crayon, Gentleman 202
Sketches by Boz 202
slave insurrection 16, 64, 69, 70
slavery 6, 7, 10, 13, 68, 69, 93, 106, 107, 180, 247, 248, 250
slaves 13, 16, 27, 37, 64, 68, 69, 70, 88, 92, 93, 94, 95, 96, 97, 98, 99, 100, 101, 102, 103, 104, 107, 109, 111, 167, 237, 243, 249, 258, 276
ski clubs 219, 224
sledding 217, 218
snowball fights 217
snowmen 217
snowshoe clubs (*see* also ski clubs) 218
Snydacker, Godfrey 158, 160, 161
Societé française de bienfaisance mutuelle (French benevolent society) 142
Sons of the American Revolution 8, 267
South, the 3, 7, 9, 10, 16, 20, 27, 48, 69, 70, 79, 80, 81, 86, 97, 102, 106, 107, 128, 133, 141, 167, 178, 199, 222, 229, 232, 233, 235, 236, 237, 239, 240, 241, 242, 243, 245, 246, 248, 249, 258, 259
Spain 9, 135, 217, 228, 229, 230, 232, 236, 237, 238, 239, 240, 242, 243, 246, 249, 250
Spanish-American War 20, 150, 151, 228, 233, 235, 237, 240, 241, 244, 249
St. Louis 126, 162, 231, 259, 260
St. Nicholas' Day 201
St. Patrick's Day 4, 129
St. Paul Winter Carnival: 1886, 1916, 1984 20, 216, 218, 220, 222, 224, 225
St. Paul, Minnesota 19, 20, 39, 215, 216, 217, 218, 219, 220, 221, 222, 223, 224, 225
St. Valentine's Day 204
"Star-Spangled Banner" 11, 140, 269
Strong, Caleb 80
Sutton, Edward F., "Ye Pilgrim Father" (poem) 287

Swabians 178, 179, 185
symbols 1, 2, 3, 4, 6, 7, 8, 10, 15, 16, 17, 20, 33, 34, 36, 47, 49, 53, 69, 72, 75, 83, 86, 93, 95, 96, 97, 98, 99, 100, 104, 107, 108, 109, 111, 112, 129, 132, 135, 147, 148, 154, 159, 161, 175, 176, 177, 179, 181, 185, 217, 224, 225, 229, 230, 231, 237, 238, 243, 249, 260, 261, 264, 265, 268, 272, 274, 280, 281, 283, 284, 285, 286
Syracuse 167

T

tableaux vivants 179, 184
Tammany Society 4, 125
Temperance Movement 6
Temperance Society of People of Color 104
Thanksgiving 84, 204
The Chutes 148, 153
"The New Roof" 52
"The Night Before Christmas" 202, 271
"The Raising
A New Song for Federal Mechanics" 53
toasts 4, 27, 30, 49, 65, 75, 79, 86, 145, 146, 147
toboggan clubs 225
tobogganing 20, 218, 219
transgression 2, 92, 108, 110
"triumphal car" 29, 38, 51
triumphalism 247
Troy Sentinel 202
Turner see gymnasts
Turner, Frederick Jackson 9, 35
Turner, Nat 70
Tusiani, Joseph 134, 135
Twain, Mark 258
tzedakah 166, 169, 170

U

"Uncle Sam" 5, 245
Union 7, 8, 20, 26, 27, 29, 32, 38, 48, 51, 56, 82, 84, 104, 145, 167, 168, 178, 180, 221, 222, 233, 234, 235, 236, 240, 243, 247, 258, 270, 279
United Hebrew Relief Association (Chicago) 160, 168
unity 2, 8, 11, 15, 18, 32, 34, 35, 39, 47, 54, 77, 79, 127, 129, 132, 133, 145, 147, 154, 159, 160, 166, 167, 168, 170, 171, 177, 178, 179, 180, 181, 182, 196, 203, 229, 233, 242, 243, 246, 249, 250

V

Van Slyke, W.A. 222
veterans 85, 142, 177, 183, 221, 222, 225, 233, 235, 238, 241, 285
Villard, Henry 221
voodoo 69, 70

W

War of 1812 4, 5, 7, 16, 72, 75, 84, 86, 87, 93, 100
Wars of Unification 183
Washington, Booker T. 239, 240, 247
Washington, George 3, 4, 7, 27, 29, 34, 35, 49, 65, 128, 179, 207
Washington's Birthday 5, 16, 75, 77, 83, 201
Watson, Guy 100
Webster, Daniel 5, 257, 271, 277, 285
Webster, Noah 30, 35
Wheeler, Joseph 232, 233
Whipple, Sherman L., "The Compact" (oration) 268, 286
"white election" 88, 92, 95, 98, 102, 105, 107, 108, 109
Whitney, Arthur B. 274, 275
Wilson, James 29, 36, 45, 48, 51, 236
winter carnivals 19, 215, 216, 218, 224
Wisconsin 18, 183, 220, 259
Wise, Isaac Mayer 163
Works Progress Administration 136
Worms 163